DON'T BE A
SLAVE
TO WHAT YOU
CRAVE

Be Slim & Healthy with The Merey Weight Loss & Maintenance Program

by

DAISY MEREY
M.D., Ph.D., F.A.A.F.P.

Published by

S.p.i. BOOKS

New York

NOTE TO READER:

The information and advice contained in this book is intended to complement and not to replace the advice and recommendations of your personal physician. Your doctor should always be consulted concerning your personal needs and before you start any new diet, nutritional regimen, exercise regimen or medical treatment. Any questions about general or specific symptoms should first be addressed to your personal physician.

An Ian Shapolsky book

For further information, contact:

S.P.I. Books
99 Spring Street, 3rd Floor
New York, NY 10012
Tel: (212) 431-5011
Fax: (212) 431-8646
E-mail: publicity@spibooks.com

10 9 8 7 6 5 4 3 2 1
First Edition

Library of Congress Cataloging-in-Publication Data available.

S.P.I. Books World Wide Web address: *www.spibooks.com*

ISBN: 1-56171-999-4

TABLE OF CONTENTS

Figures

Letters

ABOUT THE AUTHOR

Daisy Merey, M.D., Ph.D., F.A.A.F.P., is a physician who has specialized in Bariatric Medicine for 21 years. She is a Fellow of the American Academy of Family Practice, a member and diplomate of the American Society of Bariatric Physicians, a Trustee of the American Society of Bariatric Physicians from 1977 to 1999. She has been president of the Women Physicians of Palm Beach County from 1996 to the present, and the past International President of the International Academy of Bariatric Physicians (1985-1986). Born in Morocco, she now resides in West Palm Beach, Florida with her husband, John Merey, M.D. They have a son, Andrew, a daughter DeAnne, and three grandchildren, Alec, Mikala and Peter.

NOTE TO READER:

The information and advice contained in this book is intended to complement and not to replace the advice and recommendations of your personal physician. Your doctor should always be consulted concerning your personal needs and before you start any new diet, nutritional regimen, exercise regimen or medical treatment. Any questions about general or specific symptoms should first be addressed to your personal physician.

ACKNOWLEDGMENTS

F oremost, I would like to thank my family, husband John, son Andrew and especially my daughter DeAnne who gave me encouragement and moral support during the four years I worked on this book. Dr. Chris Renna was influential in showing me that neuro-transmitter deficits can influence health and disease.

I am also grateful for the technical support given by Amanda Lanthier, Linzi Zuker, and Crystal Abbuehl in putting together the manuscript. Finally, I am indebted to my numerous patients who taught me how emotions control weight and how weight loss improves their many medical conditions.

PREFACE

Does America need yet another diet book? We are already confused by a deluge of contradictory programs. High carbohydrate/low protein, high protein/low carbohydrate, or even low fat diets are being thrown at us with increasing speed. No sooner does someone tackle a program than a new, totally different, program replaces it.

The sad truth is that diets don't work for those seeking a quick fix. And one diet does not fit all! Some people are successful at certain diets, while others fail miserably.

I personally have been involved in the weight loss field for 21 years as a diplomate of the American Board of Bariatric Medicine. Bariatricians are physicians specializing in the field of weight loss.

During my two decades of practice, I have seen a parade of patients seeking to lose and maintain their lower weight. In my experience, the key to weight loss is individualization of the program. Each overweight or obese person should be able to lose and maintain weight with dignity.

The best treatment regime begins with a visit to a bariatrician. I hope that the reader, after reviewing this book and answering the four simple questionnaires, will be able to determine the best treatment for him or herself.

What differentiates this book from any other diet book is that the reader can be taught how to stop cravings depending on the foods craved and times these cravings occur. Different supplementations are described according to the hunger location (head vs. stomach or physical vs. emotional). In addition, neurotransmitter therapy for food addictions will be discussed in detail so that you can achieve the best control of your weight.

INTRODUCTION TO BARIATRICS

Does any of this sound familiar to you? You feel awful. Your head hurts. You're so short of breath that you can hardly walk without stopping several times. You avoid climbing stairs. Tying your shoelaces is a major ordeal, because your stomach gets in the way. There are no more holes left on your belt, and your clothes fit as tightly as tourniquets. You feel so uncomfortable! You avoid socializing, because you can't find anything to wear that fits and you're self-conscious about your weight. Your friends from the past don't recognize you; what's worse, you don't recognize yourself in photographs or in the mirror. You suffer from acid indigestion. You've tried many diets, but still can't lose weight, and end up discouraged and confused.

Desperation gives you the courage to finally see a doctor. What does the doctor tell you? "You're overweight!" You already knew that. After all, you have a mirror at home. Now what? Are you going to hear the usual "Exercise more and eat less" lecture?

Most doctors tell you that obesity is considered a disease, as declared in 1986 by the National Institutes of Health. Obesity may even cause or aggravate many medical conditions. You're scared, because you've already experienced episodes when you stopped breathing while asleep (sleep apnea). Relatives and friends have told you that you've even fallen asleep while seated at an important event or meeting (Pickwickian syndrome). You are aware that obesity contributes to many serious medical conditions such as hypertension, stroke, coronary heart disease, premature heart attack, mature-onset diabetes, arthritis, elevated cholesterol, gastrointestinal and respiratory problems, and cancer. You knew you had a problem before you consulted yet another doctor, but, sadly, you realize that this may not be the right doctor for your problem.

Unfortunately, not everyone is familiar with Bariatrics or the medical field of weight loss. In my 21-year practice as a Bariatrician, I've been asked numerous times why I chose this field. Many find it hard to believe, until I tell them, that my trim figure they see was once very overweight. I, too, suffered with this problem during most of my adolescence, but fortunately dropped the weight just before entering college. Knowing firsthand what my patients are experiencing, I continually scan the world to find the best treatments for them as well as for myself.

When I first began my practice in family medicine, I was overwhelmed by the amount of medications my patients consumed. They would bring into my office shopping bags full of pill bottles, the contents of which they would ceremoniously dump on my desk. Beyond this, I would see the misery in their eyes, note their difficulty walking, hear their shortness of breath, record their high blood pressure and, in many cases, list the complications of their diabetes.

Immediately, I felt that a radical change in treatment was needed and knew that the common cause for these numerous afflictions was due to their extra weight. Rather than increase the number and dosage of medications and risk encouraging serious side effects, my reasoning was to reduce the weight and cut down on the medications. This is what led me to the speciality of Bariatrics, a field in which I have become an expert.

Nearly all my patients have either reduced or overcome their dependence on medication for high blood pressure, elevated cholesterol and diabetes. How exhilarating it has been for me to discontinue their medications, and replace them with only natural products to maintain good health. The neurotransmitter theory of weight loss has also proved highly successful for the thousands of patients who are using it.

A recent patient (C.M.) came to us very overweight, with diabetes necessitating insulin injections, high blood pressure requiring several medications and a huge, non-healing foot ulcer which had been present for too long. Although skeptical at first, she followed up on her internist's order to see us; otherwise, she might not have survived!

A compliant patient, she lost a total of 80 pounds in just a few months. She had begun to exercise, and most of her blood pressure medications were discontinued. Her foot ulcer healed in a short time as her blood sugar improved. She no longer experienced shortness of breath. When she is all dressed up, she now looks wonderful. She still visits the office for maintenance and claims that we saved her life!

A young boy (D.R.) was so overweight that he could no longer find clothes to fit him. As a result, he settled for a menial job that he loathed, the opposite of his lifelong dream to be a policeman. After only six months of treatment, he shed about 100 pounds. He still comes to the office for maintenance and has not gained back any weight. Realizing his dream, he was admitted into the police academy. He attributes this new career opportunity to his successful weight loss.

I attended the wedding of a patient (D.B.) who had lost 200 pounds in our program. Still a little overweight, she was so radiantly beautiful that I beamed with pride. Losing her weight took a year, however, it was worth it, as she had found her soul mate. All the sacrifices made were justified when I saw the happiness in the eyes of both bride and groom.

Another patient (C.C.), who was quite loquacious, would come to the office in shorts hidden by huge T-shirts. She told us all about her unhappy marriage and unsatisfactory job situation. Within months of following our program she was transformed into a butterfly and emerged from her fat cocoon to become a very attractive woman, wearing beautiful little dresses and demonstrating an avid interest in make-up and grooming. As her self-confidence increased, her colleagues at work seemed to linger at her desk more frequently. Her boss finally noticed her outstanding performance and rewarded her with a well-deserved promotion. She believed her weight loss and improved grooming to be responsible for her job advancement.

Her husband, on the other hand, was extremely jealous and continued to demean her. While she was overweight, she accepted this behavior; however, as she began receiving more compliments from members of the opposite sex and her boss, she no longer tolerated the verbal abuse she received at home. When her husband refused to receive marriage counseling, she divorced him and never looked back. The last news I received from her was that she is now happily remarried and has relocated to another state. The weight loss gave her the courage to end her unhappy marriage and to attract the right person to her life.

A teenage girl (A.K.) was teased about her weight at school. She became so upset that she went to a psychiatrist and received medication for her depression. Once she started our program, she dropped her excess weight of 80 pounds. She is now the happiest, most well-adjusted, young girl we know.

A young woman (C.A.) was referred to us by her Workmen's Compensation insurance, after a work accident left her with a dislocated ankle and broken foot which resulted in serious weight gain. Because exercise was prohibited, her cravings for food grew out of control; this was especially difficult for her as she worked in a restaurant. After she began our neurotransmitter precursors and started a low fat, low carbohydrate, low calorie diet, the weight started melting off. She has lost almost 150 pounds! Because she was so positive about her program, comparing it to the other programs where she met with consistent failure, we decided to hire her. She now teaches our new patients the advantages of the various programs we offer. Although she still needs to lose more weight, her leg pains have vanished, she has a lot more energy and admits that getting dressed in the morning is no longer an insurmountable task.

This same woman could hardly walk and would circle the parking lot seeking the closest parking spot to our building's entrance. She now parks far away from the entrance and looks forward to the opportunity to walk. She has come a long way. She did it and now teaches others how to do it, and you can do it too!

NOTE TO READER:

The information and advice contained in this book is intended to complement and not to replace the advice and recommendations of your personal physician. Your doctor should always be consulted concerning your personal needs and before you start any new diet, nutritional regimen, exercise regimen or medical treatment. Any questions about general or specific symptoms should first be addressed to your personal physician.

— Chapter One —

OBESITY

I n 1986 obesity was declared a disease by the National Institutes of Health (NIH). Not only does this disease afflict over 60 million — one in three—U.S. adults, but 97 million Americans of all ages are overweight or obese. Obesity has reached such epidemic proportions that, according to Dr. Sharon Dalton of New York University, by the year 2030 the entire American population will be overweight. Former Surgeon General C. Everett Koop, who staged a war against obesity, maintains that the mortality rate of the American population could be reduced significantly by the reduction of smoking and obesity (both preventable conditions).

What is obesity? Even though obesity is defined as a weight of 20% above our ideal weight, most of us are confused as to what represents that ideal body weight. More recently the body mass index (BMI) was proposed to be the standard by which to measure obesity. Body mass index is calculated by dividing your weight by your height. To find out your BMI, you can plug in your weight and height in Table 1 on the following page.

Table 1
BODY MASS INDEX

Weight (lb)	\multicolumn{17}{c}{Height (feet, inches)}

Weight (lb)	4'10"	4'11"	5'0"	5'1"	5'2"	5'3"	5'4"	5'5"	5'6"	5'7"	5'8"	5'9"	5'10"	5'11"	6'0"	6'1"	6'2"
125	26	25	24	24	23	22	22	21	20	20	19	18	18	17	17	17	16
130	27	26	25	25	24	23	22	22	21	20	20	19	19	18	18	17	17
135	28	27	26	26	25	24	23	23	22	21	21	20	19	19	18	18	17
140	29	28	27	27	26	25	24	23	23	22	21	21	20	20	19	19	18
145	30	29	28	27	27	26	25	24	23	23	22	21	21	20	20	19	19
150	31	30	29	28	27	27	26	25	24	24	23	22	22	21	20	20	19
155	32	31	30	29	28	28	27	26	25	24	24	23	22	22	21	20	20
160	34	32	31	30	29	28	28	27	26	25	24	24	23	22	22	21	21
165	35	33	32	31	30	29	28	28	27	26	25	24	24	23	22	22	21
170	36	34	33	32	31	30	29	28	28	27	26	25	24	24	23	22	22
175	37	35	34	33	32	31	30	29	28	27	27	26	25	24	24	23	23
180	38	36	35	34	33	32	31	30	29	28	27	27	26	25	25	24	23
185	39	37	36	35	34	33	32	31	30	29	28	27	27	26	25	24	24
190	40	38	37	36	35	34	33	32	31	30	29	28	27	27	26	25	24
195	41	39	38	37	36	35	34	33	32	31	30	29	28	27	27	26	25
200	42	40	39	38	37	36	34	33	32	31	30	30	29	28	27	26	26
205	43	41	40	39	38	36	35	34	33	32	31	30	29	29	28	27	26
210	44	43	41	40	38	37	36	35	34	33	32	31	30	29	29	28	27
215	45	44	42	41	39	38	37	36	35	34	33	32	31	30	29	28	28
220	46	45	43	42	40	39	38	37	36	35	34	33	32	31	30	29	28
225	47	46	44	43	41	40	39	38	36	35	34	33	32	31	31	30	29
230	48	47	45	44	42	41	40	38	37	36	35	34	33	32	31	30	30
235	49	48	46	44	43	42	40	39	38	37	36	35	34	33	32	31	30
240	50	49	47	45	44	43	41	40	39	38	37	36	35	34	33	32	31
245	51	50	48	46	45	43	42	41	40	38	37	36	35	34	33	32	32
250	52	51	49	47	46	44	43	42	40	39	38	37	36	35	34	33	32
255	53	52	50	48	47	45	44	43	41	40	39	38	37	36	35	34	33
260	54	53	51	49	48	46	45	43	42	41	40	38	37	36	35	34	33
265	56	54	52	50	49	47	46	44	43	42	40	39	38	37	36	35	34
270	57	55	53	51	49	48	46	45	44	42	41	40	39	38	37	36	35
275	58	56	54	52	50	49	47	46	44	43	42	41	40	38	37	36	35
280	59	57	55	53	51	50	48	47	45	44	43	41	40	39	38	37	36
285	60	58	56	54	52	51	49	48	46	45	43	42	41	40	39	38	37
290	61	59	57	55	53	51	50	48	47	46	45	43	42	41	39	38	37
295	62	60	58	56	54	52	51	49	48	46	46	44	42	41	40	39	38
300	63	61	59	57	55	53	52	50	48	47	46	44	43	42	41	40	39
305	64	62	60	58	56	54	52	51	49	48	46	45	44	43	41	40	39

If you find yourself: in the dark grey region, you are considered obese; in the light grey zone overweight; and in the white region in the optimal weight zone. According to the World Health Organization (WHO) classification system, obesity is defined by the following grades:

Table 2

BMI	WHO Classification Grades
19-24	Normal
25-27	Moderately overweight (grade I)
27-30	Obese (grade II)
30-39	Severely obese (grade III)
40 or more	Morbidly obese (grade IV)

An easier method to rank obesity is a BMI of at least 27.3 for women and 27.8 for men, or simply a BMI of over 27 for both sexes. According to the NIH, BMI of 25 or more is considered overweight.

Some investigators are not convinced that the BMI is the best classification by which to study obesity and they instead rely on other indication methods.

A waist-to-hip ratio of more than one in men or more than 0.85 for women also denotes obesity. Finally, a waist circumference of more than 39 inches for men and more than 35 inches for women places that person in the obese category. A simple waist measurement may be sufficient to identify those at risk for cardiovascular disease. A waist measurement of 37 inches in men and 32 inches in women has helped identify those with elevated cholesterol levels and hypertension. Interestingly, waist-to-hip ratio was shown to be a better predictor of heart disease in Japanese men than BMI.

Overweight women may also reduce their risk of cardiovascular problems by trimming two to four inches from their waist. In this way, women may decrease at least one risk factor by 10% or more. Risk factors include a high total cholesterol, LDL cholesterol, triglycerides and diastolic blood pressure.

Waist measurement is the best predictor of type II diabetes among Mexican-Americans. Type II diabetes was 11 times more likely for those in the top quarter of waist measurement as compared to those in the bottom quarter.

The waist-to-hip ratio may be increased in people with low T3 thyroid hormone in the blood. Finally, waist-to-hip ratio may be a better indicator of risk for cataract development than BMI, according to a study involving 16,000 patients at Harvard Medical School.

Dr. Jean Pierre Depress, director of the Lipid Research Center of Quebec, Canada, performed an exhaustive study measuring visceral fat by computed tomography and concluded that waist circumference better predicts diabetes, heart disease, and syndrome X (described later in the book) than does the weight or BMI of the thousands of patients studied.

According to Dr. Kathryn Rexode, in a study published in the December 1998 *Journal of the American Medical Association*, women whose waist size approached or exceeded their hip size had three times the risk of a heart attack as women whose waists were smaller than their hips.

Not only are the waists expanding in America, but bottoms are also steadily enlarging to the point that we may run out of places to sit! According to René Sanchez of *The Washington Post*, the 18-inch per bottom measurement traditionally set by seat engineers is now considered obsolete. Theaters in Seattle are including 24-inch seats to accommodate these larger "derriéres."

The manufacturer Bemis is even promoting larger toilet seats to accommodate our larger behinds. The Ford corporation is also testing larger padded car seats to provide for those larger derriéres. Finally the stadiums in America are obliging our obese population by building larger seats. Every company in America is testing larger seats for the growing behinds, believing in the prediction that by the year 2030 we will all be overweight! A new study in Israel even equates obesity to neck size!

Without going into complicated statistics, many diseases are associated with obesity. The five killer diseases in men and women—namely cardiovascular disease, some types of cancer, stroke, diabetes, and atherosclerosis—all share the common risk factor of obesity. Diabetes affects 15 million people in the U.S. However, a 10 pound weight loss reduces the risk of diabetes by 30%.

Obesity is also a major risk factor for gallstones, sleep apnea, gastroesophageal reflux disease, osteoarthritis, digestive diseases, hypertension, heart attacks, reduced fertility and decreased mobility.

Obesity doubles the risk of hypertension, triples the risk of type II diabetes (80% of all type II diabetics are obese) and increases the risk of elevated cholesterol by one quarter. In addition, obesity increases the risk of heart disease by 60% in men and 87% in women. Obesity also raises the risk of cancer by 33%, according to the National Cancer Institute.

The most consistent evidence about an obesity relationship to cancer exists with cancers of the breast, endometrium, uterus and kidney. Less consistent results have been reported for colorectal, prostate and pancreatic cancers. The increased cancer risk may be due to an alteration in sex hormones and insulin, the hormone that regulates blood sugar. Type II diabetes has also been associated with cancer of the colon, liver, pancreas, breast and uterus. Insulin appears to promote the development of colon and liver cancer.

Obesity increases the risk of Cesarean section threefold and the risk of neural tube defects was elevated 30% in babies born to overweight mothers.

Also, emotional and psychological trauma has been documented in association with obesity. Besides sleep apnea, obese patients experience daytime sleepiness and nighttime sleep disturbances. According to Dr. John Foreyt, who specializes in the psychology of obesity, "Obesity is the number one public health concern in the United States affecting over one third of women." Obese women are also 30% less likely to become pregnant than non-obese women, according to a study of 5,300 women. Obesity increases the risk of hypertension (high blood pressure) during pregnancy by 2.4 times.

An obscure disease called pseudotumor cerebri, which manifests itself in headaches, ringing of the ears and loss of vision, occurs more commonly in obese women between the ages of 15 and 44 years. The necessary treatment for this is weight loss!

Some studies have shown an increase of up to 60% in the risk of death from all causes for obese people. In the Nurses' Health Study, a group of women age 30 to 50 were followed for 16 years and found to have an increased mortality rate from cardiovascular disease and cancer if they had gained 22 pounds or more since age 18. The least mortality was associated with a BMI of 19. Studies have also shown that 50% of all black women in America are obese. Fat loss, not weight loss, decreases the risk of dying by up to 17 %.

The economics of obesity-related diseases are staggering. In the United States, the cost to society for obesity has been estimated to be $4.8 billion in direct costs and $23 billion in indirect costs for a total of $27.8 billion. Interestingly enough, Americans spend $40 billion annually in weight loss services and products.

I am always saddened when I read in the newspaper about a famous person who died due to any obesity-related disease. When a patient comes to see me after a heart attack, I always ask why he or she did not come to see me earlier. I am also amazed at the cruelty and abuse that the overweight and obese receive throughout their lives. In school, at the job, whether married or single, in the dating game, the obese are treated unfairly.

Unhappily married women gain an average of 42 pounds during 13 years of marriage. As my patients lose weight, they are finally given a well deserved promotion or a better job; they also find or change their spouses. Their whole outlook changes from being initially depressed, shy, looking down at their feet to straightening up and smiling as they lose weight.

As their self esteem increases, these patients pay more attention to their looks, as evidenced in their clothing, makeup, etc. Therefore, when my patients tell me they want to lose weight because of health reasons, the real truth is, rather, that they want to look good! Frequently, I receive requests for rapid weight loss before a wedding, a school reunion or an important event.

Only weight loss that is maintained, however, is considered successful. By merely losing 10% of their weight, people can still significantly lessen the risk factors and severity of their diseases. According to Dr. G. Blackburn, one of the early pioneers in weight loss, even weight loss as low as 5% has been shown to reduce or eliminate disorders associated with obesity, namely hypertension, diabetes and hyperlipidemias (high cholesterol or triglyceride levels). The optimal equation is to achieve a maintained modest weight loss!

GENETICS OF OBESITY:

You're not always at fault for being overweight; in some cases you have been genetically programmed to be fat.

We cannot change our genes, but we can change our futures. Our genes may make us more susceptible to weight gain, but a fattening environment encourages the gain to occur in the first place. Some individuals, however, may possess the genes to ward off weight, no matter how many delectable foods are ingested. On the other hand, some people may be fat and have no illness associated with obesity.

Dr. David West, one of the forefathers in weight loss research, concludes that these people have a set of genes that protect them from the adverse effects of being fat. Patients who are diabetic or who suffer from high blood pressure do not just give up because of these harmful genes and die... diabetics take drugs or insulin to control their blood sugar, while hypertensive patients take blood-pressure-lowering medications. If we have a genetic tendency to be obese (just look at your own family), we have to be even more vigilant in preventing weight gain. I tell my patients to constantly be "on guard," like the Three Musketeers with their swords ready, whenever there is a possibility or circumstance that may stimulate overeating.

I also explain to my patients that life is not fair: some people can consume huge amounts of calories and remain string beans or twigs, while others, like myself, can gain weight just looking at somebody else's plate. Even though several studies were undertaken to determine the basal metabolic rate (the number of calories expended during 24 hours) of obese vs. normal weight people, no conclusive data exist. In many studies, the obese were shown to be under-burners (not burning as many calories as normal weight patients). Dr. Eric Ravussin studied for 14 years how people burn energy and how these differences contribute to weight gain. His work made him appreciate how widely metabolic rates can vary. People with the same weight and height may burn dramatically different amounts of energy each day. In evolution, those people who conserved their energy during times of famine survived better. Thus, natural selection kept fat-conserving genes in our population. Also, people with hypothyroidism, or low thyroid hormone, are under-burners; but once their thyroid hormone is adjusted, they start losing weight more easily. In my experience, I have found that a great proportion of my patients suffer from low basal metabolic rate. In contrast, recent studies by Dr. James O. Hill have shown that obese people have similar basal metabolic rates as those of normal weight.

A couple of years ago, the obesity gene, or ob gene, was found in mice. The mice with the ob gene were quite corpulent compared to the mice devoid of the ob gene. Recently, six more genes were found to be linked with obesity in mice. We can only imagine the number of genes associated with obesity in humans. A protein called leptin was also found with great fanfare in the fat cells of mice. Mice deficient in leptin levels gained weight, but when these mice were injected with leptin, they regained the svelte figures of their normal companions.

Unfortunately the leptin story cannot be extrapolated to humans. We are much more complex animals; while some patients did well with leptin injections, others failed miserably with the same treatment. In the first human trial done in 1998, leptin appeared to have a direct effect on body systems for regulating sugar within fat tissues. Even though only 10% of the overweight population is leptin deficient, leptin may be the hormone released by fat cells that decreases appetite and increases metabolism. Daily injections need to be given with reported irritation and hardening of the skin. Also, stress decreases leptin's effect and may explain why stressed patients have increased appetite and why some obese patients with elevated stress hormone levels have leptin resistance.

Leptin and obesity have also been linked to early development in pubescent girls. It is suspected that early breast development may be encouraged by leptin. Fat produces leptin and leptin is necessary for the progression of puberty. Studies have also shown an association between leptin and clogging of the arteries, or thrombosis.

Overweight girls also have more insulin circulating in their blood. Those higher levels of insulin appear to stimulate the production of sex hormones from the ovary and the adrenal glands. New studies have shown that between 50 and 70% of the obese population have insulin resistance. Insulin resistance means that even though there is insulin production by the pancreas, insulin cannot get through the cell and perform its duty of carbohydrate transport into the cell. If insulin resistance is documented, a trial of a low carbohydrate diet is quite therapeutic. Patients in this category have higher insulin blood levels and higher glycohemoglobin A1C levels. Glycohemoglobin A1C level is a more accurate detector than blood sugar level, as it measures blood sugar level in the last two months. Patients with high glycohemoglobin A1C levels have a higher tendency to develop diabetes later in life.

Skipping meals, hot water and fasting may help in decreasing insulin resistance. Some products like EPA/DHA, Omega 3 fatty acids, aminoguanidine or Goat's Rue (Galega officinalis) have been associated with decreased insulin resistance.

Insulin resistance is also associated with increased cholesterol synthesis, thus showing the link between insulin resistance and heart disease. This increase in cholesterol synthesis is no longer seen in those individuals whose insulin resistance improved with weight loss.

Finally, a recent study using electron microscopy revealed that over 50% of obese individuals had a defect in their cellular membrane. The membranes of all their cells lacked some type of essential fatty acids. A trial of omega-3 fatty acids—like primrose, borage, or flaxseed oils or better yet EPA/DHA—would be beneficial for obese individuals to restructure those defective cellular membranes. These essential fatty acids are also health-promoting and advantageous anyway. The importance of continuing this supplementation during maintenance is strongly advocated.

Genetically, sex determines the amount of fat you should carry. Women have as much as 25% fat, mostly located in the breasts (for lactation) and thighs. Men have less leeway; their fat percentage should not exceed 21% and the ideal is less than 18%. Men usually have their fat concentrated in their abdomens which gives them a penguin-like appearance.

As we age, our stomachs bulge, regardless of sex. Even though our body type most resembles the family member from whom we inherited it, and though there are a lot of exceptions to the rule, a pear-shaped type of pattern is more commonly found among women and a trunkal, abdominal, apple-shaped type of obesity is more commonly seen in men.

The female pear-shaped obesity is difficult to treat because fat in this location is more difficult to break down. In addition, fat in these areas is not considered as dangerous. Unfortunately, the abdominal or male pattern of obesity is more dangerous, as that type of fat is easily broken down and can travel through the blood vessels to induce a myocardial infarction, or heart attack. The apple-shaped obesity is also associated with diabetes and certain cancers. (see Figure 1)

Figure 1 - Apple & Pear

Female or Pear Shaped Obesity   Male or Apple Shaped Obesity

Belly fat is also an indicator of excess stress. People with abnormal spikes of cortisol due to stress have more belly fat. Cortisol (an adrenal hormone) causes insulin resistance and fat absorption predominantly in the gut. Women with visceral or abdominal obesity were shown to have lower concentrations of serotonin metabolites and other stress hormones. These lower hormonal concentrations were associated with a preference for carbohydrates. This finding emphasizes the importance of serotonin in the treatment of abdominal obesity.

The role of heredity in influencing obesity is well documented in twin studies. Twins separated at birth resemble the body type of their biological parents, not their adoptive parents. Of course, environment has some effect on obesity. I am always amazed when I see a whole family of obese patients waddling into my office, the father, mother, and children looking like they all stepped out of a Botero painting.

When only one parent is overweight, we have a dichotomy among the children between fat and thin. Even though the same foods are presented to the children, some will have a higher tendency to overeat and to snack between meals.

Finally, Dr. Bill Dietz, director of the Division of Nutrition and Physical Activity at the Centers for Disease Control and Prevention, says: "We have not clearly identified the major changes in eating behavior or activity sufficient to account for the recent rapid increase in obesity; we don't have a terrific answer." Americans may be eating a few hundred calories more, but their exercise levels are relatively the same. Dr. Kay Flegal states: "Everybody assumes it must be too much food and too little exercise, but the data does not quite fit."

In conclusion, there are many causes for the complex disease of obesity. In order to offer optimal treatment, one has to know all the underlying causes. Again, even though we cannot change our genes, we still can change our future.

Chapter Summary

- BMI determines the degree of obesity most accurately.

- Waist circumference, waist to hip ratio may predict diabetes and heart disease.

- Cardiovascular disease, cancer, stroke, diabetes, and hardening of the arteries are all caused by obesity.

- Insulin resistance is the key in the etiology of obesity and many other diseases.

— Chapter Two —

OBESITY THROUGHOUT LIFE

CHILDHOOD OBESITY AND ITS CAUSES

S ome babies weigh more at birth than others. However, according to Dr. R. Suskind, et al. overweight infants of overweight mothers weighed no more at birth than infants from lean mothers; but they weighed more at six and twelve months of age. At three months of age, their energy expenditure was already 21% lower than in normal weight infants.

A study led by Dr. Nicolas Stettler of the Children's Hospital of Philadelphia and the University of Pennsylvania found that babies who gain weight too quickly in their first four months appear prone to being overweight later in childhood. The study showed that for each extra 100 grams they put on in a month, the risk of being overweight later increased by approximately 30%.

Diabetic mothers often have babies who are bigger than usual neonates. Newborns of obese mothers with BMI's equal to or over 30 are at an increased risk for congenital malformations as compared with newborns of normal weight mothers, according to a 1998 German study.

Children of mothers who smoke are more likely to develop type II diabetes and obesity later in life, according to a new study by researchers at the Karolinska Institute in Stockholm, Sweden. The new study is the first to link prenatal exposure to cigarette smoke and an increased risk of diabetes. Participants whose mothers had smoked 10 or more cigarettes per week during pregnancy were at least four times as likely to develop early type II diabetes as those whose mothers were nonsmokers. Individuals who had smoked as teenagers also had an independent, similarly increased risk of subsequently developing diabetes. In addition, offspring of smoking mothers who had not developed diabetes were significantly more likely to be obese or overweight. The investigators speculated that smoking during pregnancy may cause metabolic dysregulation, possibly due to fetal malnutrition or toxic agents in cigarette smoke, which increases the likelihood of type II diabetes in offspring.

Some babies are hungrier than others and consume more food, whether they are breast fed or bottle fed. Infants who are mellow and easily soothed become leaner and more active children as compared to more irritable infants. Chubby babies are considered cute, as baby fat is supposed to be temporary and, therefore, excusable. The American Academy of Pediatrics does not recommend cutting down the fat intake of babies under two years of age. Some mothers who fear obesity start their babies on skim milk once they are weaned from formula feedings.

According to a study done with 9,357 children in Bavaria, the longer babies are exclusively breast fed before being switched to formula or food, the lower their chances of starting school as overweight children. The German study found that infants, given only breast milk until they were three to five-months-old, were more than a third less likely to be obese by the age of five to six years than babies given only formula from the start. Those exclusively breast fed for six months to a year fared even better; they were 43% less likely to be obese. Finally, breast fed children were found to have higher IQ's because of the possibility of higher content of DHA in breast milk versus cow's milk or formula.

Federal Health officials have issued new pediatric growth charts that more accurately reflect the nation's diversity and, for the first time, include a tool to identify children who are at risk for obesity. These new charts replace the old charts that measured height and weight since 1977. Contrary to popular belief, there has been little, if any, increase in children's height over previous decades, says Health and Human Services (HHS) Secretary Donna Shalala. "America as a whole is not getting any taller, only fatter." According to Dr. Jack Janoski, obesity before age three is not associated as much with adult obesity as being obese after age three. Children in the 85th or 95th percentile of weight are considered to be obese.

Other studies have shown that after age three, fatness was more likely to persist. Dr. Whitaker said: "The older the overweight kids were, the more likely they were to look that way as adults." For example, children who were obese at six to nine years had a 55% chance of being obese as adults. Their risk was 10 times that of children of normal weight. Those who were obese at 10-14 years had a 67% chance of being obese as adults—28 times the risk of their peers who were not obese.

Another study showed that children breast fed beyond one year had a 72% lower chance of turning out to be obese children. However, even if children were breast fed for only one or two months, they were 10% less likely to be obese by the time they started school.

A recent study showed that excessive juice drinking was associated with more overweight toddlers than milk drinking. Babies and toddlers eat what they are offered. They develop a taste and distaste for foods presented. Of course, television instills itself in the minds of children by associating toys or trinkets with cereals and cookies. Toddlers are like little sponges at this time of their lives and, with their wonderful memories, will nag parents to buy them the foods that offer those little perks. My granddaughter always asks me to take her to McDonald's. When I acquiesce, I learn she is not as interested in the meal as much as the toy that is generally featured with it. At age three, she already knew the specialties of each restaurant or destination that offered food. The minute she entered the movie theater, she clamored for popcorn. Of course, these young minds are very impressioned by the sophisticated marketing gimmicks used to attract them. In addition to commercials, smells of foods are piped throughout the movie theater and malls as a form of advertisement.

Even toddlers imitate their parents behavior; how can we expect our children to have carrot sticks if we eat french fries! Overweight children either usually skip breakfast or eat smaller breakfasts than normal weight children. Additionally some toddlers are less active than others and, as a result, can already grow chunky. If parents sit on a couch to watch television and snack, their young child will follow suit.

We always recommend that parents provide good snacking food for their children. If somebody is overweight in the family, it is best not to buy fatty cookies or ice cream for the skinny child in the family. As you might have guessed, these high fat, high calorie snacks end up in the fat child's stomach! The skinny child will generally not even touch them. The other excuse I hear a lot is, "Those snacks are not for us; they're for company." But those snacks never make it to the company's lips, because they are eaten and replaced each week, even when there is no company. Anyway, you can be sure that company will be very happy if healthy snacks are served.

Another rationalization is: "My husband likes to have some ice cream or chips after dinner." To these families, I recommend this tactic: let the father or the family member who wants these snacks go out and buy them! Never bring them to the house! Big cartons of ice cream are a magnet for the overweight member of the family. If a child is never exposed to a high fat snack, he will never crave it. My 31-year-old son, who already has his own household, recently reproached me for never giving him a chance to know how good regular cheese tasted. Because he, like me, had a weight problem, I kept only fat-free cheeses in our house. Both my children were reared on skim milk. Consequently, when regular milk was given to them, they would spit it out! Childhood obesity begins early, and therefore it is never too early to intervene. The fat child of today becomes the fat adult of tomorrow. Not only are 25% of American children considered obese, but obese children are six to seven times more likely than non-obese children to become obese adults. Dr. Jules Hirsch theorized that the body's total number of fat cells are established early in development; and while those cells may shrink, their number never changes. This theory has been challenged; not only can new fat cells develop later in life, but some unused fat cells are also lost.

The "set point" is another excuse that is often given to bariatricians. "Doctor, I used to weigh this much 10 years ago; and no matter how much I diet, when I reach this weight, I stabilize." I do not believe in set points, because set points can be readjusted by working a little harder through dietary intervention and exercise. Plateaus are good; they represent a temporary standstill while old fat is being burnt. Plateaus are followed by a downward step that represents fat loss.

People expect weight loss to follow in a linear progression

(Figure 2A). However, weight loss is better represented stepwise, as a gradual process with plateaus in between (Figure 3B). At the beginning, our weight loss phase is more exponential. Weight loss then becomes slower; the last 10 pounds are always the hardest ones to lose—almost like pulling teeth! (see Figures 2B & 3B on next page)

WEIGHT LOSS CURVES

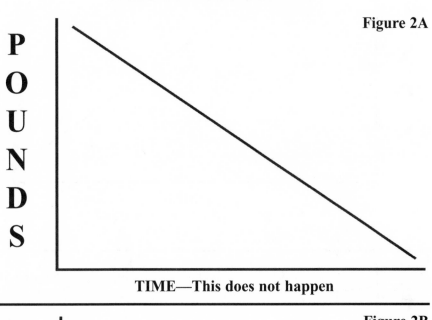

Figure 2A

P O U N D S

TIME—This does not happen

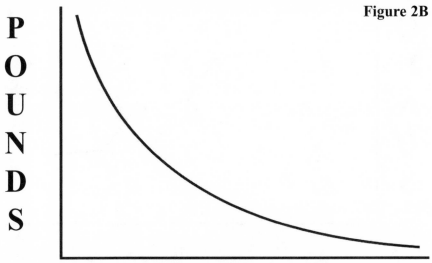

Figure 2B

P O U N D S

TIME—This is the real curve

PLATEAUS

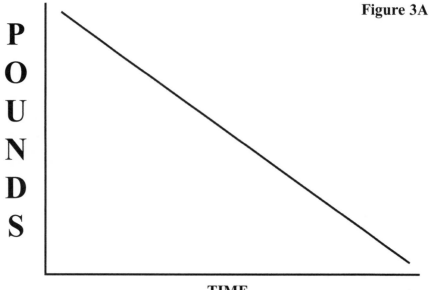

Figure 3A

P
O
U
N
D
S

TIME
Not the realistic weight loss curve

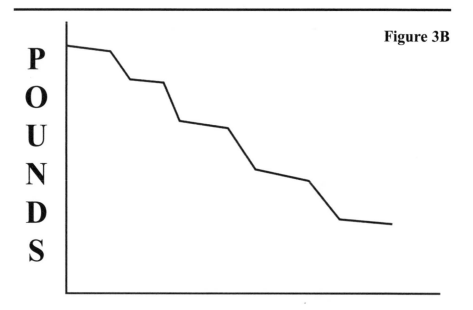

Figure 3B

P
O
U
N
D
S

TIME
Weight loss with plateaus

CHILDHOOD OBESITY

Parents also have a double standard with their children. They will eat skinny but will feed the children fat. Good parenting shows when your children look well nourished! On the contrary, we are doing a disservice to our children when we feed them fatty meals. Mom should not give her child a cookie or a sweet when the child falls down. Food does not relieve the pain; it is better to pick the child up and comfort her instead of feeding her. When we promise the child a dessert if she finishes her vegetables, the implication is that the dessert is superior to vegetables. It is best not to force the issue; if the child is hungry enough, he will finish his vegetables. Remember: blackmail begets blackmail! Children will now only eat vegetables if they know there is a dessert waiting when they finish their meal.

I personally do not see patients younger than age seven. I picked this age, because I want the child to be capable of being responsible for his/her eating problems. I refuse to see those children who are dragged to my office by the parents but who really do not want to lose weight. I interview parents and children separately, and if I find that the child is not ready, I recommend waiting another year.

I have also often witnessed confrontational behaviors between parent and child. By becoming obese, the child rebels against her/his parents. Many times the child is seeking attention. Other times, the young girl who is sexually abused by her father, uncle, older brother, stepbrother, or mother's live-in boyfriend tries to make herself less sexually attractive by becoming fat. Fat is safe for certain girls; it makes them feel less sexually attractive. Eating disorders are often associated with sexual abuse at an early age. A new study has shown that children exposed to four or more serious adverse reactions were up to 12 times more likely to become obese. Sadly, an alcoholic parent was the most common adverse exposure.

In addition, 22% of obese children reported a history of sexual abuse in childhood. A patient of mine who had difficulty with her weight and experienced problems maintaining relationships recalled being abused at age three by an uncle. She was a beautiful woman who had finally confronted this episode in psychotherapy and then lost a tremendous amount of weight. However, her relationships with men were always mixed with distrust.

In a surprising shift in thinking about kids and weight, doctors are studying the drugs Xenical™ and Meridia™, as well as the diabetes drug Glucophage™, to treat seriously overweight children. Many doctors now believe that obesity—just like cancer, heart disease or diabetes—is a grave medical problem that requires drug intervention, no matter what the age of the patient.

We should help our children become slimmer because normal weight children are healthier. Fat children have higher cholesterol levels and develop orthopedic problems earlier in life. Fat children also develop earlier sexually and do not achieve tall statures as hormones may stop their bone growth.

The Bogalusa Heart Study followed a group of children from birth. When accidents unfortunately ended some of these children's lives, their coronary arteries were dissected and observed. Those children who were overweight already showed coronary artery plaques at age seven! Dr. Gerald S. Berensen proved that heart disease in children starts early. Obesity is more prevalent in children whose parents have major heart problems by age 52 and heart disease may be passed on from generation to generation.

The same studies were done for Vietnam War casualties, and those overweight young men in their early twenties showed even bigger coronary artery plaques! Should we accept this disease in our young American population? Dr. Kelly Brownell, a behavior specialist in the field of obesity sadly concludes, "America, you are killing your children!"

The number of overweight children and adolescents has doubled in the last 20 years. In addition, adults who were obese as children have an increased risk of mortality independent of their adult weight. Some weight loss may be achieved by reducing intake of sodas, juices and excess milk. Exercise should be encouraged, but results are best achieved in behavior modification-based weight management involving both children and parents.

The timing of childhood thinness can also predict obesity. Children who reach their thinnest before age five are more likely to become fat adults than those who reach it later. The risk of obesity was lowest among children who reached their thinnest after age six. When children are thinnest before age five, parents urge them to eat and to ignore internal cues such as a feeling of fullness or only eating when hungry.

Nearly one in five kindergartners screened at 12 elementary schools in Palm Beach County, Florida is overweight. The findings could mean that the obesity epidemic is worsening and that more of the county's future workforce could be disabled from type II diabetes, a disease commonly seen among obese adults. The most recent national study estimated that 13% of U.S. children ages six to eleven are overweight. "What we're seeing in students at younger and younger ages is type II diabetes," said Anne Hedges, administrator of the district's school health program. Studies have found that children tend to maintain the eating habits they learned in childhood into adolescence. Nearly 60% of adults in Florida are obese or overweight, according to the Florida Department of Health.

Working mothers are often too tired to prepare meals at home. This is one reason that there is an increased number of fast food restaurants. According to Dr. Kelly Brownell, no house in America is farther than 15 minutes from any McDonald's. Fast food is fatty, yes; but it is also cheap, quick, available and tasty. Children quickly become addicted to fast food! Less fatty alternatives are not doing as well commercially. By the time I tried to taste a McLean hamburger, it was taken off the market. When I inquired about its fast demise, the response was that the public preferred the real thing and was not buying the less fatty hamburger. The supermarket managers tell me that the low fat products do no sell as well and have to be replaced constantly by more caloric counterparts. Sadly, the consumer does not seem to be educated enough. Very few women read food labels in the supermarket. Children definitely do not read labels. As long as there is a toy inside, the child will eat sweetened lard, which was incidentally the filling for Oreo cookies!

On my way to a meeting, I spoke to a Pizza Hut manager who happened to be sitting next to me on the airplane. I asked him why Pizza Hut has not come up with a low fat, thin-crusted pizza with more vegetables? Apparently, this had been tried before but was not very successful. He told me that the new pizzas are now bigger and cheesier. They even smuggle in some extra cheese within the crust borders.

Restaurant portions are growing bigger and bigger. Patrons look more and more stuffed; children consume these huge amounts with their parents and are only able to waddle back to their cars. In schools, I am always asked to consult on children's lunches; apparently vegetables and salads prepared in the school cafeterias are being thrown directly into the garbage cans. Favorite foods in school cafeterias are still hamburgers, french fries, and pizza, which imitate fast food menus.

Dr. Kelly Brownell proposes that fast food establishments charge a tax whenever a person orders french fries and remove the tax if a baked potato is substituted instead. This punitive method is similar to the tobacco tax. Tobacco causes many types of cancers; fried food leads to obesity-related diseases. Incidentally, obese school children were shown to eat a smaller percentage of their calories at breakfast than normal weight children did. The obese children either skipped or ate smaller breakfasts than their normal weight counterparts.

Education should be started early; nutrition classes should be given to parents so they know what foods to purchase and how to prepare the meals. Parents can also be taught what suggestions to make to their children to eat. Until parents take a firmer stand in ordering healthy foods in restaurants as well as in fast food eateries, these detrimental food practices will continue. The consumer dictates the inventory in the stores. The foods that are not bought are not being reordered and thus become extinct.

Weight loss is a family affair. Parents need to get involved. Once a child is seven-years-old, he or she should take responsibility for his or her weight loss program. Dr. Alvin Eden, a pediatrician who specializes in childhood obesity, recommends that the parents "dejunk" the house as a prerequisite for weight loss. Only good food should be available for your child. If other siblings are skinny, let them go outside for that special treat. No junk food should remain in the house. Dr. Eden allows children to eat anything they want before 8:00 p.m.; after that time, he does not allow any eating. He also recommends an exercise of the child's choice every afternoon for about half an hour. He wants this corroborated by the parents' signatures.

In my office, I prefer to handle the weight loss program directly with the child. I believe that if a parent makes negative comments about the child's eating, the child will do just the opposite. No nagging about food is allowed. (I address this point later in the chapter on pg. 47 with a letter describing how parents can help their obese child.) We require a diet diary, explaining to the child which foods are better than others and going over which foods are liked or disliked by the patient.

We then modify those favorite foods to make them healthier; we do not push disliked foods at all. We encourage color in the child's food and ask them to record how many colored foods he/she consumed during the week. We discourage bland and beige food (Barry Sears comments: "If it is white, it's not right!"). We also recommend a minimum of 30 minutes of exercise, three times or more per week, to be included in the diet diary. We first review the diet diary weekly, then every other week.

When the child goes out, we are more lenient than with their diet at home, but no bad food should be brought back into the house. No doggie bags, please! I feel that even in fast food restaurants, intelligent food choices can be made. As the child loses weight and receives compliments, he/she will be encouraged to continue the program. I have found that those children who are instructed about proper nutrition and exercise will maintain these good behaviors the rest of their lives. As a fat child and adolescent who lost my weight at age 16, I became determined not to ever be fat again. Being a fat child steered me into my profession of Bariatrics; I encourage my fat child patients by telling them I was a fat child, too. I tell them, "If I could do it, so can you!"

American children have stopped exercising. A few years ago the fitness level of American children was shown to be dismally inferior to that of other countries. Children spend an inordinate amount of time in front of televisions and now computers. Time spent playing video games is associated with higher levels of body fat, according to a study of 85 French 10-year-olds. Obesity in children was related directly to the amount of time watching television; the more hours spent watching television, the fatter the kid. Television programs are saturated with snacking commercials that stimulate children to get up and bring food to the television, the universal baby-sitter. In addition, many parents are afraid nowadays to allow their children to play in the neighborhood or in nearby parks. This is an important safety issue that is plaguing today's children because it encourages them to stay home.

Another problem is that children no longer drink water, they either drink high-calorie fruit juices or carbonated drinks. Most carbonated drinks are sweetened with high-fructose corn syrup. The consumption of high fructose corn syrup has recently been correlated with obesity, not only in children but in adults, also. Apparently, high fructose corn syrup is directly lipogenic, or fat producing.

Once a child is obese, he or she is not very motivated to exercise. Dr. Jean Mayer observed normal weight and overweight children in a swimming pool and found that while the normal weight children were swimming actively, the overweight children just chatted while holding on to the borders of the pool.

Sadly, kids' caloric intake may increase the risk of adult cancer. For every 240 additional calories consumed daily as a child, the risk of dying as an adult from all cancers is increased significantly.

The whole family should participate together in activities that expend calories, like playing ball, walking, bicycling, etc. Parents should not wait until their child is already obese. We also know that coronary artery plaques may be reversible with diet; in anthropologist Clark Wissler's experiment, monkeys who consumed a high-fat monkey chow showed coronary artery plaques. However, when these monkeys were put on a diet of low-fat chow, their coronary arteries became clean. Dr. Dean Ornish also observed similar findings in adults who were put on a low-fat diet, and whose coronary artery plaques disappeared. In conclusion, childhood obesity is never too early to treat, and it is also never too late to modify one's lifestyle. If we want to stop this obesity epidemic, we have to start today with our children; otherwise they will become our next generation of fat Americans.

ADOLESCENT OBESITY:

As a young girl enters puberty, fat distribution changes as sex hormones kick into gear. Today's young girls are very influenced by magazines showing emaciated celebrities like Calista Flockhart, Heather Locklear and Kate Moss. Young girls already begin dieting at the age of nine years and; incredibly, 40% of nine and ten-year-old females are trying to lose weight. In addition, white girls seem to be more dissatisfied with their weight than non-whites. Here are a few other facts: before adolescence, girls have about 12% body fat; overnight their fat percent explodes to 25%. The fat child and the fat adolescent are verbally and physically abused by peers. The fat adolescent may be involved in unprotected sex as she tries to fulfill her craving for love and acceptance. Sometimes in incestual relationships, fat is safe and used to repel unwanted sexual advances. Not only is the fat adolescent repeatedly humiliated at school, but she is also criticized at home by her family.

Overweight boys, however, are less concerned with weight than obese girls. Obese boys showed 50% lower vitamin E and beta-carotene levels than normal weight boys.

Some teenage girls may have as much fat in their arteries as men three times their age, according to Dr. Henry McGill, M.D. of the Southwest Foundation for Biomedical Research in San Antonio, Texas. This is due to eating a high-fat diet and smoking at an early age. Obese adolescent girls have their periods earlier than their leaner friends. Also, teen girls are less physically active than boys (who not only are more active but eat three times as much as female teens).

The condition called acanthosis nigricans in adolescents manifests itself by dark pigmented patches of skin in the neck, armpits, elbows and knees. This condition is associated with insulin resistance, a precursor of diabetes. Type II diabetes used to only occur in adults, but lately more children are becoming afflicted with this condition due to their degree of obesity.

Being overweight in adolescence increases mortality and morbidity in adulthood. According to a study by Dr. Aviva Must, overweight adolescent men had twice the risk of death compared to men who were lean as adolescents. Women who were overweight in their youth had a higher incidence of arthritis. Being overweight in adolescence increases cardiovascular risk factors like elevated blood pressure, high lipid levels and atherosclerotic plaque formation which persist into adulthood.

Ellen Goodman studied the association of TV and eating disorders in young adolescent girls in Fiji where, before 1995, the fattest girls were considered beautiful. After 1995, Fijian girls started watching programs like "Melrose Place" and "Beverly Hills 90210", and in a year and a half the number of teens with eating disorders doubled. Dr. Anne Becker, the psychiatrist who presented this research, explained that: "the acute and constant bombardment of certain images in the media are quite influential in how teens experience their bodies." Ellen Goodman adds that eating disorders are a cultural by-product and that the big success of our entertainment industry has been to export insecurity. "We can make any woman anywhere feel perfectly rotten about her shape."

If two college applications are similar, the thinner applicant will generally be admitted into the class. In a study of college students,

80% had dieted to lose weight, and 32% had dieted six or more times. According to Dr. L. Pereyra, 46% were currently dieting, even though 82% of the dieters were within their recommended BMI (Body Mass Index). On the average, they wanted to lose 11.5 pounds.

In our society, fat is equated with laziness and dirtiness. I hear the same mistaken comments over and over from those critics who shake their heads and refer to overweight people as having, "No willpower." At proms, large girls line up in the wallflower pattern waiting to be, but never, picked. No wonder these girls have no self-esteem and they are not treated any kinder at their jobs. Because fat is associated with slovenliness in employer's minds, these adolescents are not hired. A study showed an increase of accidents and absenteeism documented among obese employees. According to a new study, obesity increases absenteeism from work by 61-74%. Sick leave is 50-90% greater in the severely obese.

Approximately 10% of the cost of lost business productivity is obesity related. The estimated economic cost per million obese females is $300 million! Employers hire thinner employees, even if their qualifications are not stellar. First impressions count. Obese employees are not given their well-deserved promotions and are generally paid less; despite the fact that they are working harder. They are also taken advantage of in their relationships with the opposite sex. They have to settle for inappropriate partners, and they are mistreated more often, verbally and physically, by their spouses.

So how can we best begin to help our adolescents and young adults to lose the weight? I often give their parents the following letter (Letter 1) describing what they should and should not do to facilitate the weight loss challenge. Unfortunately, in many cases, we must follow with another communication called: "Letter to the Important Family Member or Best Friend" (see Letter 2 on pg. 48).

Letter One

13 WAYS PARENTS CAN HELP

- De-junk the house of fattening foods such as chips, cookies and candy.

- Be supportive; no one changes all one's habits overnight. Praise good dieting choices. Do not nag when your child eats something he/she shouldn't.

- In your own eating habits, set a good example for your child to see.

- Do not force the child to clean his/her plate.

- Offer to exercise with your child. He/she should exercise at least 1/2 hour per day at least three times a week.

- Remove fats from the diet. Substitute fish and poultry for beef, fresh fruit for ice cream, etc.

- Buy foods in single-portion sizes, little packets of unsweetened cereals (high protein), etc.

- Limit television viewing to one hour per day.

- Allow food to be eaten only in dining areas.

- Forbid all eating after dinner.

- Do not offer food as a reward for good behavior.

- Do not allow other family members to tease the child about his/her weight.

- Let the child know he/she is loved no matter what he/she weighs.

In cases where this letter isn't enough and the weight is not coming off, we must follow with another letter addressing other problems associated with weight loss.

Letter Two

OPEN LETTER TO THE IMPORTANT FAMILY MEMBER OR BEST FRIEND

Environment has a significant effect on the overweight person. Experiments have proven that cues like smell, sight of food, activities associated with food (watching television or movies), stress and emotional upset may trigger massive food intake.

So, if the patient is still not losing weight after receiving my first letter, I have a stronger second one that covers a another set of possible problems.

This letter goes to the most important person in the dieter's life, generally their parents or their spouse. I explain to them that if they are truly interested in helping this person, it may mean changing their own life a little, but their efforts will have an overwhelming effect on this person's weight loss results.

- Please never criticize the dieter. Ridicule, teasing, taunting or other verbal abuse does not stop an undesirable behavior. On the contrary, it will stimulate the overweight person to eat even more.

- Only comment on desirable behavior; if the dieter is losing weight, compliment him or her on how good he or she looks. If a lapse occurs, and it will sometimes happen, PLEASE SAY NOTHING!

- As the dieter needs to fat-proof and de-junk the house to achieve results in the first phase of the weight loss, do not bring foods home that he or she likes and might tempt him or her.

- Many families like to eat together; however, do not force the dieter to watch you eat things that he/she cannot have. Eating ice cream in front of the dieter is the height of cruelty. Eat the dessert after he/she has left the kitchen. Remember, many overweight people are pickers or nibblers so the less time in the kitchen, the better.

- You can also help tremendously by going food shopping with the dieter. It will prevent him/her from buying things not allowed in his/her program.

- Clean up after dinner, so that the dieter is not tempted to finish leftovers.

ADULT OBESITY:

It is difficult to believe but their are cases where family members or friends actually want the overweight person to remain overweight for various selfish reasons, and they actively sabotage his or her progress.

For example, one of my patients was doing very well in her weight reduction program. However, one week she returned to the office heavier than at her previous visit. When we questioned her, she admitted to eating a whole chocolate cake! Upon further questioning, the mother admitted to making her daughter's favorite chocolate cake to see if she had enough willpower to resist. The real reason behind this was that mom was getting jealous as her daughter became more attractive.

Another of my patients, a very attractive young woman, had lost a lot of weight and began dressing appropriately for her new figure. Her husband grew angry and wanted her to stop her weight loss program with us. He claimed that she had spent too much money. The real truth was that he was afraid that she was too attractive and might consider leaving him. Another husband brought chocolate and candies home to his wife who had lost a significant amount of weight. He also insisted on going to fancy restaurants where he ordered inappropriate foods for her. He said he wanted to reward her for losing the weight. The truth was that he was threatened by her new attractiveness.

Another of my patients was a young physician who had lost over 100 pounds and looked terrific! In the middle of the night, his wife prepared his favorite fried pork morsels which she waved in front of his nostrils as he slept. When he awoke, she shoved the food into his mouth. She said she felt sorry for him, as he was being deprived of this food. The truth was that she was insecure and afraid that he might be seduced by other women who found him so attractive.

Finally, a man weighing 686 lbs. was sent to me by the chief of a hospital from a neighboring town. When he started to lose weight, he was happy that he could find clothes and shoes to fit his body. I felt that I was doing something worthwhile by saving this young man's life; prior to seeing us, he could only sleep upright and breathe through a tracheotomy tube. Suddenly, however, his visits stopped. When we called his home, we were told that his mother could not bring him to the office anymore because she had no time. She had resumed feeding him his usual six fried eggs and 12 sausages for breakfast. We then found out the real truth: she was afraid that if he lost weight he would leave the house and possibly find a spouse which would make her obsolete.

The last example of this phenomenon involves a young woman who had repeatedly lost weight with us. Oddly, whenever she lost a significant amount of weight, her mother began to have difficulty bringing her to us. Later on, we found out that the whole family lived on this young woman's disability check which she received because of her morbid obesity status. If she achieved a normal weight, the family would lose this income and would then have to make different working arrangements. This was especially sad in light of the fact that the girl was so obese that her life was in dire danger.

This demonstrates again that obesity is indeed a family affair and that the whole family should be educated. The "Letter to the Most Important Family Member or Best Friend" (see Letter 2 on pg. 48) teaches those who would sabotage someone losing weight about the subconscious motives for this behavior. We also educate our patients about how to be firm and not to be adversely swayed by parents, spouses, or significant others. I even give my patients my home telephone number so those who are not happy with their weight loss (the saboteurs) can have someone to complain to! In the more than 21 years that I have been in practice, I have not been called once!

The same mechanisms discussed in childhood or adolescent obesity apply here, too. Obese women have a higher association with polycystic ovarian syndrome which consists of no periods, hirsutism (abnormal hair growth) and cysts in the ovaries. This syndrome is commonly linked to infertility which is reversed by weight loss.

Married men are fatter than single men; even though they drink and smoke less and use fewer drugs, most married men eat more and exercise less.

The most common adult obesity issue arises during or after pregnancy. Patients are shocked that they were able to eat as much as they wanted prior to pregnancy with no weight gain, but would become pregnant and suddenly find that the pounds continued to pile on even after delivery. A retrospective chart review of patients delivering in a rural hospital between January 1990 and June 1997 indicated that those women who are obese before becoming pregnant are at an increased risk for Cesarean delivery.

Many women lose their weight a few months after delivery while others, especially those I see in my office, seem to have difficulty shedding their extra poundage. Weight gain that is compounded by several pregnancies results in an obese and unhappy woman! According to Dr. Jennifer Lovejoy, weight gained in the first 20 weeks of pregnancy hangs on six months postpartum while the weight put on after 20 weeks is less likely to stay.

Obese women tend to have larger infants. Having children only contributes to an average weight gain of about one pound per birth. However, many variables exist in determining this. For example, black women gain more than white and due to socio-economic reasons, the unemployed gain more than the employed mothers.

These women must all understand that hormones have altered their metabolism and that they have to modify their lifestyle. Good nutritional education and exercise can help these women to lose weight and maintain their weight loss. We also recommend to pregnant women not to gain more than 25 pounds per pregnancy. Higher weight is associated with complications for the mother's health and the baby's delivery. Pregnancy per se is an insulin resistant state where the blood sugar level is low but the insulin level is high. Also, obese women may suffer from gestational diabetes during pregnancy. While small weight gain is encouraged, sweets and easily digestible starches are to be avoided. High carbohydrate diets have been shown to clog up small arteries in the placenta, causing the nutrition of the fetus to be impaired. We recommend a good prenatal vitamin with high calcium, adequate folic acid and not too high a vitamin A content. In women with high risk of preeclempsia (elevated blood pressure during pregnancy), vitamin C (1,000 mg) and vitamin E (400 IU) are recommended to prevent this condition. Neuromins, or essential fatty acids fed to pregnant mothers have been shown to increase the IQ of their babies.

Pregnant women also become hypothyroid and may require thyroid testing and supplementation. Those already on thyroid supplementation may require an increase of dosage.

In addition, mothers who breast fed their babies retain less weight over time than women who bottle feed. Breast feeding can expend 500 calories per day and may selectively reduce fat from the hips and thighs, according to Dr. C.A. Janney, et al.

During adult life, emotional overeating escalates due to stresses at the home and the work place. Men have many responsibilities, especially financial, as jobs are usually stressful and children create even more anxiety. Many mothers are single moms who juggle child rearing and jobs. Food offers comfort for the legions of stressed adults. The described discriminations continue in all aspects of their lives. Diseases start showing their ugly heads. Besides food, other addictions become strong, especially alcohol, nicotine and drugs. The "Craving Brain" does not stop at one addiction; as the addiction is fed, the financial situation plummets further. The stress increases, and the cycle inexorably repeats itself. Food, alcohol and drugs provide the escapes to promote some type of coping mechanism to continue functioning. Alcohol removes inhibitions, allowing for distraction from daily problems, and is highly addictive. We pay a high price for this addiction; alcohol undermines physical health (cirrhosis of the liver, gastritis, delirium tremens) and mental health (agitation and violence). Alcohol is very detrimental to weight loss as it is a high-caloric substance almost as high as fat (7 calories per gram of alcohol versus 9 calories per gram of fat). It also stimulates appetite and contributes to fat deposition, as evidenced by the beer belly seen in many men who are big beer consumers. Many alcoholics have difficulty staying on a nutritional program for weight loss. While obese men consume more alcohol, especially beer, obese women drink fewer alcoholic beverages but eat more fat, chocolate, candies, cake, cookies, and fewer fruits and vegetables.

Nicotine is also quite an addictive substance that may cause many cancers but stimulates weight loss. According to a new study, 80% of those who quit smoking gain weight. The average weight gain is about five to seven pounds; however, some may gain more than 25 pounds. Two-thirds of the weight gained following smoking cessation is due to an increase in caloric intake. One-third is caused by a reduction in metabolism. These people would benefit from the thyroid precursor tyrosine or from the fat-burning combination ephedrine and caffeine or, finally, from the appetite suppressant phenylpropranolamine.

A study done on obese rats showed that nicotine not only decreases food intake but also increases thermogenesis in brown adipose tissue and in the resting metabolic rate.

Reynold's Tobacco Company is currently developing new drugs that can mimic nicotine's potent effects on the brain but without deadly cigarette tars connected with smoking. These nicotinic compounds constitute a new class of powerful drugs which scientists believe can provide numerous benefits, from relieving pain to improving memory.

While average weight gain is close to 12 pounds three months after smoking cessation, those women who started and continued an exercise program reduced their weight gain to only seven pounds; thus five pounds less weight gain was achieved through exercise during those three months.

Diseases such as Alzheimer's and Parkinson's affect smokers a lot less than non-smokers. Scientists have recently learned how to identify which brain receptors are affected by nicotine. Nicotinic compounds improve both short-term and long-term memory in rats without increasing heart rate or blood pressure. Another nicotinic compound is supposed to relieve pain as much as morphine. Finally, Japan Tobacco Inc. has developed a new compound that will be the first to increase good cholesterol (HDL).

OBESITY AND AGING:

Menopause occurs four years earlier in the obese female. In the aging female, the next weight problem occurs after menopause when appropriate hormonal replacement therapy is instituted. Dr. D. Kritz Silverstein, et al. showed that hormonal replacement therapy, whether used intermittently or continuously for 15 or more years, is not associated with weight gain and central obesity commonly observed in post-menopausal women. In my own personal experience and in treating other women in this group, I have found that the post-menopausal period brings increased weight gain primarily in the breasts, waist and stomach area. Of course other factors, like aging, may also play a role in this change of body composition: the fat shifts to the center of the body, and extremities become thinner. Many women complain of weight gain even after a hysterectomy; there may be some unknown hormones in the uterus that may help with weight control. Women's responses to hormones may vary, and some do well with synthetic hormones, estrogen alone, if a hysterectomy had been performed, or an estrogen-progesterone combination for others.

At least in monkeys, it has been shown that progestins in combination with estrogens may increase fat deposition particularly in subcutaneous depots. This is the reason some gynecologists recommend progestins to be added only every third cycle.

In my office, I prefer to use natural hormonal replacement therapy. We do a complete hormonal assay and tailor the hormonal supplementation based on the results. Natural hormones made from the extraction of the Mexican Yam (Dioscora composita) are manufactured by compounding pharmacies (pharmacies that mix the compounds according to doctor's prescriptions). We use mostly estriol and some estradiol for estrogen replacement and natural progesterone instead of progestins. I have found that these hormones make my patients gain less fluid and fat and still help with symptoms like hot flashes. Most studies that show improvement in bone mass density, heart disease, and Alzheimer's disease were done using synthetic hormones. More studies are needed to show the same results with natural hormones.

As described before, our body shape changes as we age. Fat deposits itself in the abdominal area, limbs become thinner, posture changes due to osteoporosis, and gait is different due to more weight being transferred to the front. Arthritis and joint pain completely alter the body configuration. New studies using human growth hormone (HGH) injections have shown that there is a reduction in fat and improved well-being, energy and rejuvenation in older people using this product. This is a recombinant material made in the laboratory so that the risk of infection or contamination is zero. We recommend a somatomedin test or a 24-hour urinary human growth hormone level check prior to inception of therapy. And as further testing is done, dosage is increased, if needed. Preliminary results seem positive, but more data is needed to ascertain all benefits of HGH. Insulin resistance also manifests itself as more fat is stored and diabetes and hypertension follow. As we navigate through life, many obstacles are put in our way to stimulate weight gain which in turn contributes to a myriad of diseases. Treatment options vary according to the problems encountered in each stage of life.

Chapter Summary

- Infants of overweight mothers start gaining weight as early as 6 to 12 months of age.

- Smoking mothers are more likely to have obese children.

- Breastfed children (until 5 months of age) are smarter and leaner.

- Excessive juice drinking is associated with more overweight toddlers.

- Sexual abuse in children sometimes manifests itself in obesity.

- Coronary plaques occur in children as early as age 7.

- Today children are exhibiting Type II diabetes which was only seen in adults before.

- The consumption of high fructose corn syrup in many drinks or foods is fat producing.

- Obesity is a family affair; parents and spouses should be involved.

- High carbohydrate diets are detrimental to the fetuses of pregnant women.

- Careful hormonal supplementation is in order to combat adult obesity and aging.

— Chapter Three —

SYMPTOMS AND TESTS PERTINENT TO OBESITY

W hen you visit the doctor and relate to him how you are feeling, he will order some tests which include blood assays. Let me navigate you through these different tests; I will explain their significance and interpretation.

The electrocardiogram (test of the heart's contractions) will often show left axis deviation, the first abnormality in hypertensive individuals. This means that the heart is pushed to the left side and has enlarged because it has to work harder to push the blood through the bigger body. A large heart is an inefficient organ. The bigger the heart, the higher the mortality rate. High blood pressure puts you at a higher risk for a heart attack or stroke. Thus you are put on a blood pressure-lowering medication. Any medication has the potential to have side effects. Remember that blood pressure medication will reduce your blood pressure, but it only masks cardiovascular disease which may continue. On the other hand, weight loss has no side effects and will improve cardiovascular disease.

What does the panel of tests further reveal? You may have elevated blood sugar, because the insulin (the hormone secreted from your pancreas) cannot transport the blood sugar inside the cells. This occurs because fat covers the doorknobs or receptors that insulin can recognize to enter the cells. Over 50% of obese individuals are found to be insulin resistant; they produce insulin, but the insulin cannot get through the cells for proper elimination of the sugar molecules. Insulin can be compared to a bus that carries the sugar molecules as passengers inside the cell. In diabetic individuals or insulin-resistant patients, the bus cannot enter the cell and discharge its passengers, thus the sugar molecules stay outside. The pancreas continues to receive a signal to produce more and more insulin. However, this insulin is not efficient in doing its job, and insulin over-production and insulin resistance ensue. (see Figure 4)

Figure 4

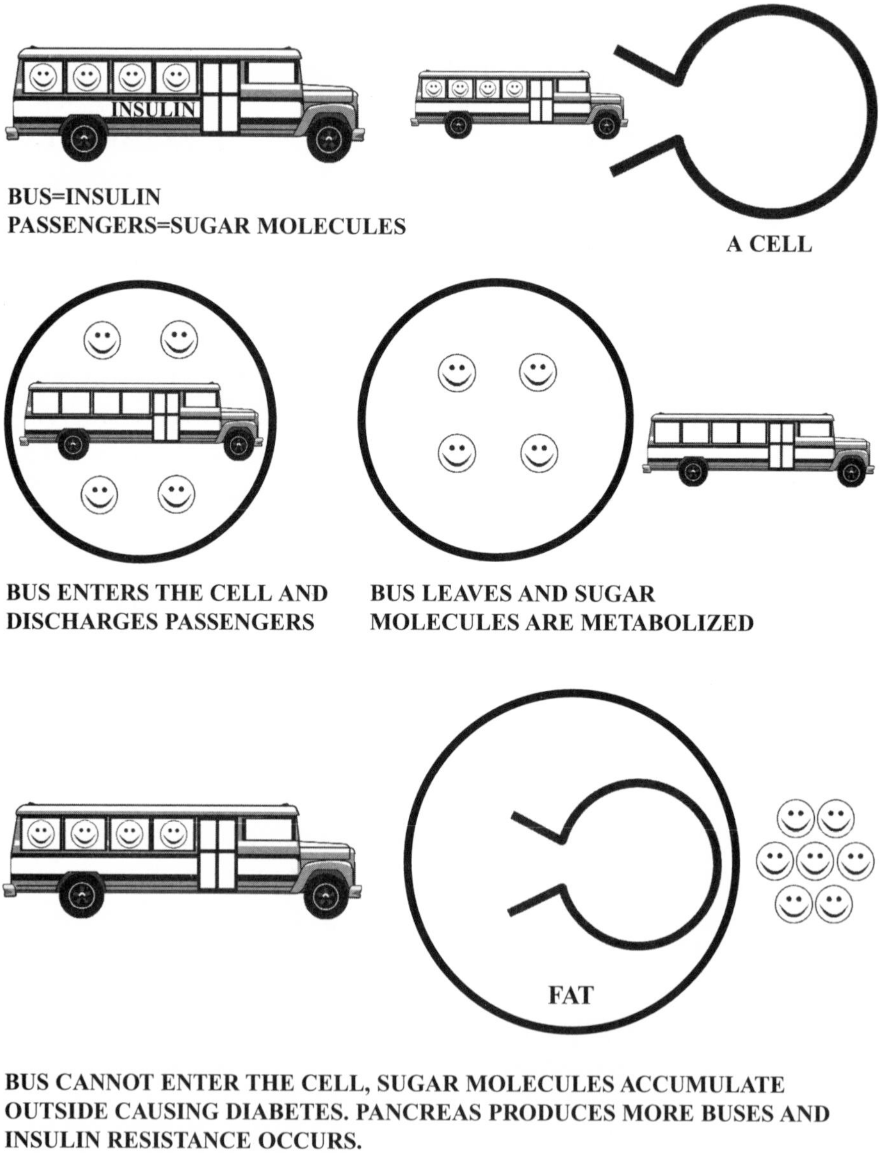

BUS=INSULIN
PASSENGERS=SUGAR MOLECULES

A CELL

BUS ENTERS THE CELL AND **BUS LEAVES AND SUGAR**
DISCHARGES PASSENGERS **MOLECULES ARE METABOLIZED**

FAT

BUS CANNOT ENTER THE CELL, SUGAR MOLECULES ACCUMULATE OUTSIDE CAUSING DIABETES. PANCREAS PRODUCES MORE BUSES AND INSULIN RESISTANCE OCCURS.

The most crucial tests to determine whether you have this problem are: a blood sugar test, a fasting insulin test, and finally, the glycohemoglobin A1C test which detects blood sugar in the last two months. A glycohemoglobin A1C of six or lower is acceptable. A glycohemoglobin value of seven or more is associated with diabetic complications (vascular and neurological problems). A number over seven indicates problems, and anything over ten is quite serious. A C-reactive protein reading over five is also quite indicative of insulin resistance and inflammation.

Diabetes affects all organ systems and is associated with increased mortality. Excess blood sugar is a key to nerve damage including numbness, tingling, and extreme sensitivity to pain. The excess sugar may also damage blood vessels and produce obstruction in the arteries that hinder blood flow to the legs. In extreme cases, tissue death involving toes and feet may occur, necessitating amputation. Kidney and heart disease are common in diabetics. Lastly, the highest cause of blindness in the USA is diabetes!

In some cases, the insulin bus with the sugar molecule passengers enters the cell but the bus cannot discharge its passengers because of a genetic defect that prevents acidification of the insulin. Then the bus and passengers exit the cell without the passengers being metabolized and insulin resistance follows.

In one test, an anti-hypertensive medication called Clonidine prevented insulin resistance, high blood pressure and elevated heart rate in dogs fed a high-fat diet, but did not affect weight gain. Dr. A.P. Rocchini, et al. concluded that "the central nervous system plays a critical role in the development of both insulin resistance and hypertension associated with...a high fat diet."

In addition, inflammation may affect susceptibility and predict the risk of type II diabetes and insulin resistance. Elevated C-reactive protein is one of the inflammatory markers that was associated with a 2 or 3 fold increased risk of developing diabetes. This inflammatory response may help explain why obesity can lead to diabetes. Besides type II diabetes, other diseases like Alzheimer's disease, cancer, heart attack and stroke may be associated with mild chronic inflammation so prevalent in the obese. Fish oils, especially the omega-3 fatty acids are effective in reducing inflammation.

Blood fats are often elevated in the obese population. These fats, if high, are associated with coronary artery disease and eventually heart attacks. High levels of fat in the blood have been shown to contribute to migraine headaches. A possible explanation is this: high levels of blood fat lead to a decrease in serotonin which normally helps keep blood vessels constricted. When serotonin levels become too low, dilatation of blood vessels in the brain causes headaches.

Triglycerides are fats that are derived from the consumption of carbohydrates (especially sugar and alcohol). Triglycerides are also elevated in diabetes; sugar molecules that do not enter the cell remain outside and are often transformed into tryglycerides. A genetic defect may also predispose people to have high triglyceride levels in their blood even if they are thin (this syndrome is called familial hyper-triglyceridemia). People with high triglyceride levels in their bloodstream should first have their triglyceride levels re-checked while they are fasting. Triglyceride values can vary depending on the last meal or drink consumed. If the triglyceride level is high (more than 200 mg/dl of blood), we recommend our patients, thin or fat, to cut down on their dietary carbohydrate consumption (no bread, no starches, no sugars). We also advise them to limit their alcohol and fruit intake.

Acording to Dr. Robert Atkins, the deadliest combination is to have both high triglyceride and high cholesterol levels as this condition increases the risk of heart attacks by 16 times. It is interesting to note a syndrome called Syndrome X, or Reaven's syndrome (named for its discoverer Dr. Reaven). The affected patients, who are obese and also have high blood pressure, are insulin resistant and have high triglyceride levels. Out of all my patients, 90% will be able to reduce their triglyceride levels through dietary intervention. The familial inherited type of high triglyceride levels, however, will be reduced with Gemfibrizol (Lopid™) or Tricor™ treatment.

The word cholesterol is the second biggest taboo "C" word after cancer. At cocktail parties, people discuss their cholesterol levels at various stages of their lives and after different dietary and drug manipulations. There is a big confusion about cholesterol. Total cholesterol levels nowadays are meaningless. The American Heart Association recommends that total cholesterol levels should be below 200 mg/dl. However, it is most important to determine the ratio between total cholesterol and good cholesterol; the ratio should be optimally below 4.5

(the lower, the better). The good cholesterol, called high density lipoprotein or HDL, is supposed to protect us against heart attacks. The higher it is, the better it is; it should be at least 35 mg/dl. An HDL below 30 carries a bad prognosis. It is said that the person who has an HDL below 30 should get a life insurance policy as soon as possible to protect his or her family. The healthiest HDL values are 55 or over for women and 40 or over for men. The measurement of serum triglyceride levels does not provide clinically meaningful information about coronary heart disease (CHD) risk beyond that obtainable by measurement of serum cholesterol subfractions alone. However, this statement has lately been challenged because high triglyceride levels may also predict CHD.

HDL is usually low in obese individuals. The best treatment to elevate HDL is weight loss and exercise. There is also some conflicting evidence pointing to the fact that red wine in moderation or even red grape juice might also help to raise HDL. This was found by studying French people who love to drink wine and whose HDL are quite elevated. However, a genetic predispositon for high HDL in the French population cannot be discarded. Fish oils have also been shown to increase HDL values. High HDL is also associated with longevity (the Methuselah gene, named after this patriarch who supposedly lived to 700 years of age).

A gene known as ABC 1 may be responsible for making a protein essential to both HDL formation and the process of unloading fats from cells and the blood. As a high HDL may be cardioprotective and as no medications are yet known to increase this lipoprotein level, this breakthrough may lead to new drugs that may reduce cardiovascular disease by 50%.

On the other hand, low density lipoprotein (LDL) was thought to be the best predictor for coronary artery disease and heart attacks. According to the Framingham studies, this substance seems to clog up coronary arteries (which are, incidentally, the size of spaghetti noodles) and is responsible for heart attacks. The LDL optimal value is supposed to be 130 mg/dl or lower. Elevated levels of LDL cholesterol were associated with the risk of dementia with stroke in elderly patients. *The American Journal of Clinical Nutrition* states that pomegranate juice can decrease LDL susceptibility to aggregation and retention.

According to the American Heart Association, six months of dietary intervention is recommended first to lower cholesterol. Dietary manipulation includes avoidance of saturated fats like fatty cuts of meats (bacon, lard, beef, lamb, and pork), some dairy products (butter, fatty cheeses, and whipped cream) and fried foods. Egg yolk consumption should be curtailed to three per week. A new study from the *Journal of the American Medical Association* recommends no more than one egg per day for healthy individuals. Diabetics are allowed less than one egg per week.

There is another substance even more atherogenic than LDL, very low density lipoprotein, or VLDL for short; VLDL (plaque former) should not be higher than 40 mg/dl. If after six months of cutting out fats, the cholesterol values have not gone down significantly, medications called statins are prescribed. They block one of the pathways of the formation of cholesterol by our bodies. The brand names are Mevacor™, Zocor™, Pravachol™ and Lipitor™. These drugs do not only lower cholesterol but may also have an anti-inflammatory role in preventing heart attack and stroke. These drugs lower cholesterol but may have side effects like muscle pain, fatigue, and loss of memory most significantly. Cholesterol-lowering drugs may also rob us of Coenzyme Q10, a nutrient for heart health, which should be supplemented whenever a statin is used.

High fiber diets, especially those rich in legumes, have also been advocated for the reduction of cholesterol. In addition, oatmeal, Metamucil™, Colestid™ granules, and Questran™ powder are used to sequester bile acids to prevent the formation of endogenous cholesterol. Niacin, too, has been used for lowering cholesterol.

Nutritional products like red rice yeast, gugulipid and policosanol have been recommended as effective cholesterol lowering medications without the side effects of the statins. Neither arabic gum nor apple pectin have been shown to have a cholesterol-lowering effect. Garlic supplementation has not yet been proven to be effective as a cholesterol-lowering substance.

However, this equation is not so simple as nearly half the people who have chest pain or heart attacks have normal cholesterol levels. New tests can help to diagnose those people who are at risk now. "Total cholesterol has pretty much outlived its usefulness as a way to predict heart disease and follow its progression," says William Castelli, M.D., director of the Framingham Cardiovascular Institute.

In the first stage of injury to the inner lining of the heart's arteries, the chief instigator is an amino acid called homocysteine. Among elderly people in the Netherlands, an elevated homocysteine level was shown to be associated with an increased risk of cardiovascular disease. Children with high homocysteine levels may also be at an elevated risk for cardiovascular disease. There is also a link between homocysteine and dementia, besides the connection to a higher incidence of heart attacks and strokes. As people with higher levels of homocysteine are twice as likely to develop Alzheimer's or dementia, by lowering homocysteine or increasing folic acid, one can prevent heart attacks or Alzheimer's. The National Institute of Health is planning a big trial with folic acid, B6 and B12 to try to slow cognitive decline in people suffering from Alzheimer's. The recommended homocysteine level is below 10. If it is higher than that, vitamins B1, B6, B12, and folic acid can reduce homocysteine levels.

The size of the LDL particles can also determine heart disease. If you have big LDL particles (or LDL pattern A), you are less likely to get heart disease than someone whose LDL bits are generally tiny and dense (LDL pattern B). LDL pattern B predicts heart disease better than cholesterol values. However, LDL pattern B can be reversed through nutritional intervention to pattern A. Again, no pastries, pastas, white bread, white rice, or sugars are allowed if you have pattern B LDL. Also, large doses of niacin can help change pattern B LDL to pattern A. The statins are not helpful in changing LDL pattern.

Recent, more complex testings from Berkeley Heart Lab, or Atherotech, can now further pinpoint the different subdivisions of HDL, LDL, and IDL (intermediate density lipoprotein) or VLDL to provide better treatment modalities for patients with high cholesterol levels.

Finally, the number of protein particles that carry the cholesterol molecules may also be a predictor for heart disease. The NMR Lipo Profile done by Liposcience checks for the number of protein particles carrying cholesterol. The company feels that the number of cholesterol carrying particles is more significant in the prediction of heart attacks than the cholesterol level itself.

A fourth predictor of heart disease is called Lipoprotein a or Lp a for short. The best lipoprotein value should be lower than 15. Presently we do not know a method, either nutritional or pharmacological, to reduce this fraction of LDL.

Recently the theory of inflammation of the inner wall of arteries has been associated with heart attacks and strokes. The best predictor for inflammation is a C reactive protein test in the blood. The statins may also help to decrease this protein. C reactive protein (CRP) may prodict cardiovascular events better than cholesterol levels in a study that analyzed 27,000 blood samples from patients participating in the Women's Health Initiative. Screening for both cholesterol, and especially CRP levels, is the best predictor of heart attack and stroke.

Obese women were recently found by Dr. G. Darietal to produce many coagulation and inflammatory products in their blood which facilitate the formation of blood clots, heart attacks and strokes. Platelet activation and low grade inflammation in these women are triggered by abdominal obesity and are reversible by weight loss.

According to the American Academy of Family Practice, cholesterol levels should be checked at about 20 years of age and rechecked at least once every five years after that. However, if you have other risk factors for heart disease you may need to have your cholesterol level checked more often. Talk to your family doctor about how often you need to be tested.

Children as young as two-years-old should have their cholesterol checked if a close relative, such as a grandparent, had heart disease before age 55 or if a close relative has high cholesterol (a level of 240 or above).

There is a common misconception about shrimp and seafood in general. Even though these foods are high in cholesterol, they are permissible for people who have high cholesterol. Cholesterol does not come from ingestion of cholesterol but rather from consumption of foods high in saturated fats.

Every obese patient who comes to my office asks to have his or her thyroid tested, and rightfully so: about one out of ten patients tested has a thyroid deficiency. The best method to determine thyroid function is a very sensitive third generation TSH (thyroid stimulating hormone). A TSH value above five (depending on the laboratory) denotes a thyroid deficiency. Of course, this test is not foolproof and many people with normal TSH levels can still have abnormal thyroid function. Sometimes checking your temperature may indicate low thyroid function. Dr. Barnes recommends taking one's temperature immediately upon awakening in the morning. A morning temperature below

97.8 degrees Farenheit may indicate hypothyroidism. A resting pulse rate less than 65 (normal 65-75) may also indicate a thyroid problem. You should keep a record of your temperatures during one week and bring them to your doctor. Low temperatures, dry skin, depression, forgetfulness, dry coarse hair, splitting nails, constipation, and loss of the lateral one-third of your eyebrows are quite suggestive of hypothyroidism. Patients mostly complain of depression, muscle weakness, weight fluctuations, and irregular periods. Headaches may also be a symptom of low thyroid function.

Free T4 (tetra-iodothyronine) and free T3 (triido-thyronine) uptakes may be better diagnostic tests for hypothyroidism. As the active form of thyroid is T3, it is paramount to check T3 in the blood. A free T3 uptake should be around 30. A value lower than 25 may point to thyroid insufficiency. Even if these thyroid tests are normal, you may produce antibodies against your own thyroid and suffer from Hashimoto's thyroiditis. The best treatment regime for this condition is thyroid hormone supplementation. The most commonly used thyroid medications are Synthroid™ or Levothroid™ (synthetic hormones). Some doctors prefer to use Armour's thyroid, a desiccated form of animal thyroid. A recent article in the *New England Journal of Medicine* (February issue 1999), found that the best treatment was a combination of Synthroid™ with triiodothyronine or (T3) or Cytomel™.

According to Dr. Christiane Northrup, T3 may also be a neurotransmitter which regulates the action of serotonin, norepinephrine and GABA (gamma aminobutyric acid) which is a tranquilizer. Hypothyroidism and depression are related on many levels. Tyrosine is needed for the formation of both serotonin and thyroid hormones. Low thyroid function can deplete the brain of serotonin, while depression can deplete the body of tyrosine and T3 hormone. Patients on this regime had a feeling of well being and energy. Low dose supplementation of T3 reduces belly fat (probably caused by low conversion of T4 to T3).

Hypothyroidism occurs more often in women at mid-life (during perimenopause and after menopause), when there is not enough progesterone. Birth control pills can also lower T3 hormone. When extra progesterone is used to balance extra estrogen, thyroid function improves. Cholesterol-lowering medications may also lower thyroid hormones, while thyroid hormone supplementation may decrease cholesterol and triglyceride levels in the blood. Dr. John Lee recommends the use of natural progesterone if the TSH is slightly elevated. Dr. Ridha Arehn's book, *The Thyroid Solution*, shows the interconnection between the mind and the thyroid gland. Finally, the basal metabolic rate of formerly obese women was found to be lower than that of the never obese females. T3 levels were 31% lower in the formerly obese than those women who were never fat before.

According to Dr. Neal Rouzier, thyroid insufficiency can be diagnosed when one has a low temperature (less than 97.6 in the morning and 98.0 in the evening), depression, hair loss, colds, headaches, and increased cholesterol. He adds that menopausal symptoms may be caused by low thyroid. He recommends also a combination of T3 and T4 (like in Armour's thyroid) even in patients suffering from congestive heart failure. Selenium supplementation is needed for proper thyroid functioning.

Another caveat is that Cytomel™ only stays in the system for six hours and therefore should be given several times a day or in a slow release form.

An individualized approach is best for therapy, as each person is different and may need different thyroid supplementation.

I would like to emphasize now the importance of individualization of treatment for all overweight or obese people, as each individual has different problems. (see Table 3)

Table 3

TREATMENT DEPENDENT ON BLOOD PARAMETERS

Blood Parameters	Tests Ideal Values	Nutrition Rx	Pharmacotherapy
Cholesterol Total	below 200	decrease sat. fats increase fiber red rice yeast polycosanol	cholestid, questran statins
HDL total	above 45 in men	increase exercise fish oil, red wine	Tricor™
	above 55 in women	increase exercise fish oil, red wine	niacin, statins
LDL	below 130	decrease sat. fats increase fiber	niacin, statins

Table 3 (cont.)

Blood Parameters	Tests Ideal Values	Nutrition Rx	Pharmacotherapy
VLDL	below 40	decrease sat. fats increase fiber	niacin, statins
Homocysteine	below 10	B1,B2,B12 folic acid	
Lipoprotein a	below 15	fish oil	
LDL pattern	pattern A	decrease carbs	Niaspan™
TGA (fasting)		decrease carbs increase fiber gugulipid	Gemfibrizol™ Tricor™
Glucose (fasting)	below 116	decrease carbs increase fiber	Glucophage™
Glyco A1C	below 6	decrease carbs increase fiber fenugreek chromium, vanadium, gymnena sylvestre	Amaryl™ Prandin™ Acarbose™ Avandia™ Glucophage™
		Natural Products	
TSH	below 5	thyroid (natural) Armour's Westhroid Naturethroid	synthetic thyroid Synthroid™ Levothroid™ Cytomel™
Free T3 uptake	around 30	natural thyroid Armour's Westhroid Naturethroid T3 slow release	Cytomel™

As evidenced in Table 3, depending on the blood tests, a pattern of dietary intervention should first be tried. People with high cholesterol levels should cut down on their saturated fat intake and substitute it with fish oil, monosaturated or polyunsaturated fats. People with high triglycerides, diabetes, insulin resistance, or pattern B LDL should cut down on their carbohydrate consumption and increase their fiber intake.

Dr. Barry Sears additionally recommends three tests to diagnose and optimally treat his patients:

1. Fasting insulin level (optimal value may be 5 to 10).
2. A ratio triglyceride/high density lipoprotein ratio, or TGA/HDL (best value is 1 to 2).
3. A ratio of arachidonic acid to eicosapentaenoic acid (best value is 1.5 to 3).

Depending on these results, Dr. Sears individualizes the treatment regimes.

The last test I do in my office is called a BMR test or resting basal metabolic study. Even though underwater weighing is the most accurate test for this purpose, I found impedance testing to be most practical for my clinic. As an electric current passes through the body, it is deflected in a different way when it passes through muscle, fat, water and bone. This test gives us two answers: it tells us the percentage of body fat, which should be less than 30% (namely, equal or less than 21% in males and 24% in females), and according to the lean body mass, the machine calculates the basal metabolic rate.

In my experience of over 21 years, I found most of my patients suffer from a low resting basal metabolic rate. In the literature, there is conflicting evidence. Though some studies find that most obese individuals have a low resting basal metabolic rate, one study recen-tly revealed no change in basal metabolic rate or burning potential in patients, between the normal weight and obese. I have always felt that there is a genetic predisposition for people to conserve energy and to store fat for times of famine. Probably during evolution those individuals who were good at conserving energy during food shortages survived, while the high metabolizers did not make it.

The offspring of my patients may resemble one parent who is fat or, conversely, the other parent who is thin. Although the children have the same environment and eat the same menu, the ones who are programmed to be fat already have this tendency at an early age. Life is not fair! Some people can eat as much as they want and remain thin; others, like myself, gain weight merely watching others eat. I find that the higher the percent of lean body mass, the higher the basal metabolic rate. Total weight is not as important as the percentage of lean body mass. (see Figure 5)

Figure 5

At 5'9" Both of These People Weigh 250 Pounds Which One is a Health Risk?

Body Fat _Not_ Weight Is the Key Factor!

In Figure 5, both men weigh 250 lbs. However, you can decide who is the healthier one. Athletes weigh a lot, but their body is made up mostly of muscle. Because of their high basal metabolic rate, for the most part athletes can eat as much as they want.

However, the majority of my patient population are not the most athletic types. They more closely resemble the second gentleman in Figure 5. The best treatment regime for this individual is to lose the fat first then build muscle mass by weight resistance training.

I have an easy tendency to gain weight; my son seems to have inherited that curse of nature called "the battle of the bulge." My husband and my daughter are quite thin and can lose weight easily just by skipping one meal; my son and I have to struggle for one week to lose the same amount of weight. It will be interesting to see how my grandchildren inherit this weight tendency. Of course, in many families the whole clan is fat, as seen in some Botero paintings. Environment also plays a big part, as children learn to eat the fatty foods their parents eat or feed them.

A German study has shown that the normal increase of metabolism that follows a meal for several hours—which is called the thermic effect of food—is blunted in obese patients. Obese people burn fewer calories after a meal, and it takes longer for them to burn those few calories. It is interesting to note that a class of blood pressure lowering agents called beta blockers reduce caloric expenditure even further. Therefore, beta blockers may be weight gain promoters in the obese. Many other medications are also found to promote obesity. Thus, the best advice is to lose the weight and take as little medication as possible.

Chapter Summary

- Diabetes, tested by Hb A1C, inflammation, tested by CRP, elevated cholesterol and triglycerides are more common in the obese.

- The different subdivisions of the cholesterol and the number of particles carrying the cholesterol molecules are better predictors for heart attack risk.

- The T3 value is more important than the T4 or the TSH to predict hypothyroidism (low thyroid state).

- Body fat not weight contributes to higher risk factors in the obese population.

— Chapter Four —

HUNGER: IS IT IN YOUR HEAD
OR IN YOUR STOMACH?

T he most commonly chanted refrain I hear in my practice is: "Dr. Merey, I'm so hungry; I'm always starved!" My new patients are startled when I inquire about the location of their hunger. Are you hungry in your stomach? Does your stomach hurt or growl before meals, or between meals? This is called physiological hunger. Or, on the contrary, does your brain tell you to eat either because it is time to eat or because others are involved in an eating activity? You may be thinking of a particular food at a certain time. On the other hand, you may be an emotional overeater; you may run to food as comfort anytime you are depressed, anxious or stressed. Hormones also may play a role in stimulating the brain's appetite control. How many times have I heard of the compulsion for chocolate or chips before menstrual periods? The epitome of food cravings is reached by pregnant women who have bizarre food predilections.

This head hunger is also defined as emotional hunger. We all can remember being stuffed to the maximum after a big meal; however, when dessert was presented, we made a little extra room in our stomachs to accommodate it. As the saying goes: "There is always room for dessert." Animals cannot be coaxed to eat more; they refuse to have another bite after they become full. We humans have this exceptional quality to stuff and stuff ourselves until pain occurs.

Why is it so important to recognize these different cues for hunger? Because a different treatment is instituted depending on the location of your hunger. It is also very crucial to determine when hunger arises. Finally, the particular food craved has repercussions in what treatment would be optimal.

As you have already gathered, there is no one treatment for everybody; I can help you individualize your program and treatment regime to best fit your needs. You will have to be involved in your cure step by step. Remember what Benjamin Franklin said, "Tell me something, I will forget; teach me something, I will remember; involve me, and I will learn!" One treatment, like one diet, does not fit all! Finally, you can only change your weight when you change your mind.

The mind affects what you eat. The decision to eat something has to be approved by your brain. Cats have an appetite regulation center in their brains that is divided into a stimulatory and an inhibitory area. If the stimulatory center is destroyed, the cat starves to death; if the inhibitory area is destroyed, the cat becomes obese. Human beings are much more complex, and probably many centers in the brain are involved in the regulation of food.

During the initial interview with our patients, we try to determine if they suffer from compulsive overeating. Compulsive overeaters are constantly thinking of food; even after they have just ingested their last meal, they start to think of their next food intake. Your stomach definitely cannot be hungry after a large meal. How can you think of more food? It becomes almost an obsession! Some type of control mechanism regulating your food intake is defective. Compulsive overeaters are out of control with regard to food. Treatment of compulsive overeaters requires drug therapy, as no dietary intervention will suffice. According to Dr. Stephen Gallo, most people don't have diet problems; they are, rather, compulsive overeaters. Trying to teach compulsive eaters to eat just a little simply does not work. Almost 90% of his patients are compulsive overeaters who compulsively eat sweets, flour products, finger foods and trigger foods (foods that stimulate you to binge).

Finally, a big segment of our patient population suffers from binge eating. Nearly 25-50% of all patients in weight loss clinics are binge eaters. Binge eating is twice as common in overweight women as compared to normal weight women. Psychological distress is probably associated with it. Binge eating disorder is characterized by eating binges not followed by vomiting. Psychiatric problems such as depression are associated with binge eating. Adverse experiences during childhood and having a depressed parent increase the likelihood of binge eating disorder. A new study has shown that 20-30% of the obese population resort to binge eating. Neither moderate nor severe caloric restriction has been associated with binge eating. In fact, weight control treatment using caloric restriction reduces the frequency of binge eating. Also cognitive therapy and pharmacotherapy (mainly Norpramin™ and Prozac™) have been very helpful.

Bulimia nervosa (binge eating immediately followed by vomiting) affects 1-2% of women. A history of sexual abuse seems to increase a person's chance of developing bulimia. This is more common among young adolescents who teach it to each other early on as a method for weight control. Nobody is born with a binge eating disease. We learn this behavior. Unfortunately, it works! Bulimics are usually young females; however, this behavior also exists in older women and even in some males. Few outward signs of this syndrome are shown in those suffering from this learned behavior. The women are usually beautiful, and only upon questioning do they admit to this syndrome. One does not know exactly how this develops; but because there is such a premium on being thin in our society, young girls are using this method to eliminate calories. When they reach college age, they become stressed out, have left home for the first time to room in college dorms, and have to produce good grades. They start eating readily-available junk food; then when they feel guilty for ingesting big quantities of fattening food or if they feel painfully full, they resort to self-purging. It becomes an obsessive compulsive behavior. Bingeing occurs, then vomiting ensues in a vicious cycle pattern. Many famous actresses have admitted to binge eating followed by purging.

The biggest problem in college nowadays is not safety on campus, rather it is bulimia. Bulimia was already described in Roman civilization when both men and women induced purging at big banquets in order to be able to eat more. A major problem in bulimia is acid reflux from vomitus. It can cause gastric ulcers and also dental enamel erosion. We have had patients suffer from irregular heart beats due to electrolyte abnormalities, especially potassium deficiency. Most patients do improve as they get older! Half of women diagnosed with bulimia recover completely with or without treatment after 5-10 years and 20% still exhibit the disorder, while the rest continue to binge and purge but to a lesser degree. Those who recover may have relapses.

Bulimia is not life-threatening, however. One particular case comes to mind of a beautiful woman who had been bulimic since adolescence. I tried many times to break the pattern of this vicious cycle to no avail. She did not want to or could not relinquish this behavior. Antidepressants helped, but when something stressful occurred, she resorted back to bulimia. She would come to our office when she had palpitations and receive potassium medication.

Problems occurred when she became pregnant, was potassium deficient, and suffered from palpitations. We rode through this pregnancy with apprehension. Thankfully, she delivered a perfect little baby boy. As far as I know, she is better now; however, whenever she gets into an uncomfortable situation, she reverts back to the bulimia. We reached an agreement; it is better to have a bulimic episode once a day rather than three times daily. It is better to have a bulimic episode every other day than daily; and, finally, it is better to have a bulimic episode once a week than three times a week. We believe in cognitive therapy: trying to recognize the factors which induce the bulimia and avoiding or modifying them. A diary for bulimic episodes and triggering factors is useful to analyze with the patient. Also, these bulimic patients are closet eaters who purge in secrecy. Interestingly enough, a smell of vomit still permeates their clothing and bodies; one can smell them even if they don't admit to this behavior. Enamel erosion on the teeth and teeth marks on the dorsum of their hands (from induction of purging, called Russell's sign) further substantiate the diagnosis. The best treatment regime besides cognitive therapy is pharmacotherapy. A small percentage (4%) of bulimics stop this behavior altogether, while 99% can only curtail it somewhat.

Finally, a more extreme form of eating disorder is anorexia nervosa. Anorexia nervosa affects roughly 0.5% of women. These patients are mostly young females who distinguish themselves as being high achievers and who, after an initial attempt at weight loss, cannot stop themselves from going into extremely low body weight. This condition is life-threatening. The anorexic patient has an unrealistic body image; she fights against treatment, is constantly cold, and can be recognized wearing layers of warm clothing in July. She delights in the control of food deprivation. A patient once told me, "You want me to give up something that I am so good at!" They all look emaciated, bony; their bodies are covered with fine hair (lanugo hair); they have severe hair loss, and lack of periods. They frequently have the stigma of the bulimic (teeth erosion, ulcers, teeth marks on their hands, smelly clothes, and palpitations). Often they have been found to have low thyroid and low magnesium levels in the blood.

I always tell my anorexic patients that periods and procreation are luxuries for the body which just seeks self preservation. To resume periods, a balanced nutritional intake is recommended. The addition of fat should be emphasized. Fat is the precursor of cholesterol which is needed for the formation of sex hormones. Because these patients have not eaten for such a prolonged period of time, potassium and enzyme supplementation are necessary. Dairy products should also be introduced slowly. Water gain is very pronounced at refeeding time and may be quite discouraging to the anorexic female. A slow increase of foods is best, along with gaining the confidence of the patients. I always shoot for one-pound-per-week weight gain. I try to be as gentle and as practical as possible. One study linked controlling mothers with a higher propensity of anorexia in daughters. It was also found that anorexic females do not want to grow up and prefer to remain preadolescent forever. There is the possibility that these young girls are afraid of being attractive to the opposite sex or even use anorexia as a deterrent for sexual advances in the family. One-third of anorexics recover fully, while 83% gain a few pounds.

Prozac reduces relapses. However, the mortality rate with anorexia is high (about 5% per decade). Reduced bone density not treatable with estrogen is quite common with anorexia.

It is quite frightening to see how the role of sexual abuse affects eating disorders. In some cases, being fat is considered safe by adolescents; in other cases, being extremely thin may detract sexual advances. I am always amazed at how much incest affects our eating patterns and also how prevalent it is among my patient population, affecting both the poor and wealthy equally.

Food is definitely associated with emotions. When I interview my patients for the first time, I am also surprised at the frequency with which women burst out crying when asked about what they have eaten that day! Yes, food is nourishment, comfort, and life; but it can also be a source of anxiety, fear, depression, compulsive behavior, and a manipulating tool!

Chapter Summary

- Head hunger or emotional hunger has to be distinguished from stomach hunger or physiological hunger.

— Chapter Five —

FOOD AS AN ADDICTION

S ome foods are just as addictive as alcohol, drugs or nicotine. Familiar foods are imprinted in our brain early in our development. There is also an innate predisposition for certain foods. In utero babies already suck sweet solutions more vigorously and turn away from salty or sour solutions. Food then becomes a comfort at birth. Whenever a baby cries, a nipple or bottle is offered. Oral stimulation is comforting. Pacifiers—and later, thumbs, gum and even cigarettes— keep our mouths busy and our brains happy.

If a child falls or skins his or her knees, the parent offers the child a treat, usually a cookie or something sweet. We quickly learn that sweet things are associated with comfort and healing of pain. Good behavior is also rewarded by a sweet treat. Finally, we are promised a dessert after we eat our vegetables; thus we learn early on that sweets are related to rewards.

Later in our development, foods are associated with certain happy memories and holidays, locking them in our brain. In Marcel Proust's autobiographical novel *A la Recherche du Temps Perdu*, the smell of a "madeleine" (a French cookie) unlocks a whole string of wonderful memories of the author's youth.

We crave these familiar foods of our childhood or youth because they are associated with pleasant activities and memories. They represent our comfort when we feel blue or down.

Mother's cooking, no matter how bad it was, is often fondly remembered as the best food by her children. Recipes are handed down from generation to generation as family heirlooms. Ethnic foods are popular, because they were introduced to us when we were children by our family.

No matter how many new foods we encounter in our lives as we grow older, we want to recapture the past and crave those foods we loved as children or young adults. Almost every holiday is associated with certain foods; turkey, stuffing, and cranberry sauce is a sine qua non of Thanksgiving. Christmas evokes the memory of ham, eggnog, and cookies. Passover would not be Passover without matzo balls and wine. Eggs are associated with Easter. What is the Fourth of July without frankfurters, hamburgers, and watermelon? Not having these foods at these holidays represents pure heresy and creates anxiety.

Certain activities are also associated with foods, because they were introduced together to us when we were children. Popcorn, peanuts, coke and candy are expected foods for moviegoers. We expect a steaming cup of hot chocolate after a skiing expedition. Beer, chips and hot dogs are standard fare for football watchers.

Even though we have not been exposed to some foods, we still may have a genetic predisposition to become addicted to these foods just as much as we may to drugs or alcohol. Once we become exposed to this addictive substance, our brain is imprinted and craves that substance even more.

A minister's wife became a widow late in life and was finally placed in a nursing home. There she was introduced to drinking a glass of wine each night. Even though she never drank before, once she tasted the wine, her craving for alcohol increased to the point that she became an alcoholic! It was later found out that both her parents had been alcoholics.

Because these memories and past experiences of food still haunt us, restricted diets cannot be maintained for long periods of time. This is why we fail so miserably. A person may know the caloric content of a lettuce leaf better than I do; however, when presented with the craved food, the person succumbs. Our intentions are good, so why can't we follow our better judgment?

Once our brain is familiarized with a particular food, it craves it like it craves drugs, alcohol or nicotine. Some people may kill, steal or prostitute themselves to satisfy their drug addiction. The same happens with food addiction! Some people will get up in the middle of the night to raid the refrigerator as a favorite food seems to call their name. They may drive a couple of miles just to get the food they crave. No persuasion can prevent them from attaining this desired treat.

We have to admit to ourselves that we have food addictions, just as we would have to admit that we have problems with other addictive substances. The best therapy is to familiarize ourselves with the foods we crave. Food cravings like all cravings are caused by a deficiency of brain neurohormones, namely dopamine and serotonin. If we feed the "craving brain," those neurotransmitter precursors, the brain will feel satisfied and will not need those substances anymore.

In my experience, the majority of those who come to see me crave carbohydrates. Fat is usually craved in conjunction with sweets. Simply put, carbohydrates are divided into two groups: simple carbohydrates (in sugars, fruits, and dairy products) and complex carbohydrates (in starches like bread, potatoes, rice, and pastas). Once carbohydrates prime the brain, the brain wants more and more. Carbohydrates have a calming effect on the brain, as they stimulate the release of serotonin, an antidepressant.

Drs. Richard and Judy Wurtman at MIT discovered a calming effect of sugar on the brain. When you feel anxious and nervous, sugar should be beneficial. When you want to go to sleep, a high carbohydrate meal should be in order. To avoid jet lag, a dish of pasta is recommended on the airplane to promote sleep during your voyage; then you arrive well rested at your new destination.

The effect of carbohydrates on the brain can also vary from person to person. Some people consume a sweet in the afternoon as a pick-up. Children are also said to have a "sugar high" after consuming a lot of sugar. Of course, the role of sugar in promoting hyperactivity is quite controversial; parents often give conflicting opinions on this subject. Personally, I feel that the reason why sugar seems to give a temporary lift is that many people suffer from hypoglycemia or low blood sugar in the afternoon between 2-4 p.m. However, this lift is temporary and needs to be reactivated with more sugar to create more permanence.

The biggest problem with carbohydrates is that they are bingeing foods. When you eat one slice of bread, you want another; you never leave with one cookie once you open the box. One slogan for potato chips proclaimed that you cannot have just one. In my practice, my patients have described going back to the refrigerator to finish a cake to its total completion or going back and forth to get one chocolate at a time until the box was empty. However, I never heard of a patient bingeing on tuna fish or turkey slices! Pure protein craving is very rare. Somehow our brain has a more potent mechanism for satiety with this food group.

Whether insulin resistance plays a role in carbohydrate cravings or not has not been proven entirely, but laying off the sugar might be the solution for a lot of people. (Cutting out excessive sugar will also help reduce frequent yeast infections.)

Fat cravings do exist, not so much as pure fats but more as fats associated with sweets (like in chocolate, ice creams) or as fats associated with protein (like in fatty meats). Many times I hear my patients commenting on craving a juicy steak. Do they crave the food or the taste? That is a good question. Steak also contains iron that is needed by many anemic patients, especially young women with heavy menstrual periods.

The foods craved may represent a dietary deficiency that some try to replenish. Children with iron deficiency crave ice or eat dirt.

Chocolate cravings are very common in women, especially during the pre-menstrual times. Chocolate has a compound similar to caffeine that acts as a natural mood elevator. Thus, just before periods when hormone levels plummet sharply, chocolate seems to balance mood swings. Coffee and tea also contain substances that keep us alert. Caffeine is quite addictive, and withdrawal headaches may ensue if caffeine has not been consumed for a couple of hours. I have also heard many times that patients reach for candy bars whenever they have headaches; strong espresso or Cuban coffee is a treatment for migraine headache. Caffeine may have a vasoconstrictive (or blood vessel shrinking) effect on those pounding headaches. The sugars in the coffee or candy bars also have a serotonin-releasing effect. We should not forget that the antidepressants advocated for the relief of migraine headaches are serotonin-reuptake inhibitors providing more serotonin at the nerve brain terminals.

Researchers are discovering that moderate amounts of chocolate might provide a number of cardiovascular advantages. According to some UC Davis scientists, "Cocoa consumption had an aspirin-like effect...Regular intake of cocoa components may contribute to a lower thrombotic (blood clot) risk." Other benefits of chocolate include reduced oxidation of dangerous LDL cholesterol. When LDL cholesterol is oxidized, it forms plaques on arterial walls more easily. In addition, cocoa flavonoids appear to relax arterial walls. This might also reduce the risk of clots and arterial blockage.

Food is a very complex substance working at the emotional, psychological, physiological and lastly at the chemical levels. Sometimes we crave foods because they contain something we lack; sometimes we crave foods because they help release some hormones that make us feel good, but sometimes we crave foods that are bad for us. We may be craving foods to which we are sensitive or against which we are making antibodies. This weakens our bodies as we spend our energy and raw materials to produce antibodies against the foods we ingest. This compromises our immune system which cannot fight the real enemy, namely cancer cells and infectious agents (like viruses and bacteria). There are two types of reactions to foods. One type is called IgE-mediated reactions in which you have an immediate reaction to the offending food; the other one is called IgG-mediated reaction which takes 24 to 48 hours to manifest itself. According to Dr. James Braly, all organ systems are affected by food sensitivities. Some patients who are refractory to any method of weight loss may be sensitive to certain foods. Foods that seem right to you may be wrong if you are sensitive to them. When I had my food sensitivities tested, I was surprised at how many frequently consumed foods (like green beans) I was sensitive to. By avoiding some foods, not only do you lose weight, but you also relieve a lot of symptoms that have been plaguing you.

Finally, because of their repetitive association with certain emotions, certain foods are consumed at times of stress, anxiety and depression. I often hear the term comfort foods describing hot foods like soups, mashed potatoes or roast beef. When one is depressed, pick-me-up foods like chocolates, ice creams, sweets and coffees are chosen. During anxiety, people describe ingesting large quantities of finger foods like potato chips, popcorn and pretzels. The continuous picking and chewing of those foods provide some type of anxiety relief, the end result being a nervous release and peace. Not only are we what we eat, but we can also control our mood by what we eat.

Protein intake has also been associated with more energy. That is why when one finally arrives in a new country after a long trip, protein ingestion is recommended to stay awake. Protein should also be consumed in the morning when we want our powers of concentration to be the highest; and skip the dessert for lunch if you want to stay awake in the early afternoon. Indulge in dessert after dinner or have a high carbohydrate meal at night to induce pleasant dreams. Have coffee in the morning and lunch and an herbal tea at night for optimal alertness during the day and relaxation and sleep in the evening.

If you are aware that you are an emotional overeater, study what emotions trigger your overeating. Is it stress, depression or anxiety that makes you eat uncontrollably? Each emotion can be handled differently; use nutritional products (described further) or even pharmacotherapy instead of food.

According to Dr. Stephen Gallo, cravings will pass. An average craving lasts between 4 to 12 minutes. He feels these cravings can be avoided by eating every 3 to 4 hours.

Many patients tell me that they eat not out of hunger or stress, but rather out of boredom; they have used this behavior repetitively, using food as a distraction or something to do. I feel that the food selected must provide some type of pleasure for it to be ingrained so deeply in that person's brain. Other activities, hobbies, or classes should be substituted at those times, instead of food. Pick activities that you like, get involved, take a warm bubble bath, write a letter, talk to a friend, watch television, talk on the phone, take a walk, paint, crochet, etc. Do not clean the house or do the ironing. Instead, reward yourself for good behavior. Keep out of the kitchen, keep your hands busy, your mind occupied; sometimes gum or a cup of hot tea can satisfy you. Just by being aware that you eat without hunger can help you make alternative plans. Keep busy at work, at home, even in leisure time.

Having a passion about something will obliterate the desire to put something in your mouth. Remember what Moliére said in *The Miser*, "Eat to live, not live to eat." Even a religious text like the Talmud has a food quote: "Fill one-third of your stomach with food, one-third with drink, and leave the other third empty." You can also develop a feeling of power by not succumbing to food, but not to the extreme of the anorexic. I feel quite mighty myself when I see other people indulging at parties, while I can control myself. One patient told me once "that nothing tastes as good as skinny feels." Food only stays in your mouth for 30 seconds, but it stays on your hips for a long time. Remember that no food, no matter how tasty, is worth the aggravation of gaining weight.

I also have my overweight patients record their favorite foods; it is impractical for me to offer them disliked foods which they will grow tired of or never consume. Favorite foods can be modified or replaced by similar healthier choices. Children respond especially well to games involving healthy foods. You may also record your favorite foods and analyze them; Brian Greer, the medical director at Renfrew Institute, who is an observant Jew, said he believes part of the problem Jews face with food is that many are struggling to fill a spiritual void in their lives. Instead of turning to God, they head to the refrigerator. Greer's suggestion is to "elevate food, so it is a connection with God." Prayers or blessings over food (wine, bread, fruit) can make a "bridge to a spiritual elevation and fulfill more than just a biological need." These thoughts were uttered in a seminar called, "Zaftig Women in a Barbie Doll World." Food is not our enemy, but our sustenance. Have fun with it! Food should not control you, you should control it!

One puzzling disease is represented by night eating syndrome (NES) which is characterized by morning anorexia, evening hyper-phagia and insomnia, and has been described as early as 1955 by obe-sity specialist Dr. Stunkard. A new study by Dr. G. S. Birketvedt, et al. showed that those suffering from this syndrome woke up more often in the middle of the night to eat as compared to normal individuals. Night eaters also had lower plasma levels of melatonin and leptin and higher levels of cortisol during the night. These investigators conclud-ed that there was a definite pattern of behavioral and neuroendocrine characteristics found in subjects suffering from NES. Dr. Joel Yager even goes further when he states that this behavior may be as uncon-scious as sleep walking.

As cortisol levels increase with the onset of additional stress, stress control may be appropriate therapy. Other therapeutic options are to increase melatonin and leptin in these patients before bedtime. Finally, serotonin levels may also be augmented for these subjects, using the neurotransmitter precursors like 5-HTP that increase sero-tonin levels in the brain. The reason these people consume high car-bohydrate snacks in the middle of the night may be to replenish their serotonin levels.

Appetite is controlled by many factors and hormones of our bodies. Besides head hunger and stomach hunger, the amount of fat stored in the body can determine the meal size. Thus, there is an interaction between long-term adiposity signals and meal-related satiety signals that control food intake.

Both leptin (secreted by adipocytes) and insulin (secreted by the pancreas) are released in proportion to the fat stored and can be thought of as lipometers. Insulin influences the secretion of leptin; however, both hormones decrease fat consumption. If food is scarce, the adipose tissue contracts, and less insulin and leptin are secreted to reach the brain. When food is plentiful, adipose mass expand and both leptin and insulin concentrations increase with consequent reduction of food intake.

Leptin levels are highest at night after a big meal and lowest in obese animals. Neuropeptide Y (NP-Y) released from the hypothalamus increases food consumption when food has not been eaten for a while. There is a battle between leptin, which decreases food intake, and NP-Y, which increases food consumption. Enterostatin, another hormone derived from the stomach and the pancreas, decreases food intake. Cholecystokinin, a peptide secreted from the gut, may lower carbohydrate ingestion and meal size. Corticotropin-releasing hormone decreases protein consumption.

The latest hormone secreted primarily in the stomach called grehlin boosts appetite by increasing upper GI motility tract.

Fat intake is increased by another hormone called galanin, while enterostatin and 5-HTP decrease fat consumption. NP-Y and insulin stimulate carbohydrate ingestion, while cholecystokinin decreases its intake.

While we have not found yet a hormone that stimulates protein consumption, we know that a corticotropin releasing hormone decreases protein consumption. However, as so many factors influence our appetite, this will be the basis in the future for the newest research in appetite suppression.

Chapter Six

QUESTIONNAIRE 1 - FOOD RECORDS WITH TIMES

To begin identifying your particular eating style, record the times you eat: for example, most people eat breakfast at 8 a.m., snack at 10 a.m., lunch at 12 p.m., snack between 2-3 p.m., dinner is usually between 6-8 p.m. Another snack is between 9-11 p.m.

Second, record the location in the chart below where you are hungry indicating either stomach hungry (SH) or head hungry (HH).

Third, record the substances you crave, such as carbohydrates, sweets, fats, salt, etc.

Please fill in the following questionnaire. (No. 1)

Times	Meals	Food consumed	Substances craved
_____Breakfast			
_____Snack			
_____Lunch			
_____Snack			
_____Dinner			
_____Snack			

For example:

Times	Meals	Hunger Foods consumed	Substances Craved
7:30 Breakfast	SH	cereal, juice, milk, coffee	carbohydrate, caffeine
10:00 Snack	HH	donut	fat/carb
12:00 Lunch	SH/HH	sandwich, chips, coke	carb/fat/salt
3:30 Snack	HH	2 oreo cookies	carb/fat
5:30 Dinner	SH	hamburger, fries, salad	fat
9:00 Snack	HH	ice cream	carb/fat

This particular example demonstrates that the person is a carbohydrate craver. He or she is also eating too much fat.

Now record your diet survey and analyze what foods you crave. You may also find a pattern of cravings. You will be surprised how much you learn about yourself in filling out this questionnaire.

Chapter Seven

NEUROTRANSMITTER THEORY OF FOOD ADDICTION: DOPAMINE DEFICIENCY OR SEROTONIN DEFICIENCY?

Neurotransmitters play an important role in health and disease; they are the brain's physiologic and psychological messengers. Although more than 40 neurotransmitters have been identified so far, the two on which we are going to focus are dopamine and serotonin. Low levels of these two neurotransmitters have been linked to many illnesses, especially obesity. Emotional illnesses have also been associated with low levels of these two hormones: namely depression, anger, anxiety, and other addictions. Genetics and aging interfere with the production of these two hormones, but also stress, illness, and poor dietary habits can deplete the amounts of these neurotransmitters. For optimal dopamine production, adequate dietary protein—namely essential amino acids, phenylalanine and its metabolite tyrosine—are needed. Tyrosine is converted to L-dopa, which in turn crosses the blood/brain barrier where it is converted to dopamine. Iron, folic acid and vitamins B3, B6, and vitamin C are necessary as catalysts or helpers to finish the production.

Figure 6: Production of Dopamine

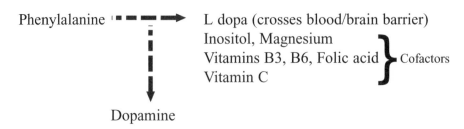

Phenylalanine → L dopa (crosses blood/brain barrier)
Inositol, Magnesium
Vitamins B3, B6, Folic acid } Cofactors
Vitamin C

Dopamine

DL phenylalanine also causes the production of tyrosine that in turn makes epinephrine, dopamine and norepinephrine which trigger thermogenesis or fat burning.

The production of serotonin requires the essential amino acid tryptophan. Tryptophan was removed from the market a few years ago because of contamination with other products, and hydroxytryptophan is used instead. Anyway, hydroxytryptophan is a metabolite of tryptophan. Hydroxytryptophan also crosses the blood/brain barrier and is converted to serotonin. Other essential prerequisites for serotonin production are magnesium, inositol and vitamins B3 and B6.

Figure 7: Serotonin production

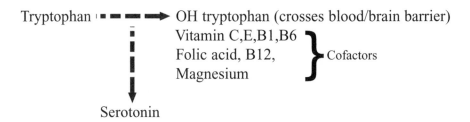

Tryptophan → OH tryptophan (crosses blood/brain barrier)
Vitamin C,E,B1,B6
Folic acid, B12, } Cofactors
Magnesium

Serotonin

According to Dr. Chris Renna, correcting imbalances in dopamine and serotonin can solve not only the problem of obesity but also anxiety and depression. Dopamine deficiency causes hunger, depression, cravings (for chocolate, caffeine, sweets, fats, and salt), and fatigue. Serotonin deficiency causes anxiety, irritability, restlessness and cravings (for breads, bagels, chips, crackers, cookies, pasta, alcohol, and cigarettes). A recent study showed that alcoholism may be mediated through the dopamine neurochemical system of the brain. Dopamine makes you feel good, while serotonin makes you feel safe.

Everybody's brain is unique: some need more dopamine, while some need more serotonin! You have to raise and balance your dopamine and serotonin levels.

Questionnaire No. 2

According to Dr. Chris Renna, cravings for:
  breads   _____
  bagels   _____
  pasta   _____
  chips   _____
  alcohol   _____
  smoking   _____
are due to low serotonin.

Cravings for:
  caffeine   _____
  alcohol   _____
  chocolate   _____
  sweets   _____
  fats   _____
  salt   _____
are due to low dopamine.

Score the number of cravings you have in each category.

Dr. Chris Renna also devised a dopamine/serotonin balance sheet. Dopamine in the right amount makes you feel energetic and less hungry. You need more dopamine when you have these symptoms:

Questionnaire No. 3

  depression   _____
  fatigue   _____
  lethargy   _____
  increased appetite   _____
  cravings for chocolate _____
  alcohol   _____
  caffeine   _____
  fats   _____
  salt   _____
  sweets   _____
Now count the check marks.

On the contrary, when you have the right amount of serotonin you feel comfortable and satiated. Now check the symptoms associated with low serotonin level.

Questionnaire No. 4

anxiety	_____
irritability	_____
anger	_____
restlessness	_____
cravings for bread	_____
bagels	_____
chips	_____
crackers	_____
pasta	_____
alcohol	_____
smoking	_____

Count the check marks here too.

Now draw your own balance sheet for your cravings and emotions. Are you dopamine or serotonin deficient? You may be both or you may have no problems at all! These cravings may vary during different times of the day, week and month. By knowing your weaknesses and positive attributes, you can use the right supplementation to achieve the best treatment for your weight loss, illnesses and ultimately health. You will then become happy, healthy, and slim!

Chapter Summary

- The lack of two neurotransmitters, dopamine and serotonin play a role in obesity.

- Cravings for breads, bagels, pasta, chips, and alcohol can be due to low serotonin.

- Cravings for caffeine, chocolate, sweets, fats, and salt are due to low dopamine.

Chapter Eight

THERAPY WITH NUTRITIONAL SUPPLEMENTS
PHYSICAL HUNGER (STOMACH HUNGER)
EMOTIONAL HUNGER (HEAD HUNGER)

O nce you have determined what type of hunger you have, you can start treating yourself. Remember: nothing is 100% accurate, and some modifications may be in order. By and large, though, you can begin your own therapeutic regime.

Half an hour before you feel hungry in your stomach, take one or two fiber pills containing sodium carboxymethylcellulose together with a big glass of water. The usual dosage is 500 mg of the carboxy-methyl-cellulose per pill. Some people require up to 2,000 mg of the fiber or about four pills before meals.

High fiber consumption, especially legumes, was shown to protect against obesity and cardiovascular disease by lowering insulin levels.

According to a study from Norway, overweight patients lost seven pounds in three months without dieting with the help of a fiber supplement compared to those given a placebo. The type of fiber, however, was not explained.

People will often consume the fiber pills before lunch and dinner when they are more commonly stomach hungry. Some individuals may need stronger medications to allay their hunger, and for this purpose, the carboxymethylcellulose is combined with benzocaine 3-9 mg per pill. Benzocaine is a stomach-numbing agent that prevents hunger pain or discomfort when food restriction is instituted.

If a burning sensation occurs after meals, some type of antacid is recommended. Tagamet™, Pepcid™, Zantac™, or Axid™, Prilosec™, Nexium™, Protonix™, Aciphex™ can be used instead of food. A recent study showed that overweight type II diabetics eliminate weight and fat when given Tagamet™ three times a day. Healthy non-diabetics also lost weight with this antacid in a previous study. The weight-reducing effect of this medication may be due to an increase of satiety via a hormone called cholecystokinin. However, as minor side effects may occur, drug monitoring by a physician is recommended.

Many patients use crackers to blot excess acid, however, this practice is detrimental to weight loss. I also find that many patients' stomachs are enlarged from overeating; these pouches can accommodate a lot more food than those in people who eat normally. The fiber expanding in their stomach, therefore, prevents overeating. As soon as the stomach shrinks back to normal size, less fiber is required. You can record in your questionnaire how many fiber pills you require to quiet down your stomach before meal time.

If you are hungry after a big meal and are constantly obsessing about food, you suffer more from head hunger. You may be craving certain foods at certain times. Record foods craved: are they chocolate, caffeine, fats, sweets, and salt? Or are they rather breads, bagels, chips, crackers, pasta, or alcohol?

Also record the times these foods are craved. Normally, patients crave these foods as snacks between breakfast and lunch, or between lunch and dinner and very often after dinner. Bring out your dopamine/serotonin balance sheet. Everybody is different, and each person will crave different foods at different times. Usually my patients crave chocolate, caffeine, fats, sweets and salt because of a deficiency of dopamine; on the other hand, they crave bread, bagels, chips, crackers, alcohol and pasta when their brain has a deficiency of the neurotransmitter serotonin.

To help you determine whether you have dopamine or serotonin deficiency, let us continue to fill out the questionnaire of our fictional patient from Chapter 4.

Sample Questionnaire 1: Dopamine Vs. Serotonin Deficiency

Meals	Food Consumed	Food types craved	Neurotransmitter Deficiency
breakfast	cereal,juice,milk, coffee	sweets,caffeine	dopamine
snack	donut	sweet,fat	dopamine
lunch	sandwich,chips, coke,	bread,chips	serotonin
snack	oreo cookies	sweets,chocolate	dopamine
dinner	hamburger,fries, salad	fat,salt	dopamine
snack	ice cream	fat,sweet	dopamine

This imaginary person, therefore, suffers more from a dopamine deficiency. We can also call it a serotonin dominance. You may be different; record your deficiencies. (see Questionnaire No. 1 on pg. 85)

Now you can determine for yourself what and when you need to replenish your neurohormones. The best treatment is to consume the neurotransmitter precursors before the cravings occur, 30 minutes to about 1 hour.

Many individuals feel a dopamine deficiency after breakfast and lunch. Serotonin deficiency seems to occur more commonly before and after dinner. However, each person has different cravings.

Dopamine is a chemical that transmits nerve impulses between synapses in the brain's pleasure center. Dopamine motivates behavior and imparts a sensation of pleasure. Addictive drugs, like cocaine, increase dopamine levels, at a rate up to 500% above normal. One report found that drinking, compulsive sex, shopping or gambling may also raise dopamine levels.

Dopamine is a natural antidepressant that gives a feeling of joy, ambition and alertness. We recommend our patients take the precursors for dopamine release in the morning, after breakfast, and after lunch.

For dopamine deficiency, we recommend 300 mg of L-phenylalanine per pill. Phenylalanine is an amino acid that transforms into a neurotransmitter in the brain (a chemical transmitter between nerve cells and the brain). Phenylalanine is turned into norepinephrine and dopamine. Phenylalanine has also been used to increase sexual interest and to decrease depression. Vitamin C, about 100-150 mg, is required for the conversion of phenylalanine to norepinephrine by the brain. Vitamin B6, between 20-25 mg, is also needed for the production of norepinephrine. (It is also a natural diuretic very useful in many of our obese patients.)

L-tyrosine (100 mg) and N-acetyltyrosine (100 mg) are also helpful in the production of dopamine. Pantothenic acid (50 mg) is also important for cellular metabolism. The formula for dopamine formation is: DL-phenylalanine 300 mg
                     L-tyrosine 100 mg
                     N-acetyl tyrosine 100 mg
The addition of a complete B-complex vitamin is helpful in achieving the best results.

On the other hand, the formation of serotonin an important chemical found throughout the body, particularly in the digestive system and blood cells in the brain can be promoted by a precursor called 5-Hydroxytryptophan. 5-HTP is made in the body from the amino acid tryptophan, and is used to create serotonin. We recommend starting slowly: 5-10 mg tablets at first, and increasing dosage to a maximum of 100 mg. Some investigators have prescribed higher dosages. I am a little concerned about prescribing higher doses, as nausea and gastric distress may occur in certain people. Some drowsiness and sleepiness have also been described by some individuals upon taking higher dosages of 5-HTP. That is why I recommend that patients to take this product later in the day before dinner or after dinner. However, if you have some cravings suggestive of serotonin deficiency, 5-HTP can be taken after lunch as well.

Sometimes it is difficult to predict whether 5-HTP will cause sedation or alertness. A number of factors are involved, including dosage, recent meal content, the time of day 5-HTP is taken, other supplements or medicines you are currently taking, your age, and perhaps the menstrual cycle in women.

Whether correcting dopamine or serotonin deficiency, one should take supplements with a warm glass of water and wait 30 minutes. If the desired response is not achieved, a second dose may be instituted; 5-HTP should also be taken with a good multiple vitamin containing

Vitamins C, E, B1, B6, folic acid, B12, pantothenic acid, and minerals like magnesium and zinc. A cinnamon-flavored powder of 5-HTP can also be placed on your tongue and be allowed to dissolved. This substance will get to your brain quicker than if you digest it. A spray of the product is also in the process of being made. This method of application will also work faster, and dosages of 1-5 mg can be implemented per spray.

Many books have been written on the benefits of 5-HTP, such as books by Dr. Ray Sahelian and Dr. Michael Murray. This substance can also be a very significant antidepressant at higher doses. In addition, it is used for muscle pains in fibromyalgia syndrome. This substance has also been advocated to be a respectable sleeping pill that puts people to sleep better than a sleep inducing drug. It also helps promote a better quality of sleep. Dr. Craig Keebler feels that 70% of 5-HTP reaches the brain and that this substance is a strong antioxidant. 5-HTP may last longer in one's system if carbidopa is added to it.

Dr. Pietr Hitzig uses 5-HTP with L-dopa as both are precursors for serotonin and dopamine. He also uses carbidopa, another anti-Parkinson's medication, to prevent 5-HTP and L-dopa from being metabolized in the body so that more 5-HTP may reach the brain. "Drug addiction, alcoholism, depression, bulimia and Gulf War Syndrome are conditions caused by serotonin and dopamine being out of balance," he feels. He adds that addicted patients lose their cravings in a matter of minutes after being given the proper combination of supplements. This combination, he claims, works for depression, fibromyalgia (severe muscle pains) and low self-esteem. My own limited experience did not show any improvements of 5-HTP when carbidopa was added to this regime.

5-HTP is also a powerful substance to combat addictions, not only food addictions as described above, but also addictions to alcohol, smoking and gambling. Just spraying the mouth with 5-HTP tryptophan may help patients to reduce or prevent many cravings and addictions.

A 1992 Italian obesity study using 900 mg of 5-HTP per day concluded "The optimal adherence to dietary prescription as well as the good tolerance to 5-HTP treatment observed suggests that this substance can be used in the long-term treatment of obesity." This is why I recommend taking 5-HTP with food, starting with a small dose and slowly increasing to a full dose over a period of a couple of weeks. I have never prescribed a dosage this high, but it is possible to use up to 900 mg for severe depression and, possibly, for some cases of difficult to treat obesity. 5-HTP is a natural product (most 5-HTP is extracted from the Gliflonia seed). Side effects occurring only at high dosages may include nausea, daytime sleepiness and reduced sex drive. Vivid dreams have rarely been associated with high doses.

5-HTP does not cause the jitteriness of St. John's Wort but rather a sense of relaxation. Some investigators have also mixed St. John's Wort with 5-HTP. I do not use St. John's Wort in my practice, as I live in Florida where many of my patients have had problems with sun sensitivities and rashes when using this product.

Some doctors have been using 5-HTP in treating fibromyalgia (dosages up to 400 mg). 5-HTP may also play a role in relieving migraines and helping with seizures. 5-HTP has also been used for multiple chemical sensitivities and in schizophrenia. Other benefits of 5-HTP have been found in treating attention deficit disorder and autism. Up to 500 mg of 5-HTP with vitamin B6 (needed for the conversion of tryptophan to serotonin) has been shown to relieve insomnia. Valerian root can also be beneficial in this regime. 100 mg of 5-HTP with 0.5 mg of Klonopin™ (a tranquilizer) has been shown to help in the restless leg syndrome. 5-HTP is also helpful for anxiety relief in a dosage of 25-50 mg.

While many people derive a lot of benefit from 5-HTP, a small number of patients may have some problems. It is then best to take it before or after dinner. And one should always take it with food to prevent nausea. Dr. Michael Murray recommends 1-2 grams of powdered ginger or a cup of ginger tea to counter the nausea; if sedation occurs, it is preferable to take the product before bedtime. If cravings occur during the day, you can balance the sedation by combining your dose with either tyrosine alone or phenylalanine or both. In addition, caffeine and Gingko biloba (40 mg/day) can be added to prevent the side effects of sedation.

Interestingly, patients who have done well with the phentermine/fenfluramine combinations will find these neurotransmitter precursors very useful. Phentermine increases the release of dopamine, and fenfluramine increases the release of serotonin. Now you can see why this combination of appetite suppressants may or may not have worked for you.

I also have in my office a capsule that contains the precursors for the formation of dopamine called Medtrim AM™ and another one which contains the precursors for the release of serotonin called Medtrim PM™. As implied in the name of the AM formula, it is used after breakfast and lunch, while the PM formula is designed to be taken before and after dinner. It is very helpful for patients who like to stay up late at night and snack until the wee hours of the night. These two formulas contain not only neurohormone precursors but also the factors needed for dopamine and serotonin release. Even though the success rate is quite high, not everybody does well with this program. Ultimately, the big benefit is that you can fine tune the release of your neurotransmitters, not only to achieve weight loss permanently but also to control illnesses and promote optimal health.

Chapter Summary

- To treat stomach hunger, a fiber which combines a stomach numbing agent is used.

- For dopamine deficiency, phenylalanine and tyrosine may be used.

- For serotonin deficiency, 5 HTP has been helpful.

Chapter Nine

NUTRITIONAL SUPPLEMENTATION USED IN WEIGHT LOSS

Bromelain: Bromelain, from pineapple, breaks down fibrinogen (a coagulation product) and has been shown to be useful in treating cardiovascular disease, so common in the obese population. It also may reduce pain and inflammation. Dosage is 500 mg three times a day. It is best to take this substance on an empty stomach

Chromium: Many of my patients complain of sugar cravings between meals, during menstruation, or after dinner.

Frequently, 5-HTP helps with carbohydrate cravings, but often we need to stabilize blood sugar levels. When blood sugar dips too low, especially after meals or at times of stress, people are more likely to look for sweets. When diabetics take blood-lowering medications, they will kill for a sweet. This does not indicate a lack of willpower but is rather a normal physiological response to low blood sugar. You know your blood sugar is low when you get dizzy, anxious and sweaty about 2 to 4 hours after a meal. If your symptoms are relieved by food supplementation, you may be diagnosed with hypoglycemia or low blood sugar.

Chromium picolinate was touted as the best product to control blood sugar fluctuations. Chromium picolinate has also been associated recently with a higher incidence of cancer. Chromium picolinate may be carcinogenic (cancer producing) because it induces chromosomal cleavage in cells and produces DNA damaging hydroxyl radicals. The American Chemical Society, in Anaheim, California, concluded

that long-term supplementation with this product may have carcinogenic potential. However, as Americans do not consume enough
chromium for carbohydrate and fat metabolism, other forms of
chromium should be investigated.

Chromium polynicotinate has been shown to stay longer in the
system so as to better exert its blood sugar-controlling effect (Figure
8). Claims of increasing muscle mass by taking either chromium compound have been refuted. However, some modest fat loss has been
shown in patients who exercised and used chromium polynicotinate.
Weight gain resulted when chromium picolinate was used instead. In
my practice, those patients who develop low blood sugar symptoms do
extremely well with the addition of chromium polynicotinate (200
mcg) at meal times. Most often this chromium is consumed at lunch
and dinner. Some patients who experience hypoglycemic symptoms
after breakfast can take it with breakfast. The maximum dosage is 600
mcg/day or 200 mcg three times a day with meals. You can continue
to record symptoms in your diary and determine if improvements in
cravings occur. Some people do well with a brand of chromium polynicotinate called Chromate™. This product has also been dubbed the
glucose tolerance factor. Some individuals can be sensitive to niacin
(from the polynicotinate) at the beginning of treatment. They may
experience headaches, flushes and nausea, but these symptoms disappear after a few days.

Figure 8

ACTION OF DIFFERENT CHROMIUM PREPARATIONS
Total Chromium Retention

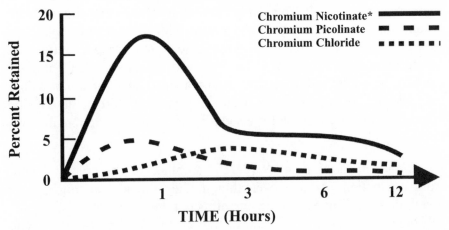

* In the form of ChromeMate® niacin-bound chromium—U.S. patents 4,923,855 and 4,954,492

Curcumin: Curcumin is the yellow pigment of turmeric. Curcumin reduces cholesterol uptake and it prevents abnormal blood-clot formation by interfering with the formation of thromboxanes, the promoters of platelet aggregation. Curcumin neutralizes dietary carcinogens and has been shown to inhibit cancer at the initiation, promotion, and progression stages of development. Curcumin also has anti inflammatory activity. A dosage of 500 to 1,000 mg of this substance is recommended daily.

Lipoic acid: This substance has been named the strongest antioxidant on the market. Lipoic acid use has been quite successful for our patients, especially if chromium never proved effective or is no longer effective. Lipoic acid has the advantage of needing only a single daily dose. No side effects have been reported with its use. I recommend taking it with the meal that begins before carbohydrate cravings occur, usually with either lunch or dinner. A dosage of 200 to 600 mg of lipoic acid may to be taken daily.

The most common times for these severe sugar or carbohydrate cravings usually occur between 2-4 p.m. or between 9-11 p.m. At around 2-4 p.m., patients are usually tired, and a carbohydrate pick-

me-up is craved. At around 9-11 p.m., patients are generally recover-
ing from the stresses of the day; dinner is over, children are put to bed,
and a sugar fix is considered a well-deserved reward after a long, hard
day. (Remember how mom used to reward you with a sweet when you
fell down, hurt yourself, or when you were a good child.) These patterns are hard to break. The candy vending machine calls you by name
around that snack time; the refrigerator with its stash of cookies or
cake or the ice cream in the freezer, also seem to be magnets after dinner. In these cases, lipoic acid has been very effective. 5-HTP at night
can also be added to this regime. Remember to take one tablet with a
warm liquid. If cravings still occur, a second or third tablet can be
taken with no ill effects; a little sedation and sleep induction are wel-
come at night!

Lipotropic amino acids (MIC): Another big complaint I hear
from my patients is that even though they do not eat much, their
metabolism is slow. Starving yourself is not the answer. Imagine yourself being a furnace: if no food or logs are put in your fireplace, you
stop burning. Still, there are patients who do everything right and even
then do not burn enough fat.

In this case, we supplement their diets with lipotropic amino acids
(methionine, inositol, and choline). Lipotropic amino acids are amino
acids (or parts of proteins) that help with the breakdown of fats.
Adding these amino acids to their regime has significantly improved
their caloric burning potential. Even after a plateau, lipotropic amino
acids seem to jump-start patients' weight loss. If you are a person who
has had problems with weight loss in the past, and you are an underburner, this may be the answer for you. All amino acids should be used
between meals, so that they are not competing for other protein brain
receptors; take them twice daily, either one hour before or two hours
after a meal, between breakfast and lunch or between lunch and dinner. These amino acids are included in our Medtrim™ formulas.

Phenylalanine: Phenylalanine is an essential amino acid. Once in
the body, it can be converted into another amino acid, called tyrosine,
which in turn is used to synthesize two key neurotransmitters that promote alertness: dopamine and norepinephrine. Because of its relationship to the action of the central nervous system, this amino acid can
elevate mood, decrease pain, aid in memory and learning, and suppress the appetite.

Tyrosine: Another substance that has proved very successful in my practice has been tyrosine which increases the basal metabolic rate of any person. Tyrosine helps in the production of the thyroid hormone, which we know is crucial for metabolism. A word of caution: do not take thyroid medication unless you need it! Many patients receive this medication for weight loss. Thyroid medication—either Synthroid™, Levothroid™ , Cytomel™, Triiodothyronine (T3 or the active form of thyroid) or desiccated Armour thyroid—are all excellent, if you are thyroid deficient. However, if taken for the sole purpose of weight loss, thyroid hormones can cause elevated heart rate, palpitations and osteoporosis (removal of calcium from the bones). Tyrosine, on the contrary, only helps with the natural production of thyroid hormone especially if iodine is added.

DHEA: Another substance that is supposed to help burn fat (thermogenesis) is DHEA or dehydroepiandrosterone. Even though the only proven benefit of DHEA has been a feeling of well-being, it has still been touted as a rejuvenator. This is due to the fact that it is the precursor of all sex hormones, namely estrogen, progesterone and testosterone. DHEA was shown to augment antibody response to foreign antigens and correct the age-related disruption in cytokines. DHEA has been used for cancer prevention and autoimmune disease, two areas of increased health risk in the elderly. Experiments on mice showed that DHEA may even be effective in improving the functioning of the immune system after severe bleeding in mice by preventing further cellular death. Because of the different extraction processes used to make DHEA, there is no standardized dose. If you do want to try DHEA, however, do not take more than 25 mg (if you are a woman) or 50 mg (if you are a man). DHEA has also been used for postmenopausal women with success. The theory is that after age 40, all our hormones decline; DHEA might be considered a fountain of youth for replenishing our declining hormones. Some individuals derive energy and a feeling of well-being by taking this precursor hormone. Others, specifically women, have shown hirsutism (hair growth on their faces) and had to discontinue the product. DHEA is the precursor for both male and female hormones, and some women experience a higher stimulation of male hormone. By stimulating the release of testosterone, some women experience increased sex drive or libido.

A new urological study suggests that DHEA may be useful for male sexual dysfunction for both erectile dysfunction and desire. Men who were given 80 mg of DHEA per day had more erections and a higher libido. It takes several months to ascertain if DHEA benefits a patient.

In a recent double-blind, placebo-controlled trial, DHEA was found to provide significant antidepressant benefits for patients suffering from major depression. Half of the trial patients given 90 mg per day of DHEA experienced improvement in depression, energy and libido.

Besides its rejuvenating properties, DHEA has also been used for weight loss and memory enhancement. We have used DHEA with bioperidine, which increases the absorption of DHEA (and permits a dosage of only 25 mg per day). Recently, 7-Keto (a component of DHEA) has been introduced to the market. The hormone enhancing properties of DHEA were eliminated, and only the beneficial effects of this product were retained, namely thermogenesis (fat burning), fatigue relief and increased memory. 7-Keto can be also used for fibromyalgia (muscle inflammation relief).

In my office, we recommend the addition of this product only if DHEA sulfate levels in a patients blood is low before supplementation. Convince your doctor to do this test for you; we recommend achieving a DHEA blood level of 150 mcg for women and 350 mcg for men. Two months later, a repeat testing is indicated to prevent high levels of this substance (maximum 200 mcg in women and 450 mcg in men); if this happens, dosage should be tapered. DHEA has also been implicated in playing a role in the immune system, in diabetes, in lowering cholesterol, in maintaining youth and health and, last but not least, in stabilizing weight. A feeling of well-being and improved memory have been reported by patients taking this supplement. Because of all these claims, DHEA has been used for diabetes, in autoimmune diseases like rheumatoid arthritis, psoriasis and lupus. DHEA is also used for obese patients, as it supposedly increases muscle mass and decreases body fat. DHEA in combination with carnitine has also been shown to increase fat utilization.

AMP, ATP, NADH, etc: Another frequent complaint among our patients is the symptom of extreme fatigue. We use adenosine monophosphate (AMP), the precursor of adenosine triphosphate

(ATP), for this indication. All bodily processes requiring energy production necessitate the addition of ATP. AMP can be given in a sublingual pill (to be dissolved under the tongue) for better absorption. AMP has also been useful for treating chronic fatigue syndrome. With the addition of vitamin B12, AMP has also helped many patients to get over a plateau in weight loss. We have used AMP very successfully for weight loss patients who have excessive tiredness (as in chronic fatigue syndrome). Recently ATP has been introduced in the market; it provides energy more directly. Another product that has been used successfully to improve fatigue is Enada (or NADH). It is the electron transport provider in the Krebs cycle of cell mitochondria, the energy organelles of the cells.

Octaconosol: Octaconosol is a naturally derived wheat germ oil concentrate. Octaconosol is another product used when patients complain of severe tiredness. It has been clinically proven to increase oxygen utilization during exercise and improve glycogen storage in muscle. As a result, it increases physical endurance, and aids in tissue oxygenation. Octaconosol may be very useful in providing energy to dieters. About 5,000 mcg of octaconosol is recommended to our patients; individuals who exercise will get a slow boost of energy when consuming this substance prior to working out.

Korean Ginseng: Korean ginseng is also supposed to help with weight loss. It is claimed to be somewhat of a rejuvenator, as it restores vigor, and is also a blood purifier. Ginseng may also interact with anticoagulation medicine. Canadian researchers reported that ginseng may play a role in carbohydrate metabolism and diabetes. The study showed that ginseng had glucose-lowering effects, especially when given 40 minutes before meals. The FDA found a significant variability in the amount of ginseng tested in the many bottles lining the shelves of health food stores. Some products may contain only 10% ginseng, while others may contain as much as 80% of this substance. Some companies use a lot of fillers; for this reason I only recommend this product from a very reliable company with good quality controls.

Guarana: Guarana extract, which comes from an herb grown in Brazil, has been touted to impart high energy, elevate moods and help with weight loss. The only caveat about guarana is that it may increase blood pressure. Be very careful with this herb; absolutely do not consume more than 1,000 mg per day. If palpitations occur, discontinue the drug immediately. The combination of Korean ginseng and guarana have been very useful at times for those patients who complain of fatigue. Take both substances in the morning as they may prevent you from sleeping if you take them later in the day.

Human Growth Hormone: Human growth hormone (HGH) precursors are amino acids that are supposed to stimulate the release of growth hormone. HGH production occurs at night while one sleeps and decreases after the age of thirty. L-arginine, L-ornithine, L-glutamine, and L-lysine are the amino acids involved in the formation of HGH. These amino acids have not exhibited any benefit in my practice. L-arginine which increases the formation of nitric oxide, a useful product in the relief of many diseases, also improves insulin sensitivity and blood vessel dilation.

Dr. Heriberto Salinas reports an increase of energy, mood and improved sleep in patients taking these precursors. A plant-derived growth hormone seems to supplement our declining growth hormone levels. This comes in a sublingual form (15 drops used three times a day). Claims have been made about the efficacy of this product in increasing muscle mass and fat loss. My experience has been quite mixed; some patients have derived a benefit of well-being from the drops, but the majority have not. We are also testing a cream version of human growth hormone, called Trans D tropin®. Beware, also, that most of the data we have about the advantages of HGH were based on using the injectable version.

Growth hormone replacement was shown to decrease body fat, cholesterol, triglycerides, and blood pressure in middle aged men. The dose of HGH was 4.3 mcg per pound. Growth hormone injections reduced abdominal fat by 25% in growth hormone-deficient men and middle-aged men. Before starting growth hormone injections, make sure your somatomedin (growth hormone level in the blood) is checked. The optimal value is between 100-125 mcg; start with only 4 units per week and increase slowly. The maximum dosage in women is 12 units per week, in men 8 units per week. Another way to test HGH levels is by doing a 24 hour urine test of this substance. Side effects of HGH injections include fluid retention and joint pain which necessitate lowering the dosage.

HGH works by increasing the basal metabolic rate and heart rate of patients. Increased cardiac workload is suspected as the mechanism of action in HGH. Growth hormone also causes fat loss and muscle gain. The increased basal metabolic rate of growth hormone injected patients may be due to higher levels of T3. Finally, growth hormone injections cause weight and fat loss and muscle gain in post-menopausal women. The possible role of HGH in increasing cancer rates has been studied extensively and no relationship has been observed.

Growth hormone levels increase significantly when insulin levels are low, about four hours after a meal. It is at this point that the fat burning potential of HGH tends to be at its daytime peak. But the largest burst of HGH is released during the early hours of sleep, there-fore our evening eating habits are crucial in maximizing this nighttime secretion. By avoiding food during the last four hours before bedtime we may enhance circadian growth hormone release and fat burning potential.

Obesity diminishes the intermittent secretion of HGH. It also causes accelerated breakdown of HGH by the body. On the other hand, sustained high-intensity exercise increases the number of HGH pulses and the quantity of HGH released.

Fasting increases both the pulsatile frequency and the amount of HGH secreted. Eating shuts it down by stimulating insulin, which opposes HGH. Over the long term, a poor diet can tremendously inter-fere with proper HGH release. The correct diet will assist in overcom-ing excess insulin in order to promote growth hormone.

Testosterone, estrogen and other hormones enhance HGH secre-tion. The amino acids L-arginine and ornithine can cause HGH release if taken in high enough amounts. Incidentally, L-arginine was shown to increase sexual desire by increasing nitric oxide (NO). It may be used as a cream to be applied to the clitoral area to facilitate orgasm.

A lot of new research is centered now on NO as this substance is a potent smooth muscle relaxant and blood vessel dilator. It also pre-vents platelet aggregation and is useful in the treatment of hyperteni-son, stroke, heart failure, impotency and other vascular disorders. L-arginine is best absorbed on an empty stomach and dosage may go up to 1 gram three times a day.

Potassium: Potassium supplementation is indicated in patients who lose a lot of weight rapidly and whose electrolytes may get depleted. We check potassium levels in the blood whenever a patient loses more than 3.5 lbs per week in women, and 4.5 lbs per week in men. The best potassium supplementation is magnesium potassium aspartate. A study was done showing that athletes, who consumed magnesium potassium aspartate before workouts, bench pressed more repetitions and had more endurance compared to those who ingested a placebo. Magnesium potassium aspartate also helps with fatigue after exercise. We recommend our patients to take this product before exercise. According to a new study from Italy, magnesium levels are lower in people who are obese, diabetic and hypertensive. Recently, scientists have suggested that an alteration of ionic metabolism, namely low mineral content in the blood, may represent an event in the pathogenesis of obesity and hypertension.

Essential Fatty Acids: Essential fatty acids are a subject close to my heart. In his book *Fats That Heal and Fats That Kill*, Udo Erasmus describes the importance of oils in health and disease. From this book, we learn that there are two kinds of healing fats: linoleic acid (LA) or alpha linolenic acid (LNA). Both LA and LNA aid fatigue recovery and inhibit platelet stickiness, thus preventing strokes and aid fatigue recovery. LNA, found in flax, sunflower and borage oils, smoothes skin, speeds learning, reduces inflammation, alleviates arthritis and eases PMS. Killer oils are cottonseed, castor, herring and anchovy oils. All oils that are heated become saturated and, therefore, harmful. The recommended doses are 3 grams of LA and 6-8 grams of LNA. Skin that has sufficient essential fatty oils (EFA) is smooth and velvety; skin that is too dry needs more EFA-rich oils. Stress, disease and sugars may increase EFA requirements. EFAs are not only effective in alleviating stress, but also may help burn fat by increasing metabolic rate.

A recent study done on women at Harvard School of Public Health supports the hypothesis that a higher intake of linoleic acid is protective against fatal ischemic heart disease. Higher consumption of oil-based salad dressings that include linoleic acid has been shown to reduce the risk of ischemic heart disease in some cases. Finally, a combination of eicosapentaenoic acid, gamma linolenic acid and antioxidants given intravenously significantly improved the symptoms of acute respiratory distress syndrome in 146 patients with infections, trauma or aspiration pneumonia.

Virgin olive oil is low in EFAs; however, it is a healer, as it has an anti-inflammatory effect. It decreases LDL, increases HDL cholesterol, and stimulates bile flow and pancreatic enzymes. Olive oil was also found to be the most thermogenic or fat burning oil in an experiment done in rats. Olive oil is also used as a cosmetic in soaps and moisturisers

Evening primrose, borage and black currant oils have a high gamma linoleic acid content. Evening primrose oil is used in weight loss, multiple sclerosis, and diabetes.

Flax seed oil is used in cardiovascular disease, cancer and diabetes. It is also used in skin diseases (dandruff, eczema and psoriasis) and in overweight patients. For healthy consumption we recommend a blend of half olive oil and half canola oil.

Essential fatty acids can also be classified as omega-3 or omega-6 fatty oils. Omega-3 fatty oils (alpha linolenic and eicosapentaenoic acid, or EPA for short) reduce inflammation and help with circulation. They are found mostly in fresh fish from cold, deep oceans (such as mackerel, tuna, sablefish, flounder, sardines, salmon, trout and bass). Omega-3 fatty oils are also provided in lesser amounts in flaxseed, black currant, cod liver and canola oils as well as soybeans.

You can determine whether you are likely suffering from omega-3 fatty oil deficiency if you have:

— cracking finger tips
— patchy dullness of skin
— mixed oily and dry skin
— rough bumps on back of arm
— dry patches on lower legs
— stiff, dry brittle hair
— seborrhea, dandruff, hair loss
— soft or brittle fingernails that split

The omega-6, non-essential fatty acids produce arachidonic acid; they increase pain and inflammation and can result in poor circulation. They are found in animal meats, whole milk, fried foods, coconut and palm oils.

According to Dr. Artemis Simopoulos, an expert in fatty acid bio-chemistry, while man originally evolved on a diet with a ratio of omega-6 to omega-3 fatty acids of almost one, today the ratio is more like 10:1 or even 20-25:1. This demonstrates how much Western diets have changed and how deficient they now are in omega-3 fatty acids.

While omega-6s are associated with cell-membrane rigidity, omega-3s contribute to the health of the cellular membranes by pro-viding cell fluidity, allowing in nutrients and letting out waste.

These healing oils should be kept in an opaque container to pre-vent denaturation and subsequent damage of these fatty acids. Some doctors also recommend a little olive oil for those patients who are on a fat-restricted program. In this condition, the gall bladder forgets to contract when no significant oil is ingested. The sludge from fat break-ing enzymes stays in the gallbladder and over time can produce gall-stones. Omega-3 fatty acids need to be supplemented in a very low calorie weight loss program to prevent heart disease which may occur if heart-healthy omega-3 fatty acid reserves are reduced. I prefer to give my patients who are on a very low-calorie diet a combination of omega-3 and omega-6 oils in one capsule to take in the morning to prevent both heart and gallbladder disease.

Hundreds of studies demonstrate that people who have a high omega-3 fatty acid diet have a significantly lower risk for coronary artery disease. Omega-3 fatty acids lower blood pressure, lower clot-ting of blood, and prevent second heart attacks.

Also omega-3 fatty acids stimulate the production of some anti-inflammatory agents that reduce insulin resistance. Besides lowering blood fats, they may even smooth out heart rhythm and reduce the risk of sudden cardiac death. Apart from helping with depression, these acids have improved ADHD-related symptoms in children with spe-cific learning difficulties.

Recently, a study showed that the membranes of the obese have a deficiency of certain fatty acids; the addition of essential fatty oils helps to restructure these membranes. Those patients who had essen-tial fatty oil supplementation lost more weight than the control group. Either borage, flax, primrose oils or best of all fish oils are recom-mended, not only during the weight loss phase, but also during the maintenance phase of weight reduction.

This supplementation must be an ongoing process to keep these membranes intact. The theory is that the fat has a better way to pass through healthy cellular membranes in order to be broken down in the little furnaces of the cell (the mitochondria). Dr. Artemis Simopoulos further explains that omega-3 fatty acids found in fish may help prevent weight gain and insulin resistance. A 30-year study appearing in the *New England Journal of Medicine* in 1997 found that men who ate 8 oz. or more of fish each week had 44% lower risk of dying of a heart attack than men who had none. Dr. Mauro Di Pasquale also writes that omega-3 fatty acids increase fatty acid oxidation (burning of fat) and basal metabolic rate and improve insulin sensitivity. A British study concluded that fish eaters weigh seven pounds less than meat eaters.

Finally Dr. Barry Sears, author of *The Zone Diet*, recommends for weight loss, disease prevention and health maintenance, the supplementation of high doses of fish oils in the form of EPA/DHA (pharmaceutical grade or purified from toxins). He feels that health food grade fish oils contain too many impurities and he prescribes a dosage of fish oils from 2.5 grams to about 10 grams per day.

Fiber: The role of fiber has also been described in detail as beneficial for weight loss. On the average, the American population consumes about 10 grams of fiber per day. For best weight loss results, 30 grams of fiber per day are recommended.

As previously described, in our office we use carboxy methylcellulose fiber pills to fill the stomachs of our patients. However, patients can be taught about the difference of fiber between soluble (more like a gel that stays in your stomach) or insoluble (more like the pieces from vegetables or fruit that come out in the stool, undigested). Many patients complain of constipation and thus could use some insoluble fiber to move stool through their intestines. Oil and water are also beneficial in making the patients eliminate. Essential fatty acids (EFAs) also help to soften the stool. We also recommend to diabetics to use fiber, as the fiber binds with sugar and carries it out of their intestinal tract.

A recent article in the *JAMA* showed that soluble fiber may decrease cholesterol, LDL-cholesterol, and triglyceride levels, and may increase insulin sensitivity. It concluded that higher fiber intake, particularly from cereal sources (oat bran), reduces the risk of coronary heart diseases in women. A diet high in legumes was shown to reduce cardiovascular disease.

I make this analogy to my patients: What is preferable, a glass of orange juice or an orange? They both contain approximately 100 calories, but the orange juice is totally absorbed. The orange has more fiber from the membranes and pulp which only allows 50% absorption (thus only 50 calories will get into the bloodstream). Therefore, a high fiber diet is recommended to our patients, salad and vegetables being the best choices, with fruit to be consumed in moderation only, preferably at the end of a meal. We do not recommend fruit juices either to our obese children or adults.

Dr. A. Burkitt found an association between a diet lacking in fiber and colon cancer; thus, many people ingest high-fiber diets for colon cancer prevention. The theory was that the harmful substances in the foods we consume had more time to stay in the intestines and produce changes (analogous to cancerous cells) during periods of constipation. However, this theory has been challenged recently as a high fiber diet did not seem to offer any protection against the disease. A combination of low fat and high- fiber diet was associated with spontaneous weight loss, but success on this program depended on how heavy the patients were; the fatter they were in the beginning, the more they lost.

Of all the fibers suggested to help prevent colon cancer, the November 1999 issue of the *New England Journal of Medicine*, in a study using pigs, found wheat bran to be the best for this purpose.

Natural Diuretic-B6: Another frequent complaint I hear from my patients, besides constipation, is: "I am retaining a lot of water!" I prefer to use a natural diuretic and reserve medications for last-resort cases. The best natural diuretic is vitamin B6. B6 also stabilizes mood, helps to metabolize carbohydrates and fat, is a stress fighter and prevents water build-up in the tissues. B6 also helps maintain the balance of sodium and potassium which regulates body fluids. B6 is best given at night in a dosage of about 25 mg. Some people may use it in the morning, if sleep is impaired by frequent bathroom visits. In our office for many years, we have used a capsule that contains both phenylalanine (described earlier) and B6.

Digestive Enzymes: Another common complaint I hear is: "Dr., I am bloated; food just stays there in my stomach" or "My belly is so swollen, I feel pregnant." First, we have to make sure the patient does not have any type of disease; in women, cancer of the ovary is always suspect. We can help patients with good digestive enzymes containing: pepsin which breaks down protein, amylase which breaks down starches, and lipase which metabolizes fats. We also recommend bromelain, derived from the pineapple, to further help with digestion. Cellulase also helps to break down the fibers from fruits and vegetables. Why help the patients to digest their food? Are we preventing weight loss? Not really, because if the patient is unhappy or has unpleasant symptoms, he/she will not remain on a dietary regime. Additionally, a happy patient will lose and maintain weight loss.

Antacids and especially cimetidine have also been used as a weight loss aid as they may decrease food intake by blocking gastric acid production.

In general, we can see that there is no one kind of supplementation for everybody. Write down your symptoms and try to approximate the best therapy from the list I have given you. (See Questionnaire No. 2 on pg. 89). Try one regime for several weeks before adding another product. Remember, these products have been tried in our office and have been successfully used by thousands of patients. If it worked for them, it may work for you. Do not take too many substances at once, as you may develop stomach irritation, diarrhea or nausea. Start with the few substances that you seem to need the most and only add more if you reach a plateau or if you have no side effects from the treatment. The only thing you have to lose is your weight. The most important thing you will learn, as Molière proclaimed in *The Miser*, is "to eat to live and not to live to eat." Hopefully, with the help of the information in this book, we will teach you how to slay the "Craving Dragon."

Chapter Summary

- Chromium polynicotinate helps balance blood sugar levels.

- Alpha lipoic acid helps with sweet cravings.

- Essential fatty acids especially Omega 3 fatty acids are helpful in reducing inflammation and obesity.

— Chapter Ten —

NUTRITIONAL SUPPLEMENTATION FOR EMOTIONAL SUPPORT

A s the mind controls so much of our eating behavior and as our emotions play such an important role, we offer some preventative measures to our patients to allay some possible problems.

Peppermint Oil: Even though most of my patients follow our guidelines to a T, unusual circumstances sometimes may occur. For instance, one might be stranded in the airport awaiting a delayed flight, where the scent of buttery popcorn, pizza or hot dogs are prevalent throughout the corridors. Another scenario might occur with the shopper who intends to buy a last-minute present but whose nostrils are tempted by chocolate chip smells wafting through the mall. The best defense for these onslaughts is provided by peppermint oil drops! On or two drops of this liquid flavor concentrate rubbed on your tongue numbs your taste buds temporarily, eliminating the urge to consume that particular food so keenly advertised.

I recommend that my patients carry a miniature bottle in their purse or pocket at all times. Packing it in a suitcase is worthless. Incidentally, peppermint oil is very helpful for pregnant women who suffer from nausea. Its added bonus is that it is not a drug and, therefore, does not possess side effects.

St. John's Wort: One of the excuses many patients have for overeating is depression. If the depression is not severe enough to necessitate a strong medication, a trial of St. John's Wort can be a logical step. In my experience, some patients have done well with this herb, while others have fared poorly. Numerous reports, especially in Germany, attest to this herb's ability to relieve mild depression. A contrasting study in the *JAMA* however, showed that St. John's Wort was not effective in moderately severe cases of major depression. Interestingly, a placebo resulted in the same effect as St. John's Wort or even a Selective Serotonin Receptor Inhibitor (SSRI). Hypericin, which is the active chemical in the herb, is not adequately standardized. Other ingredients have not been identified as of yet. Dosage is 300 mg three times a day. St. John's Wort may also increase serotonin in the brain.

St. John's Wort should not be used with other SSRIs as St. John's Wort inhibits serotonin, dopamine and norepinephrine reuptake from the brain cells and, thus, increases the amount of neurotransmitters available. St. John's wort also interferes with blood thinners, respiratory drugs and heart medications.

Side effects of St. John's Wort include dry mouth, dizziness and confusion. Besides phototoxicity, neuropathy associated with sun exposure was reported with this product.

Because it has some sun-induced toxicity, people with fair skin should avoid the sun when taking St. John's Wort. As my practice is in Florida, I am reluctant to use this herb with many of my patients. I have found that 5-HTP is a stronger antidepressant than this herb and involves no sun toxicity. A recent article in *EyeWorld* from October 1999 linked St. John's Wort with cataract formation especially in connection with bright light.

Kava, Valerian Root, and Melatonin: Many of my patients complain of stress eating. Some people may not eat at all when they are stressed, while others nervously ingest huge quantities of food without even realizing it. This is a pattern that occurs over and over again whenever they encounter a stressful condition. The best way to deal with this problem is through stress relief. We reserve tranquilizer therapy for matters of last resort. We prefer to use some anti-anxiety herbal compounds. The following three products are also effective for many patients who have difficulty sleeping and who lull themselves to sleep by eating.

Kava is a South Pacific herb which is supposed to reduce anxiety, stress and restlessness. It also facilitates sleep without developing problems of tolerance, dependence and withdrawal. Kava should not be used with alcohol or antidepressants or in pregnant or nursing women. Kava should not be taken for more than three months without medical supervision.

Kava is also neuroprotective and helps with long-term memory. Kava, which should be purchased from a reputable company, has a recommended dosage of 30-80 mg a day.

In high dosages, Kava may also be detrimental and should not be added to central nervous system depressants. Kava should not be used with tranquilizers, sleeping pills or alcohol. In addition, a skin reaction was reported in some patients taking this product. Kava was recently banned in Europe because of liver toxicity.

The Kava root capsule is not as efficient as the liquid extract. This product should contain at least 30% of kavalactones. Do not take more than 150 mg.

Valerian Root is best characterized as a mild tranquilizer. The dried underground parts of this plant possess anti-anxiety and mild hypnotic effects which make it useful in treating nervousness and insomnia. Long-term use, however, can cause restlessness, headache and sleeplessness.

We have generally had good results with valerian root for our patients with some experiencing better results than others.

Melatonin. About 3 mg in the evening may induce sleep in some patients, while others may become over-stimulated. It also can work in alleviating jet lag. Other claims that melatonin may be a rejuvenator and a cancer fighter should be taken with a grain of salt.

A recent study, though, showed that melatonin added daily to the diet of fruit flies significantly increased their lifespan due to its free radical scavenging qualities. Thus, melatonin may potentially slow the aging process in humans.

The effectiveness of melatonin remains controversial; it works mainly in the treatment of insomnia caused by circadian schedule changes (i.e., jet lag, shift work). In cases of chronic insomnia, however, it is less effective. The use of melatonin for short-term adaptation to jet lag or work shift changes may be reasonable. Over dosage of melatonin may cause sleep disruption, daytime fatigue, headache, dizziness, and increased irritability.

5-HTP also has a sedative and hypnotic effect. Other herbs should be used cautiously with this product. The best recommendation is to first try these products separately and then only combine them slowly and in small doses.

Gamma-Aminobutyric Acid: Gamma-aminobutyric acid (GABA) is an amino acid that acts as a neurotransmitter in the central nervous system. It is essential for brain metabolism, aiding in proper brain function. GABA can be taken to calm the body in much the same way as diazepam (Valium™), chlordiazepoxide (Librium™), and other tranquilizers but without the fear of addiction. It may also be prescribed for depression.

Ginkgo Biloba: This plant has been used in China for hundreds of years. By increasing the brain's tolerance for low levels of oxygen and by enhancing blood flow to the brain, this herb has been reported to improve short-term memory and concentration in those with early Alzheimer's disease. A recent article in the *JAMA* claims that Ginkgo biloba reduced the severity of dementia in some afflicted patients. This placebo controlled double blind randomized trial of 302 patients taking the Ginkgo biloba extract for dementia concluded that the herb was safe and that in a substantial number of cases it "improved the cognitive performance and social functioning of demented patients for six months to one year." This trial used 40 mg of Ginkgo, three times a day before meals, for a total of 120 mg. The improvement in the patients treated with Ginkgo was believed to be due to some components in the herb that work as scavengers of free radicals. This action prevents excessive lipid peroxidation and cellular damage, also observed in Alzheimer's disease. The active ingredients of the Ginkgo leaves are the Ginkgo flavone glycosides or heterosides.

Affliction or symptoms targeted by Ginkgo biloba include:

- Cerebral vascular insufficiency and impaired mental performance
- Alzheimer's disease
- Inner ear deafness and dysfunction, such as vertigo and tinnitus (ringing of the ears)
- Senile macular degeneration and diabetic retinopathy
- Impotence
- Premenstrual syndrome
- Depression
- Allergies and asthma
- Some cases of angina and congestive heart failure

Recommended dosage is 40 mg of the standardized product, three times a day. Some studies even advise 80 mg, three times a day. Ginkgo biloba extract needs to be taken consistently for at least 12 weeks in order to be effective. Most people report benefits within two to three weeks, while others take longer to respond. It is crucial that you purchase a standardized extract versus a tincture, because the extract contains a higher level of the Ginkgo flavonoglycerides (24%).

When Gingko was combined with phosphatidyl choline (a component of lecithin and a phytosome), absorption of the product was shown to be enhanced by three to seven times. The phytosome also increases the biological activity of the Gingko, permitting the herb to last longer in the body. Thus, it is better to chose a Ginkgo phytosome over Ginkgo alone, because the phytosome allows the herb to enhance its delivery to the body

Ginkgo biloba may be associated with spontaneous bleeding, especially if taken in combination with aspirin or coumadin. People who take garlic, vitamin E, aspirin or medications which hinder clotting, should be cautioned about potential interactions with Ginkgo products. Do not take Ginkgo before surgical procedures.

A group of 30 botanical remedy makers recently launched a project, called MVP (Method Validation Program), to develop standardized testing methods for herbal products. So far, MVP has developed standards for Ginkgo biloba, Ginseng, and Kava and expects standards for 15 other herbs in the near future. In the meantime, try to purchase products from well-known companies and check labels for notations like "Standardized," "HPLC" or "USP."

Miscellaneous Products: Finally, DHEA has been found to have antidepressant qualities. Phenylalanine, an amino acid, may also convert to tyrosine which in turn transforms itself to dopamine. Dopamine deficiency will lead to depression, lack of energy and even to Parkinson's disease. As we get older our dopamine level, like all levels of neurotransmitters, gradually declines and therefore phenylalanine supplementation is important in preserving mental health.

Omega-3 Fatty Acids from fish oils have been found to improve bipolar disorder, also known as manic depressive illness. Doses of 5.6 grams of EPA and 3.4 g of DHA were given to 30 patients during a four-month study led by Dr. Andrew Stall of Harvard Medical School. Dr. Stall stated that "This study may represent the first demonstration of an effective therapy for bipolar disorder." The patients who stayed on this supplementation continued to do well even after the study was over.

— Chapter Eleven —

NUTRITIONAL SUPPLEMENTATION FOR GENERAL HEALTH

Many patients and dietitians claim that we do not need vitamin supplementation, because they can be obtained from a well-balanced diet. With our very busy and stressful lifestyles, we certainly do not have a well balanced diet! We are happy to just survive and know that our nutritional supplementation is adequate.

VITAMINS

The following vitamins are divided into water soluble and oil soluble varieties.

Vitamin A is important for skin health and preventing night blindness. Too much vitamin A, however, can cause headaches and yellow discoloration of the skin. We recommend not to exceed 10,000 units per day. There is some controversy about vitamin A's role in cancer protection; some studies found that certain types of cancers are protected by vitamin A, while others found a negative correlation between vitamin A ingestion and the occurrence of certain cancers. During pregnancy, vitamin A consumption should be kept low so as to prevent potential birth defects. Vitamin A derivatives have been used in skin care with great success, especially with acne and in eliminating fine lines (for example Retin A™, Renova™, and Kinerase™). A study in the *JAMA* has shown that too much vitamin A may cause osteoporosis or thinning of the bones.

Beta-carotene is a derivative of vitamin A. A high dosage of beta-carotene is less dangerous than vitamin A at high consumption. The dosage should not exceed 15,000 units per day. Carotenemia or yellow discoloration of the skin can occur with too high a dosage. In patients with lung cancer, beta-carotene did not offer any protective advantage over the placebo. The explanation offered for this negative result is that beta-carotene does not work alone but needs mixed carotenoids for its cancer prevention ability.

Vitamins B1 (thiamine), *B2* (riboflavin), *B3* (niacin), *B5* (pantothenic acid), *B6* (pyridoxine), *Folic Acid* and *B12* (cyanocobalamin) are a powerful group of vitamins. B vitamins counteract the effects of stress. 400 mcg of folic acid, 500 mcg of B12 and 12.5 mg of B6 daily were shown to reduce homocysteine levels by 40% in 90 days. As noted before, high levels of homocysteine may kill 50,000 people a year from vascular disease. A dose of 100 mg of vitamin B1 or thiamine can lower homocysteine levels and be a neuroprotective agent. Its deficiency is noted in alcoholics who experience dementia. B1 supplementation is helpful with nerve pain (neuropathy) and leg cramps.

B2 or *Riboflavin* may be dosed at about 50 mg a day. A neuroprotective vitamin, it is also necessary for mitochondrial cellular function. Riboflavin at 400 mg daily prevents migraine headaches.

B3 or *Niacin* may be dosed at 50 mg daily.

Niacinamide may be supplemented at 150 mg daily. Niacin is used for tinnitus (ear ringing), for increasing cerebral blood flow and in high quantities to reduce cholesterol (1-2 grams dosage). To change pattern B-LDL to pattern A-LDL, high niacin supplementation is recommended. High niacin doses should not be given to diabetics.

If a person is sensitive to niacin, flushing and headaches can occur even at small dosages. Slow-release prescription niacin is available to prevent these side effects. In addition, an aspirin consumed half an hour before taking the niacin may prevent these reactions.

Pantothenic Acid is recommended as a cancer protector at a dosage of 400 mg daily and may also lower blood fats. Additionally, it is important for proper adrenal gland functioning, for immunity and for healthy skin and hair.

B6 or *Pyridoxine* is a natural diuretic that helps with premenstrual bloating and may also relieve carpal tunnel syndrome. The usual dosage is about 50 mg daily. It is also used to prevent kidney stone formation. Larger dosages may be used if severe problems of edema (water retention) occur. B6 deficiency is associated with irritability, insomnia, nervousness, sores and skin disorders. Pyridoxine is useful in maintaining elevated mood while dieting. As cooking destroys it, B6 is very difficult to get from food. Pyridoxine should be taken with magnesium and all the B vitamins to be effective.

Folic Acid is recommended as a protector of the heart and nervous system and also needed for red blood cell formation. Folic acid may prevent or even reverse some precancerous conditions. Dietary folate was inversely associated with breast cancer risk in a large study done in China. 800 mcg of folic acid is recommended for daily ingestion. Folic acid dosage of at least 400 mcg daily is used for all pregnant women in their first trimester of gestation to prevent neural tube defects of the fetus. Folic acid deficiency has been linked with increased risk of early spontaneous abortions.

Cyanocobolamin or *B12* helps with red blood cell and bone marrow cell formation. It is a cofactor or helper with other B vitamins in many energy pathways of the body. B12 may also relieve the stigma of vitiligo (white depigmented areas of the skin). The recommended dosage is 1 mg of B12 twice a day continued with 5 mg of folic acid, also twice a day. The role of B12 in increasing energy and a feeling of well-being is clearly documented. Some patients swear by the benefits of B12 injections. About 100 mcg of B12 is recommended daily.

Biotin is another B vitamin that is mostly used for skin and hair health. 300 mcg of biotin is recommended daily. Biotin is essential for storage of muscle and liver glucose and for fatty acid synthesis.

Vitamin C or *Ascorbic Acid* has been touted as the immune-enhancing vitamin "par excellence." Since Nobel Laureate Dr. Linus

Pauling's advice, megadoses of vitamin C have been ingested to prevent or shorten the common cold. Vitamin C acts as an antiviral by supposedly toughening cell membranes to prevent viral penetration. Vitamin C helps cells of the body (bones, veins, gums and blood vessels) grow and stay healthy. It helps the body to respond to infection and stress and to use iron efficiently. Vitamin C is also an antioxidant like vitamin A, beta-carotene and vitamin E. It helps to straighten out the wrinkles inside the coronary arteries and to prevent the development of heart attacks. Some studies have shown that vitamin C supplementation was associated with a decreased risk of heart disease and stroke. Elderly patients with bedsore ulcers improved dramatically when given 500 mg of vitamin C. This vitamin protects against osteoarthritis and helps in the synthesis of collagen of cartilage.

The first sign of vitamin C deficiency is fatigue. As deficiency continues, vein bruising, bleeding gums, poor healing, loosening of teeth and infections occur. Vitamin C is claimed to prevent the cross linking of the collagen fibers so that less wrinkling of the skin occurs. Vitamin C is one of the vitamins that help fight the eye disease macular degeneration. Vitamin C serum or cream is available for cosmetic use. Some nutrition companies market an Ester C complex that is supposed to be less acidic and offer better absorption capability. Besides its cardiovascular protection, vitamin C has been touted as a blood detoxifier and cancer fighter.

High vitamin C consumption has been associated with kidney stone formation, especially if not enough hydration is instituted. In April 1999, the NIH recommended the dietary allowance of vitamin C to be increased from 60 mg to 100 mg and preferably to 200 mg. No more than 1,000 mg of vitamin C is recommended to be consumed daily. On the other hand, Dr. Robert Hackman, who specializes in vitamin supplementation recommends high dosages of vitamin C up to 5,000 mg for pulmonary defense and to combat asthma. Vitamin C (at about 500 mg daily) enhances the benefits of exercise in adults who were depleted of this vitamin. However, the best advice in preventing cancer is to take this vitamin in five servings of fruits and vegetables a day. Those foods containing the highest content of vitamin C are strawberries, papaya, kiwi and oranges. Vitamin C recycles vitamin E, regenerating it when it becomes oxidized.

Vitamin D is important as a bone builder and as the best aid for calcium absorption. Vitamin D3 from fish liver oil is recommended in a dosage of 400 international units daily. The sun also produces a type of vitamin D on the skin at a dosage of 400 mg daily which helps calcium absorption and thus prevents a common disease in elderly women, osteoporosis. Vitamin D also helps protect against osteoarthritis in the hip.

It is interesting to note that even if they consume adequate amounts of vitamin D in pills or in liquid emulsions, those women who stay at home or wear a veil for religious purposes have a high fracture risk. A short ten minutes a day of sun bathing and exposing the face or upper arms is all that is required for best calcium absorption. One caveat is to avoid sunscreens; if wrinkling is feared, antioxidant therapy is used.

Vitamin D is an oil soluble vitamin like vitamins A, E and K. Patients with liver disease should be careful about its ingestion at high dosages. Recently, vitamin D has been shown to be helpful for people with cochlear deafness.

Vitamin E is cardioprotective in combination with vitamin C. 400 international units of vitamin E has been shown to prevent heart attacks, and no more than 1,200 IU are recommended daily. According to the *New England Journal of Rheumatology*, gamma tocopherols may be linked to arthritis of the knees; therefore make sure your vitamins contain vitamin E in the form of alpha tocopherols. A *New England Journal of Medicine* article documented a 40% reduction in the incidence of cardiac events of patients who consumed 100 IU of vitamin E. This vitamin may also retard the progression of coronary lesions. According to Dr. W. "Chip" Watkins, vitamin E levels in the blood are more important than cholesterol levels. Vitamin E may have cancer protection benefits and may also prevent certain eye diseases like cataracts and macular degeneration. The active form of the vitamin is the D-alpha not the D-L form. According to Dr. Robert Hackman, vitamin E may improve diabetic neuropathy. When healthy women deficient in vitamin E in their blood were supplemented with this vitamin, plaque deposition in their arteries was prevented. Nerve conduction velocity was improved significantly in patients taking 900 mg of vitamin E. Too much vitamin E (more than 400 IU) may be detrimental and interefere with blood clotting which may cause a stroke. Vitamins C and E may reduce the risk of preeclampsia (high blood pressure and water retention during pregnancy); 1,000 mg of vitamin C and 400 IU of vitamin E should be administered to high risk pregnant women from weeks 16 to 22 until delivery time. Beta-carotene, vitamins C, E, zinc and copper are now recommended for macular degeneration.

Vitamin K has been associated with coagulation. Hemorrhages and bleeding can result from a deficiency of vitamin K. We recommend 60 mcg of vitamin K daily. Patients who are taking the prescription medication Coumadin™ should not consume vitamin K, which counteracts the effects of the blood thinner. Vitamin K has a very important role in the maintenance of healthy bones. Thus, vitamin K from dark green vegetables may prove a very useful adjunct for prevention of postmenopausal bone loss. Vitamin K creams have also been formulated to combat bruising and spider veins in the lower extremities.

Even though many foods contain all these vitamins, taking vitamin supplements is a practical solution to guarantee that adequate supplementation occurs.

MINERALS:

Minerals are usually chelated or combined with amino acids protein components so as not to interfere with the electrically-charged cellular membranes.

Boron in a dosage of 2 mg daily is only recommended for bone density improvement.

Calcium is one of the most important minerals for health, especialy for women. Calcium is essential for proper muscle functioning and for bone integrity. One of the biggest causes of death in the adult female population is hip fractures caused by osteoporosis. We recommend about 1,000 mg of calcium in premenopausal women, 1,200 mg for pregnant or breast-feeding mothers, and finally, at least 1,500 mg for post-menopausal women. As it may increase bone fracture risk at high doses, ingestion of over 2,000 mg of calcium is detrimental.

Calcium alone and calcium with magnesium are used for blood pressure-lowering purposes; dairy products were found to prevent cancer of the colon. However, calcium and dairy products may stimulate cancer of the prostate. Many patients ask me what I think is the best kind of calcium. Even though calcium carbonate is the best absorbed calcium, we also recommend calcium gluconate or calcium citrate, especially if the patients suffer from low stomach acidity (40% of post-menopausal women) and cannot absorb calcium carbonate. No oyster shell or bone meal calcium are recommended, as they contain too much lead. Calcium hydroxyapatite is not recommended either, as it has low absorption potential. The best time to take calcium is with meals, and it is optimal to divide the dosage of calcium to two or three times a day for best absorption. Nighttime calcium is advantageous for relaxation and leg cramp improvement. The teenage girl should already start on calcium supplementation, especially if she does not consume any dairy products. Children and adolescents do not drink milk anymore, frequently opting for carbonated drinks. The high oxalate content of carbonated or diet drinks may reduce absorption of calcium into the bloodstream. Children consuming soft drinks already show low blood calcium levels. They are prime candidates for calcium supplementation.

A February 2002 article in *JAMA* equates the consumption of dairy products with lowering insulin resistance (the precursor of type II diabetes) in overweight young adults. Thus, eating dairy products may help to decrease the incidence of type II diabetes and also to lower the risk of obesity in children. While some of the components in milk such as lactose, protein and fat may increase satiety other nutrients in milk like calcium, potassium and magnesium may protect overweight individuals against insulin resistance at the intracellular level.

Calcium in the diet may accelerate fat loss in the obese population by decreasing the release of vitamin D which may induce weight gain. Dairy sources of calcium may thus exert a strong anti-obesity effect on fat metabolism and may prevent and manage obesity.

We should institute calcium supplementation early and continue forever. Some women may already consume a high dairy diet (remember that one glass of milk contains about 300 mg of calcium). Postmenopausal women would need to drink at least five glasses of milk a day to fill their calcium requirement. However, for many women who are lactose intolerant or are on a weight reduction program, I recommend calcium supplementation instead.

By contrast, in a Nurses' Health Study of 1980, hip fracture incidence was increased by 45% in milk drinking nurses. Sometimes, low fat cheeses are easier to digest than plain milk. Low-fat or fat-free yogurt does not contain as much calcium as cheese. Besides dairy products, good food sources of calcium are salmon, tuna, sardines (with bones), green leafy vegetables and tofu. As a rule of thumb, one ounce of cheese contains approximately 200 mg of calcium, exceptions are: cottage cheese and feta cheese which contain about 100 mg per cup; cream cheese with 25 mg of calcium per ounce; and finally Parmesan cheese has 70 mg of calcium per tablespoon.

Fruit juices are now supplemented with calcium (Fruitcal™) for those who dislike or cannot tolerate dairy products. An article in the *JAMA* of October 14, 2002 however, did implicate calcium enriched orange juice in a decrease of 40% of the absorption of certain medications, especially antibiotics. (Plain orange juice also prevents the absorption of the same drugs by 21% when consumed together.)

Some women also take Tums™ for their calcium intake. Tums™ contains only calcium, no vitamin D, and therefore is not the best formula for osteoporosis prevention. A better alternative is a new, tasty product called Viactiv™ which contains calcium and Vitamin D.

To test whether your calcium supplement will be absorbed into your body, drop your pill in a glass of vinegar for a couple of hours; the calcium pill that is dissolved will be absorbed, while the undissolved portion will come out of the body in the stool. Calcium is thought to be like the orchestra leader in need of a whole orchestra to function properly. The key player is magnesium.

Chromium (chelated with polynicotinate) has been discussed previously. All my diabetic patients are on this product, as it helps regulate blood sugar control naturally and decreases serum insulin. We recommend a minimum of 200 mcg to a maximum of 600 mcg daily, given with meals. Sweet cravings are significantly reduced with the consumption of chromium polynicotinate, also called glucose tolerance factor. Chromium is also helpful in inhibiting the formation of fat from carbohydrates and in regulating cholesterol production by decreasing total and LDL cholesterol.

Iodine from kelp may be supplemented at about 150 mg daily. Iodine deficiency is rare in the United States, as even our table salt contains iodine. Iodine deficiency may lead to goiter (enlargement of the thyroid).

Iron is also a very important mineral when combined with copper in the synthesis of hemoglobin (red blood cells). It is also necessary for muscle contractions. Vitamin C also enhances the absorption of iron. The dosage for menstruating women is about 18 mg daily. Men and postmenopausal women do not require iron supplementation. If not needed, iron can be detrimental, as it can cause cancer and "iron overload syndrome" in the blood. Iron may oxidize LDL cholesterol and contribute to heart attacks. Iron has also been used successfully for the "Restless Leg Syndrome" which occurs when legs twitch uncontrollably in bed.

Before iron supplementation is instituted, the hemoglobin level should first be checked; the best values are over 12 mg/dl for women and over 14 mg/dl for men. Low iron counts may be due to severe menstrual bleeding or intestinal bleeding (ulcers). A stool test called hemoccult can determine whether microscopic blood is present in the stool. Too much iron consumption can cause cancer.

Magnesium deficiency can lead to osteoporosis. Other players in the anti-osteoporosis orchestra are iron, manganese, boron, copper, iron, cadmium, molybdenum, selenium, zinc and many more.

We recommend a dosage of 500 mg daily of magnesium. Magnesium should be chelated for better absorption. Magnesium aspartate ascorbate helps protect hearing and hastens recovery from hearing loss due to loud noises. According to some investigators, the ratio between calcium and magnesium should be two-to-one; others advocate instead a one-to-one ratio of these two minerals. Magnesium deficiency has been shown to be related to high blood pressure, kidney stones, coronary artery spasms, fatigue and PMS syndrome. Supplemental magnesium may be beneficial for adults with cardiac arrhythmia, congestive heart failure, hypertension, diabetes, fibromyalgia and migraine headaches. Magnesium intake may modulate blood lipid levels, preventing plaque formation and heart attacks. For children, supplemental magnesium may be beneficial for asthma and attention deficit disorder.

Hypertensive obese individuals were found to have low intracellular magnesium levels, thus pointing to mineral metabolism defects in obesity and hypertension. Low dietary magnesium was found to be associated with insulin resistance and possibly diabetes later on in life in a sample of young non-diabetic black Americans. In patients who take diuretics, magnesium levels should be monitored and, if needed, supplementation instituted. According to Dr. Robert Hackman, both magnesium and potassium fire up the metabolism of the obese. Orange juice combined with these minerals constitutes a veritable powerhouse of energy.

We will explain later that high fracture risk may not be related to osteoporosis; some people may be osteoporotic and not have a high fracture risk and vice versa. The role of exercise cannot be emphasized enough in the prevention of osteoporosis; any exercise done against gravity, such as walking and running, helps with the remodeling of bone. Resistance training or weight lifting exercises also help to develop stronger bones in premenopausal or postmenopausal women. Incidentally, exercise was also associated with a 37% reduction of breast cancer.

Molybdenum (also chelated) may be supplemented at a dosage of 150 mcg/day. It is another member of the osteoporosis-prevention orchestra.

Potassium is also an important macromineral that decreases significantly during diuretic therapy or weight loss. A dosage of 100 mg of potassium aspartate ascorbate is recommended. Too little potassium can cause arrhythmias and palpitations, while too much potassium can kill. With magnesium and calcium, potassium also regulates neuromuscular activity.

New evidence reported by the *Harvard Health Letter* shows an association between a high potassium diet and a lower stroke risk. Out of over 43,000 men followed for eight years, the ones with the lowest risk of stroke ate an average of eight servings of potassium-rich fruits and vegetables daily.

In our office, we successfully use a combination of magnesium potassium aspartate which contains about 400 mg of each mineral. This product is especially recommended for the reduction of fatigue and also for relaxing the bronchial tubes of asthmatic patients. This complex also increases stamina in normal people and athletes before exercise work-outs. If taken half an hour before an exercise routine, endurance may be significantly increased. It is also a good product to take before any competition outdoors where one has a tendency to perspire. Most multi-vitamins are low in potassium and magnesium.

In our weight reduction programs, patients who lose a significant amount of weight have their blood potassium levels checked often.

We also recommend other minerals like *copper* (chelated) in a dose of 2 mg daily and *manganese* (also chelated) in a dosage of 20 mg daily. Copper is involved with energy metabolism, in the production of red blood cells and in facilitating iron absorption. Copper is also needed for the formation of the myelin sheaths of the nerves. In adults over the age of 50, 3.4 mg of copper daily decreased total cholesterol, HDL cholesterol and triglycerides. Copper has also been found to help macular degeneration. Manganese is necessary for normal skeletal development and maintenance of connective tissue structure. It helps to change the toxic product ammonia into urea to be excreted in the urine so as to prevent accumulation of ammonia in the brain (where it can cause dementia).

Selenium is also a natural antioxidant. We recommend a dosage of 200 mg daily in synergy with vitamin E. Selenium stimulates the formation of antibodies (proteins that act as the policemen of the defense system). Selenium has been used to combat cancer and AIDS. Selenium helps flood your body with glutathione, a potent antioxidant that "mops up" the most dangerous cancer-causing free radicals. Selenium also helps to repair damaged DNA molecules and, finally, it destroys cancer cells in the body (prostate, colon, lung, and breast). Selenium at a 200 mg dosage was associated with a 63% reduction in prostate cancer incidence; thus, all males after age 40 should supplement their diet with selenium. As selenium is an immune system booster, it is useful in patients with hepatitis B and C to prevent liver cancer.

Zinc (chelated with picolinate or methionine) plays an important role in the body's defense system. Zinc is important for the regulation and enhancement of the activity of insulin. Zinc alone has an insulin-like effect and may reduce fasting blood sugar and the rise of blood sugar after a high-sugar meal. Also, in combination with vitamin A, it plays a fundamental role in collagen formation and wound healing. In addition it is supposed to contribute to healthy prostatic function.

Zinc supplementation may be advised to patients whose blood levels show a deficiency in zinc. Zinc dosage is different between the sexes. For women the dosage is only 15 mg, while men have a higher requirement of 30 mg for improved prostate health. More than 50 mg of zinc will prevent the absorption of iron and copper. Zinc in combination with copper, beta-carotene, vitamin C, and vitamin E may retard the progression of macular degeneration according to an NIH sponsored study. Zinc lozenges have also been used for the reduction of symptoms—as well as sick days—associated with the common cold or flu.

Vanadium in the form of vanadyl sulfate is also important in blood sugar control for diabetics; the recommended dosage is 200 mcg daily.

One of the theories for aging and for chronic diseases (like cancer, heart disease, diabetes, and arthritis, etc.) is that the cellular membranes become damaged from the bombardment of electrically-charged molecules, most importantly oxygen ions. Vitamins A, beta-carotene, D and E are all oil soluble vitamins that serve as potent antioxidants which combine with the electrically-charged ions to prevent damage of cellular membranes.

Sulfhydril containing amino acids like **Glutathione, Cysteine, Taurine** and **Catalase** are natural chelators that remove detrimental substances. Anybody with cancer or a cancer history is prescribed these amino acids. Taurine helps patients after heart by-pass surgery.

Alpha-lipoic acid is the most potent antioxidant available; it is able to virtually access all body systems because of its dual solubility in oil and water. It also helps reduce blood cholesterol levels and plays an important role in controlling blood sugar levels and craving for sweets. It also improves muscle strength and energy level. It protects extracellular LDL and intracellular DNA from free radical damage. It may even improve memory. It helps to chelate excess heavy metals from the blood stream. It also inhibits the formation of sugar-protein combination molecules associated with aging and Alzheimer's disease. Thus, alpha-lipoic acid helps with cataracts, diabetes, heart and liver disease and even AIDS. We recommend a 100 mg dosage per day. I first use chromium polynicotinate for sweet or carbohydrate cravings. If this therapy is not effective, then an alpha-lipoic acid trial comes next. Alpha lipoic acid was also used successfully for diabetic neuropathy in combination with vitamin E. In Europe, alpha lipoic acid has been used for 30 years to improve nerve health, balance blood sugar, stop retinal degenerative disease, and reduce damage caused by "Syndrome X." In a study of 328 diabetics, this product reduced 30% of symptoms of hand and foot burning and numbness.

Citrus Bioflavonoids are best exemplified by *Hesperidin* and *Quercetin*. They are powerful anti-inflammatory substances working in unison with vitamin C. Bioflavonoids have been used clinically to treat and prevent allergies, inflammation, and to enhance vascular integrity. There have also been claims that these substances help with cancer. Hesperidin may dilate blood vessels, enhance circulation and strengthen capillaries. The usual dosage is 100 mg/day. Quercetin has been shown to fight cancer of the breast and to prevent metastases.

CoQ10: The beneficial effects of CoQ10 (biosynthesized from tyrosine) revolve around its ability to improve energy production and act as an antioxidant. These effects are most beneficial in the prevention and treatment of cardiovascular disease and cancer. CoQ10 can be used in congestive heart failure, high blood pressure, cardiomyopathy, angina, diabetes, periodontal disease, immune deficiency and cancer. It may also be used as a weight-loss aid requiring eight weeks for response to occur. Because of its cardioprotective effect, any patient taking chemotherapy should also consume CoQ10. CoQ10 is also advantageous in diabetes and may increase performance in athletes. A recent study at the University of California, San Diego showed that 200 mg of CoQ10 slowed the progression of Parkinson's disease by 44%. 200 mg of CoQ10 and 200 mg of ginkgo biloba improve the quality of life of patients suffering from fibromyalgia. In addition,

CoQ10 may be used in neurodegenerative diseases like Huntington's disease. The recommended dosage is about 100 mg per day (up to 300 mg can be used for severe heart disease). Because CoQ10 is a fat-soluble vitamin, its absorption is improved if eaten with a little fat. CoQ10 is also supplemented when patients are taking cholesterol-lowering drugs. CoQ10, a very fragile substance, must be stored in the refrigerator in an opaque container. The effective CoQ10 should be taken in an oil capsule, not in a tablet form. However, a sublingual tablet with better absorption properties has been put on the market recently. Finally, as a dental wash, CoQ10 is used to help with gum disease.

Goat's Rue (Galega officinalis) an herbal product and **aminoguanidine** (an amino acid) has been shown to combat glycation of proteins, thus preventing diabetes and aging.

Hesperidin can dilate blood vessels, enhance microcirculation and strengthen capillaries. The usual dosage is about 100 mg/day.

Inositol is a fuel source and an essential component of cell membranes. The usual dose is 50 mg daily. Inositol supplementation may also prevent diabetic complications. Methionine, inositol and choline are the three lipotropic amino acids that have been associated in breaking down body fat.

Lycopene, extracted from tomato, is dosed at between 10-30 mg per day. It is a potent cancer preventative agent (especially of the lungs and prostate), a defender against UV skin damage and a quencher of oxygen-free radicals. New studies have shown that men who regularly consume tomato sauce (as in pizza) have lower prostate cancer incidence. Servings of tomato-based foods over 10 weeks decreased prostate cancer incidence by 45%. One of the best sources of lycopene is pizza as the cheese increases biovailability of the lycopene. Eating cooked tomatoes, as opposed to raw tomatoes, is preferable because it provides for better absorption. Lycopene may also help with cancers of the lung and stomach. A study published in April 1999 showed that men who were fed lycopene for 30 days before their prostate operation had decreased tumor size and a less aggressive cancer.

Pycnogenol™ can be found in two sources: grape seeds and pine bark. It has been used in Europe for many years for conditions including circulatory problems of the heart and brain, capillary fragility and macular degeneration. The recommended dosage is 50-300 mg per day. In my office, we use it with great success for bruising and varicose veins. The pycnogenol from grape seed is more effective than that derived from pine bark.

STUDIES SHOWING ANTIOXIDANT ADVANTAGE:

Cancer: Free radicals are thought to initiate and promote cancer. In cell-culture studies, vitamin E and selenium inhibited transformation of normal mouse embryo cells to cancerous cells following exposure to chemicals and radiation. Vitamin C, in addition with proline, lysine and a green tea derivative prevented the metastasis of breast cancer cells, according to a recent German study led by Dr. Mathias Rath.

Coronary Heart Disease: Subjects given vitamins C and E had a decreased risk of coronary heart disease mortality by 53%. In a follow-up study of almost 88,000 female nurses, those who took vitamin E supplementation for two years had 41% lower relative risk of major coronary disease.

Pre-treatment with antioxidants, vitamin E and ascorbic acid block the effect of high plasma homocysteine levels in healthy subjects. High homocysteine levels are one of the causes of cardiovascular diseases.

A recent study in Denmark on Alzheimer's disease showed that patients taking antioxidant supplementation experienced significant improvement.

There was a 56% decrease in cataract risk in subjects who took vitamin supplements compared to those who did not. A new study from Australia showed that a diet high in protein, vitamin A, niacin and riboflavin may protect against the development of nuclear cataracts. Beta carotene, and vitamins A and C retard the progression of macular degeneration.

As you can see, one multiple vitamin pill cannot contain all the nutrients needed. We recommend taking vitamins at least twice a day with breakfast and dinner; some prefer taking them with lunch (bigger meal) and dinner. We give our patients little packets of vitamins and minerals to be taken with food; amino acids are best to be taken between meals either one hour before or two hours after a meal. Some nutrients can also be consumed sublingually (AMP or HGH). Many vitamins, minerals and special products can be consumed in a spray. The advantage of this delivery system is that it bypasses the gastrointestinal tract thereby preventing gastric irritation and facilitating absorption.

Even though there is a lot of hype about *colloidal minerals* (those extracted from the sea), according to vitamin expert Dr. Robert Hackman there is no evidence that these minerals provide any health benefits.

FRUITS:

There are many beneficial products in foods of which we are not even aware. Fruits and vegetables should be consumed for optimal nutrition and health, in addition to their good taste.

Apples contain boron which is great for bone integrity. There is some truth to the adage: "An apple a day keeps the doctor away." The June 2000 edition of *Nature* reported that 100 grams of fresh apples had an antioxidant activity equivalent to 1,500 mg of vitamin C and that whole-apple extract inhibited the growth of colon and liver cancer cells.

Black Raspberries may be effective in inhibiting the development of colon cancer in humans.

Blueberries are rich in phenolic components which protect arteries from cholesterol attack. One cup of blueberries delivers the same phenolic precursors as one glass of red wine.

Cherries: A study performed at Michigan State University determined that 20 tart cherries contain 12.5 mg of anthocyanidins (a flavonoid) and exhibited antioxidant activity similar to vitamin E; 20 cherries a day contain 10 times the pain-relieving capability of one aspirin. In addition, cherries are shown to inhibit two inflammation-promoting enzymes. These flavonoids may be responsible for the fruit's benefits for people afflicted with gout and arthritis.

Oranges have vitamin C (described above; see pg. 123) and are helpful for gum disease and for preventing cholesterol from sticking to the arteries.

Pineapple has bromelain which helps with digestion; it also has natural estrogen and manganese to prevent osteoporosis.

Pomegranates may reduce the risk of heart attacks and strokes by inhibiting the formation of blood clots and enhancing blood flow.

Chocolate has antioxidants that are good for the heart. A small piece of chocolate is better than a cracker at night.

Cranberries have certain components that kill bacteria in the bladder and urinary tract.

Garlic is a quite controversial substance. Out of 20 studies performed using garlic, 17 were positive in lowering cholesterol levels. Fresh garlic not the oil may lower total cholesterol, LDL cholesterol and triglycerides, and increase HDL cholesterol.

Kiwis keep arteries cholesterol-free because of their high vitamin C content.

Papaya has properties to help digestion and contains vitamin A and potassium. Papaya extract may be used for combating the redness and swelling of an insect bite.

Peaches also have boron, beta-carotene and vitamin C.

Prunes keep arteries clear and protect against high blood pressure due to their high potassium concentration. They reduce heart attack risk, help with constipation, and may be used as a fat alternative in baking.

Purple Grape Juice contains eight flavonoid compounds that delay oxidation of LDL (bad cholesterol) component, according to a report presented at the American College of Cardiology's 48th Annual Scientific Session meeting in March 1999. Oxidation of LDL cholesterol is the key contributor to the development of atherosclerosis. In addition to wine, simple purple grape juice can contribute to healthy cardiovascular function. Purple grape juice is already being credited with reduction of platelet activity, thus decreasing blood clots, heart attacks and strokes. In addition, it may increase nitric oxide production, a key player in improving many diseases.

VEGETABLES:

Avocados contain a high monosaturated "good" fat content. They are also a rich source of folic acid and decrease homocysteine levels. Due to the fact that they contain a hefty dose of potassium (more than a banana), they help lower blood pressure.

Barley is a potent heart medicine that contains many antioxidants.

Beets contain folic acid, iron, calcium and potassium.

Broccoli, ***Cauliflower*** and ***Cabbage*** are cruciferous vegetables that have anti-cancer and anti-ulcer properties. They produce a substance called Indole 3 Carbinol (I3C) which is a strong anti-carcinogenic product. It transforms estrogen to a non-harmful byproduct that blocks breast cancer. A stronger metabolite of I3C called DIM (also derived from broccoli) does this more effectively. Eating cabbage more than once a week cuts colon cancer odds by 66%.

Carrots are also a super food containing beta-carotene; they lower cholesterol, and fight cancer and eye disease. A carrot per day cuts stroke rates in women by 68%.

Kale has 50% more calcium than milk, is a powerful cancer fighter and also prevents macular degeneration.

Nuts contain vitamin E, magnesium, and alpha linolenic acid and are heart healthy.

Oats stabilize blood sugar and reduce cholesterol.

Onions are a major source of flavonoids which may help reduce cholesterol and prevent blood clots.

Parsley has a high concentration of antioxidants which lower blood pressure.

Soy may lower dangerous LDL cholesterol. Soy is also used to prevent cancer in men and women. Tofu and miso may be used in many healthy recipes. Soy is also useful in reducing hot flashes after menopause and in increasing bone density. Soy is used as the base for the phytoestrogens given to peri-or-post menopausal women who chose natural hormonal replacement therapy. (More about soy in Chapter 12.)

Spinach is a rich source of antioxidants and a cancer antagonist that also lowers cholesterol and prevents macular degeneration. All green vegetables like kale and chard help in the prevention and improvement of macular degeneration. Spinach also regulates blood pressure and lowers homocysteine levels, as it contains high levels of magnesium, potassium and folate.

Tomatoes are a major source of lycopene which may lower rates of pancreatic, prostatic and cervical cancer.

Fruit and vegetables contain fiber or cellulose which help reduce constipation and may lower cholesterol. A high fiber diet is also beneficial in weight loss and diabetes. A study in the October 1999 *JAMA* found a protective relationship between consumption of fruit and vegetables (particularly cruciferous and green leafy vegetables, citrus fruit and juice) and ischemic stroke risk.

How do we know which vitamins and minerals are needed for each person? Each vitamin and mineral supplementation program should be individualized. Men require less calcium and more zinc than women. Postmenopausal women need more calcium and no iron, while premenopausal women need additional iron.

A big 300-pound man would need different supplementation than a 100 pound, petite woman. Thus we check the levels of B-complex vitamins (B1, B2, B3, B6, B12, folate, pantothenate and biotin). The amino acid levels checked are serine, glutamine and asparagine; essential metabolites assayed are choline and inositol. Oleic acid level is assayed. To determine carbohydrate metabolism, we check glucose insulin interaction and fructose intolerance. For minerals, we check calcium, zinc and magnesium. Besides assaying for total antioxidant function, we also test the levels of two important antioxidants called glutathione and cysteine. These tests allow one to individualize the best nutritional supplementation for each patient.

Final Summary Table

LIST OF AILMENTS ALLEVIATED BY NUTRITIONAL SUPPLEMENTS AND FOODS

Conditions	Nutritional Supplements	Whole Foods
ADHD	DHA, magnesium, omega-3 fatty acids	
Allergies	Bioflavonoids (hesperidin, quercetin)	
Alzheimer's	Ginkgo biloba, high doses of Vitamin E	
Anti-aging	Ashwaghanda, DHEA, Gerovital, Goat's Rue, HGH, Korean Ginseng, Licorice root (Glycyrrhiza glabra)	
Anxiety	GABA, 5-HTP, Kava, Melatonin, Valerian root	
Appetite Suppression	Caffeine, fiber, 5-HTP, phenylalanine	Coffee
Arthritis	Ashwaghanda, Boswella, Cetylmyristo-late, Curcumin, Methylsulfonyl methane (MSM), Sadenosyl L menthionine disulfate (SAME)	Fish
Asthma	Boswella, Kava, magnesium, Vitamin C	Coffee
Bloating	Digestive enzymes, probiotics, licorice root	Peppermint oil

Final Summary Table (cont.)

Conditions	Nutritional Supplements	Whole Foods
Bruising	Butcher's broom, pycnogenol, Vitamin C	Citrus fruit, Kiwi
Cancer-general	Bioflavonoids, colostrum, folic acid, melatonin, MGN3, pantothenic acid, high dose of omega-3 fattty acids, selenium, shark cartilage, zinc	Cruciferous Vegetables Broccoli, etc. Garlic, teas
—breast	Ip6, DIM	
—colon and liver		Black raspberries
—cervical, pancreatic and prostate	Lycopene	Soy, tomato
Cardiovascular Disease		
—blood thinning:	Bromelain, curcumin, vitamin E and C	Pomegranates, tea
—heart attacks and stroke:	fish oils (omega-3 fatty acids)	Pomegranates
—heart strengthening:	CoQ10, Magnesium, Potassium	Dark chocolate, fish
Cataract	Vitamins A, B2, Niacin	
Cholesterol	Copper, Gugulipid, HGH, Niacin	Blueberries, garlic, oats, purple grape juice, red grapes, red wine wheat bran
Constipation	Fiber, fish oils	Fruit, vegetables
Cravings		
—for caffeine, fats, salt, sweets:	Phenylalanine, B6, lipoic acid, Chromium	
—for starches:	5-HTP	

Final Summary Table (cont.)

Conditions	Nutritional Supplements	Whole Foods
Diabetes		
—General:	Alpha lipoic acid, chromium polynicotinate, Funugreek, Goat's Rue, Gymnema sylvestre, Vanadium sulfate	Maitake mushroom
—neuropathy:	Alpha lipoic acid, inositol, N acetyl cysteine	
Depression	DHEA, GABA, Vitamin E, Ginkgo, Omega-3 fatty acids, St. John's Wort	Coffee
Endurance	AMP, ATP, carnosine, magnesium/ potassium aspartate	
Fat burning	DHEA, HCA, HGH, guarana, lipotropic amino acids (methionine, inositol, choline), vitamin B6	Coffee
Fatigue	AMP, ATP, Ashwagandha, DHEA, Enada(NADH), Guarana, magnesium/ potassium aspartate, Vitamin B12	Salt Coffee
Fibromyalgia	CoQ10, ginkgo, magnesium	
Fluid retention	Gotu kola, vitamin B6	
Hair problems	Biotin, fish oils, pantothenic acid, Saw palmetto (for male pattern baldness)	Seeds, nuts
Headaches	Feverfew, petadolex, riboflavin	
High homocysteine	B vitamins (B1, B2, B6, B12, Folic Acid)	
Hypertension	Calcium, magnesium, potassium	Avocado, dairy products, garlic, parsley, spinach
Immunity	Echinacea, goldenseal, selenium, vitamin C, zinc, MGN3, Colostrum	Maitake mushroom

Final Summary Table (cont.)

Conditions	Nutritional Supplements	Whole Foods
Impotence	Arginine, Ashwaghanda, DHEA, Ginkgo, Yohimbine	
Inflammation	EPA, Omega3s, curcumin	Celery, blueberries, cherries blackberries, strawberries, raspberries
Infections		
—Bacterial and Viral:	Echinacea, goldenseal,olive leaf, Omega-3 fatty acids	
—Urinary tract		Cranberries
Intelligence (I.Q.)	DHA, omega-3 fatty acids	
Kidney stones	Folic acid, magnesium, Vitamins B1 and B6	
Leg cramps	Ginkgo biloba, iron	
Liver detox	Sylimarin (milk thistle)	
Macular degeneration	Beta carotene, lutein, Vitamins A,C,E, Zinc	
Memory	Acetyl carnitine, Ginkgo biloba, phosphatidyl choline, phosphatidyl serine, vinpocetine	
Menopause	Black cohosh, Mexican wild yam, soy	
Metabolism (low)	DHEA, 7 keto, tyrosine	Teas, coffee, Yerba mate
Neural tube defects (prevention)	Folic acid (for all pregnant women)	
Neuromuscular activity	Calcium, magnesium, potassium	
Nightblindness	Vitamin A	
Osteoporosis	Calcium, copper, magnesium, manganese, molybdenum, soy, vitamin D	Dairy products, Sardines, tofu

Final Summary Table (cont.)

Conditions	Nutritional Supplements	Whole Foods
Parkinson's	IV glutathione daily, CoQ10	
PMS (mood swings)	Black cohosh, calcium	
Prostate	Lutein, lycopene and pygeum	
Sinus infections	Bromelain, calcium, echinacea, vitamin C, zinc	
Skin	CoQ1O, fish oils, Vitamins A,C, zinc	Fish
Stress	All B vitamins (Bl,B2, B3, B6, B12) Folic acid	
Tinnitus	Niacin	
Thyroid	Iodine, tyrosine	
Vitiligo	B12	
Wound healing	Gotu kola, vits A, C, zinc	

Chapter Summary

- Consumption of dairy products may lower insulin resistance and prevent diabetes and obesity.

— Chapter Twelve —

HERBAL MEDICINE

T he following is a quick overview of herbal products as they affect weight and health.

Ashwagandha, also known as *Indian Ginseng*, is a medicinal herb from the roots and leaves of the Withania Semnifera shrub. Considered a tonic for building energy, especially in the obese and fatigued population, it can also increase an athlete's endurance and vitality. Useful for inflammatory conditions like arthritis, it has also been used as a sex tonic.

Black Cohosh (Cimifuga Racemosa) is very important for the reduction of hot flashes in the postmenopausal woman. Many women complain of weight gain after menopause, especially if they consume synthetic hormones. Black cohosh can ease menopausal syptoms with less weight gain reported; black cohosh in small dosages can be used by women suffering from PMS and mood swings. Black cohosh suppresses the secretion of a hormone from the pituitary gland that usually promotes hot flashes. The recommended dosage is from 80-160 mg/day; most women use the product twice a day.

Boswella is an herbal product that improves blood flow to the joints by restoring the integrity of damaged blood vessels. It is used for arthritis, lower back pain and sports-related injuries common in obese persons unaccustomed to exercising. Boswella relieves the pain and swelling of benign prostatic enlargement. Boswella in a dosage of 300 mg per day has been helpful in treating asthma.

Bromelain has also been used for colds and sinus infections, as it breaks down protein. Better breathing, decreased inflammation and swelling, and improvement with pain and headache are associated with this pineapple derivative. It also helps in digestion.

Curcumin or ***Turmeric*** is a spice that is an anti-inflammatory and used in conjunction with boswella. They all may have an immune enhancing property beneficial to cancer patients. Turmeric and boswella improve symptoms of rheumatoid arthritis and osteoarthritis.

Echinacea is known to strengthen the low-immune system of those who are dieting. Researchers at the University of Munich showed that echinacea increased production of T-lymphocytes by up to 30% which led to enhanced immune systems. It may also inhibit virus production in addition to halting bacterial growth. However, the latest study published in *JAMA* did not show improvement in the duration or severity of colds in those taking Echinacea.

Fenugreek and ***Gimnema Sylvestre*** are two herbs that are useful in controlling blood sugar. We have used them successfully in our diabetic patient population.

Feverfew extract has also been associated with reduction of headaches. A new nasal spray containing this extract has been formulated to relieve headache symptoms more quickly.

Garlic, also considered an antioxidant, is supposed to reduce hypertension and help with infections. Garlic is touted as an anti-cancer agent. It did not, however, produce a reduction in cholesterol in the latest 1998 *JAMA* study. However, other older studies have demonstrated that garlic may have a modest cholesterol reducing effect.

Ginkgo Biloba is a supplement that increases cerebral blood circulation and helps support mental alertness and memory, especially in older individuals. Ginkgo biloba in a dosage of 80 mg three times a day is a good leg cramp reliever for the elderly. In addition Gingko is therapeutic for patients suffering from strokes, asthma, macular degeneration, diabetic retinopathy and tinnitus (or ringing in the ears). In a dosage of 240 mg it prevents sexual dysfunction that may occur with the selective serotonin reuptake inhibitors (antidepressants).

Goat's Rue (Galega Officinalis) is a natural aminoguanidine preventing glycation or cross-linking of proteins with carbohydrates. This process helps with sugar control and anti-aging.

Gotu Kola (Centenella Asiatica), by promoting healthy connective tissue, can help with varicose veins and hemorrhoids. Gotu Kola can help with swollen ankles and it also improves memory, heals burns and wounds, and even combats cellulite!

Gugulipid Capsules: Over 20 clinical studies have been published on the lipid-lowering effects of gugulipid. This product lowers total cholesterol, increases HDL cholesterol, and decreases LDL cholesterol and triglycerides.

Hydroxycitrate (HCA) is an organic compound derived from the dried rind of the Garcinia cambogia fruit. In one study, patients who took HCA with chromium polynicotinate lost 2 1/2 times more weight than those who took a placebo. Another study showed that high doses (1320 mg) of HCA suppress the appetite and stimulate thermogenesis (fat burning). A recent study in the *JAMA*, however, did not find a relationship between HCA consumption and weight loss.

Ipriflavone, a derivative of the isoflavones found in plants, has been shown to significantly slow bone loss in postmenopausal women. Two Italian studies demonstrated a reduction in vertebral fractures in women taking ipriflavone. Considered safe, it can be used with estrogen for a synergistic effect. A double blind study of almost 100 postmenopausal women taking ipriflavone 200 mg, three times a day for two years, showed a significant decrease in bone loss. Ipriflavone stimulates bone formation, and may be used to promote repair of injured bone and decrease bone pain.

Licorice Root Extract (Glycyrrhiza Glabra) has a reputation for promoting health and longevity by supporting the metabolism of the adrenal hormone. It also helps patients with acid reflux, a common symptom in the obese.

Maitake Mushroom may also have anti-obesity effects according to author Nadine Taylor in her book *Green Tea*. It may also prevent a rise in blood insulin and blood sugar levels in rats. However, this study should be extrapolated with caution to humans.

Mastic (Pistacia Penticus) may alleviate stomach distress and help with oral health.

Policosanol is a mixture of chemicals isolated from sugar cane (Saccharus officinarum). It has a dramatic cholesterol lowering effect by inhibiting cholesterol synthesis. If red rice yeast and gugulipid do not reduce cholesterol sufficiently, policosanol may be tried. A combination of all three products is optimal to decrease cholesterol. Policosanol lowers LDL cholesterol, raises HDL cholesterol and even lowers triglycerides.

Red Rice Yeast is an herbal statin that, in combination with a low fat diet, has been shown to reduce cholesterol significantly without side effects.

Saw Palmetto Complex, which contains pygeum, lycopene and lutein besides saw palmetto, may improve benign prostatic hypertrophy and cancer of the prostate. Results of a prospective analysis showed that high lycopene levels were associated with lower prostate cancer risk. Pygeum inhibits the reaction to make dihydrotestosterone (the more potent testosterone hormone) and may prevent or slow the growth of the prostate. Finally, saw palmetto complex is also offered to post-menopausal women who suffer from male pattern baldness which might be caused by too much dihydrotestosterone.

Soy Isoflavones (Genistein, Daidzein, and ***Glycitein)*** may be found in tofu, boiled soybeans, soy milk and miso. Soy sauce is too salty and is isoflavone free. The consumption of soy foods has been associated with low rates of certain diseases like coronary heart disease, hormone-dependent cancers (such as breast, prostate and colon), osteoporosis, and problems associated with menopause. Soy isoflavones are part of a class of plant hormones (phytoestrogens). Soy is a bone builder. Although Asian diets are lower in calcium then those in the West, Asian women are less prone to develop osteoporosis due to their large consumption of soy products. To be active, soy products must be digested in the gut. Other functions of soy are:

- *Cholesterol fighter*. In Italy cardiologists prescribe soy protein for patients with high cholesterol as it raises HDL cholesterol and lowers LDL cholesterol. Dozens of studies have proven that eating as little as 47 g (about 1.5 oz), of soy foods can lower total cholesterol levels an average of 9% and LDL 13%.

- *Menopause easer*. Soy may have the potential as a natural alternative to hormonal replacement therapy. Recent studies have found that soy products can keep vaginal tissues moist and healthy and counter hot flashes. A study at Wake Forest University found that when menopausal women consumed 20 grams of soy protein powder everyday for six weeks, the severity of their hot flashes and night sweats was reduced significantly. Also, improvement in vaginal dryness was noted.

- *Cancer preventor*. In animal studies, rats were less likely to develop breast cancer with genistein (one of the isoflavones of soy). Genistein has also been shown to inhibit the growth of human prostatic cancer cells in the laboratory. Researchers at the University of Alabama recently completed a pilot study on whether eating soy can prevent prostate cancer in elderly men. So far, studies are quite positive. Evidence presented in the *Journal of Nutrition* (1995) claimed that diets containing large amounts of soy products are associated with reduction of breast, colon and prostate cancers. However, one study done recently showed that isoflavones of soy may promote rather then retard breast cancer in some women. Obviously, further studies are needed to clarify these contradictory results.

- *Obesity fighter*. Soy protein powder was used successfully in obese patients to lose weight. The FDA recommends eating about 25 mg of soy protein a day.

Despite all of the positive benefits of soy isoflavonoids, a new study has shown that they do not reduce blood pressure.

St. John's Wort is often called Nature's Prozac. However, because of its variability in potency according to the brand chosen, selecting from a well-known pharmaceutical company is recommended. This product is useful for the obese patient who eats when depressed. St. John's Wort was shown in German studies to raise serotonin levels and may even keep this hormone active between meals to prevent snacking.

Sylimarin or ***Milk Thistle*** is a good detoxifier of the liver for patients with liver disease (like fatty liver in the obese, in alcoholics and in people suffering from hepatitis).

Teas: Many studies have linked regular tea consumption to a small but significant decrease in heart disease and cancers of the digestive tract and lung. New research shows that the beverage contains antioxidants that are more potent than those found in fruits and vegetables. In humans, tea has slowed the progression of precancerous oral lesions and reduced the spread of breast cancer to the lymph nodes. A new study in the *American Journal of Epidemiology* has shown that people who drink one or more cups of tea a day seem to have half the risk of myocardial infarction as non-tea drinkers. Tea leaves contain antioxidants that reduce platelet aggregation and reduce LDL cholesterol. Both green and black tea offer antioxidant benefits, but green tea is 10 times more effective in blocking an enzyme known as t-NOX, a tumor promoter. Black or green freshly-brewed tea (from bags or leaves) is best. Polyphenols in green tea may lower cancer risk at a variety of sites and even inhibit tumor growth.

Black and green tea not only inhibit tumor growth but also prevent metastasis by reducing inflammation and free radical formation. In addition, green tea may reduce muscle cell death in mice with muscular dystrophy through its strong antioxidant activity.

Green Tea may also promote weight loss in rats. However, the dosage for humans would be equivalent to 20 cups of green tea per day. Bloating and gas are some side effects of excessive tea drinking. Because of its high fluoride content, tea protects against tooth decay, cavities and gum disease.

Green tea increases the number of calories used up as well as the amount of fat burned, according to a study by A.G. Dullo, et al. performed on 10 men who were given capsules of green tea extract containing 50 mg of caffeine and 128 mg of green tea polyphenols, the noradrenaline output (similar to dopamine) was 40% higher in the green tea than in the placebo consumers. However, we do not know whether it was the polyphenols or the caffeine that caused this calorie boosting effect.

Tea may not only cause weight loss but also reduce the risk of a heart attack by 44% in people who drink one or more cups of tea per day compared to non-tea drinkers.

Besides suppressing appetite, green tea may speed up the rate at which the body burns fat. A green tea extract was shown to prevent metastasis in breast cancer cells cultured in vitro in a study by Dr. Mathias Rath.

Black Teas include English Breakfast, Darjeeling and Orange Pekoe. Green tea is served more often in the Orient and in Asian restaurants in America. Oolong tea is a cross between black and green teas. Formosa Oolong grown in Taiwan is the highest grade of the teas. According to a recent study from Japan, young mice that were fed Oolong tea powder with a high-fat diet gained only 16% more weight than mice fed a diet of low-fat rat chow. Oolong tea was found to increase the release of fat from fat cells and reduce the absorption of dietary fat. Oolong tea is reported to have a cholesterol and triglyceride lowering effect and has been shown to reduce weight gain. Milk, lemon, and sugar are not usually added to Oolong tea as they inhibit the antioxidant properties. How many cups of tea are needed? Nine cups of green tea are suggested to reduce cancer of the lung and five cups to lower cholesterol and protect against heart attacks. Scalding hot teas or bottled teas may not be as beneficial. Green tea polyphenols may be concentrated in pill form. Drinking tea has also been associated with an increase in bone density so needed in postmenopausal women.

Valerian Root is also a good sleep-inducing medication that is useful for night eaters who have difficulty falling asleep. Valerian root could be called Nature's Ambien™ or Nature's Halcyon™, as it helps patients experience a more restful sleep without the heavy sedation of drugs.

***Wild Mexican Yam* (or *Dioscora composita)* is responsible for the production of natural hormones most resembling the physiological hormones produced by the premenopausal woman. Estrogen and progesterone can be extracted from the yam to be used as capsules, sublingual tablets (called troches), sublingual drops or as cream to apply on the pubic or inner thigh areas. These are products specially made by compounding pharmacies.

Lately, however, a natural progesterone compound from peanuts called Prometrium™ has become available in regular pharmacies; in addition, a natural estrogen product made from wild Mexican yam and a soy product called Cenestin™ is available and is being used quite successfully by some women.

We have come a long way, baby! Every woman can now decide, with the help of her physician, the most comfortable hormonal replacement therapy for her. She can then become an educated consumer who is knowledgeable about all of her options.

Chapter Thirteen

AN OVERVIEW OF DISEASES ASSOCIATED WITH OBESITY AND THEIR TREATMENT

T he number-one disease associated with obesity is *type II diabetes*, also called mature-onset or non-insulin dependent diabetes. Of all type II diabetic patients, 80% (15-million adults) are obese! Diabetes is defined as a fasting plasma sugar of 126 mg/dl or greater. Signs of diabetes include: frequent need to urinate, drowsiness, nausea, extreme thirst, hunger and blurred vision. Minorities such as Native Americans, Hispanic Americans and Pima Indians have high rates of diabetes because it generally targets the so-called thrifty genotype selected for survival in less plentiful environments. In addition, insulin resistance and a low metabolic rate define a prediabetic phenotype. Insulin resistance is common in those populations with hypertension, coexisting with significant cardiovascular disease.

In 1994, the American Diabetes Association decided not to impose any type of diet on diabetics but rather to institute a weight loss recommendation for overweight patients. An individualized approach to each patient was advocated. However, it was discovered that foods containing carbohydrates raise blood sugar concentration. Starches are 100% glucose. Cornflakes and rice (including rice cakes) and other highly-processed cereals raise glucose concentration after a meal more rapidly than any other food studied. Therefore, a reduction in readily-digestible starches should be emphasized.

Fiber's role in diabetes is controversial. A low fat diet is also recommended for diabetics with an emphasis on olive and canola oils. An increase in dietary protein, associated with a corresponding decrease in digestible starches, seems to work the best. A dietary protein intake of about 20% of total daily food is not harmful.

Exercise is also beneficial for the obese diabetic. An optimal routine of 30-40 minute sessions, five times a week is recommended. Proper footwear and socks are important to minimize trauma to the feet. Proper hydration is also essential (17 ounces of fluid, two hours before exercise). Severe diabetics and older patients should exercise only mildly. In a recent study of over 1,400 diabetic women, greater physical activity was associated with a substantial reduction in the risk of type II diabetes. Thus, the common recommendation was 30 minutes of moderate intensity physical activity each day.

In our office we have been very successful in instituting higher protein, lower carbohydrate and lower fat programs for our type II diabetic patients. Avoidance of fried foods, potatoes and alcohol has also been recommended. Chromium polynicotinate (400-600 mcg) taken with meals keeps blood sugar levels constant.

Lipoic Acid, the popular antioxidant, has also been shown to reduce sugar cravings. Lipoic acid may prevent damage to the lenses of diabetic rats. Fenugreek and gimnema sylvestre are two herbs that have also been beneficial in lowering blood sugar levels.

If everything else fails, the best pharmacotheurapeutic agent has been *Glucophage*™, as it does not increase weight gain. Insulin should be avoided at all cost, as it is a potent appetite stimulator. We have to be careful with other oral hypoglycemic agents that will increase appetite and induce weight gain which is the number one enemy for diabetics! *Precose*™ or *Acarbose* causes minor weight loss in diabetics due to lower absorption of foods. Side effects are abdominal pain, diarrhea and flatulence. Diabetics are requested to keep food diaries to list blood sugar levels at various times of the day. Correlation between foods and blood sugar elevations can then be made by the diabetic patient.

At a recent meeting of the American Academy of Clinical Nutrition, three diets were offered to type II diabetics: one advocated a high fat, low carbohydrate composition; the second showed that a high carbohydrate, low fat program was more successful at reducing blood sugar; finally, a high protein, low carbohydrate dietary intervention was recommended. High glycemic foods that increase blood sugar the most are potatoes, carrots, and white bread and should be reduced in type II diabetics. An insulin index of 38 common foods was found in the November 1997 issue of the *American Journal of Clinical Nutrition*. This insulin index of foods is similar to the glycemic index of foods. The more carbohydrates and sugar a food contains, the higher the insulin index; while more fat and protein in a food correlates with a low insulin index. Refer to Table 5 (see pg. 193) for a glycemic index of foods.

On the other hand, Dr. Barry Sears recently recommended using the glycemic load for obese and diabetic patients. The glycemic load is the ratio between the glycemic index of a food divided by the amount of carbohydrates the food contains. This glycemic load may even be more accurate than the glycemic index.

The American Diabetes Association recommends three meals and three snacks per day. Sugars, fried foods and juices are to be avoided.

Besides diabetes, the obese individual may be plagued by *heart disease*, hypertension and hyperlipidemias (which include high cholesterol and high triglyceride). For those afflicted with high cholesterol, we recommend a low-saturated fat intake. A high triglyceride report is accompanied by a reduction of refined sugars and starches. In severe cases, some fruits and all fruit juices are limited.

Vitamins B1, B6, Folic Acid, B12, E, and *C* are advocated for heart disease. Niacin has been helpful in changing the dangerous pattern LDL-B to pattern LDL-A, as described in chapter 3. Soluble dietary fiber has been shown to reduce total cholesterol and LDL cholesterol concentrations. Approximately 10 grams of fiber per day is required to show a significant effect. *Whole grains* such as oats are also effective in reducing cholesterol levels. *Gugulipid extract* reduces cholesterol and triglyceride levels. *Pantothenic* (900 mg) reduces cholesterol and triglyceride levels. *Red rice yeast* and *Policosanol* have also been shown to decrease cholesterol levels.

Omega-3 Fatty Acids (like those in fish oils) are associated with reduced incidence of cardiovascular disease. Fish oils have been found to reduce triglyceride concentrations, decrease blood pressure and to even prevent inflammation and blood clotting.

Salt Restriction may be advantageous to those patients who retain fluids (edema) and who suffer from *hypertension. Calcium, Magnesium* and *Potassium* are all minerals that help lower high blood pressure.

As mentioned above, *CoQ10* (150-300 mg) has been very useful for heart disease, congestive heart failure and angina. CoQ10 also is effective in diabetes, cancer, pulmonary edema and shortness of breath. Once consumed, it takes 4-12 weeks for CoQ10 to decrease blood pressure (50 to 150 mg per day is recommended). It even helps with heart palpitations.

B6 is a natural diuretic helpful in cases of water retention. In most cases, *water* ingestion is recommended to flush the system of toxic products.

Red Wine, even *Red Grape Polyphenols*, help raise HDL cholesterol, the good cholesterol. However, the two key factors for increasing HDL are weight loss and exercise.

Gastroesophageal Reflux is very common among our obese patients; the extra abdominal fat raises the diaphragm with hiatal hernia occurring frequently and acid indigestion ensues. 90% of those afflicted improve dramatically when they lose weight. Antacids are frequently used. We recommend that our patients have small frequent meals throughout the day, stop smoking, cut down on alcohol and avoid coffee and tea. We also advocate an increase in protein-rich foods and an avoidance of high fat foods. Symptoms improve dramatically when patients avoid tomato products, citrus juices, citrus fruit, peppers, onions, garlic, peppermint, spearmint, cinnamon and chocolate.

As everyone differs, a diet diary that charts one's symptoms will teach patients which foods to avoid.

Licorice-DGL (Glycyrrhiza Glabra), called the natural Tagamet™, is a great treatment for *ulcers.* Six to nine capsules (200 mg per capsule) are recommended per day. Mastic is another product successful in treating reflux. Other interventions include: not sleeping flat but elevating the head of the bed, not wearing tight-fitting clothes, and preventing constipation. Sometimes digestive enzymes may help with the bloating and gas which is common in the obese. Carbohydrates can cause bloating, especially apple juice and yeasty products like breads, donuts and bagels. A food-sensitivities blood test may also help in determining which foods are offenders for each person.

Celiac Disease may be associated with obesity and diabetes. Depression is the most common symptom in celiac disease. Liver enzymes may also be elevated. There has been an increase in the risk of lymphoma and of thyroid disease in those affected by celiac disease. Dermatitis herpetiformis (tenacious rash of the skin) may also be associated with celiac disease. A positive gliadin test confirms the diagnosis. A gluten-free diet that eliminates wheat, rye and barley may result in miraculous recovery. Elimination of dairy products has also proven beneficial for this condition. A complete food sensitivity study might be advantageous for those affected by celiac disease symptoms.

Arthritis is all too common with obese individuals, as the extra weight seems to affect the joints, especially in the lower extremities. According to Dr. Felson of Boston University, the biggest risk factor for osteoarthritis of the knees and hips is obesity. Weight loss appears to lower the risk of radiographic and symptomatic osteoarthritis and even ameliorates symptoms.

In addition, excess fatty tissue may produce abnormal levels of certain hormones which affect cartilage or underlying bone in such a way as to predispose to osteoarthritis. According to Dr. Timothy McAlindon, a specialist in this disease, vitamin D and, to a lesser extent, vitamins C and E may protect against osteoarthritis. Antioxidant therapy has also shown promising preliminary results against the disease. Low vitamin D intake was associated with a three-fold increase in the progression of osteoarthritis.

We recommend a dietary regime devoid of meats as certain meats may produce inflammatory responses. Chocolate, caffeine, sugar, wheat, corn and dairy products may be deleterious for this condition.

Fish is allowed, because it contains the good healing fats, eicosapen-taenoic (EPA) and docosahexaenoic (DHA) acids, which are natural anti-inflammatory substances. Nightshade vegetables like potato, tomato, pepper and eggplant may be avoided in certain cases with great success. We have great success with **Glucosamine Sulfate** in dosages of 1,500 mg per day, either by taking a 500 mg pill three times a day or a packet of soluble powder (1500 mg) once a day. One caveat is that the addition of chondroitin sulfate prevents the full absorption of the glucosamine. Therefore, I recommend glucosamine sulfate to be taken alone. Glucosamine can also be administered successfully through weekly injections. Consumption of 1,500 mg of glucosamine a day for three years was followed by improvement in pain, stiffness and physical function in a Belgian study led by Dr. Jean Yves Reginster.

Other natural anti-inflammatory products are available to help with arthritis like **Turmeric** or **Curcumin.**

EPA/DHA seem to alleviate inflammation of the joints. Boswella serrata is another plant with anti-inflammatory and analgesic effects.

Methylsulfonylmethane *or (MSM)* is widely promoted for pain and arthritis in a new book called *The Miracle of MSM*. Though there are lots of glowing testimonials from people who have tried it, there is no scientific proof that it works.

Sadenosyl L Methionine Disulfate *or (SAME)* is another product that helps with arthritis and depression.

Cetyl Myristolate has been advocated as an anti inflammatory product for this condition. For severe pain and while waiting for these natural products to take effect, we recommend a new class of anti-inflammatory drugs called **Cox II inhibitors**, which do not irritate the stomach as much as the nonsteroidal anti-inflammatories.

Many obese patients suffer from **emotional problems**. Even though obese people are perceived as being happy, in a good mood and funny (often cracking jokes about their extra poundage), they are gen-erally quite insecure. Deep down they may show signs of depression, anxiety and insomnia.

For depression, I prefer to first recommend a trial of natural medications. I start with **St. John's Wort** in certain cases; **Tyrosine** and **Phenylalanine** are other treatment approaches. **5-HTP** has been used very successfully in our practice for this indication. Remember to start with low doses and increase the dosage slowly.

GABA (gamma aminobutyric acid) is a natural anti-depressant with relaxing properties as well.

If a trial of these natural medications has not been successful, or if the depression is quite severe, pharmacotherapy is then instituted. I am very partial to the serotonin reuptake inhibitors like Prozac™, Zoloft™, Paxil™, Serzone™, Celexa™, and Effexor™. Wellbutrin™ has also worked well for our obese population. We have to remember that serotonin reuptake inhibitors can increase weight gain after four months of usage. They may cause sexual dysfunction. In my practice, I recommend Effexor™ or Wellbutrin™. Topamax™ is an anti-epileptic agent which works as an anti depressant agent which helps in weight control.

It is always difficult to decide what came first, whether the depression caused the weight gain, or whether the weight gain prompted the depression. In many cases, as the patient loses the weight and feels better, natural products can help wean patients off their medication. This process has to be implemented only under a physician's supervision.

In addition, light sources and sunny scenery are natural approaches for combating depression. We do not recommend the use of Elavil™, as it is a potent appetite stimulator.

Anxiety is also common among the obese. Food seems to help with anxiety, just as it staves off depression. **Valerian Root** (one to three tablets at night) are used for this indication. **5-HTP** and **Taurine**, an amino acid, are also used to promote a mellow mood without sedation. It also prevents excessive sensitivity to noradrenaline or dopamine which manifests itself by jitteriness and overstimulation. One can become calmer with **magnesium** at a dosage of 500 mg. If the anxiety is severe enough, pharmacotherapy may be used in certain cases; the best medications are Buspar™, Xanax™ or Ativan™. The smallest dosages of these drugs are recommended first.

The obese also have difficulty *falling asleep* and often wake up in the middle of the night. These sleep difficulties may be due in part to anxiety or depression. These sleep problems also affect eating behavior, as high food ingestion may occur at night. To break this vicious pattern of night eating, melatonin, or valerian root, may be tried. My patients have been very successful with 5-HTP taken before and after dinner. Sometimes a combination of these natural products can bring relief to our patients. Calcium taken at night may also be helpful as a calmative (remember the practice of drinking warm milk before bed time).

Occasionally, a mild sleeping pill like Ambien™ taken after dinner may also break the pattern of night eating.

A new medication, Sonata™, may help patients go back to sleep for four hours if they wake up in the middle of the night. No hangover is observed the next morning.

In rare instances we have had patients who have risen from their beds to sleepwalk to the refrigerator and consume enormous quantities while sleeping. The only telltale signs of this surreptitious eating are the empty containers discovered the next morning. These patients definitely need help, not only from spouses or relatives, but from professionals such as psychiatrists, neurologists, or physicians specializing in sleep disorders. Obviously, forbidden foods should not be stashed in the refrigerator to tempt somnambulic eating.

Many obese patients suffer from sleep apnea: they stop breathing while asleep! Weight loss is also the best therapy for this disease.

A *decrease in libido* occurs frequently among the obese, mostly due to psychological reasons. The obese person does not feel sexy or sexually responsive, as he/she is ashamed of his/her body. Hypertensive or anti-depressant medications may also cause a lack of sexual interest and impotence. Diabetes, too, can be associated with these symptoms. A sorting of all these factors is in order to determine the best treatment options. Medications may be switched to avoid this problem, and weight loss effectively enhances self-esteem and sexual responsiveness. Finally, there are some natural options available to treat this troublesome problem. Ginkgo biloba, choline, the amino acid arginine (which increases nitric oxide, the dilator of blood vessels) have all been used for these symptoms. Yohimbine, in a dosage of 5.4

mg three times a day, is used to counteract anorgasmia, or lack of orgasm, a side effect of antidepressants. DHEA has also been found effective in enhancing the libido. A lack of hormones can also cause decreased sexual desire. Men and women affected by this problem should undergo hormonal testing. Women react especially well to **progesterone** and **testosterone** supplementation. Men are very successful with testosterone, if the levels of this hormone are found to be low. Males with prostate cancer should not take supplemental testosterone, as this hormone may stimulate the prostate gland. This notion has been recently challenged as cancer of the prostate occurs in men when testosterone levels are low. There is always Viagra™ to come to the rescue!

The overweight patient often complains of *fatigue and lack* of energy. My usual response is that this person is carrying a significant amount of extra weight that may cause this tiredness. Depression may also manifest itself by fatigue. Weight loss is definitely the best treatment modality. My patients always comment on how much better they feel after weight loss. Their energy level soars exponentially with the weight loss. Multiple vitamins, especially *C* and *B12*, have been great energizers and some patients swear by the benefits of B12 injections.

Magnesium Potassium Aspartate supplementation has been associated with an increase of energy and higher performance in all exercise tasks. For patients losing weight quickly, potassium supplementation has been very useful. In some cases, the addition of salt for low blood pressure and fatigue has been miraculous. Caffeine consumption has also been tried in some cases of tiredness associated with sleepiness.

Ginseng, guarana, and *ephedrine* are herbal products which have been beneficial in alleviating fatigue in many patients.

Octaconosol has been also implemented in those patients on low carbohydrate diets with low energy.

Protein usually increases our energy levels, while carbohydrates are more relaxing. Ketosis, or the breakdown of fats, also stimulates a feeling of well-being and high-energy.

Finally, certain products have been associated with energy-increasing properties. ***DHEA*** was found to give patients a feeling of well-being and increased energy. ***Adenosine Monophosphate*** (AMP), associated with the alleviation of fatigue, also helps in breaking down body fat; it comes in sublingual tablets or in injections. ***Adenosine Triphosphate*** (ATP) is now also available. ***Magnesium malate*** (1,200-2,400 mg) has also been used successfully to relieve fatigue in chronic fatigue syndrome.

L-carnitine (500 mg) is also used with 100 mg lipoic acid, N acetyl cysteine, and essential fatty acids. L-carnitine has an important role in burning fat for energy. Lastly, 5-HTP has also been very useful for combating fatigue. Remember to take this product in a low dosage first, preferably in the evening.

Enada (NADH) is a new, over-the-counter product promoted for chronic fatigue. NADH plays an important role in the production of energy in cells and may also increase the production of dopamine, norepinephrine and serotonin. A recent Georgetown University study showed a small benefit in about one-third of patients with fatigue. The recommended dose is 5-10 mg per day. NADH may improve energy in some cases and does not have any known harmful side effects.

Obese patients also suffer from ***low immunity***: they experience frequent infections and colds which, in turn, necessitate long antibiotic usage. This prolonged antibiotic therapy may promote yeast infection. The extra fat is also responsible for a high incidence of cancer in the overweight population.

Many obese patients who are also diabetic experience impaired healing due to their elevated blood sugar. Foot ulcers, yeast infections and candidiasis are very commonly found in our diabetic overweight patient population. The best therapeutic regime for those ailments is weight loss which also reduces blood sugar.

There are a few immune boosters; ***Beta 1, 3, 1, 6, Glucan*** (3 mg capsule) that strengthen the immune system by activating immune cells called macrophages (powerful Pac men who gobble up all foreign bodies like viruses, bacteria and parasites).

Olive Leaf Extract in 500 mg capsules has been found to have a unique antiviral action. In his latest book, *Olive Leaf Extract*, Dr. Morton Walker writes that olive leaf extract prevents such viral diseases as Epstein Barr, herpes, and even HIV. Vitamin C also strengthens the cellular membranes to prevent viral penetration into the cells.

Vitamin E and *Ginseng* have been reported to increase immunity in the elderly. Zinc, selenium, and vitamin B6 supposedly help with immunity, but studies are still inconclusive. Zinc inhibits the growth of viruses. Selenium enhances white blood cell proliferation and differentiation to make those cells better microorganism killers. B6 increases the quality and quantity of antibodies.

The role of *echinacea* is quite controversial, as there are claims that this herb increases cytokine production in human macrophages. However, a recent study in the *JAMA* did not find an improvement with cold symptoms in those patients taking echinacea.

Folic Acid and *B12* also help with the production of white blood cells. *Vitamin A* is both an anti-tumor and an anti-viral agent.

MGN3 (a rice bran derivative) and *colostrum* ("nature's first milk") have been found to be successful immune enhancers. MGM3 has even been shown to help with cancer.

Dietary factors like essential nutrients, antioxidants and flavonoids may also enhance immune function. Optimal immune function requires a healthy diet that has adequate amounts of protein, and is low in fats and refined sugars.

Adequate protein is essential for optimal immune function. Eating as little as four ounces of carbohydrate may reduce the ability of white blood cells to destroy microorganisms. During an infection, therefore, sugar consumption, especially in the form of juice, is discouraged. Do not give juice to your children when they have a cold. Cholesterol and triglycerides can also depress immune function. Alcohol and consumption of allergy-inducing foods can be detrimental to our optimal immune function as well.

Caprylic Acid capsules have been advantageous in treating candidiasis. According to Dr. William Crook's book, *The Yeast Connection,* the best therapeutic regime is achieved by avoiding foods that are high in sugar, packaged or processed. Also, foods containing yeast, such as breads, bagels and pastries, should be eliminated. Cheese, alcoholic beverages, condiments and vinegar-containing foods should be restricted. Anti-fungal medications should be used only if all else fails.

Finally, there exists a connection between *cancer* and obesity. For cancer prevention, a good multiple vitamin with anti-oxidants is advocated. Lipoic acid is used for this purpose. We also recommend decreasing iron and iron-rich foods. Charbroiled foods (especially meat) are also carcinogenic. Omega-3 fatty acids, flax seed oil or fish oil capsules have been used successfully in high doses for cancer patients.

Inflavonoids, like quercetin and hesperidin, are supplemented in patients afflicted with cancer. Soy product consumption has also been associated with a reduction of cancers in the uterus, breast and prostate.

Green tea has some cancer-fighting properties and antimetastatic properties. **Ip6** with **inositol** is another new cancer fighter available today. This product has been studied extensively by Dr. M. Abulkalam Shamsuddin, a biochemist. Ip6 works as an anti-cancer agent in malignancies of the breast, colon, liver, lung, muscle and skin. For healthy individuals, 1-2 grams of Ip6 is recommended. Up to 8 grams a day may be used for high risk or cancer patients. DIM is even more potent.

One of the most common complaints I receive from my female patients is that weight increases as a result of pregnancy or menopause. A new study of 5,600 women from the NHANES project has shown an increase of about one pound per birth per woman. Weight gain was higher in black versus white women and in non-smokers and those who had low physical activity. Thus, high or low hormone levels have a significant role in obesity.

Even though there is no physiological explanation, women complain of weight gain after a hysterectomy. In our office, we recommend *natural hormonal supplementation* of formulas prepared by compounding pharmacies using mostly extractions of the Mexican Wild Yam called Dioscora composita. We have found that natural hormonal supplementation as opposed to synthetic hormones is associated with less weight gain and water retention. Natural progesterone is also a mood elevator and a natural diuretic. *Black cohosh* helps with hot flashes, *ginseng cream* alleviates vaginal membrane thinning, and phytoestrogens in soy products prevent cancer formation. Natural testosterone enhances libido in women as well. In general, water retention is treated with B6 first, then Aldactone™ is used next, as it does not deplete the electrolytes in our bodies.

Many other conditions are associated with weight gain. *Smoking cessation* is often associated with a 10 to 20 pound weight gain in some patients. Tyrosine supplementation has been very useful in helping with this condition. Peppermint oil drops have also been helpful. 5-HTP may reduce the cravings for smoking. The combination of ephedrine and caffeine may help prevent weight gain after smoking cessation. Phenylpropranolamine may also reduce weight gain after discontinuation of smoking. Nicotine gum addition has resulted in equivocal results. The latest anti-smoking device is nicotine lollipops that help some people. Intense dieting utilizing a very low calorie diet showed the highest rate of smoking abstinence and weight loss after a four month, placebo-controlled study.

Many overweight patients suffer from *poor circulation* in their legs, and, in many cases, *horse chestnut seed extract (escin)* has been useful. In 13 controlled trials of horse chestnut seed extract, a decrease in the swelling of the leg, calf and ankle circumference was found. Therapeutic benefit was derived from 100-150 mg of escin daily (escin is the active component of the extract). Horse chestnut seed extract may work in the degradation and synthesis of the protein and sugar molecules in the cellular membranes of blood vessels.

Improvements in the appearance of varicose veins was achieved by *pycnogenol* and *vitamin C* supplementation. *Gotu Kola* has also been recommended for treatment of varicose veins and hemorrhoids.

Another common complaint is frequent attacks of *gout* and *gallbladder disease* during the rapid weight loss phase in some obese patients. A high protein diet and rapid weight loss can be associated with an attack of gout. Nonsteroidal anti-inflammatory medicine is the best immediate treatment. If uric acid levels remain high, colchicine or allopurinol may be administered during the weight loss phase.

In low calorie diets, if no oil is consumed by the patients, the gallbladder does not contract; stone formation may stimulate a gallbladder attack. Oil, aspirin and finally Actigall™ may be used to prevent this complication.

Because of the extra weight, obese patients have *difficulty breathing*; they may have *asthma* more frequently and puff and pant more easily than normal weight people. A high protein diet seems to be most effective for alleviating these symptoms. Good hydration is quite important; coffee and tea consumption are also helpful. The best treatment intervention, however, is weight loss. For asthma and chronic obstructive pulmonary disease, vitamins A and C are recommended. Vitamin C in a dosage of 500 mg improves asthmatic attacks produced by exercise. B6 is also effective to prevent wheezing, especially in children. Magnesium, too, improves bronchoconstriction and may be used in a nebulizer. Sweet drinks or juices are deleterious in these conditions as they decrease immunity. Gastrointestinal complaints are similarly treated with weight loss.

Kidney stones also occur with frequency in dieters. Drinking fluids prevents this condition. Exercising may dehydrate the patients even further. I don't recommend consuming more than 1,200 mg of vitamin C daily, as higher doses of this vitamin are associated with kidney stone formation. A low oxalate diet is sometimes recommended also for prevention: excessive amounts of cocoa, chocolate, tea, tomatoes, almonds, spinach, peanuts and soybeans are to be avoided. Folic acid, B6 and magnesium supplementation are often effective in preventing this problem.

Because many obese patients complain of a *lack of memory*, we recommend a broad spectrum nutritional support which includes Acetyl L-carnitine 500 mg, Gingko biloba 80 mg, DMAE (dimethylaminoethanol) 100 mg, choline 150 mg, Neuromins or DHA (docosahexaenoic acid) 300 mg. This formula is to be taken twice daily. Acetyl L-carnitine stimulates the production of acetylcholine (key neurotransmitter in brain function). Phosphatidyl, at a dose of 300 mg daily, and serine also abate memory loss by improving cognitive function and facilitating communication between cells.

Vinpocetine also has been used successfully in our practice to improve memory loss as it enhances blood circulation and oxygen utilization in the brain. Finally, DMAE may also be a memory enhancer as it increases acetylcholine production.

The role of obesity in cancer has been overlooked by the general population. The American Institute of Cancer Research undertook a massive study, to be published in 2003, to determine the link between diet and cancer—and especially between obesity and cancer.

Obesity may cause, in certain individuals, the body to produce increased amounts of insulin and other hormones which may lead to rapid cell proliferation. The most convincing evidence that exists today links obesity with five specific cancers: breast, colon, endometrium, prostate and kidney.

Breast Cancer: Stored fat may produce more estrogen which may, with the additional insulin release, stimulate breast cancer production. As cancer of the breast becomes more prevalent in post-menopausal women who gain weight, avoidance of weight gain after the menopause should significantly decrease this risk.

Colon Cancer: When people consume excess calories, toxic products from food and the environment may get trapped in the body's fat instead of being excreted. As abdominal fat may secrete more insulin and as men tend to store more fat around their waist, men are at a higher risk for colon cancer.

Gastroesophageal Cancer: This cancer is more common in the obese. Acid reflux, which occurs often in the overweight population, may expose the lining of the esophagus to constant irritation and damage which ultimately leads to cancer.

Pancreatic Cancer: A study from the September 2002 issue of the *Journal of the National Cancer Institute*, led by the Dana Farber Cancer Institute of Harvard Medical School, suggests a possible link between high starch diets (such as potatoes, rice and white or rye bread) and pancreatic cancer in overweight, sedentary women. Dr. Charles Fuchs, the senior author, explains that excess insulin may play a role in the development of this very aggressive cancer. Only 4% of people with this cancer survive five years. Although this study involved only women, these findings may apply equally to men.

Prostate Cancer: Prostate cancer, the most common cancer in men, is also more prevalent in the obese as abdominal fat may trigger the release of insulin and sex hormones, which may also stimulate the more rapid division of prostatic cancer cells.

Kidney Cancer: Kidney cancer may be more common in obese females as excess estrogen from fat may stimulate kidney cells to grow and divide more quickly.

Uterine Cancer: Research has also implicated higher levels of estrogen, estradiol and testosterone with the increased risk of cancer of the uterus (specifically, the lining of the uterus, the endometrium) in overweight women who gained their weight after menopause.

However, the risk was even higher if obesity was present in the third decade of life.

Finally, obesity expert George Bray, speaking at the International Research Conference on Food, Nutrition and Cancer in July, 2002, stated: "Fat in our gut, hips or love handles does not just sit there" but rather is a very metabolically active substance producing all kinds of hormones and "growth factors" into the blood stream. As a result, an obese person's cells are encouraged to grow and divide at an accelerated rate. While being overweight and inactive may account for one-quarter to one-third of most cancers in the world, even a few extra pounds may increase cancer risk.

The best treatment for many of the ailments that plague our obese population is weight loss. However, we still can help alleviate these problems by using natural methods first and relying on drug therapy if symptoms persist.

Chapter Summary

- 80% of all type II diabetic patients are obese.

- Obesity in certain individuals may cause the tendency to produce hormones that may lead to cell proliferation and cancer (breast, colon, gastroesophageal, kidney, pancreatic, prostate and uterine).

— Chapter Fourteen —

NUTRITIONAL REGIME

"There is no love sincerer than the love of food."
—George Bernard Shaw

"Let food be your medicine and let medicine be your food."
—Hippocrates

Despite the fact that diet and health books and articles are sprouting like mushrooms, Americans have never been fatter! The majority of people fail miserably in their attempts to lose weight because obesity is as complex a disease as is its treatment. One diet simply does not fit all!

Some patients do well using balanced dietary intervention, others are successful in cutting fat intake, while others need to go on a low carbohydrate diet to achieve optimal weight loss.

In my opinion, it is not the diet that counts but rather the control of our brain chemistry that stops the cravings for certain foods. I have found that many of my patients suffer from insulin resistance; if their blood insulin levels, glycohemoglobin A1C levels, or C reactive protein levels are elevated, I feel justified in putting them on a low carbohydrate program.

I also find out whether the patient binges on certain foods. In my 21 years of experience dealing with the obese, it is rare for me to find a patient who binges on pure protein. Most of my patients crave either sugars or carbohydrates. Some of them crave fat, but usually it is in combination with carbohydrates. A few may also crave salt.

Chocolate or ice cream, which constitutes a combination of fat, sweets, and probably other chemicals like caffeine, are the most commonly craved foods.

No matter how elaborate our diets are, if the patient dislikes the foods prescribed, we will meet with failure. I give my patients an extensive questionnaire to determine what foods are liked and disliked. I try to avoid disliked foods and incorporate the favorite foods in their dietary regime. If possible, I also attempt to modify the preparation of these foods or to find similar-tasting alternatives.

If I were to give all of my patients the same diet sheet, that paper would most likely be tossed in the garbage can. The USRDA food pyramid concept emphasizes a low fat, high carbohydrate diet, which may be beneficial for some but deleterious for others as far as weight loss goes. Here, protein is used more as a flavoring, but the main staple is carbohydrate consumption. The only advantage of the food pyramid, if any, is the low fat recommendation.

I also hate reading in magazines about complicated menus that dieters need to follow for one week, two weeks, or even up to one month. First of all, who has such fancy ingredients at home? As for myself, I do not store cilantro or ground ginger in my kitchen. In my opinion, the less the patient is in the kitchen, the better. Some affluent individuals find success in spas where prepared foods are offered and where they are exercised and pampered all day long; however, results are temporary and usually lost when the patients return to the reality of their everyday lives. At my office, we have devised dietary plans based on the patients' wants (weight loss desired) and needs (physical and emotional make-up).

We perform a body fat composition test on all our patients. The machine, depending on the percentage of lean body mass, calculates the basal metabolic rate (the number of calories consumed in 24 hours). Ethnicity may affect the accuracy of bioelectric impedance analysis. Lean body mass was underestimated in white women and overestimated in black women because of their greater bone mineral content. In addition, black women have a lower metabolism and lose less weight than white women. A low basal metabolic rate (less than 2,000 calories) labels the patient as an underburner. An underburner patient needs tyrosine supplementation to help increase the burning potential. Ephedrine and phenylpropranolamine may also increase thermogenesis, or burning of calories. A low basal metabolic rate is also another reason why a low carbohydrate diet is justified. The analogy of the fireplace is apt for such underburners. The protein is represented by logs fueling the fire in the fireplace, while the carbohydrates are depicted as water which stops the fire. (see Figure 9)

Figure 9

Body's Fireplace

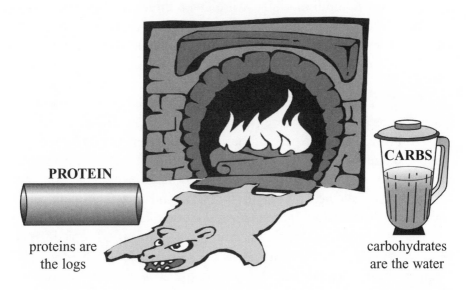

PROTEIN   CARBS

proteins are   carbohydrates
the logs   are the water

To lose one pound of fat, you need to consume 3,500 calories less a week or roughly 500 calories less per day. Sometimes a small amount of slow release triiodothyronine or Cytomel™ is added to hypothyroid patients already consuming thyroid supplementation to increase thermogenesis. Armour's thyroid, which contains both T3 and T4, has been very helpful for a lot of people.

If a patient wants to lose 50 or more pounds, a low calorie diet (LCD) is first tried. A low calorie diet constitutes about 1,000 calories a day. A very low calorie diet represents an intake of only 500 calories per day. Even though very low calorie diets (VLCD) are the most effective method for quick weight loss, I use mainly low calorie diets, as patients seem to stay longer on these programs and, thus, achieve permanent success. Very low calorie diets combined with behavior modification have caused maintained weight loss for five years. Intermittent use of VLCD for about two weeks at a time also helps to keep the patients motivated. We find that our patients do better when they stay on the VLCD for a longer time. Side effects of VLCD include hair loss and muscle fatigue. Nutritional supplements that contain dissolved protein and vitamins have been very successful in our practice. These products have little fat and carbohydrates and seem to be veritable logs in our patients' fireplaces.

A few years ago, an experiment was devised by using two groups of obese women, both of whom were given three balanced meals per day. Both groups were hospitalized to prevent cheating. One group was given an additional three nutritional supplements as snacks per day. Those women who had the three meals plus the three supplements a day lost more weight than those who had just the three meals. The conclusion drawn from this experiment was that the dissolved protein and vitamins helped the obese patients to burn their calories better!

Dr. Pi Sunyer, an expert in obesity control, compared five weight loss treatments and found that the most successful method for weight loss was the liquid diet, followed by the low calorie diet with appetite suppressants, followed by part liquid/part food diet. The worst outcome was associated with the reduced-calorie diet.

Because protein supplements represent the logs in a fireplace, it is better to consume as many as possible. ***Starving*** definitely stops the fireplace from burning, and thus no weight loss is achieved. In our office, no limit is given to these nutritional supplements; however, most patients consume at least five to six supplements per day. I have had some patients who have taken up to 20 supplements per day and still have lost a significant amount of weight. Our slogan in the office is: "The more shakes you take, the more weight you lose."

A recent study also proved that patients taking ***meal replacements*** lost more weight than these on a low calorie diet. According to a new study by B.J. Rolls, et al. the caloric density of foods rather than the fat content affects the amount of food a person eats. While the fat content of the food did not stimulate eating, the high-calorie dense foods increased the consumption of food. The low density foods contained 30 calories per ounce, while the high density foods (like some cheeses, some meats and desserts) had 45 calories per ounce.

This brings us to the conclusion that *calories are not created equal*. One gram of fat consumed is equivalent to nine calories, and four calories are ingested when you eat one gram of protein or carbohydrate. Thus fat has twice as many calories as protein or carbohydrate. One gram of alcohol is the equivalent of seven calories (almost as high as fat). Even though there are many popular diets that recommend a relatively high fat intake, I still have a revulsion to high fat consumption. We have been so brainwashed against fat that it is hard for me to swallow these fatty foods! As mentioned before, essential fatty acids are beneficial for health purposes; omega-3 oils are especially recommended for good nutrition and, also, for weight loss. Essential fatty oils are needed, also, to preserve the integrity of the cellular membranes. These oils are necessary for keeping the gall bladder working and the heart healthy during low fat diets.

The American Heart Association recommends that the consumption of fats should comprise 30% of our total calories. These 30% fat calories should be subdivided into 10% polyunsaturated, 10% monosaturated, and 10% saturated fats. The normal American diet is usually close to 50% fat calories. The Mediterranean diet contains olive oil, a monosaturated oil that seems to be beneficial for heart disease and longevity. Olive oil, in southern European countries, is not heated, (the heating of oils produces saturation). Other healthy oils are canola or rapeseed oil. Polyunsaturated oils are also better than saturated fats, but their consumption has been associated with cancer.

Table 4

PERCENT SATURATION OF COMMONLY-USED FATS

Oils	Monosaturated	Polyunsaturated	Saturated fatty acid
Olive oil	74%	8%	13%
Canola	55%	33%	7%
Corn	24%	59%	13%
Safflower	12%	75%	9%
Sunflower	20%	66%	10%
Peanut oil	46%	32%	17%
Margarine fat	59%	18%	19%
Palm oil	37%	9%	49%
Coconut	6%	2%	86%
Palm kernel oil	11%	2%	81%
Tuna fat	26%	37%	27%
Chicken fat	45%	21%	30%
Lard	45%	11%	40%
Butter fat	29%	4%	62%
Beef fat	42%	4%	50%

We should choose oils that are primarily represented in the mono-saturated category and that contain little saturated fat. We know that saturated fat intake is associated with: an increase of cholesterol formation in the body, heart attacks, and heart disease.

The worst offenders are coconut and palm kernel oils with a saturated fat content of over 80%. The best oils are either canola or olive oil. For optimal health I recommend a combination of half olive oil and half canola oil. Safflower and sunflower oils are also acceptable choices; however, corn oil which contains mostly omega-6 fatty acids should be restricted. Flax and borage oils are very useful essential fatty acids that are good healing oils.

For best preservation of the oils, keep them in the refrigerator in an opaque container to prevent denaturation. Try not to cook with them; just drizzle them on top of food to enhance their flavor. Even though there are exceptions to the rule, high fat diets have frequently been associated with weight gain. Normal weight men, consuming 900 calories or more of fat, gained weight and fat. A high fat diet promoted weight gain in women with a predisposition to obesity, according to a six year study in 1995. Decreasing fat intake causes the most weight loss. Patients who lost the most weight reduced their fat intake the most (less than 40 grams of fat). High fat diets induce greater food intake and weight gain than high carbohydrate diets.

Meals with high fat content have less of a satiating effect than previously thought. Not only the level of hunger, but the nutrient content of the food as well, may dictate meal size. According to a study by psychiatrists Drs. A. Golay and E. Bobbioni, lean control groups consumed a diet with energy balance while the obese had a diet with no energy balance between fat, carbohydrate or protein. Fat oxidation (or breakdown) did not occur in the obese or the post-obese individuals. In this group of people, dietary fat also induced overconsumption and weight gain. For some reason, these individuals do not adapt appropriately to dietary fat and, therefore, fat storage is increased. Carbohydrate oxidation is also impaired. A low fat diet, plus aerobic exercise, proved to be the best way to lose weight in their group of obese men.

In a meta-analysis of 33 studies involving a total of 1,257 men and 920 women, a reduction of dietary fat was accompanied by weight loss. For every percent reduction of dietary fat, there was a corresponding 0.5 pound weight loss.

Some individuals have done well with high fat, low carbohydrate diets, but high fat diets have resulted in some patients experiencing elevated cholesterol levels and heart disease. High fat diets have also been associated with some cancers like breast cancer. Additionally, people cannot stay on these dietary regimes for a long time. They crave carbohydrates with a vengeance even more!

Of course, those patients who come to see me have been unsuccessful at these programs. I probably do not get to see those individuals who have done well! Even if weight loss is achieved, maintenance is not documented. In these cases, my motto has always been: "Only weight loss that is maintained is successful weight loss."

In my practice, I teach my patients to cut down their fat percentage to 30% of their total calories, and preferably to 20%, if possible. There are days when deviations from this formula occur; but staying within this range is beneficial, not only for weight loss but also for weight and health maintenance as well. We teach our patients the percentages of fat in their foods; we recommend fat-free products as much as possible: fat-free tuna, fat-free cheeses and fat-free snacks.

Beef, prime rib, brisket and short ribs have about 75% fat content and should be consumed very sparingly. Ground chuck, cube steak, rib steak, rib roast and T-bone steak are better with about 60% fat content; beef tenderloin, chuck roast, rump roast and flank steak are better choices with about 50% fat content. The best choices in beef cuts are sirloin steak, bottom round steak, or top round steak (all broiled) with fat percentages of 38% to 21%.

Remember that there are two kinds of fat: the visible fat that can be cut off from the meat, like the fat around the steak, and the invisible kind that marbles the meat and greatly increases the fat content (like in a filet mignon). We should also note that meats contain aldehydes which accelerate the aging phenomenon.

Pork can vary in its fat percentage according to its cut; bacon, chops, spare ribs and sausage are high in fat (about 80%). Top loin, loin chop, blade center loin, sirloin chop, blade shoulder steak and canned ham average a fat percentage of 60-70%. Center rib and lean pork roast are closer to 50% fat content. Canadian bacon and cured ham steak have the lowest fat percentage of 34% and 3% respectively. Regular hot dogs have close to 80% fat content. Boiled ham is better at 70% fat content.

Lamb cuts are high in fat (close to 80%). Veal ranges from 60% fat in cutlets and rib roast to 30% fat in rib chops, blade steak, loin chops and rump roast.

Poultry is always a good choice. However, goose or duck with skin can have a fat percentage of 60%, while chicken or ground turkey lower their fat percentage to 50%. But the winner is chicken breast without skin with only 24% fat. White turkey meat is another excellent choice with 24% fat content. Turkey salami, turkey pastrami and turkey ham have a higher percentage of fat ranging from 40 to 60%. Regular salami, liverwurst and bologna are much worse with a percentage of 80% fat.

Fish is a better choice, as it contains the EPA or eicosopentaenoic acid or omega-3 fatty acids. EPA is reported to protect against heart attacks and prevent platelet aggregation which leads to blood clots, heart attaks and strokes.

Lake trout or tuna canned in oil have a fat percentage of close to 80%. Herring, bass, and Chinook salmon have a fat percentage of roughly 70%. Mackerel (both Atlantic and Pacific) has a fat percentage of about 50%; swordfish and pink salmon have a fat percentage below 30%. Trout, scallops, crab and raw clams have a percentage of below 20%. Haddock, cod, sole, flounder, shrimp, lobster, halibut, snapper and tuna canned in water have a fat percentage of less than 10% and should be used as staples in our diets.

Dairy Products also vary in fat content according to the product.

Cheeses such as Neufchatel and Brie are 90% fat. Cheddar, Bleu, Gouda, Muenster, Swiss, American and Camembert range from 70 to 75% fat. Parmesan, feta and mozzarella (part skim) cheeses are close to 60% fat, while cottage cheese ranges from 14% to 30% depending upon whether it is creamed, and 2% or 1% on whether it is low fat or fat free.

Whole milk has 50% fat content, 2% milk has 37%, skim milk has less than 20%, and low fat yogurt has 26% fat content.

American consumption of cheeses has climbed since 1972. Not counting cottage cheese, Americans consume 28 pounds of cheese (cheddar and mozzarella especially) per year.

There are many fat free or low fat cheeses available in the market that can be substituted for the real thing. While these cheeses do contain calcium, salt is substituted for fat. People who suffer from water retention should be wary of an over-consumption of these products.

A new study showed that excess salt can lead to osteoporosis; while cheese may be beneficial to prevent bone loss, salty cheeses may prove detrimental. However, dairy products were recently found to decrease insulin resistance and, thus, are beneficial in diabetics or pre-diabetics. Lactobacillus (a friendly bacterium) also called probiotic may be found in yogurt and milk. It has been shown to help with migraine headaches, autoimmune diseases and stomach ulcers caused by the bacterium called Helicobacter pylori.

Nuts also vary in their fat content; macadamia, pecans and hazelnuts have the highest fat composition (over 90%). Almonds, pistachio, walnuts, peanuts, sunflower seeds and cashews are healthier with a fat percentage of close to 80%. However, almonds, hazelnuts, pistachios and pecans contain a large percentage of heart-friendly monosaturated fat (as in olive and canola oils). Subjects who ate almonds showed a decrease in LDL cholesterol. In a Harvard Nurses' Health Study, women who ate five ounces of nuts per week showed a 35% reduction in heart attacks. Five trials demonstrated that walnuts may also lower cholesterol and, thus, even in small amounts they can protect again heart disease. According to Frank Saibes, M.D., nuts help dieters to stay on their diets, as they may alleviate cravings and prevent snack scavenging. Recently, a diet high in nuts and peanut butter was shown to be beneficial for women suffering from type II diabetes. In my experience, however, whenever patients start consuming nuts, they overindulge in this product and actually experience a weight gain.

Avocados represent the only vegetable with high monosaturated fat content 80-90% (180 calories for 2 tablespoons). *Peanut butter* is 80% fat. *An egg* contains 60% fat percentage (located in the yolk).

It is important to remember that most bingeing foods (most cookies, crackers, cakes, donuts, regular ice cream) are in the 50% or higher fat percent range.

Even though the recommended daily intake of fat is about seven teaspoons, only 250 calories of fat are needed. Thus, one should read nutrition labels carefully. The preparation of foods may also help cut down on the fat content of your meals. It is a good idea to prepare meals with monosaturated or polyunsaturated sprays that lightly coat pans. Do not fry or cook with oils, as they become saturated during cooking. A recent study done in Stockholm, Sweden links potato chips, French fries, breakfast cereals, chips and other fried carbohydrate foods with a substance called acrylamide which might be cancer-producing. The suspect of this possible carcinogen may be a naturally ocurring amino acid that when heated with certain sugars may produce acrylamide. This might explain the relationship of certain cases of cancer caused by food.

Purchase cooking utensils like pots and pans with coated finishes to help cut down on the use of fats and oils; steam vegetables and skip fattening sauces completely. Use lemon juice, herbs and salt-free spices to enhance flavor; use microwave and slow ovens as much as possible. Be creative with salad dressings and marinades and skimp on the oils!

In the last 15 years, more and more fat-free products have been created. Oddly enough, people may be eating more fat-free but are still getting fatter! Fat-free products have calories also, and too much consumption of these products can still lead to obesity. Many fat-free products are deceptive, as they technically contain components of fats (diglycerides or triglycerides) even when they are labeled as fat-free.

Other investigators have touted fat as a satiety inducer. Fat stays in the stomach longer and slows down gastric emptying. Alcoholics consume fat to delay the absorption of alcohol in the bloodstream. I personally have found fiber to be superior in slowing gastric emptying than fat. Just like fiber, fat has an important role in colonic health, as it helps to move food through the intestinal tract. While some fat should be incorporated into our dietary regime, we recommend mostly uncooked monosaturated or essential fatty oils not to exceed 30% of our total calories.

In addition, the *American Journal of Clinical Nutrition* has published two supplements in the last several months about dietary fats. A summary of these papers follows: Omega-6 fatty acids and linoleic acid (in corn, soy, safflower and sunflower oils) may promote breast cancer in mice and in non-estrogen dependent humans. Omega-3 fatty acids (in flax and fish) and monosaturated fatty acids like olive oil may inhibit colon cancer and protect against breast cancer, while dairy, poultry and vegetable oils do not. Omega-3 fatty acids may reduce insulin resistance, lower blood pressure and triglycerides. A high carbohydrate, low fat diet is not recommended for diabetics, because it increases already elevated triglyceride levels.

Trans-fatty acids found in partially hydrogenated vegetable oils like margarine and vegetable shortening decrease HDL cholesterol, inhibit the metabolism of fats, and may cause heart disease. They do so by impairing artery dilation and and by hardening the arteries. They are said to increase the risk of diabetes. Food labels may not list trans-fatty acid content. Its consumption should be reduced to a minimum, as it is estimated that trans-fatty acids kill 30,000 people a year. The Food and Drug Administration is not taking lightly the fact that trans fatty acids increase LDL cholesterol and, therefore, promote heart disease. New labels may be required to list the amount of trans-fatty acids. Margarine, especially the hard stick form, contains the highest trans-fatty acid content and raises blood fats the most. French fries also contribute to 75% of the trans-fatty acids consumed in America, according to Dr. Alice Lichtenstein. French fries, as we read before, may actually be cancer producing! Other sources of trans-fatty acids are cookies and crackers. Recently McDonald's removed the high trans fatty acid content from their french fries.

Olestra is a fake fat that helps to decrease fat intake. It reduces the absorption of fat soluble vitamins. It decreases 5% of the cholesterol ingested, but has no effect on triglycerides. Unfortunately, Olestra does not cause weight loss. Some gastrointestinal upset may occur if large amounts are consumed.

Plant stanols moderately decrease serum cholesterol by inhibiting cholesterol absorption and by decreasing cholesterol synthesis. Benecol™ is a canola based margarine supplemented with a plant stanol ester, from the Finnish pine cone. Many studies have shown that this product has reduced total and LDL cholesterol levels by 10 to 15% in individuals who suffer from high cholesterol. These studies showed that triglyceride and HDL cholesterol levels remain unchanged. Even better cholesterol-lowering results have been experienced by people consuming this type of margarine, in addition to medications. Not only margarine, but salad dressings, cream cheese spreads and candy bars will sweep the United States and Europe under the Benecol label. There are two kinds of Benecol margarine, one that is suitable for cooking and one that is best for spreading. At least at home the 98 million Americans who are cholesterol concerned will be using these products. However, when eating out we will have to make concessions as no cooks or chefs are using these fake fats, yet.

"Take Control"™ is another margarine from plant stanols that blocks cholesterol absorption in the intestine. For optimal effects, three tablespoons of each margarine are needed.

According to a November 1999 *JAMA* article, plant stanols contained in these new margarines may decrease LDL cholesterol. However, they may produce plaque deposition in the arteries. Burping and gas may also hinder their effect. Therefore, the good effects of these stanols may be counteracted by negative consequences.

According to Dr. Michael Murray, flaxseed oil or fish oil also increase the effect of 5-HTP. Omega-3 fatty acids are necessary for proper functioning of serotonin in the brain. Conversely, diets low in omega-3 fatty acid levels have been associated with depression, probably due to improper serotonin functioning.

Investigators like Drs. Golay and Bobbioni claim that ingested fat may alter body fat and weight regulation. A low-fat diet is best for the active weight loss phase. They recommend not to go below 20% fat intake because below this percentage, fat storage may occur.

On the other hand, an elevated intake of high fructose corn syrup may cause lipogenesis or fat formation. In his book *Protein Power*, published in 1998, Dr. Michael Aedes cites two reasons why Americans are getting fatter. One reason is the ingestion of trans-fatty acids from partially hydrogenated oils. The second explanation is the consumption of all the high-fructose corn syrup found in sweetened drinks and processed foods. His best recommendation to avoid obesity is, thus, to avoid processed foods.

PROTEINS:

Most studies show that high protein diets are the most efficient method for losing weight, decreasing the appetite, and helping maintain a high metabolism while losing weight.

I recommend the consumption of lean proteins, as described above, to my patients. Lean proteins are to be eaten three times a day at meals and may be incorporated into two more snacks if needed. Proteins constitute the logs needed to ignite the fire in our body's fireplaces.

Shrimp and lobster are lean proteins with low-saturated fat content; they do not raise cholesterol content and constitute good choices for consumption. Dissolved proteins in nutritional supplements are even more efficient in producing weight loss, especially if the proteins are mixed with dissolved vitamins. This combination enhances weight loss significantly.

Egg whites, low fat cottage cheese, fat free cheeses, chicken or turkey slices, shrimp, lobster, veal slices, most fish, chicken, or turkey breast (broiled or grilled), tuna in water, sardines in water and chicken in water are our best lean protein choices.

Overweight men ate fewer calories when they consumed a high protein diet compared to a high carbohydrate diet. They also consumed less fat. Patients who need to lose 50 pounds or more are put on a program called PSMF, or protein-supplemented modified fasting. Patients in this program are only allowed to consume nutritional supplements that contain a high protein, low carbohydrate and low fat formula. Potassium supplementation and essential fatty acid addition are required to stay on this program. Patients may stay in this program for a maximum of 12 weeks; then after a two-week holiday, they may engage in another 12-week continuation of the program. The lean protein consists of a milk protein called casein and egg white protein called albumin. Soy protein may also be added to the formula.

Electrolytes, vitamins and minerals are incorporated to make this product a complete food. The first program was called Optifast™, because it was supposed to provide the "optimal fast." The protein prevents the patient from going into negative nitrogen balance, and losing muscle mass. Up to 100 grams of protein, or one gram per kilogram of weight, are consumed per day. The main rationale is to keep the patients in ketosis (explained below) with just a minimum of carbohydrate intake (about 100 grams a day).

Ketosis means that the patient has used up his sugar storage and is breaking down his fat reserves. Protein is used by the body as a last resort means of fuel during prolonged fasting. (see Figure 10)

Figure 10

Physiology of Fasting

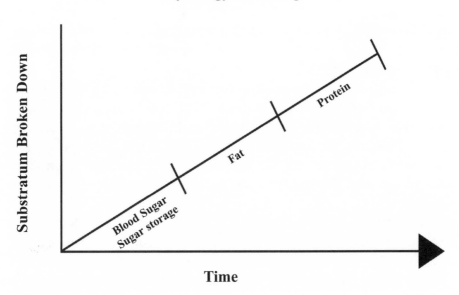

During fasting, the body first uses blood sugar or sugar stored in muscle or liver, then if the fasting continues fat is used, and only at the end, protein is broken down. Protein is what our bodies are mostly made of and our bodies try to preserve protein to the end. Ketosis manifests itself by showing dark coloration in urine keto sticks, also by causing bad breath relieved by peppermint oil or gum. Ketosis also gives patients a feeling of well-being and energy. After 48 hours on the fast, patients do not feel hungry; to the contrary, they feel elated and energetic as they burn their fat storage. Optimal weight loss that is rapid and painless is achieved with this method. However, patients need to be monitored closely by physicians trained in the use of PSMF. Electrolytes and medications like insulin and diuretics have to be checked often. In the last twenty years, thousands of patients have been treated successfully with no significant side effects. Only potential mild side effects are reported and are reversible: hair loss, mild hypotension, tiredness and muscle cramps. Many imitation formulas improved upon the original Optifast™. These include: Procal™, Medifast™, HMR™, Bariatrix™, Robard™, and Pro Amino™, just to name a few.

The ketosis of fasting is much milder than the ketoacidosis found in diabetics and is definitely not harmful. Oprah Winfrey became the poster child for Optifast™, proving that the program works. Patients do lose weight, especially if they are motivated enough to stay on the program. However, if no maintenance program is offered, those patients may gain weight easily if they resume their old eating habits (as evidenced with Oprah).

Not all patients are put on a complete fast; some are put on a semifast with one or two meals a day, but still with nutritional supplements consumed as the third meal (usually breakfast) and snacks between meals. However, the less food and the more nutritional supplements consumed, the greater the weight loss. The different supplements are chosen according to the lifestyle, taste and food preferences of the patients.

There is no contraindication for the patients to consume one or two health shakes for the rest of their lives; a morning supplement helps the patient to start the body's fireplace burning for the whole day. The high protein supplements give the dieters a lot of energy and a feeling of well being.

The other advantage of the nutritional supplement programs is that there is no decision-making about food; in addition, no possibility of cheating is allowed. As the protein supplements are only presented in single packets, patients learn about portion control. In addition, the rapid weight loss is very stimulating to those patients who are so thrilled with their new looks that their self-confidence soars.

Thus, a complete fast is recommended for the very obese and one or two meals, in addition to the nutritional supplements, are advised for the rest. One or two supplements a day prevent patients from gaining their weight back. One caveat is that commercially-available supplements may contain a higher carbohydrate content than those available at physicians' offices.

These high protein programs have been shown to work well in my practice and in thousands of offices of physicians who specialize in the field of Bariatrics. Certainly patients cannot stay on these programs forever, but many studies have shown that weight regain happens less frequently in patients treated by bariatricians.

According to a study from Germany, patients lost five times as much weight after three months of using meal replacements as those using conventional diets. Obese children also lost weight on high protein, low calorie diets (100 grams of protein, 25 grams of carbohydrate). Later on, after three months, the children were given 90 grams of carbohydrates. According to Cathy Nonas from the Obesity Research Center at St. Luke's Roosevelt Hospital in New York, the recommended intake of high quality protein is 50 grams for women and 63 grams for men. However, in a reduced calorie diet, the suggested intake is 72 to 80 grams per day. Eating inadequate amount of protein (less than 40 grams per day) causes cardiac arrhythmias. A maximum of 100 grams of carbohydrates per day is permitted. I always counsel my patients that this method represents just a temporary bridge to get them quickly to their thin island (see Figure 11). Maintenance constitutes the removal of the bridge (see Figure 12 on pg. 186).

Figure 11

Weight-loss is a bridge between the fat and thin islands.

Figure 12

Maintenance is removal of the bridge.

I also do not recommend the high protein program for the rest of one's life. Ingesting over 100 grams per day of protein for a prolonged period of time may hypothetically cause kidney or liver overload and possibly kidney stones. Also, there have been claims that a high protein diet may leach calcium from the bones and contribute to osteoporosis. In my own practice of 21 years, I have never encountered these problems. Dr. Robert P. Heany, who has studied the role of protein, in bone loss for 30 years, concludes that "excess protein intake may not adversely affect bone." He adds that calcium intake, reduced consumption of caffeine, oxalate restriction from diet drinks, and hormonal replacement are keys in combating bone loss. A calcium-protein ratio of more than 20:1 is adequate for protection of the skeleton. No heart problems have ever been associated with high protein diets. Also, when one weighs all the increased risk factors and the higher mortality associated with obesity, one sees that these side effects are minimal compared to the whole picture.

Calcium supplementation to prevent osteoporosis and periodic blood work-ups to determine any liver and kidney abnormalities are routinely done for people on this program.

Finally, as high protein diets do not work for everybody, some patients might suffer from extreme fatigue at the beginning (maybe for one week). If the patient is motivated, the best treatment regime is to wait one to two weeks for symptoms to improve. Octaconosol may also bolster low energy as well as NADH.

I have also experienced problems with patients who are strict vegetarians and who do not eat meat, fish, dairy or egg whites. Vegetables which contain protein are then recommended like corn, beans and tofu with a light sprinkling of some nuts. Other vegetables and salads are also allowed, but low fat preparation is still recommended.

Dr. Michael Eades also recommends a high protein diet to block insulin oversecretion. He limits carbohydrate intake and is not worried about good fat intake, only bad fat consumption. He also claims that low carbohydrate diets are good for ulcerative colitis, Crohn's disease, rheumatoid arthritis and multiple sclerosis. Maintaining a high protein content in an energy restricted diet reduces the fall in energy expenditure that can happen with low calorie diets. A high protein diet was shown to increase energy expenditure more than a diet high in carbohydrate or fat. Also, high protein diets may stimulate T3 thyroid hormone formation and increase thermogenesis (or caloric burning).

Dr. Barry Sears balances protein and carbohydrates one to one at every meal to control insulin levels (the Zone diet).

While barbecuing and grilling may produce heterocyclic amines (cancer-causing agents) that are produced from the fat dripping on the hot coals and then wafting forward, marinating the meats for one-to-two hours may reduce these carcinogens by 67%. Different marinades were tested, like Hawaiian teriyaki and Indian turmeric-garlic by Dr. Partibha V. Nerurker from the University of Hawaii Cancer Research Center. She found them all beneficial and, thus, suspects that the liquid content of the marinade may add moisture to the meats and fish and prevent them from burning too much.

It is unrealistic to believe that patients are not going to be tempted by foods in front of them, especially when high carbohydrate foods are easily available, cheap, and store well as they require less refrigeration.

CARBOHYDRATES:

High or low carbohydrate diets can cause weight loss, but low carbohydrate diets have shown slightly better results in the active weight loss phase. Carbohydrates are divided into two big groups: simple sugars and complex carbohydrates.

Simple sugars are found in the sugar bowl (from grapes, beets, or sugar cane, and called glucose or sucrose) or in dairy products (called lactose) and finally in fruits (called fructose). These sugars are easily absorbed, and we already discussed that high fructose corn syrup may be lipogenic (a fat depositor).

Breads, pastries, rice, potatoes and pasta comprise complex carbohydrates. These have to be broken down into sugar molecules for absorption and, thus, require more energy. Some people can consume these products without repercussions, while others have difficulty achieving weight loss while eating them. Those people who have bingeing tendencies should analyze which product category they are more apt to crave. 90% of the time, carbohydrate consumption for breakfast may stimulate hunger the whole day. When teenage boys were fed high glycemic index breakfasts, they consumed more calories for lunch than those who had a low glycemic index breakfast like a vegetable omelet.

According to a few studies, a low carbohydrate diet improves blood lipids and insulin levels, in addition to causing weight loss. The diet consisted of a high protein, high fat, low carbohydrate program with no caloric restriction. Weight loss was associated with an insulin drop as well as a decrease in cholesterol and triglycerides. On the other hand, a high starch diet caused weight loss in normal weight women, because they avoided sucrose and fat.

Researchers have found that obese people eat carbohydrates to reduce depression. A carbohydrate-rich meal relieves depression in carbohydrate-craving obese patients. As carbohydrates increase serotonin levels, patients self-medicate themselves with carbohydrates to relieve their depression and feel happy and positive. Carbohydrates stimulate tryptophan to enter the brain and increase the production of serotonin. The subconscious desire to feel good makes people eat more carbohydrates and less protein. However, Dr. Richard Wurtman pointed out in *Obesity Research* in 1996, that animals given medications to increase serotonin release did not indulge in carbohydrate consumption.

Most of our complex carbohydrates come from refined grains which are devoid of fiber nutrients. Look for the word "whole" when buying complex carbohydrates. Enriched or wheat flour means they are a refined product.

Today Americans consume 115 lbs. of sugar per person per year. Many individuals exhibit bloating. Eliminating yeasty foods like breads, pastries and donuts seems to alleviate bloating and gas. Many patients have demonstrated sensitivities to yeast. A food sensitivity blood test may uncover this as well as many other food allergies. Those who are insulin-resistant or who have high glycohemoglobin A1C, or high insulin levels in their blood and those with the deadly pattern B-LDL should restrict their carbohydrate intake.

Dr. Robert Atkins feels that carbohydrate restriction decreases insulin resistance, edema, bloating, flatulence, irritable bowel syndrome and gastroesophageal reflux. In addition, it controls yeast overgrowth and increases cancer survival.

Carbohydrates also make up healthy nutritional products like legumes, grains, fruit and vegetables. I counsel my patients to remove the beige, bland foods from their plates—cereal, bread, bagels, white rice, pasta and potatoes. I ask them instead to put color in their plates. Green comes from green peppers, spinach, kale and lettuce; red from tomatoes, red peppers and beets; yellow from squash and corn; orange from sweet potato, carrots and oranges; purple from cabbage and eggplant; and blue from blueberries and plums.

My young patients are supposed to count the colors they have daily in a sort of game to introduce them to different foods. Vegetables and salad materials provide bulk to fill our tummies; they work very well to assuage the stomach hunger that is very common in certain patients.

Beans (black, kidney and garbanzo), a staple in vegetarian diets, can also be used in moderation as a sprinkling on other vegetables or salads. Too much of the starchy vegetables like corn and peas can be detrimental for weight loss. Again, a 1/4 cup is all that is allowed per meal. Other vegetables can be eaten without limits.

Grains: Cereals are best chosen without the sugar frosting or coating. Skim milk, not whole milk, should accompany them. The best choices of cereal are those that provide a high protein percent. A single serving size is adequate.

Fruits: There is a lot of controversy about this food product. Some diets recommend them, while some forbid them. I feel that during the active or restricted weight loss phase, fruits should be not allowed. Fruits are full of fructose which elevates glucose, causing hunger for the whole day. As patients lose weight, we allow some fruit: 1/2 grapefruit may be added to breakfast, an apple or orange may be incorporated at the end of lunch or dinner. We reintroduce the fruit at the end of the meal rather than as a snack, because the absorption of the fruit is delayed when it is consumed with other foods. We recommend all fruit, except the very sweet ones like bananas, grapes, cherries and watermelon, after the active weight loss phase is successfully completed. We also advise against drinking juice, as juice does not contain the fiber and pulp found in fruit that cuts down the absorption of fructose by 50%. Patients who suffer from diabetes, high triglyceride or pattern B LDL cholesterol also do well with these dietary restrictions.

Finally, I use the law of "what is better?" for myself and teach it to my patients. It is better to have a parfait glass filled with fresh berries than a piece of chocolate cake. Incidentally, berries are often available as a dessert in many restaurants (of course, you should order it minus the whipped cream). We also do not recommend dried fruits, as they are quite caloric and have a high sugar content.

The other issue that has created a lot of controversy is starches like bread, white rice, pasta and potatoes. We have to analyze ourselves. I know that for myself and my staff, whenever bread is part of a meal, after eating a few slices, we continue foraging for food the whole day.

White bread, rice and pasta are nutritionally very limited; they are just bulk in our stomach. They can be low fat, but they do not bring us much vitamins and minerals. A high rice diet was associated with obesity in 457 Japanese 10-year-old children. The author of this study suggested that high rice consumption may be an early warning sign for future obesity. I personally have a problem with pasta; whenever I have a pasta meal, the next day I show a weight gain on the scale of a pound. As I am aware of it and am resigned to it, I plan a more restricted dietary intervention the next day. Half of a baked potato with one's meal is acceptable on occasion, as the potato is high in vitamins and minerals. However, french fries are best to be banned from the strict weight loss phase.

Chips, crackers, popcorn and pretzels are the snacking foods of choice for most Americans. We eat them without even knowing what we are eating. The same occurs with the bread basket at the restaurant; people are not even aware of it and wolf down all of the bread, crackers or chips put in front of them. Morsel sized, easily available food is a dieter's nemesis. It is better to have to work for your food, so that you can savor each morsel (and hopefully eat less). Try eating a fresh artichoke leaf by leaf; a half a lobster on the shell also provides an hour of digging and savoring the meat. Of course, the meat should not be dunked in butter! To prevent aimless carbohydrate eating, I recommend not buying these foods for the house. If they are available at the restaurant table, ask the waitress to immediately remove them, and order a healthy replacement such as your salad, as soon as possible.

As you have already gathered, I do not adhere to one specific nutritional plan. Study yourself first for one week to see what foods you crave and use the supplements I have described to alleviate the cravings. Do not starve yourself, as you will stop your body's fire; highly-restrictive eating rarely leads to sustained weight loss. Denial results in overeating, according to Gorgia Kostas, MPH, RD. If the physician tells the patient not to eat chocolate, he or she will often just go home and eat some with even more gusto.

I initially recommend a low fat, low carbohydrate diet and increased protein at the inception of the weight loss program. Many patients want to know how many carbohydrates they can consume and still stay in ketosis. Of course, everybody is different: some individuals may have less than 100 mg of carbohydrates per day; while others do not show color in their urine keto sticks unless they cut down to a carbohydrate count of 50 mg per day. Dr. Jean Pierre Flatt found that the more carbohydrates one consumes, the less fat one burns; to burn fat some people need to restrict carbohydrate to 50 grams or less. Dr. Robert Atkins recommends less than 30 grams of carbohydrate in the beginning of his program (called the induction phase). Most carbohydrates are not usually converted to fat, despite a popular belief, unless fat intake falls below 20%.

Of all the carbohydrates, the one most easily converted to fat is high fructose corn syrop. High fructose corn syrup is the biggest fat storer or lipogenic product available. High fructose corn syrup also raises insulin more than a fructose and glucose mixture. The dramatic increase in the consumption of high fructose corn syrup (in sodas, juices, cookies and baked goods) may be one of the reasons Americans are getting fatter and fatter.

In accordance with scientific opinion, I never believed previously in food combinations. However, recently a new article showed that when combined with a high glycemic carbohydrate, even protein may be stored as fat. Dr. Atkins also believes that carbohydrates may help proteins to be stored as fat. Protein and starch constitute the staples of the American diet: for example, hamburger with a bun, steak with potato or fries, or chicken and rice. Thus, avoidance of high glycemic carbohydrates should be even more reinforced.

Exercise can also put color on one's urine keto stick. When we continuously fill our meals with refined sugar, the insulin switch turns on and its opposite hormone, glucagon, does not begin working. Glucagon hastens the breakdown of stored fat into energy. The glycemic index of foods was used a few years ago to assess those foods that were converted to sugar most easily in diabetics. Glucose has the highest index with 100. Finally, Dr. Barry Sears feels that the glycemic load is even more significant and recommends keeping one's glycemic load below 3,000 in any one meal.

Table 5

GLYCEMIC INDEX OF FOODS

Foods	Glycemic index
Puffed rice	130
Rice cakes	130
Glucose	100
White bread	100
Whole wheat bread	100
Russet potatoes	98
Grape nuts	98
Carrots	92
Rolled oats	90
Beets	88
Honey	88
White rice	82
Brown rice	82
Bananas	82
White potatoes	81
Pasta	79
Whole wheat pasta	78
All bran	74
Pinto beans	60
Peas	49
Grapes	45
Oranges	40
Navy beans	40
Apples	39
Tomato soup	38
Chick peas	36
Pears	36
Yogurt	34
Whole milk	32
Skim milk	32
Lentils	29
Peaches	29
Grapefruit	26
Plums	25
Soy beans	15

Table 6

GLYCEMIC LOADS OF VARIOUS TESTED CARBOHYDRATES

Source	Typical Volume	Grams	Glycemic Index	Glycemic Load
Fruits				
Apple	1	18	54	972
Apple juice	1	29	57	1,653
Apricot	1	4	81	324
Banana (medium)	1	32	79	2,528
Cantaloupe	1cup	15	65	975
Cherries	10	10	31	310
Grapefruit	1	10	36	360
Grapefruit juice	8oz	22	69	1,518
Grapes	1cup	15	66	990
Kiwi	1	8	74	592
Mango (medium)	1	33	80	2,640
Orange (medium)	1	10	63	630
Orange juice	8oz	26	66	1,716
Papaya (medium)	1	28	83	2,324
Peach	1	7	40	280
Pear	1	21	54	1,134
Plum		7	56	392
Raisins	1cup	112	91	10,192
Watermelon	1cup	11	103	1,133
Legumes				
Black Beans (boiled)	1cup	41	43	1,763
Black Bean soup	1cup	38	91	3,458
Chickpeas (boiled)	1cup	46	47	2,162
Fava Beans (boiled)	1cup	34	113	3,978
Kidney Beans (boiled)	1cup	40	39	1,560
Kidney Beans (canned)	1cup	38	74	2,812
Lentils (boiled)	1cup	32	43	1,376

Table 6 (cont.)

Source	Typical Volume	Grams	Glycemic Index	Glycemic Load
Navy Beans (boiled)	1 cup	38	54	2,052
Pinto Beans (canned)	1 cup	36	64	2,304
Soy Beans (boiled)	1 cup	20	26	520

Breads & Pasta

Bagel, small	1	38	103	3,914
Bread, dark rye	1 slice	18	109	1,962
Bread, sourdough	1 slice	20	74	1,480
Bread, white	1 slice	12	100	1,200
Bread, whole wheat	1 slice	13	99	1,287
Croissant (medium)	1	27	96	2,592
Hamburger bun	1	22	86	1,892
Kaiser roll	1	34	104	3,536
Linguini pasta (thin)	1 cup	56	79	4,424
Macaroni	1 cup	52	64	3,328
Pita bread	1	35	81	2,835
Pizza	1 slice	28	86	2,408
Spaghetti	1 cup	52	59	3,086

Starches, grains, & cereals

Barley (boiled)	1 cup	44	36	1,584
Bulgur (cooked)	1 cup	31	69	2,139
Cheerios	1 cup	23	106	2,438
Couscous (cooked)	1 cup	42	93	3,906
Corn, sweet (canned)	1 cup	30	79	2,370
Corn Chex	1 cup	26	119	3,094
Corn flakes	1 cup	24	120	2,880
Grapenuts	1 cup	108	96	10,368
Oatmeal (slow cooking)	1 cup	24	70	1,680
Potato, red (boiled)	1	15	126	1,890
Potato, white (boiled)	1	24	90	2,160
Potato, white (mashed)	1	40	100	4,000
Rice cakes	3	23	117	2,691

Table 6 (cont.)

Source	Typical Volume	Grams	Glycemic Index	Glycemic Load
Rice Chex	1cup	22	127	2,794
Rice Krispies	1cup	22	117	2,457
Rice, white	1cup	42	103	4,326
Rice, brown	1cup	37	79	2,923

Dairy Products

Source	Typical Volume	Grams	Glycemic Index	Glycemic Load
Milk (low-fat)	1cup	11	43	473
Soy milk	1cup	14	44	616
Honey	1tbs	16	83	1,328
Power Bar	1	45	83	3,735
Snickers Bar	1	36	59	2,124
Table sugar	1tsp	4	93	372

*Excerpted from "The Omega Rx Zone: The Miracle of The New High-Dose Fish Oil" by Dr. Barry Sears.

The lower the glycemic index, the less the sugar and insulin response. Dr. Ritchie Shoemaker feels that rice cakes are the worst in increasing blood sugar. He feels that the higher the amylase content of starches, the better the insulin response. He recommends eating soybeans, plums, grapefruit, peaches, lentils, yogurt, peas, chickpeas, tomato soup, apples and navy beans. However, he warns about variables in the glycemic index depending on the methods of cooking the food and the fruit ripeness. The addition of free fatty acids and magnesium also lower the glycemic index of foods.

As mentioned before, high glycemic index or high glycemic load foods increase insulin overproduction and cause insulin resistance and eventually type II diabetes. Recently, pancreatic cancer has also been linked to a high starch or high glycemic load foods in overweight sedentary women. The risk of developing pancreatic cancer was increased 2-3 times in those women consuming these foods. Obese women who consumed a high intake of fructose had 57% increase in this lethal cancer. These findings may apply to men as well. Other cancers like breast, gastroesophageal, prostate, kidney and uterus may also be linked to a diet elevated in high glycemic load carbohydrates.

As the patient loses weight, I start introducing carbohydrates slowly: fruit at the end of meals, more starchy vegetables and finally some starches at the end of the refeeding list. If the weight loss continues and no weight regain occurs, I proceed to introduce a little bit of fat. In general, I am very adamant against fat intake and fried foods.

In maintenance, patients are not seen as often but still record a diet diary; we are imperfect human beings, so indiscretions are allowed as long as we go back the next day to our healthy balanced program. To falter is not to fail!

Incidentally, both books, *The Zone*, written by Dr. Barry Sears, which recommends a ratio of 40% protein, 30% carbohydrate and 30% fat and *Protein Power* written by Dr. Michael Aedes, have received a lot of criticism and condemnation from many groups and associations.

Dr. Sears recommends a carbohydrate/protein ratio of 1:1. He describes the optimal meal as one-third of the plate filled with lean protein, and the other two-thirds made up of mostly vegetables and certain fruits. Dr. Robert Atkins advises that there is an initial carbohydrate level for each person at which that person will lose weight. He is very strict with regard to the amount of carbohydrates consumed (up to 30g each day) during the induction, or beginning phase, of the weight reduction.

The next complaint my patients voice frequently is: "Dr. Merey, I want a natural eating program!" They do not realize that the American diet as it stands today is the most unhealthy, unnatural, overprocessed conglomeration of fatty foods imaginable. Our ancestors ate more unrefined foods, less fat and more fresh produce. According to a recent survey, Americans eat 50% of their calories from carbohydrates, 15% from added sugars, 33% from fat, 3% from alcohol and only 16% from protein. Consumption of grain products rose by 40%, ready-to-eat cereal consumption increased by 60%, and popcorn and corn chips intake increased by 200% in the last 20 years. Milk ingestion has decreased and carbonated soft drink consumption has risen. Grape and apple based juice mixture intake increased by 300%. 57% of Americans eat away from home on any given day. Foods most commonly consumed are pizza, bologna, ravioli, and Mexican foods and they are all usually drowned with carbonated soft drinks.

We also have more knowledge now about phytochemicals, which protect us against cancer and are found in green and cruciferous vegetables. Finally, lycopene, the red pigmentation in tomatoes, may prevent and help in prostate cancer. This may represent the tip of the iceberg; more studies will surely extol the virtues of fruit and vegetables in the future.

The other frequently-asked question is *how many meals* should we consume a day? An old experiment showed that optimal weight loss was achieved when patients were given three meals a day. In my practice I recommend at least six meals a day (three meals and three snacks between breakfast and lunch, lunch and dinner, and finally after dinner). I find the after-dinner snack very beneficial for night eaters. Frequent eating of at least five small meals a day was associated with lower weight in men but not in women. However, frequent eating was associated with more physical activity in both men and women.

On the other hand, according to Stephen Gullo, Ph.D., author of the book *Thin Tastes Better*, three meals a day are better than five for maximum weight loss. Just a little trigger food may stimulate people to have more. According to Dr. Gullo, "Every addict can be moderate; however, they can't stay moderate very long." He also adds, "that an increase in frequency of meals leads to an increase in quantity."

Late day eating is not more likely to cause weight gain than eating earlier in the day, concludes a new study by researchers who analyzed the weight gain of 2,600 men and 4,600 women after 10 years. On the other hand, in another study, nighttime fasting was associated with 15% of weight loss in obese women who did not restrict their calories from 6:00 am to 5:00 pm. 92% of the women who continued to fast at night maintained their weight-loss habits. The conclusion of this study was that obese women burn less fat at night than lean females do.

I also do not force a patient to have breakfast if this person generally doesn't consume this meal. At the beginning of the weight loss phase, I recommend a portion of protein at each meal and preferably with their snacks.

The scale is the yardstick for nutritional changes. It also tells me whether I have been able to slay the "craving dragon." The other recommendation is to drink about eight glasses of water a day to help our kidneys and liver to remove the toxic products we ingest daily. Eight glasses of water a day will:

1. Reduce swelling and water retention.
2. Help burn fats and carbohydrates.
3. Help provide more energy.
4. Help remove waste products.
5. Avoid constipation.
6. Help reduce hunger.
7. Reduce the possibility of bladder cancer.

Alcohol is another culprit in discontinuation of many diet programs. One gram of alcohol is the equivalent of seven calories. Check the proof of the alcohol; if the proof is 10, there are 10 grams of alcohol per ounce, or 70 calories per ounce. Remember that a glass of alcohol has about three to four ounces, thus one can calculate the caloric content of one night's damage starting with cocktails, dinner wine and maybe after-dinner liqueur. Alcohol may decrease our inhibitions, while our food consumption increases exponentially.

Wine consumption, however, has been linked with lower weight in certain women. The theory is that alcohol increases levels of leptin, the hormone that reduces appetite and increases metabolism. Red wine polyphenols may also increase HDL (the good cholesterol) levels.

Consumption of alcohol (three beers or two glasses of wine per day in men and two beers or 1.3 glasses of wine per day in women) raises blood pressure. However, red wine has been shown to reduce the risk of coronary heart disease by increasing HDL cholesterol and decreasing platelet aggregation. The risk of heart attacks was decreased in regular drinkers as compared with non-drinkers. As there was no advantage in drinking wine, beer or any other liquor, ethanol was suggested to be responsible for the reduced risk of heart attacks.

The above advice is a bit limited, as it applies to the weight loss phase. However, as the patient loses weight, the dietary intervention becomes less strict; one slice of bread and one starch are introduced with the meal. As dessert is hard to resist, we recommend not to order a dessert but rather to sample a friend's, partner's or spouse's dessert. I prefer that the patient has only one meal away from home per day. When patients are traveling, I recommend that they should be careful, but should not continue on a strict diet. I do not expect any weight loss but just weight maintenance. Even before the patient has achieved his or her ideal weight, a refeeding program is instituted; patients are given more carbohydrates, and we stop at the amount of carbohydrates at which the patient can still maintain his or her weight.

At home, if the woman is the food preparer, she should stay in the kitchen as little as possible. Lots of mischief can happen when cooking is accompanied by tasting.

I have a lot of patients who consider themselves garbage cans: not only do they have to eat up everything on their plates ("empty plate syndrome"), but they also have to finish every other family member's plate. This is derived directly from one's upbringing when parents forced children to finish their food, even when they were not hungry. This is a good time to learn from our mistakes and to avoid doing the same to our children. If the child does not want to eat, leave him or her alone; he or she will eat when hungry. Forcing children to eat when they are not hungry at an early age has incredible repercussions later on in their lives.

Another problem encountered by weight loss patients is the fear of low calorie sweeteners. Information was circulated about the possibility of brain damage, lupus, multiple sclerosis and Alzheimer's disease in people consuming Nutrasweet™. There is no foundation for these claims. Presently, 100-million adult Americans consume foods containing low calorie sweeteners which can provide a significant psychological benefit to dieters by satisfying their desire for sweet taste without adding calories. Dr. Katherine Porikos and colleagues showed that people who unknowingly had their sugar substituted with cyclamates showed a significant weight loss. An experiment done with rats by Yokogoshi, et al. showed that aspartame did not affect serotonin release and did not alter neurotransmitter activity. Aspartame does not increase insulin release, either. There are claims that problems occur due to the metabolism of aspartame into methanol and formaldehyde. But more methanol and formaldehyde are produced from the metabolism of fruits and vegetables than from aspartame. A new study found that Nutrasweet™ is surprisingly effective for weight loss and maintenance. This study stated: "Data from well-designed clinical trials have shown that aspartame is not associated with weight gain and can facilitate weight loss." All side effects were refuted.

Saccharin has also been cleared of its association with bladder cancer. New sweeteners, called sucralose (Stevia) and acesulfame potassium (Splenda™), have recently been approved by the FDA. Both products are   incorporated in chewing gum, cough drops and Pepsi-One (the one-calorie drink). Stevia is a non-caloric sweetener that has not been approved in America yet on the grounds that the herb is an unapproved food additive. However, Canada and European countries use it successfully. Splenda™ is being incorporated into a lot of products successfully.

Diet drink sales average $54-billion a year! A moderate intake of low calorie sweeteners can be consumed without fear.

Although very popular, caffeine has also been much maligned, besides the fact that caffeine is the most widely used psychoactive drug in the world. Caffeine is contained not only in coffee but also soft drinks and, to a lesser extent, tea. Instant coffee contains 60-85 mg of caffeine, while brewed coffee has 65-120 mg. Other drinks are also high in caffeine, such as Mountain Dew with 55 mg, Coca Cola with 45 mg, Pepsi Cola with 37 mg and Snapple Iced Tea with 48 mg. A new category of herbal drinks and beverages —called, for example: Think, Power Energy, Aqua Java, Krank 20, Surge, Jolt, and Kick (just to name a few)—also contain significant amounts of caffeine.

The National Coffee Association reports that the number of coffee drinkers has increased by five million since 1991. Sensitivity to caffeine generally differs from person to person, as some individuals may be more affected by it than others. 80% of Americans ingest caffeine everyday with an average intake of 200 milligrams. "Moderate use of caffeine is not life-threatening, but caffeine is not benign either," said Roland Griffiths, Ph.D. Adverse side effects of coffee may include insomnia, anxiety, irritability, heartburn and indigestion. Caffeine has also been linked with osteoporosis, as it may prevent the absorption of calcium. Whether or not coffee may increase blood pressure is controversial. Coffee has also been associated with an increase in homocysteine levels in the blood. Coffee does have some addictive potential, too, as demonstrated by the withdrawal symptoms of insomnia, anxiety and severe headaches when its use is discontinued quickly. Whether or not it is addictive, many people depend on a coffee jump-start in the morning. People who drink four-to-five cups of coffee have higher blood pressure and show elevated stress related hormones (epinephrine and norepinephrine) in their blood, according to a 1999 study done in San Diego by Duke University. Cholesterol levels are not affected by filtered instant coffee; however, espresso or non-filtered coffee may be responsible for some elevation in cholesterol. In addition, coffee is not the diuretic it was considered previously.

Coffee intake may not be so bad for health after all. A recent Harvard study showed that women who drank six or more cups of coffee per day were less likely to have a heart attack than women who consumed fewer than six cups. In another study, heart attack risk was found to be 16% lower in people who drank four cups of coffee or more per day compared to those who drank one cup or less per week. Finally, decaffeinated coffee drinkers were more likely to suffer a heart attack when they drank one or more cups per day compared to non-coffee drinkers. The latest study from May 2000 led by Dr. G. Webster Ross, et al. has shown that coffee consumption is inversely related to the risk of Parkinson's Disease (a severe debilitating neurological disease). As caffeine may be a nervous stimulant, regular exposure to caffeine may counteract the aging related neurodegenerative processes that cause loss of dopaminergic neurons. In addtion, niacin contained in coffee may be neuroprotective. Besides coffee and tea, cola and chocolate may also provide similar benefits.

Caffeine has additional benefits, such as:

Pain Relief: Caffeine and aspirin or caffeine and Tylenol™ have shown better pain relief than aspirin or Tylenol™ alone. As caffeine constricts blood vessels, it is used successfully to treat migraine headaches.

Diabetes Control: Diabetics can better recognize low glucose warning signs when they consume coffee.

Liver Problems Diagnosis: Caffeine can be used as a tracer to help assess liver function.

Symptomatic Gallstone Disease: 46,000 men who drank two-to-three cups of coffee per day showed a decrease in symptomatic gallstone disease. According to the *JAMA*, coffee may even prevent gallstones and gallbladder disease in men.

Athletic Performance Boost: Caffeine enhances endurance in sports like running, skiing and cycling.

Weight Loss: When added to ephedrine, between 100 mg to 200 mg of caffeine is used for anorectic control.

Short Term Memory/Free Radical Damage: Coffee may even improve short term memory and be a strong antioxidant that protects against free radical damage. Smelling freshly-brewed coffee may even improve your health, as the coffee aroma may contain as many as 300 antioxidants and may give us the same benefits as eating three oranges. Because coffee contains theophylline, it may be of some help in asthma relief.

In summary, every physician has his or her own way to treat the very complex disease that is obesity. Not only is it true that one diet does not fit all, but each doctor may have a different program that best suits his/her personality and beliefs.

Now armed with this extensive knowledge, you will be able to make intelligent food choices and manage your weight in the best way possible. We wish you: "Bon Appetit!"

Chapter Summary

- Protein constitutes the logs in our body's fireplace, while carbohydrates represent the water drowning the fire.

- Starving stops the metabolism from burning calories.

- A combination of 50% olive oil, 50% canola oil is optimal oil supplementation.

- For every 1% reduction of body fat, there is a corresponding 0.5 lb weight loss.

- The body uses blood sugar and stored sugar for fuel, then it uses fat; protein is only used as a last recourse.

- Low fat, low carbohydrate, and high protein weight-loss programs have been most successful.

- The glycemic index of foods and/or the glycemic load of foods tell which foods increase blood sugar the most and therefore may contribute to insulin resistance and obesity.

— Chapter Fifteen —

PHARMACOTHERAPY

As previosly described, 80% of my patients achieve and maintain weight loss with neurotransmitter precursors (dopamine and serotonin). However, 20% of our patient population needs a little more help. They may require a jump start for a temporary situation, or their cravings may be so severe as to require pharmacotherapy. In our office, we only use drug therapy as a matter of last resort or if the patient already has a history of having used stronger medications.

We first use over-the-counter medications (OTC), especially if a patient's BMI is below 30 (in the white region in Table 1). Our first line of OTC medication is *phenylpropranolamine* (PPA). It comes in doses starting with 37.5 mg, then 50 mg for a quick burst of appetite suppression, and lastly, 75 mg dosage in a slow release form that lasts longer. We usually use the 75 mg slow release appetite suppressant. Sometimes this anorectic drug may be combined with fiber (carboxy methyl cellulose). I do not recommend this combination, however, as the fiber may prevent the absorption of the drug. Often PPA is used with benzocaine (which numbs the stomach) containing from 3 to 9 mg per capsule. One pill may be used between breakfast and lunch and another between lunch and dinner. PPA works synergistically with the neurotransmitter precursors. PPA may stimulate the metabolism through thermogenesis. According to Dr. A Halperin, et al., PPA causes more weight loss than either ephedrine plus aminophylline, T3 thyroid hormone or yohimbine.

Side effects associated with PPA include hypertension, palpitations, and elevated heart rate (tachycardia) in certain patients. Even seizures have been recorded on rare occasions with PPA ingestion. Therefore, careful monitoring by a physician is recommended, especially if the patient suffers from high blood pressure.

Dosage of the drug can be readjusted, and timing of ingestion may be changed for earlier in the day if patients experience insomnia or difficulty falling asleep.

Some of the OTC medications containing PPA have been removed from the market.

Ephedrine, or *Ma Huang,* an herbal derivative, is included in many OTC medications for weight loss. The FDA limits its consumption to 24 mg per day. Abuse of this product has been linked with hypertension, headaches, seizures, palpitations, and even rare cases of deaths attributed to heart attacks and strokes. People should be warned against taking this substance if they suffer from heart disease, glaucoma, hypertension, hyperthyroidism, diabetes or prostate enlargement. One report has linked ephedrine with kidney stone formation. While three-fourths of the effect of ephedrine is as an anorectic (appetite suppressor), one-fourth of its effect constitutes thermogenesis or fat-burning potential. In our office, ephedrine has been used successfully when patients reach a plateau and have a harder time losing weight. Ephedrine's action is increased when combined with aspirin, caffeine or theophylline (an asthma medication). These combinations increase caloric expenditure by 18% and may even cause a preferential loss of abdominal fat.

Different experiments have shown the positive effects of ephedrine and caffeine on weight loss. Obese monkeys given this combination, even though they were not restricted calorically, burnt 21% more calories at night. Levels of T3 thyroid hormone were increased by 10% in those animals. The dosage used was equivalent to 20 mg of ephedrine and 200 mg of caffeine in humans.

The combination of ephedrine (10 to 20 mg) and caffeine (100 to 200 mg) was found to be safe and effective for treating 16-year-old obese adolescents who lost approximately 20 pounds in five months.

According to a new study, ephedrine and caffeine increased the amount of time to exhaustion in obese men riding a bicycle by an average of 39%. This combination could probably be used to increase the amount of time that overweight people are able to exercise.

Supplementation with magnesium and potassium may also help to protect against cardiovascular problems.

In addition, *ephedrine* and *caffeine* are quite effective asthma medications. It is interesting to note that the risk of asthma is at least three times greater in people who are roughly 35% overweight. As the incidence of obesity increases, so does the risk of asthma. Ephedrine and caffeine may help both conditions, asthma and obesity, at the same time. Ephedrine, caffeine and aspirin combinations have been shown to be associated with even more weight loss. Most research has shown that the best dosage for this combination is 20 mg of ephedrine and at least 100 mg or, better yet, 200 mg of caffeine.

In my own practice, I give my patients one-half of a tablet of the 25 mg ephedrine to be taken with either a cup of coffee or a caffeinated drink at around 2:00 p.m. As an extra bonus, this combination gives a boost of energy to patients and may allay cravings for snacks in the afternoon.

It is imperative though to check blood pressure and pulse periodically when patients take this combination. Metabolife 356 contains 12 mg of ephedrine and 40 mg of caffeine per tablet; the usual dose is two tablets twice a day up to eight tablets a day which definitely exceeds the FDA proposed limit of 24 mg per day of ephedrine. This product should be used with extra caution.

Synephrine, a product derived from *Citrus aurantium*, has also been added to ephedrine and caffeine in order to achieve even greater weight reduction. Unfortunately, synephrine does not suppress appetite nor does it increase basal metabolic rate.

Finally, two other products in combination are being used for weight loss. *Herbal Phen/Fen* contains ephedrine and St. John's Wort which is also supposed to raise serotonin levels in the brain. In addition, this latter herb contains a product (catechin) similar to green tea. It might be cheaper, however, to combine ephedrine with green tea.

Phen Cal is another product that has been used for weight loss. It contains large doses of DL phenylalanine (900 mg) and tyrosine (1,000 mg) to increase levels of dopamine and norepinephrine in the brain. 5-HTP in the amount of 5 mg is included to raise serotonin levels. Three pills a day would only contribute to 15 mg per day of 5-HTP, too small an amount to cause a difference.

I personally prefer to separate dopamine and serotonin-releasing precursors to give patients more possible choices and treatment opportunities. I recommend taking instead the dopamine releasing precursors during the day and the serotonin ones in the evening or late at night.

*Garcinia Cambogia (*or ***HCA)*** has also been touted as an effective natural appetite suppressant. Numerous articles and even books have described studies proving the relationship of this product with weight loss. As late as 1997, Dr. Carol Straughan recommended two to four tablets of HCA for her patients to suppress afternoon cravings. However, the latest study done in the *JAMA* of November 11, 1998, concluded that Garcinia cambogia failed to produce significant weight loss and fat-mass decrease beyond that observed with the placebo. Dr. Steven Heymsfield also observed no additional weight loss in patients who received this herbal extract.

Grapefruit: Anecdotal information has linked this product with weight loss. If this were true, coffee and grapefruit would be the optimal breakfast for weight loss. Unfortunately, no hard data has confirmed the efficacy of grapefruit in weight reduction. If anything, it is still better to consume a half of a grapefruit rather than the juice in the morning; the fiber in this fruit will fill the stomach preventing the consumption of something worse.

Finally, some of our patients may qualify *for appetite suppressant medications*. The American Society of Bariatric Physicians has written guidelines for anorectic drug use. To initiate therapy, BMI needs to be equal to or over 30 for a normal otherwise healthy individual (see Table 1 on pg. 22) or equal to or over 27 in an individual with associated diseases like type II diabetes, hypertension, abnormal glucose tolerance, atherosclerosis, osteoarthritis, gallbladder disease, breast cancer or sleep apnea.

The other criteria for starting drug therapy is a body fat percentage equal of over 30% in females or 25% in males. To start drug therapy, I use the smallest dosage first, before the time the patient is hungriest. The clinical response of the patient dictates whether an increased dosage is necessary. Optimal weight loss is about two pounds per week. If the patient does not achieve a 12-pound weight loss in three months, which is the equivalent of one pound per week, drug appetite suppression is discontinued for at least two weeks and alternative methods are offered to the patient. Appetite suppressants are controlled substances and should be dispensed or prescribed by a physician who specializes in weight control. To enhance the effectiveness of anorectics and to allow me to decrease the dosage of appetite suppressants, the natural neurotransmitter precursors are also used in tandem.

Appetite suppressants are to be used only as a last resort and only if patients constantly think of food with cravings so severe as to interfere with the quality of life of the fat person. In 1996, the National Task Force on the Prevention and Treatment of Obesity published a recommendation that pharmacotherapy should be used very cautiously and not routinely or indiscriminately. Most of the anorectic medication work through the release of dopamine and serotonin. Two defunct medications—*Pondimim*™ (or fenfluramine) and *Redux*™ (as dexfenfluramine)—are used to increase the release of serotonin. The only medication that seems to help the release of both dopamine and serotonin is *Meridia*™ (sibutramine). Unfortunately, we have not found this drug to be as successful as expected. The latest kid on the block, *Xenical*™ (or orlistat) is the new non-controlled substance working not through the mind but through preventing, by 30%, the absorption of the fat ingested daily.

Generally, most of these drugs have very low addiction potential. The most addictive is *Melfiat*™ or phendimetrazine. In my experience, I have not encountered any addictive tendencies in patients taking the drug.

There has been an association between Pondimin™ and Redux™ with heart valvular disease and the very rare condition called primary pulmonary hypertension. However, as time passes, the relationship between these side effects and the drugs weakens.

One of the oldest and most widely used anorectics agent is *phentermine*, the generic form for many brand names like Adipex™, Ionamin™, etc. Even though there is the possibility of a link between phentermine and possible heart disease, this connection has not been confirmed in our office. Phentermine is often combined with hydrochloride; however, the resin combination is longer lasting.

Dosages of phentermine. The drug dosages vary from 15 mg, 18.75 mg, 30 mg and finally 37.5 mg per capsule or pill. These medications are slow released. Phentermine is contraindicated for patients with heart disease or hypertension. Caution should be exercised in starting this drug in hyperthyroid patients. Some nervousness, anxiety, palpitations, dry mouth and finally insomnia are the most common side effects encountered in our office. Some urinary retention, nausea, GI distress, constipation, diarrhea and rashes have been infrequently associated with this medication. In our office, if the patient needs a burst of energy, phentermine is the medication of choice. However, we start with the smallest amount possible, such as the slow release 15 mg in the morning. Because of the possibility of insomnia, I do not recommend taking this drug too close to bedtime. In a new study done in rats, phentermine was shown to increase dopamine, but not serotonin release, in the brain. Dosage may also be increased to 15 mg of phentermine twice a day or 30 mg in the morning and 15 mg in the afternoon.

Another medication that has been quite successful is ***Tenuate***™ or diethylproprion. This drug has the distinction of being the only appetite suppressant that may be used in hypertension. Also, as patients lose weight, their blood pressure lowers itself. Diethylproprion exists in two dosages: the 25 mg and the 75 mg. The 25 mg dose works quickly but does not stay in the system as long as the 75 mg, which is in the slow release form. We individualize the dosage according to the patient's hunger. A 25 mg diethylproprion is given after breakfast and after lunch, if the individual is hungry for lunch and dinner. Sometimes, as with phentermine, a slow-release diethylproprion is administered in the morning, and, if needed, a booster of a 25 mg medication is recommended in the afternoon to cover dinner and maybe after-dinner hunger. Constant reevaluation of the clinical response dictates dosage and timing of the drug. Each person is different and metabolizes the drug differently. Whenever a patient tells me that he or she is still hungry, I adjust the dosage by asking what time the medication was taken and when the person experienced hunger again. This way I can calculate how long the drug stayed in the person's system. Also, natural neurotransmitter precursors taken in conjunction with diethylpropion may enhance their action. Dr. Craddock noted that chronic use of both diethylpropion and phentermine deplete the brain of noradrenaline. Thus, supplementation with the amino acid *L-tyrosine*, the precursor of dopamine and noradrenaline, may help prevent this.

Side effects of diethylpropion include headache, nausea, dry mouth, nervousness, anxiety and urinary retention. Caution should still be exercised with patients taking other medications, especially thyroid supplementation. Diethylpropion is contraindicated in glaucoma and within 14 days of taking a monoamine oxidase inhibitor. Some individuals prefer the brand name Tenuate™, while others swear by the generic. However, this drug affects neither mood nor thermogenesis, and does not give any extra energy, associated with phentermine. Both phentermine and Tenuate™ have not been associated with any addiction potential in the multiple studies done throughout America. Very rarely has dependence occurred at very high dosages only. Phentermine and diethylpropion are considered to be schedule IV controlled substances in the same category as cough medications. Diethylpropion may be used in obese patients who suffer not only from hypertension but also from diabetes, and cardiovascular disease. Continuous administration of the drug for four months resulted in the best weight loss. Patients taking diethylpropion continuously for six months lost 35% of their excess weight.

However, 30 mg phentermine was found to be 32% more effective than 75 mg diethylpropion, during a three month study. Diethylpropion may be also used in children and adolescents. 50 mg of diethylpropion helped 85% of obese children to lose five pounds in two months without dietary restrictions. Obese adolescents lost 11.3 pounds in 11 weeks when taking 75 mg of the sustained release diethylpropion.

Both phentermine and diethylpropion can be made into lollipops which work immediately to allay hunger, but do not stay long in the system. Thus, they can be used for dinner and after-dinner hunger.

In order of efficacy, phentermine is the most potent anorexiant, followed by diethylpropion and phendimetrazine.

Mazanor™ or **Mazindol** is another appetite suppressant used in dosage of 1-2 mg. Because of its many side effects, the drug is no longer used.

The only appetite suppressant medication that falls in category III of controlled substances (and is considered the most addictive) is **phendimetrazine,** also known as **Phenzene**™ **or Melfiat**™. We only use this medication as a matter of last resort. The slow release 105 mg capsule is taken once a day and only the 35 mg may be used three times a day before meals. This drug does not cause any nervousness or insomnia; it is well tolerated and suppresses the appetite of most patients. No addictive problems have been encountered in our office. While diethylpropion and phendimetrazine decrease the number of meals eaten per day, phentermine does not. Diethylpropion and phendimetrazine decrease the size of the first meal, while phentermine does not.

Meridia™ or **Sibutramine**, another relatively new medication, was awaited with great anticipation, as it increases the release of both dopamine and serotonin (similar to the defunct phen-fen combination). Meridia™ comes in two dosages: starting dose of 10 mg and subsequent dosage of 15 mg (if the 10 mg is not effective). Meridia™ is contraindicated for hypertensive patients, as it may increase blood pressure, thus necessitating close physician monitoring. Some patients who took this drug experienced irritability and mood swings. In addition, this medication cannot be given in combination with a class of antidepressants that increase serotonin (like serotonin reuptake inhibitors). Some patients did exhibit modest weight loss, especially if the medication was used as an adjunct with nutritional education and exercise prescription. Meridia™ took the edge off one's appetite, but did not deliver the full suppression that it was intended to give. It was shown that there are Meridia™ responders and non- responders. One third of patients generally lose 10% of body weight, one-third can lose 5%, and the last third less than 5% while taking 15 mg of this drug. One out of 20 patients loses no weight at all and should not continue taking this drug. At least 1% of the weight (or four pounds per month) needs to be lost to justify continuation of this medication. Meridia™ seems to increase fat loss and decrease muscle loss. Meridia also has the distinction that it can be used for one year as well as for maintenance purposes. The most common side effects of Meridia™ are headache, dry mouth, insomnia and constipation. It also may increase blood pressure. Meridia™ is more effective in men than in women and in younger men than older ones, as testosterone sensitizes the body to the effects of this medication.

According to a new study from Brazil, Meridia™ (sibutramine) may be more effective when combined with Xenical™ (Orlistat). Dosages were 120 mg of Xenical™ three times a day with meals and 10 to 20 mg of Meridia once a day.

Xenical™ or *Orlistat* is the newest medication approved by the FDA. It is not a controlled substance and does not work on the mind, but rather, blocks the absorption of 30% of the fat consumed (70% of the fat being absorbed anyway). This 30% of fat has to go somewhere, so in certain cases it finds its way as an oily fecal discharge in underwear and is accompanied by smelly gases. It works as an aversion technique because patients taking this drug punish themselves and their dinner companions if they ingest a high fat meal. Most side effects, especially gastrointestinal complaints, generally occur in the first three months. Soon patients learn how to regulate their eating to restrict fat. However, with all the new fat-free products available and with the carbohydrate cravings experienced by most of our patients, I feel the drug's use may be limited. A whole fat-free Entenmann's cake or a box of cookies could be consumed with impunity. Fat soluble vitamins E, K, A and D absorption may also be hampered in the high fat consuming population. Therefore, it is recommended to take vitamins in the evening for best absorption, if one is taking this medication (three times a day before meals).

Metamucil reduces the gastrointestinal side effects of Xenical™ (Orlistat), according to a study from the University of Sao Paulo Medical School in Brazil.

However, in studies done in 1998, Xenical™ was associated with a 6% weight loss in diabetics (versus 4.2% in controls) with an 8-9% weight loss after one year (as compared with 5.8% in controls) with a 5% loss after two years (versus 1.7% in the placebo group). Most importantly, Xenical™ seems to help prevent weight gain and, finally, it may even increase fat loss. Xenical™ may lower cholesterol but may increase triglycerides. Xenical™ may be destined to play an important role in the high fat-consuming population.

A quick comment on the combination phentermine/fenfluramine and Redux™ (dexfenfluramine) is in order now. While, as described above, phentermine increases the release of the neurotransmitter dopamine, fenfluramine and dexfenfluramine stimulate the release of serotonin from the brain. Michael Weintraub, M.D. thought of the popular phen/fen combination while stuck in the airport between conferences. Phentermine, he thought, is an upper and fenfluramine is more of a downer; thus the combination would possibly be perfect in balancing moods. Fenfluramine was very effective in curbing carbohydrate cravings and compulsive overeating. Side effects were thought to be minor: nausea, diarrhea and temporary loss of memory. The diarrhea from Pondimin™ was canceled by the constipation produced by phentermine. Dexfenfluramine, or Redux™, was also introduced in America in 1997, after being used in Europe for many years. Dexfenfluramine was then thought to be the better derivative of fenfluramine. Patients did well on it, and the medication was approved for one year maintenance. Obese diabetics were quite successful with Redux™. In the last months before its recall, Redux™ was also used with phentermine to stimulate release of both dopamine and serotonin.

Unfortunately, there were cases linking fenfluramine and dexfenfluramine with valvular diseases of the heart and, most ominously, with a possible lethal condition called primary pulmonary hypertension. These findings, though rare, produced a recall for both medications and a mass hysteria among dieters. As time elapsed, the heart problems were shown to be less severe than originally reported. It should be emphasized that close to 300,000 obese people die every year form obesity-related causes. Therefore, many patients would happily take the risks to continue their successful weight loss. As a result of all the above-mentioned negative correlations, a bad name has become associated with all appetite suppressants, and the obese have lost some confidence in weight-loss physicians.

Both Pondimin™ and Redux™, if taken with the serotonin reuptake inhibitors in high doses, could have caused a syndrome called serotonin syndrome which manifests itself with agitation and tremors, and could, if untreated, be lethal. The antidote for this condition is Periactin™ (an antihistamine) which should be given as soon as possible.

Serotonin Reuptake Inhibitors

Another group of medications that have been used for weight control are the *serotonin reuptake inhibitors (SSRIs)* class of antidepressant medications. They are very effective for the obsessive-compulsive overeaters, for the bingers and, finally, for the depressed patients who overeat when they experience low moods.

Prozac™, the first of this group of SSRIs, has been beneficial for eating disorders especially in higher doses (40-60 mg per day).

In addition, *Zoloft*™, *Paxil*™, *Effexor*™, *Serzone*™, *Wellbutrin*™ and *Celexa*™ have been used successfully in the depressed overweight patient. Each person should be analyzed for the best medication according to their accompanying medical conditions and moods. If the patient is also anxious, I prefer to use Paxil™. If the person is more calm, Prozac™ is recommended.

Effexor™ is a stronger antidepressant as it releases both norepinephrine and serotonin.

Serzone™ is given to patients who have difficulty sleeping or experience sexual problems (frequently experienced by those taking other SSRIs).

Celexa™ and *Lexapro*™ are the new antidepressant medications on the block and reserved for those individuals who do not do well with other antidepressants.

Wellbutrin™ is not actually in the class of SSRIs but has been used successfully in depressed patients. A serious side effect of Wellbutrin™ is an increased incidence of seizures. Wellbutrin™ is also used when patients do not respond well to other antidepressant medications. Recent data have shown that Wellbutrin™ may be useful in weight loss even with no dietary restrictions.

Luvox™ is another drug used for obsessive-compulsive personalities and could theoretically be used for obsessive-compulsive overeating.

Finally, I have had good response with **Zoloft**™, which does not cause either anxiety, insomnia or excessive drowsiness.

Each medication works differently with each patient and it is necessary in some instances to wait for eight weeks to reach maximum response. Some of the side effects already mentioned are anxiety, insomnia, drowsiness, sleepiness and sexual problems (lack of orgasms and low libido). Changing medications in the same class may offer some relief; prescribing antidepressants from another class may also be successful.

It is very important to use antidepressants only if the overweight patient exhibits symptoms of depression. In addition, even though some overweight patients lose weight at the beginning when using this class of antidepressant administration, the effect is temporary, lasting only four months. Unfortunately, after the four months are over, weight climbs up with a vengeance. Wellbutrin™ has the distinction of helping patients lose weight.

Recently, **Topomax**™, an anti-epileptic drug that also helps with depression, was shown to cause weight loss as a side effect.

Various doctors have tried the combination of appetite suppressants and SSRIs. The theory for using this combination is that the appetite suppressants available in the market today increase only dopamine, and the SSRIs inhibit (as their name implies) the breakdown of serotonin at the nerve terminals.

Dr. M. Anchors coined the name "phen pro" for the combination of phentermine and Prozac™ (20 mg). He feels that the phentermine— Prozac (fluoxetine) combination is more effective than phentermine alone. The optimal dosage for weight loss is 20 mg of the generic fluoxetine as the 10 mg does not work. In addition, higher doses of fluoxetine used in depression are not effective for weight loss. Other physicians have used all the other SSRIs with phentermine with different dosages and different degrees of success. There is a lot of controversy surrounding this combination, as serotonin release was thought to be responsible for heart valvular damage and the lethal primary pulmonary hypertension condition. Blood studies done in patients taking Prozac™

failed to show increased serotonin levels. Phentermine alone, diethyl-propion and even phendimetrazine may have a slight increase in heart valvular disease.

The combination of SSRIs and anorectics, however, should be used with caution and frequently monitored to prevent any problems in the future. New combinations using an SSRI, an anorectic and 5-HTP have also been tried with success. However, one should be watchful for signs heralding the serotonin syndrome as previously described.

Dr. Paul W. Medve, a bariatrician from Ontario, Canada, has been successfully using the combination phentermine, Prozac™ and L-tryptophan. The L-tryptophan is used for sleep induction and can only be found in compounding pharmacies in the U.S. Dr. Jerry Darm prefers to use phen-Wellbutrin™ in a dosage of 15 mg of phentermine and 150 mg of sustained release Wellbutrin™ SR twice a day at noon and at 5 p.m. He also reports that patients had feelings of strangeness or painful tingling and burning sensations in fingers, toes, ears and nose which necessitated stopping the medication. Trazodone (a tranquilizer) also helps with bedtime insomnia. Dr. Darm feels that Wellbutrin™ alone, or in combination with phentermine, reduces the cravings and improves appetite control. Wellbutrin SR™, mostly used for depression and to help people quit smoking, has been studied by Duke University Medical Center psychiatrist Dr. K. Golay for weight loss. Maximum dosage was 200 mg twice a day. However, women who took the drug lost 6.21% of their body weight in eight weeks. Wellbutrin™ works by increasing norepinephrine and dopamine, not by increasing serotonin. The study is continuing, and results will be published soon.

A recent study has shown that calcium blockers like nifedipine may increase fat burning potential, or thermogenesis, in some patients due to the ability of this class of drugs to increase the release of nora-drenaline.

Of course, each physician will find his best treatment modality for cravings and control of food addictions. Also, each patient will constitute a therapeutic challenge; but each individual should know that there are many available programs including food, herbal products, amino acids, neurotransmitter precursors, as well as, anorectic drugs, antidepressants and combinations of the above. Thus, we should never give up in our quest for losing weight, but rather, try again and again until the optimal solution is found.

In addition, new medications are in the works and doctors will be able to answer more of your weight problems in the near future.

NEW DRUGS AND ANTI-OBESITY MEDICATIONS UNDER DEVELOPMENT

Beta 3 Adrenergenic Receptors are supposed to increase the breakdown of fats or thermogenesis (fat burning). Beta 3 receptor agonists may offer promise in the future for the treatment of obesity; however, they act by stimulation of brown adipose tissue encountered more in the rodent than in the human model.

Bromocriptine or ***Ergoset***™ (a quick release form of the hormone) causes weight loss, improves glucose tolerance and reduces insulin levels according to a four-month study by Drs. A.H. Cincolta and A.H. Meier. Dosage was 1.6 mg to 2.4 mg given at 8 a.m. Bromocriptine also increases dopamine release, but decreases lipogenesis (the conversion of carbohydrate to fat). Because it decreases insulin secretion, lowers hemoglobin A1C and increases insulin sensitivity, it may be the ideal drug for diabetics. It also helps to lower triglycerides, cholesterol, blood sugar and free fatty acids. The most common side effect is slight nausea. Other side effects include headaches, nasal congestion, drowsiness, dry mouth, constipation, dizziness, psychosis with hallucinations, delusions and confusion, as well as fainting episodes.

Agouti-Related Protein was shown to be higher in leptin-deficient mice and may regulate body weight through the adrenal gland and the hypothalamus.

Amylase Inhibitors have been shown to block the breakdown of starch and thus reduce caloric intake from carbohydrates. Amylase inhibitors have mostly been beneficial in diabetics by preventing high blood glucose levels, but their effect on obesity have been minimal.

CART, an appetite-suppressing protein found in the brains of rats, was named because it represents a cocaine/amphetamine regulated product.

Cholecystokinin is a peptide that slows gastric emptying and decreases appetite. However, most studies were done in mice and correlation to humans has not yet been determined.

Ciliary Neurotrophic Factor stimulates receptors in the leptin pathway that suppress food intake and lower body weight by possibly blocking Neuropeptide Y gene expression. This substance may be helpful in patients who do not respond to leptin injections.

Corticotropin Releasing Factor (CRF) works on stress receptors in the brain to decrease appetite and regulate metabolism. Studies have shown that leptin may modulate the secretion of CRF from the hypothalamus and that an imbalance between leptin and CRF may contribute to obesity. Experiments were done in rodents only. Genetically-engineered antibodies are supposed to destroy fat cells and thus affect permanent weight loss. Rats maintained the loss of 10% of their body weight for three months after being injected with these antibodies.

Galanin stimulates food consumption. An anti-galanin product may be in the works.

Glucagon Like Peptide 1 inhibits gastric emptying and limits food intake. It may be useful in the treatment of diabetics, but its effect on human weight loss is not yet known.

Grehlin released by the upper intestinal tract stimulates appetite; thus, an anti-grehlin appetite suppressing substance is being investigated.

H3 Histamine Antagonist enhances histamine release in the brain and suppresses food intake. However, this product was only shown to suppress appetite in animals.

Human Growth Hormone fragment may increase breakdown of fats and elevate resting energy expenditure. Preliminary studies done on animals are promising, but no research has been conducted on humans yet.

Human Steroidal Hormone may also cause the body to store less fat and produce more energy. This substance promoted weight loss and insulin sensitivity in obese animals. Studies are underway on obese and diabetic persons.

Leptin may regulate body fat and cause weight loss. Obese mice are leptin deficient, while most obese humans have high leptin levels in their serum, but have low levels in the central nervous system. Moderate weight loss is achieved in those patients who are responders, and who do not mind daily leptin injections.

Leptin Promoters are similar to leptin injections but in an oral formulation. These promoters do not circumvent leptin resistance in some patients.

Leptin Receptor: Some patients have speculated that leptin resistance may be due to inefficient transport of leptin across the blood-brain barrier. This product may prevent leptin resistance.

Lipase Inhibitors are similar to Xenical™ in that they prevent the absorption of fat.

Melanocortins are hormones that work with leptin and Neuropeptide Y to suppress the appetite. Neuropeptide Y elevation has been associated with obesity in rats. Studies are being done to determine whether melanocortins may work in obesity, diabetes and syndrome X.

Neuropeptide Y inhibitor may block Neuropeptide Y which signals the body to burn more sugar and less fat and to consume more foods. Rats injected with Neuropeptide Y inhibitor lost weight. However, because of elevations of liver enzymes, studies were halted. New derivatives of this substance are now being researched.

Serotonin 2c Receptor Agonists may produce weight loss. These products showed a small but significant reduction in body weight in a small group of obese patients by producing satiety. These agonists may work similarly to 5-HTP.

Tub Genes (genes that are associated with obesity) have been found in obese and diabetic mice who had normal food consumption.

Uncoupling Proteins (UCP) are heat-generating proteins that raise metabolism and burn white adipose fat, most commonly found in humans. There are three uncoupling proteins—UCP1, UCP2, and UCP3—that have been identified. These proteins waste calories by uncoupling them before they are converted into energy. Olive oil was the best oil to stimulate the uncoupling of these proteins.

According to Dr. Eric Ravussin from the National Institute of Diabetes, Digestive and Kidney Diseases, uncoupling proteins waste energy in the process called thermogenesis. By increasing UCP activity, one can boost metabolic rate. UCP1 is present in brown fat and, thus, is not applicable in humans. UCP2 is found in brain, muscle and fat cells, and UCP3 is mostly active in muscle cells. UCP3 is regulated by diet and hormones. Low UCP3 was found in hypothyroid rats and it has been suggested that UCP3 may explain the effects of thyroid hormones on thermogenesis. There is evidence now that a defect in UCP3 may also be associated with a slow metabolism and obesity. More research is needed to apply this knowledge to an obese population.

Leptin helps the production of this protein (also found in humans) and blocks Neuropeptide Y (potent appetite stimulant).

The insulin-blocking drug ***somatostatin*** helped patients lose weight after radiation (usually radiation to the head causes a weight gain of two pounds per month until adulthood). Whether somatostatin can help other obese patients lose weight would be interesting to investigate. Even though somatostatin treatment requires three injections daily, a new study using this drug will begin soon.

Table 7

SIGNALS THAT AFFECT EATING

Substance	Source	Appetite	Metablolism	Fat Storage
Bombesin	Gut	↓		
CCR	Gut	↓		
CRF		↓		
Glucocorticoids	Adrenal	↑		
Grehlin	Gut	↑		
Insulin	Pancreas	↑	↓	↑
Leptin	Fat cells	↓		↓
Orexin		↑		
Neuropeptide Y		↑	↓	↑
PPY	Gut	↓		

It is interesting to note that there are opposing hormones involved in satiety control. Bombesin, CCR, CRF, leptin and PPY decrease appetite while glucocorticoids, grehlin, insulin, orexin and neuropeptide Y all stimulate the appetite. When stress is significant, glucocorticoids prevail and CRF cannot exert its anti-eating effect.

According to Dr. S.C. Woods, et al., there are so many different signals involved with appetite that "finding a magic bullet for the treatment of obesity may be unrealistic." Interventions directed at multiple targets might be necessary to achieve and maintain weight loss.

Most of these hopeful medications either help with appetite control, with increasing basal metabolic rate or in preventing the absorption of certain foods.

Many years will be needed before tests are completed and medications are approved and implemented. However, obese patients should never lose hope, for doctors and scientists are at work on a possible solution to their problems.

Chapter Summary

- Over the counter appetite suppressants include phenyl-proprandamine and ephedrine combined with caffeine.

- For drug therapy, one should consult bariatricians who subscribe to the anorectic guidelines. Medications include phentermine, diethylpropion, phendimetrazine, Meridia™ and finally Xenical™.

- Antidepressant medications have also been added to appetite supressants to enhance their effect (Prozac™, Paxil™, Zoloft™, Wellbutrin™, Celexa™ and Lexapro™).

- New medications for appetite suppression and for burning potential are on the horizon.

— Chapter Sixteen —

OTHER UNUSUAL METHODS FOR WEIGHT LOSS

A *romatherapy*, especially aversion aromatherapy, has been used with some success for weight loss. In 1995, Hirsch and Gomez used pleasant sweet-smelling odors to create a feeling of well-being, calm, and weight loss. Recently, favorite high-calorie foods like pizza, cakes, candies, french fries, chips and cookies were purposely associated with noxious odors like pure skunk oil, in order to deter people from eating them. In a recent aversion experiment, subjects lost an average of three to five pounds in two to three months. Patients generally regained the weight after discontinuation of therapy.

Aversion Therapy has been used by many other experimenters. In its mildest degree, patients flock to doctors who hurl insults at them and criticize them if they don't lose weight. I have seen refugees from these programs come crying to my office after they were called ugly and fat by my predecessors. In a very masochistic way, some individuals need or crave these treatments. I have heard of physicians tearing favorite family pictures or heirlooms when their patients do not meet their weight goal expectations. I have even seen them send substantial amounts of money in checks written by the unsuccessful patients to their least favorite organizations (like the Ku Klux Klan, the National Rifle Association, Unrestricted Gun Possession supporters or Prolife groups).

My late mother used to go once a year for a check-up to this physician who scolded her because she was overweight. Of course, her blood pressure and her blood sugar remained high and she never did anything about her condition; but she felt better, almost cleansed, by receiving this verbal flagellation. Every year she felt she needed to go see this doctor to expiate her sins, the same way pious people turn to confession. This psychological cleansing lasted her the whole year.

Other more violent aversion techniques have been used to prevent patients from failing on their diets. Electric shock was used to treat obesity in the 1950s and 1960s. Even as recently as 1997, some doctors admitted to whipping some patients who strayed from their diet.

In his book *Scentsational Weight Loss*, Dr. Alan R. Hirsch describes "how *odors* may have a direct effect on the satiety center in the brain so that people become full faster. The brain may be fooled into thinking that if it smells the food, it does not need to eat it." Smelling the odors may become a substitute behavior to eating. Odors may also relieve anxiety and produce an increased sense of well-being. The three smells used by Dr. Hirsch were peppermint, banana and green apple. Test patients were told to sniff the odors three times into each nostril whenever they felt hungry. Those who were responders lost weight of about five pounds per month. But 25% of those tested had a smelling impairment and were non-responders and, therefore, were not successful with their weight reduction.

Other smells, like apple spice, nutmeg and vanilla, tend to reduce anxiety. Lavender causes a more relaxed state, while jasmine may increase alertness.

The preliminary studies done in our office using banana, green apple and peppermint sniffers were not successful with our group of patients. However, Dr. Hirsch is in the process of carrying on a big experiment with thousands of people to determine if odors can truly help control our appetite!

Hypnotherapy directed at reducing stress may help patients to lose a few pounds and maintain small weight loss, according to a study from the National Service Hospital in the United Kingdom. However, the total weight loss achieved was quite modest.

In her book on hypnosis, Dr. DeBetz described her success in treating overweight patients. I have tried this technique on my patients but have not found it particularly useful in my practice. Some patients are better candidates than others for hypnosis. The doctor's personality and beliefs in this procedure influence the ultimate outcome.

Patches have also been used for weight control purposes, just as patches are used to deliver transdermal medications like hormones, anti-seasickness medication and nitroglycerin. Diet patches contain an iodine-containing herb called fucus or bladder wrack which may stimulate the thyroid to promote weight loss. There is no evidence that these patches work and iodine supplementation may be dangerous to some patients if not needed.

Bariatric Surgery is reserved for the morbidly obese patient with a BMI of 40 who has failed all other attempts to lose weight. Of course, any surgery has the possibility of complications or side effects. Without going into excruciating details on the surgical procedures, suffice to say there are two main purposes in bariatric surgery. One technique consists of stapling the stomach to create a smaller pouch to shrink the capacity of this organ. A feeling of fullness is thereby achieved with less food. A balloon inserted into the stomach also achieves the same principle of artificial fullness. These techniques work temporarily as the stomach pouch may enlarge over time and more food can then be ingested by the patient. The balloon technique may on occasion strangulate the stomach, requiring a second emergency surgery.

The second surgical technique involves avoiding the ileum, a part of the colon where absorption of food occurs. Patients eat as much, but food is eliminated in the stool. Also, the dumping syndrome (severe diarrhea) may occur after meals. Besides not absorbing their nutrients, these people suffer from vitamin and mineral malabsorption (most dangerously potassium deficiency). Some vitamins like B12 must be supplemented through injections and a follow-up with a health professional well versed in these problems is a necessity.

However, some patients may achieve success with any of the surgical procedures described above. Gastric bypass surgery has been shown to decrease the risk of dying from diabetes by 78% in the morbidly obese. Type II diabetics respond well to this procedure.

Weight loss surgery causes an average weight loss of 18% of body weight compared to 11% with diet and drugs, 7% with diet alone or diet and group education, according to a study analyzing six years of data from an obesity program in Madrid, Spain.

While patients who underwent Vertical Banded Gastroplasty lost

87% of their excess weight after six months, those who were given Laparoscopic Adjustable Gastric Banding lost 50% of their weight. Another study showed that, after a year, the patients who underwent laparoscopic gastric banding lost 50% of their weight; after two years there was a loss of 62%; and after four years of 68%.

Some other anecdotal techniques used in the past include jaw wiring, devised by Dr. Garrod in England. Patients could consume thin foods through a straw only. However, weight regain was the norm as soon as the jaw wiring was removed. In addition, acupuncture, ear devices, belts, thermal wraps and finally sweat booths have not been proven to provide reliable weight loss.

Even though some studies showed that ear acupuncture helped in weight loss, this technique was also combined with diet and exercise. A review of four trials using acupuncture showed no effect on body weight.

Cellulite Treatment constitutes one of the most sought-after therapy. Women, especially, are plagued with these dimpled fat deposits in the thigh and buttock areas (in the pear shaped obesity). Men suffer more from the abdominal cellulite or fat deposit in the true apple fashion. No matter how much or how hard these people exercise or diet, these saddlebags do not disappear. Herbal wraps, creams, pills and finally surgery were tried for these stubborn spots. Sweat booths were first devised to make patients lose these extra fat deposits. However, the ladies only lost fluid which was regained the minute they started drinking water. Herbal wraps also have been used with not too much success. Concoctions of vitamins, minerals, mud and algae from the sea have not been efficacious either.

A few years ago, a combination of caffeine and theophylline (an asthma medication) was shown to decrease these unwanted fat deposits in the stomachs, thighs and buttocks of women. The so-called "thigh creams" were manufactured by all pharmaceutical companies. We found some patients to be better responders than others, and fantastic results were achieved by some. The problem of this treatment is that continuous therapy is needed to conserve results.

A new pill, Cellasene, has been touted as a cellulite fighter. This medication only contains essential fatty oils (like borage and fish oils), herbal products like gingko biloba, sweet clover, grape seed extract and bladder wrack. Cellasene may be harmful, as it contains iodine from bladder wrack; it may also increase bleeding in patients taking aspirin or warfarin due to the sweet clover and ginkgo biloba. The cellulite-melting effect of this product is quite doubtful. Cellasene is supposed to increase blood flow to the skin of the thigh area. While an Italian study showed a reduction of thigh size in 40 women, the data has not yet been published.

Endermologie and Silk Light are massage treatments that use devices resembling vacuum cleaners to run over the cellullite-ridden areas. Many applications are needed to show a very modest improvement. However, both procedures have earned the FDA approval for better appearance of cellulite. According to Dr. Harold J. Brody, "The potential benefit is not worth the effort or the money."

The most effective cellulite-attacking technique is liposuction, where fat is sucked out from the most objectionable areas of the body. A low-fat diet is the key to preventing recurrence of the same problem later. Liposuction is not innocuous, and complications— even death— may occur.

In Brazil, the dimpling of the cellulite is improved by silicone injections. There are two products that have received a lot of attention, especially among athletes who seek a larger musculature.

A study performed by Dr. Morton Maxwell using a minimum of 15 grams of *pyruvate* in combination with dihydroacetone (which converts itself to pyruvate in the body) was shown to have some beneficial effect on weight loss and muscle enhancement. The few human trials have used 19-44 grams of pyruvate to achieve weight reduction and muscle mass increase. The product sold in health food stores contains only six grams of this substance. Though no benefit can be derived from this small dose, some anecdotal evidence exists that even six grams of pyruvate may be helpful.

Creatinine Powder has been embraced by athletes seeking to enlarge their muscle mass. Eight weeks of creatinine supplementation (5.4 grams plus 33 grams of carbohydrate) improved exercise performance in 24 college football players. A recent study showed benefits in patients with neuromuscular disease who took 10 grams of creatinine monohydrate for five days, followed by another five days of 5 grams of this substance.

Creatinine, an amino acid derivative present in meat and fish, was reviewed in the *Medical Letter.* In one short-term study, use of creatinine increased body mass primarily through increased water retention. A summary of 31 studies of short, high intensity tasks suggested that oral creatinine modestly improved performance. These positive findings were only found in the laboratory, not in the actual field.

Androstenedione, a precursor of estrone and testosterone, may enhance testosterone formation, but the effect of muscle mass increase remains to be established. Androstenedione may have similarly adverse effects as testosterone and its use has been banned by many athletic organizations.

Plastic containers contain a compound called *Biphenol (BPA)* which may make us fat. BPA may mimic natural estrogens. A study done in mice showed that these animals weighed more when their mothers were exposed to this substance. In humans, the amount studied would be similar to normal exposure of dental sealants and to food in plastic lined cans. These results were presented by Dr. F.S. Vom Saal, et al. on the subject of "Estrogens in the Environment." Even though no human studies have been done, I would feel more comfortable taking my milk from a cardboard carton than from a plastic jug.

There are some drugs that may stimulate weight gain or water retention. *Hormones*, like estrogens, especially the synthetic ones, may increase weight in the breasts and in the middle areas of the female bodies.

Insulin increases weight by a dual mechanism: it increases appetite, but it also stimulates fat storage via lipoprotein lipase.

Other oral medications for diabetes, like the *sulfonylureas*, may also stimulate weight gain, probably by increasing appetite when blood sugar becomes too low. They have been given to patients for intentional weight gain.

Cortisone also increases appetite and makes patients retain water.

Antidepressant medications may also make patients gain weight. Elavil™ is very notorious in stimulating appetite. Patients have gained significant weight while on this medication. The SSRI's (like Prozac™, Paxil™, or Zoloft™) have a weight reduction effect for the first four months. Subsequently, patients gain weight after prolonged administration. The only antidepressant which does not increase weight after continuous use is Wellbutrin™.

*Gabentin (*or *Neurontin™)* has also been associated with weight gain in many patients.

Valproic Acid (an anti-seizure medication) has been shown to cause obesity in 50% of female patients. Weight gain may be progressive and associated with high insulin levels; this in turn may lead to higher male hormones levels and polycystic ovaries.

Zyprexa, an anti-psychotic medication, has deleterious effects on weight.

Finally, there are some medications called protease inhibitors, used in AIDS patients, that have the same effect on body type as the aging process. The patients have a shift of fat towards the center, while the extremities remain emaciated. They are called "Buffalo humps" and "protease paunches." Another description by doctors is "apples on a stick." These protease inhibitors raise blood sugar and cholesterol levels. Dr. Gabriel Torres helped one patient to lose his hump with human growth hormone injections. An interesting finding would be to isolate the product responsible for this selective weight gain and find its antagonist.

There are patients who are at a normal weight but who already have the symptoms of the obese: hypertension, high lipids in the blood, hyperglycemia and insulin resistance. They are metabolically obese but normal weight individuals. These patients also need to be treated, as these diseases have dire consequences. Treatment includes diet, exercise and pharmacotherapy.

Lots of unknowns plague the field of obesity study, and more research and trials are needed to uncover all these clues. Hopefully, in doing so, more knowledge will be gathered to treat our very large and complex obese population.

Chapter Summary

- Many drugs can increase weight gain.

— Chapter Seventeen —

BEHAVIOR MODIFICATION

T hrough behavior modification, health professionals work with
   patients to change and manipulate personal habits in order to
achieve a common goal which, in this case, is weight loss. A partner-
ship is thus formed between the physician or health-related professional (nutritionist, dietitian, behaviorist, psychologist or nurse) and
the patient.

According to *Obesity Research Update* of July 1998, behavioral
therapy causes 10% weight loss after 4 to 12 months (which is double
the amount needed to change the comorbidities of obesity).

No one specific therapy is superior to another. The more frequent
the visits and the longer the visits with the health professional, the
greater the weight loss. Extended therapy for one-and-a-half years is
more successful than therapy lasting for five to nine months.

Weight regain occurs more often without continued behavioral
intervention. Combining behavior therapy with other weight loss
measures maintains the weight loss for up to one year. After three to
five years, those benefits are lost if no continued behavior modification is used. Motivation is the key to successful weight loss. Self monitoring is crucial for successful weight loss.

John Foreyt Ph.D., director of the Behavioral Medicine Research
Center at Baylor College of Medicine in Houston, recommends keeping a *food diary* to break the diet-binge seesaw. Patients should be
taught to keep a diary of their eating behavior and exercise regime.
The food diary should also include when foods were eaten and what
triggered an overeating behavior. The mood or the emotions at the time

of those high-caloric food intakes may also be recorded for further discussion. Exercise type, intensity and length can be added to this weekly diary sheet. Some individuals are given one-week diet diaries, while others are given two weeks worth. We may give a maximum of four weeks of diet diaries. When people go away on a trip or for the summer, we recommend that they fax us their food and exercise diary with their weight recorded each week.

Although most individuals do not always record the information accurately, the point is to make the person aware of his/her obesity-related activities. Consistently, research has shown that self-monitoring improves outcome. Patients report self-monitoring as one of the most helpful tools in controlling weight. *Obesity Research Update* claims: "Lose more by writing it down."

Weight should only be checked once a week in the morning after getting up from bed with no clothes and on an empty bladder. Some people are devastated when they gain even one pound a week. There are many reasons for this possible increase and the plateau curve should be looked at again. It is normal to gain sometimes as long as the general weight curve is downward.

Menstruation Time is often associated with a weight gain of two pounds. *Constipation* may also be responsible for one pound of weight gain, and water retention from a salty meal can cause a two pound weight increase. Exercising adults also may gain muscle mass which weighs one-and-a-half times as much as fat. If this occurs, take your measurements at three places: bust circumference, waist and hip measurements. If these have improved, then you are definitely doing something positive for yourself and should disregard this fluctuation of weight. Look also at Figure 5 (see pg. 69) which shows that actual weight is less important than measurements.

THE IMPORTANCE OF SELF-MONITORING:

Weight recording has always amazed me; patients record their weight on a board in the hallway and change it every week. Often patients will return to the office to change the weight on the board, even though they are almost a half an hour away from our office. We also make our patients look at themselves every week in the "skinny mirror" (a mirror designed to make them look 20% thinner). Patients love to primp in front of this mirror and condition their brain to a thinner image.

It is important that the overweight patient keep an accurate report of their diet diary on a weekly, twice monthly, or monthly basis. These should be discussed with a health professional. One can review foods they have eaten and realize a previously unrecognized behavior or a pattern to overeating. Cravings also can be met with the appropriate treatment using the neurotransmitter precursors.

We teach our patients *cognitive therapy* to help them to understand what is causing their dieting woes! We make them fill out questionnaires which ask:

— Is it in your head or is it in your stomach where you are hungry?

— Do you eat whenever you are depressed?

— Do you eat when you are anxious?

— Do you consume more food whenever you feel insecure or angry?

—Does a fight with your mother, spouse or best friend trigger off a feeding frenzy in you?

Emotional overeating is extremely prevalent among the obese. We can only treat weight if we know what is in our minds! Understanding the triggers for our overeating is half the battle of the bulge!

Stimulus Control is very important for certain patients. The most quoted example is from the patient who knows that they always buy a pastry when they pass a certain bakery. The obvious solution is to take an alternate route.

However, my patients tell me that even if they bypass the bakery, they still may go out after dinner and buy some sweets at a 24-hour convenience store. Stimulus control may be helpful, but sometimes the "craving brain" shows its ugly head; then only neurotransmitter precursors or pharmocotherapy will do.

FOOD SHOPPING:

The list below is our recommended "Staples to Have at Home" list. (see List 1)

List 1

STAPLES TO HAVE AT HOME:

Entrées:	1. Egg substitutes that can be frozen or refrigerated and used as needed.
	2. Canned tuna, chicken or sardines (all in water).
	3. Deli style chicken or turkey slices to eat as needed (low sodium preferred).
	4. Ready to eat, roasted, skinned and boneless chicken breasts.
	5. Ground turkey with as little fat as possible.
	6. Fat-free, low-sodium soups or broths, either canned or in packets to reconstitute as needed.
	7. Fat-free or low-fat cheeses.
	8. Shrimp, lobster or imitation crab meat (surimi).
Vegetables:	1. Frozen vegetables including: chopped spinach, broccoli, cauliflower, green beans, squash, asparagus, carrots and kale, etc.
	2. Canned vegetables such as green beans, kidney or navy beans, peas, black beans, garbanzo beans, corn, chopped tomatoes, tomato sauce, mushrooms, roasted peppers, artichoke and eggplant already marinated. (Always look for the low-sodium variety.)

      3. Pre-washed greens in a bag and any other salad material preferred.

Condiments:
1. Fat-free parmesan cheese.

2. Extra-virgin olive and canola oil in an opaque container.

3. Low-sodium soy sauce.

4. Lemon juice and balsamic vinegar.

5. All kinds of spices like dried herbs (parsley, oregano, dill) or garlic powder (not the salt), ground pepper and paprika.

6. Fat-free mayonnaise and mustard.

7. Ketchup and red sauce for seafood.

8. Coffee, tea, skim milk, sweeteners, fat-free hot cocoa.

Desserts:
1. Nutritional supplements may be made as dessert (they are also high in protein).

2. Nutritional bars (also high in protein).

3. Sugar-free Jell-O.

4. Fat-free, low-sugar puddings.

5. Frozen mixed berries or individual bags of different berries, depending upon preference.

6. One sponge or angel food cake (keep it frozen until needed).

7. A box of fat-free cookies—only for emergencies.

Prepare a list for shopping and find a buddy to accompany you to shop. Never buy on an impulse and never go to the store hungry. Use preventative medicine: eat something before you leave the house. Give yourself only half an hour in the store and do not meander in the aisles which may offer temptation. Whatever you forgot to buy, wait another week to purchase it. Shopping too often for food stimulates buying more items than are needed.

Only buy enough for the week; do not buy too much perishable produce that needs to be eaten before it spoils. I repeat again: "You are not a garbage can!"

Introduce different colors in your diet; frozen and canned foods are permissible, as they last longer. Bulky foods like salads and vegetables or even fruit are more filling than pretzels and fat-free cookies. Avoid processed foods, sweets and bingeing foods. Know what foods you cannot resist and give them away as soon as you receive them as gifts. Chocolates are always a problem food for the dieter!

Many times patients have confessed to eating a whole box of cookies that they found miraculously in their cupboard. These foods needed to be purchased, brought to the house, and put away by this person. Those craving foods did not just climb from the supermarket shelves into the shopping cart drive themselves to the house and then hoist themselves into the cupboard!

Non-dieting support persons should only buy allowable staples for the house. No exceptions are permitted for other members of the family. No inappropriate temptations for the dieter to find should be left in the house.

HOME COOKING:

Cooking should be simple and uncomplicated; the less the dieter is in the kitchen, the better. We recommend the dieter to eat slowly in order to fully savor the flavor of the foods. The non-dieting partner could prepare the nutritional supplements for the person who is on a weight-reduction program. The same person could clean up and wash the dishes to prevent leftovers from ending up in our dieter's stomach.

If a crisis occurs, let the parent or partner find the sheet with the neurotransmitters and help the dieter with the right supplementation. When women have inflexible partners, they have to make several meals: one for the husbands, one for the children, and a healthy alternate for themselves.

Women who are also working are often too tired to make all of these meal preparations and, therefore, they often succumb to take-out or prepared foods for the sake of simplicity. This is the reason why staples purchased at the store are so important in weight control. Once a week, for instance on Sunday, healthy foods can be prepared or frozen to be re-heated during the week.

Intelligent Food Selections can happen anywhere! In addition to support from family members and friends, it is also essential for one to learn when problem times arise (refer to Questionnaire No.1 on pg. 85) and to be prepared to handle them. Good snacks and activities should be planned at the time when problems occur, usually in the afternoon or after dinner.

Distraction and *delay* tactics can do wonders in postponing cravings which generally only last a maximum of 15 minutes. Set the table, put a pretty mat on it, get a nice dish, wipe the silverware and the glass. Cut the food into little bites. By that time, you have forgotten your need to have the desired food.

The dieter should only eat in the designated areas of eating: the kitchen or dining room. You may eat with your family but you should fill your plate with food that is served directly from the stove or microwave and not from food that is available in serving plates on the table. Have a salad to start and fill your plate with one-half vegetables and one-half lean protein. Do not place the serving bowls on the table or you may be tempted to help yourself to second or third helpings.

Hot soup constitutes a wonderful comfort food: use a tomato base and add as many vegetables as you have available. Keep it ready always whenever you are hungry. For some reason, soup appears to have a unique ability to quell hunger by being psychologically satisfying. Even though soup contains the same calories as cantaloupe, people prefer soup. Good choices are tomato, vegetable, minestrone, onion soup (without cheese) and fat-free consommé.

If you are a night eater or a television watcher, bring out just one snack or a cup of hot tea, hot cocoa or coffee into the living room or bedroom. Leave dirty dishes until the next morning. Do not return to the kitchen.

Unfortunately, television watching has been linked to childhood and even adulthood obesity. Children who watched four hours or more of television daily had a greater body mass index than children who watched two hours a day, according to a new study by researchers at the Johns Hopkins University School of Medicine.

A decrease in television watching and eating between meals was associated with a weight loss of 3.1 pounds in middle-aged men compared to a weight gain of 3.1 pounds for others. This study encompassed almost 20,000 middle-aged male health professionals during a four year hiatus.

In a study published in the *American Journal of Public Health* in February, 1998, the fatter men and women watched the most television. For each hour of television watching, half a pound of weight gain could be expected in high-income women.

Television watching at home stimulates the most snacking, especially night eating. People should not be hungry at this time, as they just had a big meal. Yet this is an association, a learned behavior, almost a reflex to grab for food during the commercial breaks.

SNACKING:

"Snack often, at least every four to five hours," says Terrie Brownlie MPH, RD, the director of Nutrition at Duke University Diet and Fitness Center. We teach our patients to keep the fireplace burning by putting low fat, high protein logs every three to four hours. We also recommend a snack in the afternoon (when our blood sugar dips) to prevent ravenous hunger at dinner time.

The most commonly snacked foods at night are ice cream, cookies, chocolate, popcorn, pretzels, chips, nuts and beer.

Very rarely do individuals consume natural fruit; but they must be aware that dried fruit like raisins, apricots and dates are high in calories and too sweet. Nuts in excess may also increase calories. We recommend cutting fruit into small pieces and savoring each morsel, one at a time. All kinds of berries are permitted and most fruits are allowed in moderation except grapes, watermelon, cherries and bananas which contain too much sugar.

Another tactic is to keep an icy bowl of water in the refrigerator into which you can add cut pieces of vegetables like broccoli, cauliflower, carrots and celery, the night before. These crispy crudités are wonderful and healthy for snacking. Healthy energy bars can also be kept frozen, with only one brought out and cut into very small bites to consume slowly.

Chocolate is another craving food, especially at night and during PMS attacks. One effective aversion technique is to read about how disgustingly chocolate is made (see Letter 3 on next page).

Letter 3

CHOCOLATE ANYONE?
From Dr. Tom Cooper

"Almost everyone with a weight problem has a chocolate problem, too. It seems that candy bars don't grow on trees after all! Over half of the chocolate we consume comes from Cacao trees found in West African countries like Ghana, Nigeria, Ivory Coast and Cameroon. The Cacao tree grows in a lush tropical environment that has a number of fungi and insects which are enemies to this plant. It is necessary to spray the trees with a number of control chemicals, including organic and potentially toxic fungicides that may remain in small amounts in the harvested cacao beans.

• The Cacao trees produce a certain number of seed pods each year. These pods are harvested, and the cacao beans are removed manually by local indigenous people. They are then spread out on the jungle floor and allowed to ferment (a nice way to say rot) for five to six days in the jungle heat and humidity. There is nothing to keep insects and small animals from nesting and feeding among the beans while they are exposed to the elements. It is common to find animal droppings, dead insects, and animal hairs in this fermenting collection of cacao beans.

• After they have stayed like this for the required period of time, they are packed in jute or plastic bags and stored in harbor warehouses until it is time to load them into the holds of ships for transportation to this country. In the warehouses and the ship holds, they are again subjected to the ravages of resident rodents and insects. The Cacao bean is a rich source of fats and carbohydrates and is relished by both kinds of pests.

• The resulting mixture of cacao beans, insect fragments, rodent droppings, leaves and rat hairs is unloaded in this country and is taken to one or another of the various chocolate processing factories. A conscientious effort is made by these companies to remove as many of these contaminants as they possibly can, but the thousands of tons of raw material processed each month make properly cleaning the raw commodity a virtual impossibility.

- To quote the FDA manual: 'The action levels are set because it is not now possible, and never has been possible, to grow in open fields, harvest, and process crops that are totally free of natural defects.' You can translate natural defects into hairs, insect fragments and animal waste. There is, and I know you will be comforted to know this, a level of contamination at which the FDA will seize a product and not let it be sold.

- If 100 grams (about three ounces) of chocolate exceeds an average of 60 microscopic insect fragments or one rodent hair, when six similar samples are analyzed, or if any one sample contains more than 90 insect fragments or three rodent hairs, then this sample will be rejected by the FDA.

- Animal waste is normally the color of chocolate and cannot be tested for with any great accuracy. Nobody is hurt by this contamination, since the hairs and insect fragments are partly protein, but the aesthetic aspect of chocolate with all this possible filth mixed in may make you less likely to eat it. When you bite into a candy bar, the crunch may not come from peanuts, but from something else."

A little piece of dark chocolate is satisfying; a dozen low-fat frozen semi-sweet chocolate chips may do the trick of assuaging the chocolate craving. A cup of diet hot cocoa can eliminate the chocolate desire. Also, only dark chocolate has antioxidants called polyphenols that may allay heart disease.

Only a few words will be mentioned now about exercise, because a later chapter will focus on the subject exclusively. Exercise may be a wonderful distraction for the snacker. Exercise can also be a family affair as misery loves company and overweight people may dislike exercise. A walk, a dance with one's spouse or a bowling night may be suggested to the dieter when he or she seems to falter.

Eating Out is the dieter's nemesis. Often, I am told by my patients they can control their eating at home; however, all hell breaks loose when they go out to eat.

Restaurant Eating can be tamed with prevention. Do not go hungry to a restaurant. Have a healthy snack prior to going out. In the old days, mothers gave their daughters a snack prior to going to the ball so that they would appear to be dainty eaters. Take your fiber pill or your neurotransmitter precursor medication. Try to pick the restaurant in advance and call to order from your house. The best bets are fish places or continental cuisine.

In my opinion, however, any restaurant anywhere can make a healthy meal that you may have. Make the waiter your friend; ask about the specials and about substitutions. Whenever I go to a restaurant, I ask the waiter what is broiled without fat. Also, substitute the starch with vegetables.

An important rule is to know what you are going to order in advance. Do not be swayed by what other people are eating in the neighboring tables, especially if they themselves are rotund. Stick to your plan, and even better, be the first one to order. I am always amazed when I take the lead in the ordering circle; once I start, most of my dinner companions follow suit with my order. If you do not especially care for any entrée on the menu, you may make a meal from two appetizers. I brainwash myself and my patients into thinking that food is not that important.

Generally, buffets are meant for overeating and should be avoided. On cruises, those buffets enlarge people's waists in no time. And try to forget about any midnight buffets!

Alcohol is caloric and may remove the inhibitions of the dieter. Only one glass of wine or preferably a spritzer is recommended. Do not allow the waiter to pour more than one glass of wine. And as explained in Chapter 14, have the chips, crackers or bread removed from the table as soon as possible. You may order a diet drink and a salad right away. If the food is not prepared the healthy way you want it, politely return it; do not settle for fatty or salty food!

A few tests will determine how healthy your food may be:

• *The Crunchy Test:* Anything that is crunchy or crispy in your mouth may be fried; do not eat it and return what is left immediately!

• *The Shiny Test:* Whenever you touch a food, and your fingers look shiny, there is obviously too much fat in it. Whenever the food is swimming in fat and you have requested it dry, you may have another option besides returning the item: you can ask for several paper napkins and squeeze your entree on them. Better for your napkin, and not for your stomach, to receive the extra fat!

Desserts provide a red flag to our dieters. Some patients are wonderful throughout their meals; but as soon as dessert time rolls around, they cannot resist their favorite sweet which they consume with coffee or tea and, ironically, artificial sweetener.

I recommend ordering one dessert for the table and passing it around so that everyone has a chance to taste a small amount of this forbidden concoction.

Another tactic is to order a plate of berries or fruit. Sherbet or sorbet constitutes yet another possibility. American dessert is famous only for its pies. I personally love apple pies. The best tactic here is to eat the fruit and to leave the crust, which is full of fat, untouched. Fat-free desserts are plentiful. People eat them in great quantities without realizing that they are still quite caloric!

As portions in restaurants are getting larger and larger, it is a good idea to cut the food in half and to request a "doggie bag" for future consumption the next day. Some patients may not do well with "doggie bags," however, as there are some who consume them on their way home or when they arrive home!

We have provided a general recommended list of what to eat in restaurants (see List 2).

List 2

RECOMMENDED RESTAURANT EATING:

- Be assertive, do not eat the food that is on your plate if it is not the way you asked for it. Return your food until it is right.

- Be the first one to order so as not to be swayed by other people.

- Dressings and sauces should be ordered on the side.

- Ask about food preparations and substitute more vegetables for the starches.

- Ask for the protein dishes to be grilled or baked instead of fried or sautéed.

Sample Choices For Different Menus In Different Restaurants:

Breakfast: egg white or egg substitute omelet (may contain vegetables), fat-free or low-fat cottage cheese, fat-free cheese, high-protein and low-fat cereals with skim milk.

Lunch: salad with a protein, fat-free or low-fat dressing, grilled chicken breast, turkey, or fish on salad.

Dinner: seafood appetizer, dinner salad with fat-free or low-fat dressing, grilled, boiled, broiled, or baked protein with as little fat as possible. Eat as many vegetables as possible, try to limit the starch. If you need an alcoholic beverage try a spritzer (a little wine and a lot of carbonated water).

Traveling tip: Call the airline two days in advance and order a special low-fat meal.

List 3

ETHNIC RESTAURANT EATING:

American   Grilled meats, salad and vegetables, fruit cup.

Chinese   Shrimp, chicken or vegetable chop suey-type dishes are
the best choices. Miso soup or vegetable soups are also
good choices. Limit rice and avoid fried rice and egg
drop soup.

Cuban   Salad, "palomillo" steak grilled, broiled chicken, eye
round slices or "ropa vieja," limit rice, beans and
plantains.

French   Steamed mussels (no butter) or shrimp appetizer to start,
salad with dressing on the side. Bordelaise sauce (wine
sauce) is better than Hollandaise or Béchamel (these
are more fatty); the best choice is poached filet of sole.

Greek   Shish kabob, Greek salad, "Tzatsiki", and "Plaki" are
healthy choices. Avoid lamb, phyllo dough, caviar and
babaganoush dishes.

Italian   Chicken or fish cacciatore style (red sauce), marinara or
marsala sauces on veal or chicken or turkey are better
choices. Avoid Alfredo sauce (full of butter and cream) or
scallopini (buttery) or parmigian (cheesy).

Japanese   Vegetable soup, and pickled vegetables are good choices.
Sashimi, sushi, nabemono, teriyaki (chicken and shrimp),
tofu, and miso soup are encouraged. Tempura (fried) or
soy sauce (salty) should be avoided. Request light soy
sauce if you must use it.

Steakhouse Leaner cuts of meats should be requested; like London
broil, lean ground round or eye round slices. If no
vegetables are served, have just half a baked potato and
avoid french fries.

Fast Food Chicken breasts grilled on salad with fat-free dressing,
yogurt or fruit dish if possible.

Should you dine alone or in the company of others?

There is some controversy about that. According to Dr. Barbara Rolls, Nutrition Professor at Pennsylvania State University in University Park: "When female friends get together for a meal, they consume about 50% more calories than when they dine alone." We may be letting our inhibitions down when we are among friends. Dr. Rolls noticed that the excess calories in this instance came from desserts. She recommends skipping dessert or ordering fruit instead.

On the other hand, Deborah Kesten, MPH, author of *Feeding The Body, Nourishing The Soul* (Conari Press 1997), recommends eating with others as often as possible. According to her research, social interaction enhances our lives and may even strengthen our immune systems.

School Lunches are also quite caloric and laden with fat calories. I prefer my young patients to bring their own lunches which should consist of turkey, tuna, fat-free cheeses with vegetables (these can go inside a pita bread pocket) accompanied by a healthy bar and/or a fruit. Fat-free yogurt or pudding may be other alternatives.

Office Lunches are also best if they are brown-bagged, as better control is achieved this way. A big salad with a lean protein should be brought to the workplace. If going out for lunch is desired, then the same format discussed previously when going to a restaurant is recommended. Mid-day eating should be devoid of carbohydrates which are more sedating and sleep inducing. A lean protein at lunchtime might keep you more alert.

Fancy Foods: I was once asked by the dean of a major medical school to write a book about the best choices to eat when one is offered fancy fare. "Daisy, which is the lesser of two possible evils?" he asked. This gentlemen travels a lot and, of course, he is wined and dined wherever he goes. He further prodded, "Is it better for me to have the Duck à l'Orange or the Filet Mignon?"

Portion sizes and food preparation vary tremendously according to the restaurant; however, I would recommend having the duck well-done as the better option. I would then scrape off the sauce and eat only the breast. The duck does not need to be finished! If he had a special desire for the filet, he could divide it and have only half of the portion. I always recommend a fish entrée, even in fancy restaurants. One can request a broiled, poached or grilled piece of fish; sauce should be added on the side. If the sauce is already there, scrape off as much as you can or blot the piece of protein on a paper napkin (and place ithe oily napkin on the butter dish, where it belongs!).

Bad Appetizers: Caviar, foie gras and patés are high-fat, caloric appetizers. Every restaurant can always provide a good healthy salad. Croutons and bleu cheese pieces can always be left uneaten. In addition, instead of fried foods or starches, one can always request a double order of vegetables.

Good Main Courses, Bad Main Courses: For main courses, here are a few rules to keep in mind: veal marsala is better than veal scaloppini. Veal paillard is better than the veal chop. Chicken cacciatore is better than osso bucco. Marinara (red sauce) is better than Alfredo (white sauce). Livornese or puttanesca sauces contain tomato sauce and are less caloric. A sprinkling of parmesan cheese is better than Parmigian sauce. Finally, sautéed is better than fried. Now armed with all this new knowledge, you can lose weight at the fanciest restaurants.

Afternoon or after-lunch cravings are very common in people whose blood sugar plummets. When this happens, bowls filled with sweets at the workplace attract too many hands in the afternoons. Have your own healthy snacks stashed in your drawer and do not even look in the direction of the unhealthy office candy bowl.

Vending machines flash their tempting presence every afternoon. One snack may follow another, as the cravings increase "crescendo" style. This is another reason why bringing your own snacks is important and will save you from these dieter's disasters!

PARTIES:

Going to eat at somebody's house presents a great challenge to the dieter. Bringing along a contribution of a low-calorie dish of vegetables, salad, crudités or even a plate of grilled chicken breasts will ensure that you have something healthy to eat.

Help the hostess serve the hors d'oeuvres and minimize temptation by keeping one hand occupied with the passing tray, while the other hand holds the napkins. Help with the serving and cutting at the buffet table. Sit down at the end of the table near the kitchen to allow you to get up often. (The more often you are getting up to help, the less time you have to nibble and over-eat!) Fill your plate with salad, vegetables and a little meat. Pass up second helpings. Chew your food slowly and focus on being scintillating company and honing your witty conversation. Be sure to tell a few great stories. Do whatever it takes to minimize your eating time. And do not finish the food on your plate in order to prevent second helpings from being piled high on your dish. Just because the foods are being placed on your plate does not mean you must eat these second portions that you don't want or need! When dessert arrives, firmly state that you have no more room to eat, "not even another bite!" Profusely thank the host or hostess for the food prepared and ask for recipes, even though you might not have cared for the food. It will distract the hostess from noticing your non-empty plate!

Be the first to clear the table and dishes and to bring them to the kitchen. Help with dishes and with coffee or tea service. Do anything to distract you from eating!

HOLIDAY PARTIES:

At your house:

Keep low-calorie foods at your house, substitute recipes to decrease fat, and sugar; use egg whites, cocoa instead of chocolate, and artificial sweeteners for your baking. Be creative, but do not obsess about food! Remember, presentation of the food is very important. Have as many colors of foods as possible. If sauce is required, serve it on the side. If you are the host, you will be so busy serving everybody else that you will probably eat only after everybody leaves. Do not keep leftovers in the house! After the meal, prepare a whole stack of paper plates and have the guests help themselves to their favorite foods. Cover them with foil and have your guests take their individual goodie bags home with them! If you still have leftovers, take some the next day to the office to treat colleagues and staff. Desserts left in the house will call out your name until they are completely consumed.

At somebody else's house:

If you are a woman, wear a purse on one arm and hold a diet drink in the other hand, so that you have no empty hand for eating. Again, use your conversational skills to the best of your abilities. Tell stories, jokes, keep your mouth full with gum. Peppermint gum may make you feel more awake and alert, according to Dr. Alan Hirsch. Turn your back to the buffet and be the last to serve yourself. Survey the whole table before you put even one morsel in your mouth; you may find better, healthier food choices at another corner of the room!

List 4

HOLIDAY EATING: UNDER CONTROL

Here are some tips on controlling your weight during the holidays. Remember that this is not the last time you will be offered a serving of dressing or gravy. Life is full of upcoming holidays, and your goal is to keep yourself healthy for the many others to come.

- Plan ahead, have a variety of low-fat foods available in the house.

- Don't deprive yourself of special holiday foods that you like. Deprivation can result in self-pity that may cause you to dump your efforts to control holiday calorie intake and eat more. Instead, remind yourself that moderation is the key to success.

- Don't skip meals—especially breakfast.

- Don't use the holidays as an excuse to bring all sorts of high calorie foods into the house. Bring in treats only for special occasions and decide in advance what you will eat at holiday gatherings.

- If baking has always been a part of the holidays for you and your family, continue the tradition, but plan to give the leftover baked goods as gifts. Keep them wrapped in foil and in the freezer until gift giving time so you won't be tempted to sample. Use less sugar in your recipes and add artificial sweeteners in your baking.

- Enjoy holiday meals, but make them in a lighter way. Try steamed vegetables instead of heavy casseroles, crisp vegetables instead of limp ones smothered in cheese sauces, string beans, brussel sprouts, or broccoli with pearl onions.

- Avoid high-fat dairy products. Make dips and sauces by blender-izing low fat cottage cheese. Use low fat or skim milk in holiday recipes.

- Use egg whites. Two egg whites can replace one whole egg in many recipes.

- Don't baste the turkey. Place it breast down on a rack and let it baste in its own juices for a moist, tender result.

- Don't eat the turkey skin. Turkey skin contributes to one-third of the fat in a typical serving of turkey. The breast has fewer calories and less fat than dark meat.

- De-fat drippings before preparing gravy. First put them in the refrig-erator and then remove the hardened fat that collects on the top.

- Eat a low-calorie snack before a party to enable you to face party fare without feeling ravenous. Have a protein supplement, a low-fat soup, coffee, tea or hot cocoa (no cream soups). You may also have turkey, chicken or fat-free cheese slices. Seafood and crunchy vegetables are another option.

- When you get to the party, instead of a mixed drink, try a wine spritzer (one-third wine and two-thirds sparkling water or club soda) or, better yet, a club soda with a twist of lime. Alcohol stimulates appetite and overeating. Even one to two drinks can lower blood sugar and increase hunger, not to mention the high calorie content of the alcohol and the mixer!

- Take smaller portions: choose a small salad plate; you can always go back for more.

- Don't be first in the buffet line; start eating later but finish when everyone else does. Promise yourself that you will make only one trip to the food table.

- Eat slowly: taste your food, chew slowly, eat one-half of the food on your plate, then take a 10 minute break and evaluate your hunger.

- Add exercise to your holiday plans. Start exercising now and get the bonus of stress relief while burning calories and excess fat during this hectic time. Chose an activity you enjoy.

- Get your sleep. Some people are so sleep deprived during these times that they eat to give themselves energy, when what they need is sleep.

- Give yourself the gift of a healthy body. Don't stuff it with too many empty calories from cakes, nuts, gravies, chips and dips or alcohol.

- Again, fill your plate with salads, vegetables, sliced turkey or shrimp, which is a very low-calorie, low-fat food. Pile seafood on your plate with a dash of red sauce. Tuna and grilled chicken are great food choices. Broiled fish is available in many buffets.

- Often you can scrape off the sauces surrounding the entrées. The only pasta sauce allowed, if needed, is the marinara kind (red sauce). Avoid creamy sauces. Always be moderate when eating pasta.

- If dessert looks good, decapitate the whipped cream dollop; eat the filling and skip the crust. You do not have to finish everything on your plate as a taste will suffice. Many times the food looks better than it tastes. This is an excellent reason not to eat it! It is especially not worth to eat mediocre food to gain unwanted weight.

  Nothing tastes as good as skinny feels!

When you eat out, company can sometimes be advantageous and sometimes deleterious. You often feel you have to keep up with your friends by eating and drinking as they do.

You may lack self-confidence and be embarrassed to be the only one not drinking alcohol or not ordering an appertizer. You must find the strength to stand up for your principles and your health! Once alcohol removes your inhibitions, you will give in to your friends' urgings. You will generaly drink and eat even more. If this is a pattern that occurs frequently, use different techniques to prevent this self-defeating behavior. Only diet drinks or iced tea should be consumed. Again, be the first one to order. Keep a clear head, even if others around you may be losing theirs.

When friends or relatives cajole you into eating something you should not, even though they know you are on a diet, do not go out with them anymore. They are not true friends! They are your weight loss saboteurs! Only supportive relatives or friends should be included in your eating-out expeditions.

Many overweight patients are ashamed to go out and prefer to stay home instead, like Cinderellas. I recommend that my patients go out and have fun. I do not want them to be hermits; however, I like them to knock food down from its pedestal. Dr. Audrey Cron, Professor of Nutrition at Columbia University, advises: "Find a substitute for food." Go to the movies, go dancing or walking with your friends and relatives. Also, bring your own healthy snacks.

Vacations are often contemplated with ambivalent feelings of pleasure and apprehension by those who have weight problems. Travel holidays are not an excuse to overeat. On the contrary, seeing new countries or places should stimulate more non-eating activity. Visit the sights, the museums, and mingle with natives. Food should be the last thing on your mind. Trying the local cuisine is pleasurable, but should always be done in moderation.

While on vacation, bring some healthy snacks from breakfast to avoid lunch altogether. Snacking often during trips is permissible, as long as healthy food is used. I have often transported healthy personal snacks to foreign countries in my briefcase and suitcases.

Low-fat or low-calorie meals can also be ordered from airlines two days in advance. Consume a meal at home before taking the airplane. Boats often have heart-healthy menus from which to choose.

Pick your meals from the healthy categories of the menu as often as possible. Buffets on boats are to be avoided as it is difficult to be moderate when there are no limits. I always recommend ordering from the menu. Just because something is free, it still has calories. A little taste of this and a little taste of that surely add up to too many calories. Drinking water is very important for keeping hydrated and avoiding fatigue.

Food has the same calories, whether it is consumed in Paris, London or Madrid. Upon your return, you will have to face the scale, along with the self pity and depression wherever the weight was gained. I recommend to my patients taking a trip not to gain or lose weight, but, rather, to maintain it. Upon returning from your travels, you can get stricter. You would be devastated if the clothes you brought on a vacation no longer fit. The purchase of bigger clothes is strongly prohibited. A few days of careful eating will keep things constant and put an end to the upward girth.

COMMITMENT

To keep dieters focused, the following tactics are recommended. Remove all your clothes and stand naked in front of a full-length mirror. Do you like what you see or are you shocked to see all these rolls and flabby areas?

Joan Jacobs Brumberg, a Cornell University women's history professor who has studied young women and their body images, feels that the root of all evil is the bathroom where mirrors reflect our not-so-perfect bodies, and where scales are kept. She feels that bathrooms constitute the ideal place for us to obsess about our weight.

On the contrary, I feel that we need the mirrors and the scales to remind us of our status and transgressions.

Fitting rooms in stores represent gentle reminders of our weight and size. Larger-sized women or girls have difficulty finding attractive clothes. I had a patient who, after being successful with her weight loss, could squeeze into size-eight pants. She was so proud that she put the size label on the outside of her clothing for all to see.

One of the most depressing facts in a woman's life is to go up a size. We agonize about it all day. However, if we can fit into a lower size, we are floating on cloud nine the whole day.

The most humiliating, belittling, humbling experience for a woman is to try on a bathing suit. This experience transcends race, color and creed. Only groans and moans are heard in the fitting rooms during bathing-suit season. We feel vulnerable trying to squeeze into those skimpy pieces of clothes. Understandably, many of my new patients' visits were prompted by ill-fitting bathing suits.

Another patient has told me that whenever she feels that she does not need to lose weight, a trip to the store to try on white pants brings her down to reality and bolsters her determination to continue on the program.

PSYCHOLOGY & DISTRACTION TIPS FOR WEIGHT LOSS

Because we want to remove the possibility of your returning to your fat island, big clothes should be eliminated from your wardrobe as soon as possible. Smaller clothes should be brought from the back of our closets where they were buried and exiled, as soon as the others get too loose. This technique is called "burning our bridges."

Another strong motivating tool is reviewing old pictures and pasting a thin and beautiful one of yourself on the refrigerator door. Whenever you open the refrigerator, this motivating picture should hit you in the eye!

Whenever you go shopping, buy a piece of clothing that is a little tighter and put it in front of your closet to admire. Everyday try on this tight item, until the day when it is finally comfortable and a big victory has been achieved.

Sometimes going to a restaurant with a tight belt will prevent too much eating, as slight physical pain might curtail your overeating behavior.

Distraction tactics are also successful for some. I play games with myself all the time to minimize my food intake. I will eat this particular food after I finish one or two tasks. By the time I have finished my various work activities, my craving has disappeared. Retreating to the bathroom while the dessert cart is wheeled to your table is another scenario. When you return from powdering your face, the cart will be gone! I have actually seen people doing exercises in the restaurant bathroom, to prevent confrontation with a favorite dessert!

When we are lonely, unhappy, or after we have had a fight with the boss or a relative, we often turn to our unconditional love: food. When you are feeling down or just in the mood to binge, try to find things that you enjoy doing which provide non-edible rewards.

I like to take a bubble bath and just luxuriate in the warm, scented water. According to dermatologist Dr. Dennis Gross, "The warmth of the water helps dilate your blood vessels, increasing blood flow to achy muscles." Playing a sport, a game, taking a walk, or going dancing may be better choices than an unhealthy trip to a restaurant.

Calling a friend or writing a letter may also serve to absorb some of our attention. Any creative project that we love may hinder our eating attempts. Busy people do not have time to think about food. Even shopping may sometimes make us forget about cravings.

Massages may relieve tension and stress. According to a study of 50 adults at the Miami School of Medicine, the group who was given a 15-minute massage showed a significant decrease in their stress hormones as compared with the group who was instructed to relax only. Even though a professional massage is best, a self-massage may also relieve tension and anxiety and promote alertness. Dr. M. Hernandez Reif, who headed the study, recommends sitting up straight in a chair, then tilting your head to the right, bringing the right ear to your right shoulder and with your right hand, reaching across your chest to the left shoulder. Rub the fleshy area where your neck connects to your shoulder in a circular motion for a minute or two. Slowly work your way up to the left side of the neck, feeling for areas that are hard or sore. When the neck feels better, tilt your head back up. Now tilt your head to the left and repeat the massage on the right side.

Sometimes just reading women's magazines with lots of pictures distracts my patients from eating. They find it a relaxing activity to combat the pressures of the day. Some people enjoy listening to soft music which also has a calming effect.

Do not skimp on sleeping time, especially while dieting. Sleep deprivation makes you more irritable, and you may compensate by feeding yourself to get more energy. Carbohydrates may make you even more drowsy. According to Dr. John Winkelman, associate medical director of the Sleep Disorders Service at Brigham and Women's Hospital in Boston, "You need seven to eight hours of sleep a night to feel your best." Not getting enough sleep may affect mood as well as productivity. However, exceptions to this rule exist. Many students who cram for exams keep themselves awake and alert by eating and drinking coffee. When finals are finally over, their waists have increased exponentially!

Some individuals use other coping mechanisms, like meditation and relaxation techniques to reduce stress, especially if they suffer from stress-induced eating.

Emotions can play havoc with our best intentions. Feelings of deprivation and of injustice often accompany obesity. "Why is it that my co-worker or spouse can consume 3,000 calories and remain a string bean, while I gain weight by just deviating a little from my program?" my patients often ask me reproachfully. I can only answer that life is not fair. We have received a set of genes from our parents that govern not only our physical appearance but also our basal metabolic rate. I motivate my patients by saying, "Just because we have lousy metabolism genes, we cannot give up; on the contrary we have to fight even harder."

We need to focus on realistic goals: our body type may be improved but not changed radically, as we cannot all look like Marilyn Monroe, Elizabeth Taylor or Cindy Crawford. Gradual changes and improvements are all that can be expected. We recommend a weight loss schedule of two pounds a week. I always tell my patients that I wish I was a magician who could instantaneously melt their fat with a magic wand. However, they have to work to lose their weight, and I will be their determined coach.

Readers can enlist their own support system, either within their family or from their best friends. According to Dr. John Foreyt, "Support systems rank among the top five factors in both weight loss and, more importantly, weight maintenance." He adds that the best support system is provided by the family (spouses or children).

When dieters do not have support, they falter. Spouses (especially husbands) should be made cognizant of this fact. Let them read Letter 2 (see pg. 48). Harsh criticism from parents, spouses, bosses or co-workers is counter-productive and can also halt weight loss success. Only very strong people can withstand these obstacles.

To be able to ward off all these negative feelings, the obese individual must love him or herself. Self-esteem may be very low at the beginning; however, as weight loss progresses, the patient realizes that he or she is capable of improvement and is not so bad after all!

It is a good idea to write down your goals and to look at them daily. Divide your goals into little steps, as we described the small steps on the bridge from fat island to thin island in Chapter 14 (see Figure 11 on pg. 185).

Also write down on an index card at least five positive characteristics about yourself. For example, you may realize that you are a good person, a generous person, a good mother, a good daughter, or a good worker, etc. Whenever you falter in your dieting challenge, read aloud these positive comments about yourself.

After each 10 pound weight loss, treat yourself to a non-edible reward: a scarf, a movie, a bottle of perfume, a manicure, etc.

One of my patients who is married to a very supportive husband, receives a piece of jewelry at each 10-pound weight loss landmark.

If you do not love yourself people will treat you poorly. In addition, also, self-assurance is contagious and will earn you the respect of others. Accept admiring glances from the opposite sex as a compliment. You do not have to act on these compliments. Many women actually begin to regain their weight as soon as they feel themselves too attractive to the opposite sex. I always advise that you lose weight for yourself and not for anybody else. If somebody from the opposite sex becomes too pushy, you always have the prerogative to say "no." You worked hard to achieve your goal—do not let some stranger ruin it all!

Accept your limitations: you are not perfect, but neither is anybody else. You may sometimes err, but do not give up. I always tell my patients that we expect little slip-ups in weight gain during holidays, travels, birthdays, etc. But some of my patients are mortified when a slight weight gain occurs!

As long as the general weight loss curve goes downward, we can accept these minor transgressions. They will occasionally happen again; thus, resignation is in order. Even though one battle may be lost one week, the war is not over. We pick ourselves up from our bootstraps, we dust ourselves off and continue with a stricter program for the next few days. I have coined this "The Indiscretion Day-After Diet." (see Letter 4)

Letter 4

THE INDISCRETION DAY-AFTER DIET

Just because you went off the diet one day, doesn't mean you have failed your program! One battle lost does not mean you've lost the war. We know there are birthday parties, festivities and invitations that will occasionally interfere with you following your program faithfully. However, we have devised a program to allow you to continue your weight loss as if you had not had that indiscretion. This is called "The Indiscretion Day-After Diet." Here is what you do:

- You go on a more restricted program that includes meal replacements, water and potassium supplementation for a couple of days. For a few more days, you continue with this program but add a meal (lean protein and vegetables only; no starches). Continue the strict program until you have lost the weight you have gained.

- Remember, if you go off your diet one day, it is up to you to get back on track by following the above instructions the very next day.

- It is not your fault that you are overweight; however, it is your responsibility to fight the fat!!!

Recent weight gain can be lost very rapidly, as soon as the person goes back on track. Relapse prevention may be secured by positive reinforcement of your looks and your improved health status.

I go over my patients' blood work-up at the beginning of their program. Each time we do a new blood work-up, we compare it to the original ones. The body fat composition test also improves greatly as weight decreases. As fat percentage is lowered and muscle mass increased, basal metabolic rate soars. Patients can eat more without gaining weight.

This lower fat percentage, higher metabolic rate and weight loss fills us with a sense of empowerment. Not only do we receive admiring glances from the opposite sex, but we notice our increased power at work. Our colleagues and bosses treat us with more respect. We now only need to take vitamins and nutritional supplements, as opposed to when we first started and had to consume a whole bagful of medications with associated side effects.

We feel so good, so full of energy, we can exercise better and do all the things we could not accomplish previously. For one of my patients, playing ball with her children was a major victory. For another, putting on a pair of jeans called for a major celebration!

Are we going to give up all these advantages and go back to our fat selves? The majority of individuals who had experienced a major weight loss preferred to lose an arm or an eye rather than regain their weight!

For those of us who have been there and have been subjected to the usual humiliation and discrimination, we are not ready to go back to our "fat islands." However, as situations sometimes arise beyond our control, I have devised the five-pound regain rule. Each of my patients is not given a definite ideal weight but rather a five-pound range with which to play. For example, we might tell you that "you should weigh between 125 to 130 pounds." It is easier to maintain this range, as parties, vacations, birthdays, etc. may all add a couple of pounds to our weight, in spite of our best intentions.

I find that allowing an extra five pounds makes it easier for the patient to maintain weight. The minute you step on the scale in the morning and you notice you have gained these five pounds, a red light should start flashing in your brain stating: "Back off and return to a stricter program for a week!"

"It is easier to lose five pounds than it is to lose 50 pounds," I tell my patients, and I tell you, the reader, too. My patients are supposed to call and return before greater harm arises. I advise the reader to go back on a stricter regime with more protein, less fat, and no carbohydrates for one week. Also, depending upon your needs, you may need to increase the neurotransmitter precursors.

No one claims that weight loss is easy. However, if your weight loss is important to you, if you are committed, if you have a good support system and you are aware of your dieting woes and how to solve them, you will be successful!

I tell my patients that I have never had a failure in 21 years and, therefore, I do not expect her or him to become my first! In the same way, I challenge the reader of this book; I will not allow you to become a failure either!

Finally, according to Dr. John Foreyt, problem solving is an important component of behavior modification. Hopefully, this chapter has helped you solve problems in the dietary department. The next chapter will cover in detail problems associated with exercise.

Chapter Summary

- Behavioral therapy is helpful in weight loss.

- Self monitoring, as in a food diary, is important in tracking nutritional intake.

- Cognitive therapy and stimulus control are taught to our patients.

- Lists for food shopping, home cooking, restaurant eating and parties are provided.

- Good snacks are also incorporated into the eating plan.

- Commitment tactics are also offered like problem solving and controlling emotions.

- A support system is key for the dieter.

- The Indiscretion Day after Diet and the Five Pound Weight Regain rule are important reminders for those who occasionally falter.

— Chapter Eighteen —

EXERCISE

W hether young, old, obese or thin—everyone extols the virtues of exercise. Frequently, my patients will excuse their lack of weight loss to less exercise. However, fewer than one-fifth of U.S. adults engage in vigorous exercise, a fraction that has not increased since the 1980s. Sadly, only 30% of people continue to exercise within a year of beginning, and 70% drop out. We do not know the relationship of exercise to weight loss. In addition, few people know what, when, and how much exercise is optimal for weight loss and maintenance. Let us now examine the pros and cons of this activity and debunk all the myths associated with it.

Exercise is not a pleasurable activity for many of us. Even though the number of joggers has increased significantly in the last few years, these individuals do not look happy or wear smiles. They have a pained expression; they puff and pant while sweat pours down their faces!

According to Dr. Grant Gwinup, professor of the Division of Endocrinology and Metabolism at Irvine Medical Center in Orange, California, exercise is an unnatural activity for mankind. The only exercise primitive man did was to flee from predators. No wonder dietary alterations are more easily accepted than following an exercise regime.

If, with a lot of coaxing, we convince our patients to exercise, the sad truth is that if they stop they become "de-trained" and worse off than if they never exercised at all. This was shown by Dr. Judith Stern, professor and director of the Food Intake Laboratory, University of

California at Davis, in her experiments with rats. Therefore, introducing patients to exercise may be detrimental to their health and weight if they discontinue it at a later date.

A few intrepid scientists found that fitness, like weight loss, has a genetic predisposition. Therefore, some people find it is easier to get fit than others. Some people may inherit an ability to gain muscle strength and to grow large muscles, while others may struggle and not achieve noticeable results. Exercise physiologist Claude Bouchard of Laval University in Saint Foy, Quebec, put a group of 47 young men on a training program for 15 to 20 weeks. While some men showed 100% improvement in their maximal oxygen uptake (which measures their fitness level), others showed no change. Heart size, muscle fiber size and performance after 90 minutes of exercise stayed the same in the non-responders, even after 20 weeks of regular exercise at a frequency of five times a week.

The conclusion was that some people may lead a completely sedentary life and yet are fit and have the ability to grow muscle very easily, while others despite tremendous efforts, are never able to achieve large defined muscles. Dr. Bouchard found that 10% of people he studied could not improve their fitness level with exercise. They did not improve their endurance or even lose a gram of fat. Therefore, there is a strong genetic link between changes in endurance, fat loss and muscle gain. In my experience, I have also noted that some patients develop rippling muscles with ease whenever they exercise, while others who perform the same exercise maintain puny little muscles.

STARTING AN EXERCISE PROGRAM:

First and foremost, you should get medical clearance.

You should purchase a good shoe or sneaker with padded heels and heel support. The shoe should have good arch support, a flexible sole and plenty of toe room. The upper part of the shoe should be leather or nylon to allow the foot to breathe.

To get the maximum benefit from your exercise you should know how to find your target heart rate. To make it easy, just subtract your age from 220 and take 60-80% of that number to get to your target heart beat zone.

Multiply by: 0.60 if you are a beginner
                          0.70 if you are an intermediate exerciser
                          0.80 if you are an advanced exerciser

The target heart rate can be measured at the wrist with the first two fingers of the other hand.

A five-to-ten minute warm-up is beneficial before starting any exercise; stretching is then recommended. To prevent a possible strain avoid stretching cold muscles. At the end of the exercise, stretching may also be helpful to prevent stiffness and increase flexibility.

To start, the best exercise is walking, especially for the obese. A caveat: do not use ankle weights when walking.

Very heavy people have to be very cautious with exercise. In my practice, I have seen many obese individuals who have been injured with exercise. Walking on a uniform surface is the safest aerobic exercise. Vigorous movement with arms and legs is recommended; shoulders should be relaxed, hips should be even, and knees and feet should point forward. Sometimes walking in a swimming pool is easier for the very obese.

At week 1: we recommend 10 minutes, twice a week.
At week 2: we increase to 10 minutes, three times a week.
At week 3: we go up to 15 minutes, three times a week.
At week 4: we can go up to 18 minutes, 3 times a week.
At week 5: 20 minutes may be done, 3 to 4 times a week.
At subsequent weeks, the minutes of walking are slightly increased, but the frequency stays at four times a week.

Any dizziness, lightheadedness, chest or arm pains should be followed by discontinuation of the exercise and a clearance from a physician. Knee or ankle strains must heal before exercise is reinstituted.

No one kind of exercise fits all. There are responders versus nonresponders to exercise. Many investigators have shown that exercise has remarkably different effects on different people. When people exercise regularly for three or four months, their bodies can change dramatically. Their hearts and muscles get stronger, and they can exercise harder for longer periods of time. However, not everybody fits in this category!

The effectiveness of exercise may vary dramatically from person to person. The best advice I can give is that you should perform an exercise that you enjoy, one that can be done with a buddy or with your family. It is best to exercise using realistic goals so as to continue this activity for the foreseeable future.

Exercise appears to boost sexual health. Sexual dysfunction that is often attributed to age may actually be caused by a sedentary life style. Men and women who exercise have been shown to have increased sexual activity.

Each new year brings out new dietary and exercise resolutions with great anticipation. For a couple of weeks we exercise until we drop out, and like a balloon, our enthusiasm deflates. A lot of exercise equipment is purchased for the holiday season, and by February it is covered with dust or has become the most expensive clothes hamper in the world.

YOUR LEVEL OF FITNESS

You should also determine your level of fitness before you start your exercise program. For cardiovascular endurance, run or walk for one mile. The ideal time to do this should take you less than 7.5 minutes. If your time is 7.5-9 minutes, your endurance is high; a mile run for 9-10 minutes points to moderate endurance; however, if it takes you longer than 10 minutes to perform this, your endurance is poor.

You can also score your muscle strength by doing the following two simple tests.

Chair Dip Test: Sit on the edge of a chair or bench, place your hands in front of the chair's edge, place hips forward until they clear the seat, lower hips toward the floor until elbows are bent at right angles. Pause, then raise the body up until arms are straight; four seconds are needed to lower, and two seconds are needed to raise your body. 10 chair dips at one time are considered excellent; seven to nine dips are very good; four to six dips are average, and fewer than four dips are considered poor performance.

Leg Squat Test: Stand four to eight inches in front of a chair, feet hip width apart. Clasp arms over chest, keep back straight and bend the knees, lowering the body until your butt touches the seat while keeping your heels on the floor. Take four seconds to lower and two seconds to raise your body. The ideal number of squats is 25 or more; between 20 to 24 you are doing fine; between 15 to 19 you are considered average; but below 15 squats, your performance is poor!

The advantages of exercise are numerous. A beneficial association between exercise and the avoidance of many diseases has also been described in the previous chapters. In 1992, the American Heart Association named physical inactivity as an independent risk factor for cardiovascular disease. Exercise improves cardiovascular circulation by bringing down low density cholesterol and increasing high density cholesterol components. In a 10 month study of 34 sedentary men and 70 women between the ages of 43-45 years who were put on an exercise regime of 257 minutes per week for men and 209 minutes per week for women, HDL cholesterol increased by 15% in men and 5% in women, and LDL cholesterol level (especially the oxidized dangerous kind) decreased by 10% in men and 11% in women. The exercise program consisted of walking (70% of the time) with other activities like skiing, biking, and dancing (30% of the time).

In another experiment, even without weight loss, exercise showed a modest rise in HDL of 10% and a decrease in triglycerides of 7%, after one year. Dr. A.L. Dunn, et al. conducted a two year study involving sedentary men and women who were put on intensive therapy for six months and either a lifestyle physical activity or a traditional structured exercise program for 18 months.

Both the lifestyle and structured activity groups had significant and comparable improvements in physical activity, cardiorespiratory fitness and blood pressure. Although weight stayed the same, the percentage of body fat was reduced. The structured exercise group received an exercise prescription of 50-85% of maximal aerobic power for 20 to 60 minutes, five days a week for six months in a fitness center. The participants in the lifestyle group did at least 30 minutes of moderate physical activity on most days of the week. The activity, behaviorally based, was adapted to each person's lifestyle. The benefits were the same in both groups lasting 24 months. Physical activity can provide options beyond the traditional fitness center-based recommendations for those individuals who dislike vigorous exercise, who have no access to gyms, and who claim not to have time. Couch potatoes may improve their heart and lung fitness by doing daily activities like cleaning, raking leaves or climbing stairs.

Dr. J. Kelly Smith, et al. conducted a study that concluded that moderate intensity exercise (70 minutes at least twice a week) decreased the cell production of cytokines with predominantly athero-genic properties while augmenting the production of cytokines with predominantly atheroprotective properties. The data suggest that long-term physical activity may protect against ischemic heart disease in people at risk for such disease.

Dr. Ross E. Anderson also devised a 16-week program for obese women using dietary intervention and additionally either structured aerobic exercise (three step-aerobic classes per week) or a moderate intensity lifestyle activity of 30 minutes (like walking) most days of the week. Results showed both groups lost the same amount of weight and fat percentage. Blood pressure and blood lipoprotein levels also decreased substantially in both groups. One conclusion is that any kind of exercise, if performed regularly, is better than being sedentary. The other result is that those women, who continued to exercise after the study, maintained their weight loss, fat decrease, and improvement of blood parameters.

J.E. Manson, et al. and J.P. Helmrich, et al. already showed in 1991 that physical activity reduces the occurrence of non-insulin dependent diabetes mellitus and that type II diabetics improve when they committed to an exercise program.

Acording to *Obesity Research Update* of October 1998, exercise not only reduced the risk of type II diabetes in those with a BMI greater that 25, but it also resulted in a modest weight loss of four to seven pounds. Walking was found to be the most appropriate form of activity for the obese diabetic. Exercise has also proven beneficial in preventing cancer of the colon, as found by C. Bouchard, et al.

In addition, studies have shown a 37% reduction of breast cancer in exercising women. According to Dr. Christine Friedenreich, a speaker at the Intenational Research Conference on Food, Nutrition and Cancer, exercise is becoming "a primary means of preventing can-cer and improving cancer survival." She feels that exercise per se decreases the over-production of sex hormones and reduces body fat deposits making it harder for "dietary carcinogens" to be stored long term. Also, exercise may speed the transit time of the food going through the colon and decrease the secretion of bile acids (both factors involved in colon risk). Dr. Friedenreich recommends for cancer prevention a minimum of 30 minutes of moderate to vigorous intensity activity per day, for a least five days a week. She adds: "The key is to get moving and keep moving."

Aerobic exercise in the form of a treadmill has also been shown to reduce mortality. According to Dr. Andrea Dunn, a 10% increase in treadmill performance may result in a 15% reduction in mortality. Another study showed that each one-minute increase in maximum treadmill time decreased mortality by almost 8%.

According to Dr. J. Foreyt's 16-month study, people who took 45-minute walks, three times a week, reduced their bingeing potential to zero.

We see conflicting data regarding exercise's role in weight loss. A moderate amount of aerobic exercise slightly reduces the body weight by 2% of overweight black women after aerobic training sessions, three times per week for 18 weeks.

On the other hand, after a lengthy research of 493 studies, W.C. Miller, et al. concluded that diet plus exercise causes as much weight loss and better weight maintenance than diet alone; and both are superior to exercise alone. After 15 weeks, the average weight loss with diet and exercise was 24.2 pounds compared to 23.5 pounds with diet alone and 6.4 pounds with exercise alone. Weight loss maintained after one year averaged 18.9 pounds with dieting plus exercise, versus 14.5 pounds with diet alone. Therefore, in this study, dieting alone caused more weight loss than exercise alone.

However, daily walking with no dietary restriction may cause moderate weight and fat loss. Daily walks from 20 to 43 minutes for one year resulted in a modest weight loss of 10 pounds. While physical activity may decrease body-fat in men, according to Dr. Westerkerp, et al. who analyzed 122 studies, a decrease of body-fat percentage does not occur in exercising women.

In a study using 970 normal-weight female twins, weekly one-hour moderate intensity exercise accounted for 2.2 pounds of body fat loss, while two hours a week was followed by a difference of 3.1 lost pounds of body fat.

We know that basal metabolic rate is increased by a higher muscle mass. Researchers from the Mayo Clinic have shown that the more muscle mass one has, the less weight that person gains from overeating.

Muscle usually burns one-and-a-half times more calories than fat does. However, according to *Obesity Research Update* of October 1998, exercise has little or no effect on diet-induced thermogenesis. During dieting, weight loss consists of 10-30% muscle loss. Weight-lifting during dieting does preserve muscle mass but, interestingly, it does not affect basal metabolic rate. Another complicating factor is, as shown by Dr. Liebel, et al. in 1995, that a 10% decrease in weight is accompanied by a 15-16% reduction of basal metabolic rate. Thus something in the dieting process prevents exercise from increasing thermogenesis.

A new study from Appalachian State University in Boone, North Carolina, has shown that moderate exercise is not associated with significant weight loss. Again, diet plus exercise groups lost a significant amount of weight, while the exercise control groups did not.

A group of 128 obese females were randomly assigned to four treatment groups: diet alone, diet and aerobic exercise, diet and strength training, and finally, diet plus strength training and aerobic exercise. This study was done to determine whether one kind of exercise was more helpful than others for weight reduction. All women received the same diet and behavior modification advice. This experiment showed that obese women lost as much weight with diet alone than with any kind of exercise, even strength training.

Even though evidence is strong that exercise alone does not help weight loss, it is crucial for successful *weight maintenance*.

In a ten-year old follow-up study of 2,564 men and 2,695 women, ages 19 to 63, in three towns in Finland, modest weight gain was seen in both groups who did not exercise (an average of 5.5 pounds per year per man versus 3.7 pounds per year per woman). However, both women and men who maintained their weight engaged in vigorous activity twice or more a week. Thus, keeping active throughout life may prevent weight gain.

A study done in 1998 showed that to minimize weight regain in women, at least 80 minutes of moderate exercise or 35 minutes of vigorous exercise was needed daily. According to this study, the results of exercise are not linear (you don't automatically improve a certain amount due to the same amount of exercise) but rather, they show a threshold-like effect whereby one reaches a certain threshold and it can take substantially more work to get to the next level.

The latest studies in 1999 link diet and exercise to maintaining 50-60% of weight loss during a two-year period. Dr. R.L. Weinstein concludes that diet, rather than reduced physical activity, is a major reason for the rapid increase in obesity that is occuring in the new millennium.

While 20 or more minutes per day of vigorous exercise, such as jogging, swimming or cycling were touted as optimal in the 1960s, lesser quantities and intensities of exercise or physical activity can also lead to health benefits (cardiorespiratory fitness, body composition, and blood pressure reduction). However, in both studies done by Dunn, et al. and Anderson, et al., greater beneficial effects on cardio-vascular disease risk factors and fitness were observed among participants who maintained higher activity levels. There is, thus, a dose-response relationship between higher intensity exercise and health improvements (the greater the amount of exercise, the greater the benefits). Furthermore, as both studies had longer follow-ups (two years and 68 weeks respectively), we can derive that long-term health benefits require long-term behavioral changes.

In the 1980s, the theory was that high intensity activity was not followed by weight loss, only by blood sugar decrease. Sustained slow intensity activity was associated with fat loss. The exercise was supposed to take 10 minutes for the information to be relayed from the brain to the mitochondria, the little organelles that produce energy in the cells. Thus, at least 30 minutes of slow, sustained exercise was supposed to promote fat loss.

On the other hand, another study showed that high-intensity exercise reduces body fat in women better than low intensity physical activity. Low-intensity exercise that caused a heart rate increase of below 132 beats per minute was done 40-45 minutes, four times a week. High-intensity exercise that rased the heart rate above 163 beats raised per minute was also followed by a decrease in saturated fat and cholesterol. The percentage of body fat decreased in the high intensity group (27% down to 22%) but did not change in the low-intensity group (22% versus 21%). However, even though body fat was reduced in the high-intensity exercise group, body weight did not change in either group.

Moderate or high intensity exercise was more beneficial in improving cardiovasaclar disease in men than the low intensity physical activity, independent of the duration of the exercise. Thus intensity rather than duration is more important in reducing CHD risk in men.

Another study showed that exercising for 90 minutes or more per day decreases the immune system, while exercising for 30 minutes daily improves the immune system.

According to Dr. Grant Gwinup, to derive optimal cardiovascular benefit from aerobic exercise, one must exercise at least one or more hours. He feels that the first half-hour is considered a cardiovascular warm-up. He also recommends exercising at least one-half hour, twice daily, preferably in the morning and in the evening. This regimen accounts for an after-burn period of several hours following each exercise session. Daily or every other day exercise is suggested.

According to a study of 13,000 middle-aged men at the New York School of Public Health, cardiovascular benefits appeared to stabilize after an hour's worth of physical activity daily. These men were exposed to "moderate" exercise which was defined as rapid walking, gardening, home repairs, dancing, and home exercise for about one hour daily. Gardening for over an hour did not result in better health than gardening for 45 minutes.

There is also a dichotomy between *aerobic exercise* and *resistance-weight training*. *Aerobic exercise* uses oxygen and is mostly represented by walking, running, jogging and dancing programs. Even though aerobic exercise is advantageous for cardiovascular health and longevity, it does not help with weight loss; on the contrary, it decreases resting basal metabolic rate. Thus, aerobic exercise is an inefficient method for losing weight or fat. Also, aerobic exercise ceases to burn extra calories when one stops exercising. It also burns 20% muscle mass and thus decreases basal metabolic rate, which is dependent on lean body mass. Dr. Gwinup found that swimming and aquatics may increase weight as evidenced by chunky swimmers, and he attributed this to cold water possibly lowering body heat which promotes growth of an insulating layer of fat.

On the other hand, *anaerobic exercise* or *resistance training* or weight lifting increases burning potential by 15%. It was calculated that anaerobic exercise burns over 500 times more fat than aerobic exercise. Resistance training also has an after-burn effect that burns calories long after one stops exercising and even during sleep. Two hours after this exercise, a 12% increase of caloric burn occurs. Twice weekly weight lifting is sufficient, as the third day of this exercise does not offer extra benefit. Muscles need at least 48 hours to recover.

A Tufts University study showed that women who do not do resistance training lose five pounds of muscle, 10% of bone mass and gain 10 pounds of fat every 10 years. By age fifty, the same women have lost 30% of their bone mass, have gained 20 pounds of fat and lost 10 pounds of muscle. Men also lose muscle, bone mass, and strength if they are not involved in weight lifting. If you do not use your muscles, you lose them.

The more bulk one has, the less fat we see! The best resistance equipment is free weights, mainly dumbbells which exercise 90% of the body's muscle. A qualified personal trainer is essential to optimize anaerobic exercise. However, some people can utilize Nautilus or Universal machines very efficiently on their own.

Resistance training, if done properly, should not take more than 30 minutes per session. The basic routine is to exercise larger muscle groups before small ones. Chest exercises should be done before triceps moves. Do squats and lunges before leg curls or extensive calf raises. Also note: whenever one lifts weights, it is important to bend the knees for back protection.

Dr. David B. Jack recommends a split routine: exercising legs and abdomen two days a week, then concentrating on the upper body the other two days. To keep yourself stimulated, if you can do 15 repetitions on a certain weight, it is best to go to the next weight and do 12 repetitions only. It is very important to do sets *slowly*; flex or lift for two seconds and extend or lower for four seconds. The best technique is to come to a complete stop, pause and contract the muscle. With the machine, feel the weight stack almost touch but do not stop the action at the end of the extension phase. A set of 8 to 12 repetitions should take a total of 30-70 seconds.

Muscular growth occurs during a 5-10 minute time period. However, it continues 30-40 hours after stimulation. Do not rest longer than 15-20 seconds between machines.

Strength in all exercises should be doubled in about six months, and the maximum potential is probably reached within 18 to 24 months. Though women possess about two-thirds of the strength of men, they are as able as men to develop muscle mass. According to Dr. M.E. Nelson, strong women stay young.

For osteoporosis prevention, a mixture of aerobic excercise and resistance training are recommended. Resistance training should be performed first and followed by aerobic exercise because the resistance training has an after-burn energy that continues during the aerobic phase.

Popular machines, called ab rollers, offer minimal results. Sit-ups do not flatten abdomens either.

The number one equipment for cardiovascular advantage is the *treadmill*. Spinning, recumbent bicycles, rowing and ski machines are other alternatives. Classes in yoga, Pilates, kick-boxing, Tai chi and Tae kwan-do also seem to provide benefits to body and mind.

Two to four short bouts of 10 minute exercise throughout the day (five days a week) are more efficient in weight loss (19.6 pounds in five months) compared to a single bout of 20-30 minute exercise (where only 14.1 pounds were lost in the same amount of time). The difference may be due to better program adherence by those women who used small increments of exercise that could be implemented throughout the day. Both groups were asked to eat a reduced-calorie and lower-fat diet. However, without dieting, short-bout exercise is not effective in losing weight for women. Again, several studies confirmed that a minimum of 80 minutes of moderate exercise a day is required to prevent weight regain in women.

Belly fat, rather than thigh fat, was preferentially lost in those exercising women. *Age* is also not a barrier for exercise. A study by Dr. Wayne W. Campbell of men and women between the ages of 56 and 80 years showed that lifting heavier weights in fewer repetitions changed their body composition. Dr. Campbell also recommends only doing 8-12 repetitions of a specific weight before resting. He recommends two basic exercises for the large muscle groups in the upper body and two in the lower body. The subjects did bench presses and lateral pull-downs for the arms, chest, shoulders, hamstring curls, and knee extensions for the lower body.

Sometimes mixing longer walks, which build endurance and cardiovascular health, with shorter ones, which permit recovery of muscle fatigue and are less time consuming, breaks the monotony of the exercise routine.

Also, exercises have been designed for a particular body shape which either resembles a pear or an apple. *"Pears,"* who tend to gain excess weight in the thighs and buttocks are better off with a workout that incorporates lower body moves right along with a moderate intensity walk.

"Apples" who pack on pounds in their midsection need interval walking and strengthening exercises (with weights). Interval walking uses bouts of three minutes of low to moderate intensity walking. Rest periods between sets of exercise should not be too long (two minutes maximum), as too long a rest does not provide muscles with the stimulus to grow, while a too-short rest stresses and breaks muscle fiber. Body builders claim that short rest stops build stronger muscles.

As already mentioned, there was a 20% reduction in breast cancer risk in women who spent seven hours or more a week engaged in moderate exercise. The rationale for this study of 85,000 nurses, published in the October 1999 *Archives of Internal Medicine*, may be a reduction of estrogen attributable to the exercise.

DISSADVANTAGES OF EXERCISE

Exercise may actually be detrimental to immunity. Often after a stressful competition, athletes succumb to sickness (especially colds). According to Dr. David Nieman, heavy training increases one's susceptibility to respiratory infections (notably within two weeks after a competition or race). A single bout of heavy-duty exercise seems to throw the immune system out off kilter. Stress hormones that become elevated during heavy exercise may, in addition, weaken the immune system. Natural killer cells which represent the first line of defense in immunity are lowered after heavy exercise. However, moderate exercisers fared better in immunity than sedentary people. Thus, even here, moderation is the key.

Dr. D. Donahue concurs that moderate amounts of exercise do not make a cold better or worse. Rigorous exercise, however, temporarily weakens the immune system and can make colds linger.

If symptoms are above the neck (runny nose or sneezing), moderate exercise is not harmful. If symptoms include those below the neck (coughing or body aches), it is best to take an exercise break.

If not done properly, however, exercise may leave you weak for periods of approximately one month. Wearing out the muscles may manifest itself by soreness and swelling especially if eccentric movements are made, such as using the arm while gradually lowering a weight from shoulder level. This type of improper exercise happens more with inexperienced exercisers who may overdo it during weekends.

Finally, a study led by Dr. S. Giri and published in the November 1999 *JAMA*, showed that overweight sedentary people are 30 times more likely to have a heart attack during exertion than at any other time. Out-of-shape people should exercise with caution and check with their doctors first. If the body is not used to exercise and suddenly gets challenged, the circulatory system becomes stressed; blood pressure and heart rate increase and may lead to a heart attack. Even modest amounts of structured physical activity may result in transient subclinical myocardial damage associated with mild heart enzyme elevations.

Sometimes an exercise monitor may be helpful for weight loss. Dr. Daniel Sufer of Johns Hopkins University showed in an eight-month study that those patients who were put on an activity monitor lost an average of 24.2 pounds compared to 14.4 pounds for those without a monitor.

EATING AND EXERCISE

What should be consumed prior, during, and after exercise?

Before exercise, a low glycemic index, carbohydrate-rich meal should be eaten to promote sustained carbohydrate availability.

During exercise, moderate glycemic index carbohydrates are recommended.

Post-exercise, high-glycemic carbohydrate-rich foods may enhance glycogen storage by promoting greater glucose and insulin responses. The supplementation of 500 mg of vitamin C helped the treadmill performance of nine individuals with low vitamin C status. Magnesium potassium aspartate has also been very useful to patients before workout sessions. Carnosine may contribute to the improvement of high intensity exercise performance by buffering acid-base balance in skeletal muscle and preventing lactic acidosis.

Because it lays the groundwork for adult activity in the future, childhood exercise is of great concern to me. American children fare poorly compared to those in other countries. Children tested in the 1980s by the President's Council on Physical Fitness achieved poor scores. For example, 50% of girls and 30% of boys ages six to twelve cannot run a mile in less than seven minutes. 55% of girls in the same age range cannot do one pull-up, while 40% of boys can do just one. 40% of boys ages six to fifteen cannot reach between their toes.

According to the Youth Risk Behavior Surveillance (YRBS) of 1997, only two-thirds of U.S. high school students reported participating in three or more bouts of physical activity during the previous seven days. One-half of students did not meet the standards of stretching and strengthening exercises. Fewer girls than boys meet the standards for vigorous physical activity.

With each increasing year of age, activity levels tend to decline.

PHYSICAL ACTIVITY GUIDELINES FOR CHILDREN:

Guideline 1 = Elementary school children should accumulate 30 to 60 minutes of exercise on most days of the week.

Guideline 2 = Physical activity should last between 10 to 15 minutes or more and include moderate to vigorous physical activity. Brief periods of rest should be interspersed with the activity.

Guideline 3 = Extended periods of inactivity are inappropriate.

Guideline 4 = A variety of physical activities is recommended.

Some deterrents for incorporating exercise into our lives include lack of time, lack of motivation to "move it," lack of an appropriate or safe place to do it, tiredness or feeling more hungry after exercise. However, according to studies done in 1982, moderate exercise does not increase caloric intake or hunger.

One does not have to exercise all day long; small, short bouts of exercise are sufficient.

Changing our whole outlook towards exercise may be quite helpful. This is not an all-or-none situation. Every little bit helps. A study showed that a sign put in front of the airport escalators that encouraged stair climbing resulted in more people taking the stairs.

In our daily lives, we can find many simple ways to increase our activity. Let us have only a few telephones in the house, so that we can walk to a phone; climbing stairs whenever possible is suggested; do not always use the television's remote control and get up from the couch to change the channel; when shopping, do not search out the closest parking place near the door, but rather, take a farther spot and walk. Exercising while driving or sitting at work is also possible.

ENDORPHINS

Endorphins are brain chemicals released during exercise. They make us feel better and less depressed.

Think about the activity that your body likes and go for it. Dancing, gardening, house cleaning, mowing the lawn, and walking the dog are exercises, too. Activities can be done anywhere in the house for those who do not have time to go to a gym. Incidentally, all exercises are more fun if accompanied by music.

HOME EXERCISE ACTIVITIES FOR THOSE WITH LITTLE TIME:

• While you brush your teeth for one to two minutes, bend and straighten your knees and do the toothbrush tush-push for two minutes.

• Stand with your feet apart, grab your towel and hold it tight behind your head while exerting your arm muscles, bend side to side, repeat 12 times on each side.

• To help dry your hair after the shower, stand with your feet apart, bend from the waist and let your hair down. Use your free arm to reach for your toes. Switch arms and use the other arm to reach for your toes. Repeat until hair is no longer dripping wet.

Table 8

CALORIES BURNED PER 10 MINUTE PERIOD OF
DIFFERENT ACTIVITY

Activity	wt 125 lbs	wt 175 lbs	wt 250 lbs
Sleep	10	14	20
Conversation (sitting)	15	21	30
Housework	34	47	68
Walking 1.8mi/hour	29	40	58
Walking 4.4mi/hour	52	72	102
Climbing stairs	146	202	288
Running 6.8mi/hour	118	164	232
Cycling 13mi/hour	35	124	178
Racketball/Squash	95	124	164
Cross-country skiing	98	138	194
Downhill skiing	80	112	160
Swimming 66ft/min	40	56	80
Tennis	56	80	115

EASY EXERCISES TO BE DONE IN THE KITCHEN:

Triceps Toners: Grasp a can of soup, stand with elbow bent and pointing upwards, hold soup can behind your head, palm facing forward. Keep upper arm stationary, exhale and extend arm upward. Repeat 20 times then switch arms.

Can Openers: Stand with feet shoulder-width apart and parallel. Extend arms forward at chest level, a soup can in each hand. Open arms to the sides, then close them. Repeat 12 times, exhaling as you open.

Leg Exercisers: While doing dishes, strengthen those legs. Raise one leg to the side, hold for 10 seconds. Repeat. Do repetitions and switch legs often. You may tie a sock stuffed with a soup can around each ankle to create more resistance when you lift your legs. You can do this during workouts, at work or even while watching television.

Arm Circles: Stretch arms out to the sides, shoulder high with palms up and make backward circles in the air. Start with 10 repetitions, increasing as time and energy permit.

Waist Whittler: Sitting tall, stretch arms overhead and interlock thumbs. Lean first right and then left. Do five repetitions.

Sit Downs: Sitting tall, stretch arms overhead. Bend down and touch the ground. Do 16 repetitions.

Chair Jogging: Jog in place as fast as you can for two minutes, holding the back of a chair for support.

High Kicks: Hold the back of a chair for support and straighten one leg as high as you can. Return to starting position. Alternate and do 10 repetitions.

EXERCISES TO BE DONE IN YOUR BEDROOM:

Relaxation exercises stretch muscles and relax you for your night's sleep.

Stretch: Lie on your back, arms over your head, toes pointed. Reach as far as you can and inhale. Hold for a count of three, flex your ankles and hold again for a count of three. Do three repetitions.

Handling Hamstrings: Lie on your back with left knee bent and left foot flat on mattress. Extend right leg, toes pointed. Raise the right leg and grasp the right knee with your hands. Stretch hamstring and hold for a count of three. Flex ankle and hold again. Switch legs. Do three repetitions.

Lower Back Release: Lie on your back, bend knees and grasp with both hands. Stretch gently. Do three repetitions.

Any type of *dancing* burns calories and brings enjoyment. Do not worry what steps you use, just have fun!

Exercise is what you make of it! For weight loss, dietary intervention is the key. For maintenance, exercise is the most important step to achieve success.

Only maintained exercise matters, therefore pick an exercise you enjoy and keep on doing it as long as you can.

Remember, strong people are slim, healthy, and forever young. So, enjoy!

Chapter Summary

- There is a strong genetic predisposition for some people to improve endurance, fat loss and muscle gain with exercise while others will not improve any of these parameters, no matter how much they exercise.

- Physical activity improves cardiovascular disease, blood pressure, lowers blood fats, prevents cancer and boosts overall longevity.

- Exercise does not help with weight loss where dietary inter vention is key; however, it is the key factor for weight maintenance.

- Optimal exercise includes one hour five times a week and combines aerobic with weight lifting (resistance) activities.

- For exercise to be effective it needs to be continued, otherwise one becomes more unconditioned than if one had never exercised previously.

Chapter Nineteen

MAINTENANCE

C ongratulations! You have reached or are close to your ideal body weight! We are very proud of you! You have successfully won many battles, but, unfortunately, the war against FAT is not yet won. You have crossed the bridge and have finally landed on your "thin island." Now let us remove the bridge and let it float away, as never, never do we want you to return to your "fat island" again. When most formerly obese individuals were interviewed, they said they would rather lose an arm or an eye than regain their weight.

Remember what I said before:

"Only weight loss that is maintained can be considered successful weight loss!"

Successful maintenance is defined as retaining 50 pounds of weight loss for a minimum of five years. Some people do not need to lose that much weight, and others may need to lose even more. However, reducing 5-10% of one's weight significantly decreases the severity of the numerous diseases associated with obesity.

By regaining our weight, we lose all our advantages: our physical looks, our psychological well-being, and our health benefits. Let us not return to the Cinderella stage with no coach, no horses, and a tattered dress after the stroke of midnight! She had also experienced beauty, class and the charming company of the Prince before she was changed back.

Weight does not just pile on quickly again. It creeps up on us gradually until we are right back to where we started. Most weight is regained within three to five years of lifestyle change and within one year of drug intervention. Unfortunately, only 5% of clients at commercial weight loss centers maintain this weight loss. Bariatricians have a higher success rate of 40%. However, my patients who continue coming during the maintenance phase are virtually all successful!

In addition, an article in *Obesity Update* of 1993 showed that long-term contact helped patients maintain weight loss. According to a study spanning three years by Dr. Robert Kanter, director of the Northwest Clinical Nutrition Center in Seattle, longer periods of treatment helped patients maintain their weight loss. Dr. Kanter stated that as "obesity is a chronic disease, it makes sense to have a chronic treatment."

Being accountable to a health professional, a faithful friend or an interested family member is crucial for long-term commitment. Even a psychologist or therapist may help you to discuss problems associated with overeating.

On the other hand, the vast majority of my patients have learned the lessons that have been outlined in the previous chapters.

Obesity is to be treated as a disease for the rest of your life. We will constantly fight the battle of the bulge, but we are now armed with the right weapons. We realize what our enemies are, thanks to cognitive thinking and filling our questionnaires (see Chapters 6 and 7, pgs. 85-90). We know how to use our neurotransmitter precursors and how effective they are as they lead us gradually across the bridge to our "thin island." Our rewards for being thin are innumerable. We love ourselves thin and we can find the strength within to get to our reasonable thin body weight! And most importantly, we are not going back!

I personally have maintained a weight loss of about 70 pounds for over 30 years. My children, my husband, and my friends do not know me fat! I don't want my patients to see me fat! This adolescent obesity led me in the direction of the field of Bariatrics, shortly after I opened my medical practice. I do not want to go back to my fat self, and I will not allow my patients or you, the reader, to regain weight. The fat girl of yesterday became the thin doctor who specializes in weight loss today.

Let us go over and analyze the secrets to long-term weight loss.

NUTRITION AND MAINTENANCE:

Dr. S.M. Schick, et al. studied 438 people who lost an average of 66 pounds and kept it off for five years. A low-fat, low-calorie diet (from 1,300 to 1,700 calories) was responsible for the weight loss maintenance.

Another study by Stoubs, et al. concluded that it is easier to maintain weight loss (70% of the original weight) by eating a low-fat, high carbohydrate diet than by trying to follow a fixed, low-calorie diet for one year. After two years, 65% of the patients in the low-fat group maintained their weight versus 40% in the low-calorie group.

A high-vegetable, low-meat diet, along with regular exercise, may be the best method for someone to maintain weight loss, according to a large study of 79,236 healthy white adults during a 10 year interval. Weight gain was less common in those who ate at least 20 servings of vegetables per week, took a vitamin E supplement and ran one to three hours per week.

Weight regain was more common in those who consumed red meat at least three times per week and in those who stopped smoking. In women, weight loss was associated with walking four hours or more per week. These activities were associated with lesser results in men.

Thus, even though high-protein, low-fat eating seems to be optimal for weight loss, for weight maintenance, a low-fat diet seems to work the best!

By contrast, a study reported in 1984 showed that patients who continued using protein supplements did better with maintenance. Protein supplements tend to reduce appetite and smooth out blood sugar levels. In addition, a German study that gave patients defined meal replacements for two years was successful on long-term weight maintenance and in improving the associated co-morbidities (medical conditions associated with obesity).

Carbohydrates can be introduced slowly in the nutritional regime. It is best to add one carbohydrate per meal; fruits are introduced first, and starches are used last.

I personally find that whenever I have pasta or bread, my weight goes up approximately one pound the next day. I expect it and adjust my dietary regime accordingly the next day.

Alcohol consumption may also be easily analyzed for its weight gain effects. Weigh yourself after one, two, or three alcoholic drinks a day or a week; stop your consumption at the amount that does not increase your weight.

Especially during maintenance, the list found in Chapter 17 (see List 1 on pg. 236) should be reviewed and copied. Take the eating-out guides (see Lists 2 and 3 on pgs. 245-246) with you. All these tactics have been successfully used by me and thousands of my patients.

EXERCISE IN MAINTENANCE:

According to Dr. John Foreyt, the single most important tool for successful weight maintenance is exercise. While exercise alone was shown in Chapter 17 not to be effective in weight loss, exercise may be important to fight off weight regain.

The amount of exercise needed to minimize weight regain seems to be quite vigorous. Women required a minimum of 80 minutes of moderate exercise or 35 minutes of vigorous exercise per day to maintain their weight loss according to *Obesity Research Update* of June 1998.

According to Dr. T.S. Vasilaras, et al. walking 20-50 minutes per day does not help to prevent weight regain following weight loss on a VLCD. For nine months, 72 women who had lost almost 30 pounds, were assigned to three groups: one where they received dietary counseling weekly; one, where besides the counseling, they walked 20-25 minutes daily; and one where they walked 35-50 minutes daily plus the counseling. There was no significant difference between the groups in weight regain (between 9 to 13 pounds in nine months).

This study did not take into consideration whether the women develop more muscle mass from the walking regime and whether their measurements were better, as shown in Figure 5 (see pg. 69).

"Maintenance of fat loss is extremely difficult...even with relatively intensive training," confirmed a study by W.J. Pasman, et al. Men in the study, who trained three to four times per week, regained 52% of their weight, while those who did not train gained 74% of their weight back.

Behavior Modification In Maintenance:

The ground rules of behavior modification in weight loss that were laid in Chapter 17 apply in maintenance, also.

Planning is the key to weight regain prevention! Review all materials in previous chapters that pertain to you. Continue with the neurotransmitter precursors and food supplements that helped you in the weight loss phase. Also, know your obstacles to weight loss, so you can fight them. Avoid those foods that may cause you to binge; have snacks during menses or stressful times; and do not socialize with people who are your "weight loss saboteurs." Instead, seek the company of supportive family members and friends. As soon as these tactics become a reflex, you won't even need to think about them.

I, personally, am so brainwashed that I'll never bring forbidden foods into my house. I read the labels of everything I buy! For relapse prevention, we have to understand that we are humans and that indiscretions may occur. According to Dr. Scott Rigden: "To falter is not to fail." If an error is committed, do not get discouraged; just correct the mistake as soon as possible.

Read about the five pound weight regain rule. A red light with a bell should signal our brains that it is time to go back to the stricter weight loss phase whenever the five pound regain is exceeded. Do not wait until you have gained a significant amount of weight to return to the stricter program. Do not purchase bigger clothes. Suffer in those tight clothes until you lose these extra pounds.

According to Dr. John Foreyt, there are four factors that can predict relapse.

1. *Emotional State*: Negative feelings like anger, depression and anxiety may sabotage weight loss. Know which feelings may stimulate you to overeat. Learn how to conquer those negative feelings in non-edible ways. Food is not the cure for problems. A diet diary that includes feelings may make you cognizant of those negative thoughts.
2. *Social Situations*, such as travel and meetings, may also lead to relapse. Planning is the key here. Pre-order your allowed foods from the airlines beforehand. Carry permissible snacks with you in case of flight delays. Just in case the breakfast in

the meetings consists of danishes or donuts, get up a few minutes earlier to eat your healthy cereal or egg-white omelet in the coffee shop. Hunger does not make you a good philosopher, so prevent it as much as possible by planning.

To prevent weight gain during traveling, offset extra calories with more vigorous exercise.

Restaurant eating was discussed in Chapter 17 and can be controlled. Eating at other people's houses can be controlled by bringing your own food, choosing appropriate foods, and discarding your personal "forbidden foods." Not going anywhere hungry is another helpful tool; you will be more rational whenever you food shop, eat out or go to parties if you have a snack beforehand to assuage your hunger.

Nonetheless, food enjoyment constitutes one of life's pleasures. Sometimes we succumb to a wonderful meal, whether it is home cooked or gourmet chef-prepared. We enjoy our meal, and one or two pounds may creep up on our weight the next day. This is permissible as long as we correct our regime during the next few days.

This reminds me of the story of Danielle Darrieux, one of the most beautiful and talented French actresses. She dieted all week so that on weekends she could enjoy her refined favorite dishes prepared for her at gourmet Parisian restaurants.

Many people have the same attitude: we diet at home but once out, indiscriminate eating is allowed. The specialties of each restaurant are ordered, regardless of caloric or fat content. Holidays, or occasions like birthdays, weddings, and anniversaries, are excuses to allow ourselves to misbehave.

Moderation and planning are also the key here. Exercise and eat lean before the occasions. Being a couple of pounds leaner to accommodate the extra calories then removes the guilt of overeating.

If all else fails, there is always tomorrow. Do not allow more than two extracurricular meals per week.

The scale is, as always, our yardstick. Weigh yourself weekly. On vacations or when out of town, weigh yourself the day after your return.

3. ***Testing the Boundaries***. You have lost the weight and now feel you can "get away" with some cheating. Many people think that weight loss is a cause for celebration with all the foods that they previously restricted from their diet. This was evidenced by Oprah Winfrey who gained back her weight quicker than the time it took her to lose it through the VLCD program.

Many individuals can get sick when they consume high-fat foods after they have been on low-fat programs for several months. Some may even get gallbladder attacks, necessitating gallbladder removal. Many lack the enzymes to break down fat. That is why a little fat is recommended during the strict weight loss program. The re-feeding program should also be a slow, gradual process.

It is virtually impossible not to cheat on certain occasions; especially if no other foods are available. However, do not cheat as a test game. You are only cheating yourself, and weight regain may not show its ugly head right away, but eventually, it will come back with a vengeance. Again, subscribe to the five pound regain rule.

No matter what weight-loss program you follow, you will regain the weight if you are not careful. Again, as food only stays for 30 seconds in your mouth, is it worth gaining weight for only 30 seconds of pleasure? If you had a bad day, follow the day-after indiscretion program (as described in Chapter 17, Letter 4 on pg. 259) the next day.

4. ***Life Stresses***: Marriage, children, job situations, illness and financial problems can all divert us from the right path. Analyze what conditions led you astray. Did eating help the situation? Often people eat to provide some type of solace or comfort, as learned from their childhood.

Sometimes we get even with the person who triggered the stressful situation by overeating. There is no rational excuse for this! We get so stressed by these situations that we forget the importance of our weight maintenance.

When stressed, we put our own selves at the bottom of the totem pole, and these stressful circumstances are magnified. Stress control—by analyzing these situations, by relaxation techniques, by exercise or anything that works for you—should be applied as soon as possible.

Remember, you need to first love yourself for others to respect you. Self-esteem is the key to achievement. Be selfish occasionally. Take care of yourself. You will be a better parent, child, spouse, worker if you indulge yourself in some self-improving non-edible treats. You can exude confidence if you are self-confident.

Positive self talk, looking yourself in the mirror, receiving all the compliments from your new figure make life worthwhile. Be good to yourself, list all your good qualities and personal achievements. Next time you recognize a wonderful quality or performance, reward yourself with a non-food reward. Do not be too critical if you err sometimes; nobody has a mental scale to weigh you and judge you with. Always try to do your best, and the weight will come off and stay off.

Chapter Summary

- Low-fat, low-calorie diets seem to be the best for maintenance. High-vegetable, low-meat but high-fish diets are also optimal.

- Emotional state, social situations, testing the boundaries and life stresses may all be instrumental in relapse.

— **Chapter Twenty** —

LONGEVITY AND ANTI-AGING TECHNIQUES

T hroughout the centuries, besides the quest to transform common metals into gold, the search for the fountain of youth has obsessed mankind. Spaniard Ponce de Leon invested in a trip to Florida just to look for this miraculous fountain. Fantasies of Shangri La or Brigadoon, whose inhabitants never age, have stimulated the minds of many authors.

Stopping the aging clock or at least delaying its inexorable ticking has been the object of exhaustive research in the field of rejuvenation and ultimately immortality.

Longevity has been steadily increasing, thanks to medical technology, better hygiene, pharmacotherapy (especially antibiotics) and healthier nutrition. While a few hundred years ago the normal life expectancy of the population reached a maximum age of 30 to 40 years, nowadays centenarians are becoming more and more numerous, even doubling during the past decade. In 1996, normal U.S. life expectancy was 73 years for a male and 79 years for a woman.

According to a census report, four out of five U.S. centenarians are women. Iowa had the highest percentage of residents in their 100s, followed by South Dakota. Besides these two states, Nebraska, Kansas, Minnesota, Connecticut, Massachusetts, Mississippi, Montana and the District of Columbia were the top 10 states where centenarians live. The estimation is that there are now 70,000 people age 100 or older, almost double the 1990 census count of 37,000 centenarians.

Dr. Tom Perls, a principal investigator for the New England Centenarians study, said that genetics may play a role in clustering these people in a *"longevity belt"* that spans from Minnesota to Nova Scotia. Dr. Perls also feels that women age slower than men, and the onset of cancer, stroke and Alzheimer's may be delayed in women by 10 years.

Interestingly, many centenarians show **mysterious patterns of good health**. The rate at which people die rises from middle age up to and through the 80s. But then death rates decline. After age 110, the death rate drops back to that for people in their 80s. The oldest woman recorded was Jeanne Calmet of France who died at 122 years of age. The oldest man, named Shirechiyo Izumi, who was from Japan, reached the age of 120 years and 237 days in 1986. It seems like those people who make it to 95 are strong enough to run a while longer. Those who reach 100 do not suffer from **dementia**, contrary to previous studies suggesting that centenarians would suffer from dementia 100% of the time. Dr. Margery Silver and Dr. Perls in their book *Living To 100* showed that 25% of 100-year-olds still have no dementia. Fewer men than women suffer from this illness. Cancer is extremely rare in the group studied; women centenarians are childless or had children after age 40. Centenarians, both men and women, seem to manage stress effectively by bouncing back readily from life's crises. Therefore, the elderly are not only living longer but are healthier.

According to Dr. Perls: "Some of us have supergenes that may protect us from cancers and Alzheimer's. The genetic evidence of slow aging is seen in extreme old age running in families."

Aging may be slowed beginning in youth. Very late menopause past the fifties occurs in women centenarians.

Are we programmed then to die at a certain age? This is a controversial subject. However, many tendencies to diseases are inherited. Cancer, for instance, is stimulated by oncogenes (special genes that will in time contribute to cancer).

Alzheimer's and osteoporosis are preventable but inherited conditions. A study by Dr. Mulnard and colleagues investigated the role of estrogen replacement therapy in the treatment of Alzheimer's disease. They believe estrogen may improve verbal explicit memory.

A team of Italian scientists have recently reported a **gene that controls life span in mice**. This gene prevents production of a protein that destroys the cell when exposed to oxygen damage. By altering a single gene in the mouse's genetic makeup, the mice lived longer. A drug may be manufactured to block this self destructive protein. Dr. Pier Paolo Pandolfi of Memorial Sloan Kettering who helped engineer the study, said that this drug in the form of a cream may even reverse wrinkles and blemishes of the aging skin. Experts on aging believe that this gene may be found in humans.

In contrast, scientists at the Baylor College of Medicine in Houston, Texas raised the shocking possibility that aging may be a side effect of natural safeguards that protect us from cancer, at least in mice. The study raises the question of whether any attempt to slow down aging would be likely to raise cancer rates. Among other things, the research raises the possibility that younger people treated with chemotherapy for cancer may be subject to premature aging. The mice treated with chemotherapy had a 20% drop in life span.

On the other hand, the ultimate method to reaching immortality is *cloning*. The birth of Dolly, the ewe, shook the world when it was discovered that it was created from the cells of the udder of a six-year-old sheep.

The question remains, however, as to whether Dolly will live a regular life span, or if she will suffer from an early demise close to her six-year old genetic twin. The latest developments have shown that Dolly is suffering from arthritis at the early age of 5.5 years, while other sheep usually develop arthritis around the age of 10-11 years. Otherwise, Dolly remains a healthy animal who has given birth to six healthy lambs. Dr. Ian Wilmut comments, "We will never know in the case of Dolly whether her condition is because she was cloned or whether this is an unfortunate accident."

Her telomeres, which represent the tips of her chromosomes, are shorter than other sheep of the same age. This shortening may herald a shorter life span. The length of a cell's telomeres is associated with cell division, aging and cell death. Most cells keep on dividing to stay alive. The longer a cell's telomeres, the more divisions the cell has remaining, and the longer it has left to live. As a cell divides, telomeres shorten, and life expectancy diminishes. When telomeres cannot protect the DNA from damage, the cell dies. Shortening telomeres may trigger the unraveling of chromosomes which may lead to aging and death. Thus, even though Dolly is only 3-years-old, her cells may be 9-years-old.

As normal sheep live from 12 to 14 years, there is a lot of interest in determining whether Dolly will die earlier with its six year older genetic twin or experience a timely demise. The whole rationale of cloning is to keep the genes alive forever, as cells are immortal in tissue-culture experiments.

In fact, human cells grown in a test tube double up to 50 times before dying, a process that takes about 11 years to complete, roughly the maximum laboratory life span we can expect under optimal conditions.

Dr. Alexis Carrel kept chicken cells growing and multiplying in a culture for 35 years by feeding them chicken embryo extracts. He intentionally destroyed his cultures to prevent their overgrowth.

I remember working in tissue culture with He La cells that were disseminated from laboratory to laboratory and survived many years in a frozen state. These cells came from a tumor of a patient who had died a long time ago; however, those cells will continue proliferating forever.

Dr. Paul Niehans, glandular expert, was the first to grind up and inject fetal cell extracts to cure diseases and to increase longevity. Clinique La Prairie in Switzerland still offers intramuscular injections of fetal sheep cells to the very wealthy to perhaps retard the aging process. Fetal sheep liver cells are preferred, as they may contain active substances that control the growth and development of the fetus. Even though there are no controlled studies to prove the efficacy of fetal sheep cell injections, patients report a feeling of increased energy and well-being. Fetal pig tissues are being used in the United States to treat Parkinson's disease, and insulin-producing pancreatic cells from pigs have been tested in human diabetics. A good possibility appears to be that transplanted cells, either from humans or animals, will be a standard in the near future.

A new study reported in the July 1999 issue of the journal *Nature Biotechnology* used brain stem cells from mice grown in the laboratory and transplanted them into Parkinson's disease afflicted patients. These transplanted cells produced dopamine, which is lacking in Parkinson's patients.

Human Embryonic Stem (ES) cells were first grown in tissue culture last year. These sex cells come from the previous generation of germ line cells and represent an immortal lineage that connects the generations of all living beings on the planet. Only germ cells are immortal; the rest of the cells do not share this amazing property. Telomerase is an enzyme controlled by a gene that is turned on for immortal cells and turned off for mortal cells.

According to Dr. Michael West, these stem cells can differentiate into all types of tissue and might be used one day to grow new organs. Damaged cells, like those occurring in heart attacks, may be replaced by young cells as a therapy for aging. Lack of telomerase causes the cells to age; but if the telomerase gene is turned on, immortality occurs.

Dr. West further states that even an old cell, if put into an egg cell, may be made young again, like a clock that has been rewound. Thus, he theoretically proposed that, for a very old person, new transplantable tissue may be made just like the tissue posessed at birth. New cartilage for arthritis, new blood cells for leukemia and even neurons for some neurological disorders may be manufactured for each elderly patient.

Fat cells can be changed into nerve, heart, bone or any kind of cells, if grown in a specific enviroment with different nutrients, vitamin and mineral supplementation.

Cryotherapy keeps cells alive in a dormant state for long periods of time. Even blood components, sperm, eggs and embryos are kept frozen for better preservation. Some people believe in the premise of freezing their bodies and thawing them at a later date.

Several *"longevity genes"* have been identified lately. A gene that stimulates premature aging was found in Werner's Syndrome which ages people rapidly. Canadian studies have shown that inserting certain genes in the cells of fruit flies increased their life span by 40%. Dr. Gabrielle Boulianne, who headed the study, concluded that: "Just one gene targeting one type of cell has a huge impact on aging."

Dr. Hayflick found in his tissue culture experiment that when the cells were starved or fed less nutrients, the cells survived longer.

Food restriction in rodents extends life span, reduces incidence of tumors and suppresses oxidative damage to proteins, lipids and DNA in several organ systems. When alternate feeding for two to four months was given to adult rats, life span was extended. In addition, their brain was also more resistant to metabolic insults through toxins and drugs.

In general, *lean people* live longer. In a study by Dr. J. Stevens, et al. in 1998, the greatest longevity was associated with a body mass index between 19 to 22.

A 26 year study by Lindsted and Singh encompassing 5,062 white males reported in 1998 that the risk of death from all causes was lowest among the leanest and increased with increasing weight. A 1997 Nurse's Health Study done in America showed that the leanest nurses suffered from fewer diseases and enjoyed longer lives.

Later, a bell-shaped curve was found to better represent mortality versus age in obese individuals. Young people fared better when they were lean; however, in the older population, the very thin died earlier.

These older people may have been sick already and suffering from lack of appetite before their death. The other possibility could be that some fat is beneficial for longevity in the elderly population.

A new German study of more than 6,000 obese patients over almost 15 years concluded that the risk of death increased with body weight, but that obesity-related mortality declined with age at all levels of obesity in both men and women.

Scale weight is a poor measure of our elderly population's weight. As people age, they suffer from sarcopenia, a condition where the body favors fat at the expense of muscle.

People also age slower when consuming less fat, something that affects circulation and cardiovascular disease. Meat-eating is associated with aging, as it contains aldehydes that stimulate wrinkling of the skin by stimulating the cross linking of the collagen fibers.

Tobacco and *Alcohol* may also stimulate aging. In addition, sedentary lifestyle is also responsible for accelerated aging, because exercise helps with circulation and with hydration of the vertebrae of the back.

Consumption Of Food Groups And Nutrients

An Italian study examined the association between the consumption of specific food groups and nutrients and five year survival. Researchers used a food frequency questionnaire to survey 160 independent living residents in a geriatric home. Individuals consuming *citrus fruit* at least twice a week had an adjusted risk of dying that was half that of individuals who consumed citrus fruit less than once a week. The adjusted relative risk of mortality was less than 40% in those who drank *milk* and *yogurt* at least three times a week, compared to less than once a week. Longevity was increased by 20% in *espresso coffee drinkers* (one to two cups weekly), compared to those who drank espresso less than once a week. Longevity went up to 35% for intake of over two cups a week of espresso coffee, compared to less than one cup a week.

High intake of ascorbic acid, riboflavin and linolenic acid were associated with 50-60% decreases in mortality risk. **High consumption of meat** was associated with an almost tenfold higher risk of mortality. The study showed that the consumption of citrus fruit, milk, and yogurt, and low consumption of meat are associated with longevity.

The Sun And Your Health

Finally, *avoidance of the sun* is advocated to prevent photo aging of the skin. Tanning booths are just as detrimental as the sun. Antioxidant therapy may counteract the effects of the sun if exposure is unavoidable. It is interesting to note that sun exposure, by providing effective vitamin D, is necessary for osteoporosis prevention and for lowering the risk of cancer of the colon, breast and prostate. This sun-derived vitamin D cannot be supplemented either by diet or pills.

Declining levels of hormones may also play a role in the many ills associated with aging and may even have a direct relationship to aging itself. The hypothalamus of the brain may be controlling not only the endocrine system but also the aging process. As aging may be associated with a slowing of the cellular metabolic rate, thyroid hormones may also regulate aging. Thyroid levels are best checked through T3, T4, T7 and TSH testing in the blood. Better results are achieved by 24-hour urinary thyroid hormone test. Thyroid supplementation will restore energy, mood, bowel function, and help with depression, dry hair, skin and nails. A combination of T4 and T3 seems to be the optimal supplementation to enhance all of these benefits, as many people cannot convert T4 to T3, the active thyroid hormone. Recently thyroid hormone, especially T3, was shown to enhance tumor growth. Thus, in cases of people who already are afflicted with cancer, a trial of thyroid hormone reduction or suppression would be recommended.

HORMONE REPLACEMENT THERAPY

Many scientists believe in hormonal replacement therapy (HRT) during the aging process. Natural estrogen and progesterone supplementation are advocated for postmenopausal women who, as a result, look significantly younger than non-hormone taking females. HRT decreases morbidity and mortality associated with aging. In addition, it improves quality of life by decreasing mood swings, urogenital atrophy and pain with intercourse caused by poor lubrication and atrophy of the vaginal walls. HRT also decreases dementia and Alzheimer's disease. Women also benefit from estrogen/androgen combinations and as result they experience positive moods, a feeling of well-being, and ultimately, an increase in libido.

ESTROGEN

Estrogen may also help with fractures, especially of the hip. Mortality may be as high as 30% within a year after a patient is hospitalized for a hip fracture. Even urinary incontinence from aging may be improved with HRT.

Amounts as small as 0.3 mg of estrogen may be effective in preventing post-menopausal symptoms and eliminating negative side effects. Negative side effects associated with HRT include blood clot formation, endometrial cancer (prevented by progesterone administration), small increased risk of breast cancer (but with a favorable prognosis), hypertension and possibly weight gain. Positive side effects linked to HRT include improved sexual function, healthier skin and hair, improved memory, delayed dementia, decreased depression and mood swings, improved quality of life and finally, longevity. In addition, both estrogen and progesterone are helpful in osteoporosis prevention.

Dr. Bernard Cantor calculated that "there will be 20-million women entering menopause by the year 2005." These women will be demanding services encompassing hormonal and alternative therapies.

Estrogens are most commonly given in a conjugated form, such as **Premarin**™. One active form of estrogen is **17B estradiol**. It is not well absorbed when taken by mouth and is mostly destroyed by the liver. However, 17B estradiol is best absorbed through the skin in the form of estrogen patches, or the newest estrogen/progesterone combination patch. According to Dr. Neil Goodman, transdermal estrogen supplementation is the optimal treatment. Dr. C. Richard Mabray believes that menopause is an insulin resistant stage of our life. His studies showed that hysterectomized rats had a decrease in leptin, the hormone that prevented fat storage. Dr. Mabray recommends estrogen patch therapy in the perimenopausal stage of a woman.

Physiologically, human estrogen can be synthetically reproduced with a combination of **estrone** (10%), **estradiol** (10%) and **estriol** (80%). Dr. Jonathan Wright developed this formula and called this combination *"Triest"* with dosage ranges from 2.5 mg to 5 mg per day. Other doctors use a combination called *"Biest"* made of estradiol and estriol without the estrone, which is high in obese and postmenopausal women. I personally favor this combination as well. While estrone and estradiol may be associated with cancer, estriol has an anticancer activity.

Even though **estriol** is a weak estrogen, a 2-4 mg dosage improves postmenopausal symptoms. Estriol does not cause proliferation of the uterus and, therefore, does not lead to cancer of the uterus. It also prevents, rather than promotes, breast cancer and is, therefore, safe even for women with breast cancer. A controlled trial of intravaginal estriol in postmenopausal women prevented recurrent urinary tract infections probably by modifying the vaginal flora.

Estrogens may activate specific brain regions involved with memory in postmenopausal women. A urinary estrogen test indicates whether or not a female patient has a tendency to have breast cancer. The estrogen form that is a breast cancer protector is 2 hydroxy estrone; while the 4 hydroxy estrone or 16 hydroxy estrone are the cancer promoters. We recommend the use of **indole 3 carbinol** (a very concentrated product coming from broccoli) or its stronger metabolite called **DIM** (diindolyl methane) that will change the bad estrone to the good one and help to prevent breast cancer.

According to Dr. John Lee, progesterone alone is sufficient for osteoporosis prevention, while estrogen alone just relieves postmenopausal symptoms. According to Dr. D.L. Feldman, et al., lack of progesterone may be partially responsible for postmenopausal osteoporosis.

Dr. J.C. Prior, an expert in normal replacement therapy, also recognizes the active role of progesterone in bone metabolism following much clinical data.

Dr. Joel T. Hargrove recommends the micronized version progesterone derived from soybeans; 200 milligrams of micronized progesterone is the normal dose.

Prometrium™, derived from peanuts, may be used for those women who fare poorly with progestin. Most of the side effects of progestin, besides weight gain, are bloating, depression and severe bleeding. Prometrium™ improves heart disease by increasing HDL and lowering LDL cholesterol. In addition, it may also protect the uterus from cancer. It may be sleep inducing and it is recommended that it be taken at night.

A combination of ***estrogen*** and ***progesterone*** may make patients gain more weight than estrogen alone. As progesterone may stimulate weight gain and water retention, some endocrinologists recommend only using it every third cycle (Dr. Mabray) or to start estrogen supplementation without it and then use it as needed, according to the symptoms of the patient (Dr. Goodman).

Some foods or plants called ***phytoestrogens*** are capable of relieving postmenopausal symptoms. Soy is the best known example; however, cashews, peanuts, corn, almonds, alfalfa, apples and pineapples may have estrogenic activity. Ginseng may also be used as an alternative to estrogen. Ginseng may allay stress and anxiety and allow better sex. In certain people, however, ginseng may cause high blood pressure, anxiety and insomnia.

Damiana may also stimulate the production of male hormones in both sexes. Wild Yam may also be a good source of progesterone, while licorice root may contain some estrogenic activity. Soy and its component genistein may have a cancer- protecting effect. Low doses of soy, however, did not help with osteoporosis.

Testosterone supplementation has also been advocated as one of the ways to combat aging in men. The theory is that testosterone levels decrease as men get older; however, testosterone supplementation may be dangerous if levels of this hormone are normal. However, if testosterone deficiency is documented, testosterone, either orally, by patch, by cream, or by injection, may increase a feeling of well being and augment libido. Testosterone may also be used in women to increase libido.

Androstenedione, a precursor of testosterone, has recently been marketed as a product for increasing blood testosterone concentrations to be used as a natural alternative to anabolic steroid use.

However, an eight week trial done in 1998 showed that androstenedione does not increase serum testosterone levels or skeletal muscle fiber size and strength. No increase of lean body mass or fat mass decrease were found. On the contrary, the androstenedione group showed a decrease in the "good" HDL fraction of cholesterol. Though the study was performed in young males, there is no reason for older men to ingest this product.

Dehydroepiandrosterone (DHEA) is another hormone secreted by the adrenal glands which may be involved in aging. DHEA deficiency was correlated with aging, and high levels of this hormone were associated with increased longevity in 1996. DHEA's roles in improving obesity, cardiovascular disease, immunity, osteoporosis, diabetes, and, finally, depression were previously discussed. DHEA is, however, not the purported "aging pill," and side effects may occur. DHEA potentiates the action of thyroid hormone; thus, less thyroid hormone must be given with DHEA supplementation. It should be used with caution, as more extensive trials are needed to establish its safety and efficacy. However, new studies have linked DHEA supplementation with improvement in depression. DHEA may be a precursor of cortisol, besides estrogen and progesterone. The recommended dose is 30-90 mg of DHEA a day for the treatment of resistant depression.

Dr. Joel T. Hargrove only corrects deficiencies of estrogen, progesterone, testosterone, and DHEA by supplementing them in appropriate amounts for women who exhibited low levels of these hormones. In women, he assays estradiol (estrogen component), progesterone, DHEA and testosterone blood levels. In men, however, only DHEA and testosterone levels are checked.

Dosages of DHEA usually range from 12.5 to 50 mg daily. In a recent study, women with higher levels of DHEA showed evidence of less risk of breast cancer and better functioning immune systems as they get older.

Evista™ or *Raloxifene* (a designer estrogen) has been shown to improve osteoporotic conditions slightly. In addition, the risk of invasive breast cancer was decreased by 76% during three years of treatment with this drug.

According to Dr. Eugene Roberts, *pregnenolone* secreted by the adrenal glands, may be the most potent hormone for memory enhancement by activating the neuroreceptors necessary for effective memory. By the age of 75, 60% less pregnenolone is produced than at age 35. Pregnenolone may also be a biomarker of aging. Pregnenolone may be not only a powerful memory enhancer but also an antidepressant as well. Dosage is 10 to 100 mg per day taken in the morning. More clinical trials in humans should confirm the data.

To prevent Alzheimer's or for people suffering from this disease, the natural product *galantamine* is very helpful. *Acetyl carnitine* and *phosphatidyl serine* are considered to be life extenders and in Europe, *Lucidril* and *Piracetam* are used as extremely powerful rejuvenators for the mind and body.

During times of stress when the body is deprived of cortisol, an extract from licorice known as *Glycyrrhiza glabra* (in doses of 25-100 mg per day) may improve many conditions that plague the elderly population like colds, flu, fatigue, allergies and asthma.

Melatonin, produced by the pineal gland, has been called the anti-stress hormone as it regulates other hormones. Dosage ranges from 750 mcg to 6 mg and it is to be taken at bedtime.

The role of melatonin is mostly to prevent jet lag and induce sleep. Test tube studies have shown that supplementation of melatonin in large doses may be effective against free radicals. However, the claims of melatonin as an anti-aging agent have been questioned, and further studies are needed to substantiate them. Melatonin has also been implicated as a cancer-fighter.

Possible side effects of melatonin may include confusion, drowsiness, headache and constriction of blood vessels which may be deleterious to people with high blood pressure.

Human Growth Hormone (HGH) is a synthetic recombinant version of the hormone that is produced in the pituitary gland and plays a critical role in hormonal child development and growth. Many researchers now feel that HGH decline may play an important role in the aging process of some individuals. According to Dr. Daniel Reidman, "the effect of six months of HGH hormone on lean body mass and adipose tissue were equivalent in magnitude to the changes incurred during 10 to 20 years of aging." Dr. Ronald Klatz, author of *Grow Young with HGH* and president of the American Academy of Anti-Aging Medicine, comments that "HGH is the most powerful anti-aging agent out there." He also predicts that human lifespan may reach 130 years. HGH may stimulate the breakdown of body fat, stimulate the immune system, increase the level of blood sugar for energy and may help accumulate protein-building amino acids. Additional advantages of HGH may include better exercise performance, lower blood pressure, lower cholesterol, fewer wrinkles, better memory, better functioning and regrowth of major organs (which usually shrink with age).

Injections of growth hormone caused weight loss and fat loss in postmenopausal women. A small but significant increase in muscle mass was also observed.

As 75-million baby boomers are hitting middle age, the number of individuals who will take HGH is projected to double every year for the next 20 years. This is no small feat as these youth-extending injections cost an average of $20,000 annually.

Joint pains, diabetes, insulin resistance and carpal tunnel syndrome have been reported with a high dosage of HGH use. People who have had cancer must be cautious in trying the product, as HGH may stimulate some cancers. This notion has been refuted recently. Other forms of HGH are sublingual drops and a transdermal cream which may be quite effective. Physician monitoring is very important either through 24-hour urinary output of HGH or through blood testing of IGF1 or Somatomedin.

A sublingual form of HGH-releasing agents contains a combination of amino acids and key nutrients that may make growth hormone more effective in the body. This nutritional product may not produce any adverse side effects, according to Dr. Ronald Klatz. The transdermal version called Trans D Tropin™ may be more effective.

Another theory for aging proposes that high insulin levels may be deadly. Trials have shown that elevated insulin levels are intimately linked with symptoms of aging such as obesity, diabetes, cardiovascular disease, and even cancer.

Dangerous insulin resistance may go unnoticed for 40 years. While aging may be the most common cause of insulin resistance, our lifestyle may also accelerate its progression by excessive sugar consumption (115 pounds on average per person per year in the U.S.). Diabetes is the end stage of insulin resistance, resulting in one death every three minutes in the United States.

Because glucose tolerance gradually declines with age, by age 70 almost everyone develops some level of diabetes which may ultimately cause premature death. To prevent insulin resistance, the consumption of low glycemic index foods is recommended. *Pyridoxine* (B6) may also prevent complications of diabetes by inhibiting the glycosylation (or the combination with sugar) of proteins. *Aminoguan-idine* and the herbal product *Goat's Rue* (Galina officinalis) both prevent glycation of proteins.

N acetyl cysteine also may protect against diabetic complications. *Vitamin E* may improve insulin action and glucose sensitivity. *Vitamin C* may also protect the cellular membranes of diabetics. *Chromium* between 400-800 mg and *vanadium* between 50-150 mg per day have been linked positively with insulin and blood sugar control. *Fenugreek* is an herbal product which lowers blood sugar naturally. *EPA/DHA* or *fish oils* improve insulin sensitivity. Insulin resistance can be best measured by testing the blood. The best treatment is avoidance of carbohydrates in the diet.

Some life extension experts are even advocating very low carbohydrate diets with low glycemic index. Longevity, weight loss and reversal of conditions associated with aging were associated with the consumption of less than 50 grams of carbohydrates per day. When sugar levels are low, the body uses fat as fuel (in a process called lipolysis). Fat utilization may be also measured by the levels of ketones in the blood or urine.

The *glycosylation theory* of aging is similar to this concept. The attachment of sugar molecules to cellular proteins leads to the ultimate malfunctioning of the proteins. This is best exemplified through the effects of Alzheimer's disease where the nerve endings are covered by this combination of sugar and proteinaceous material that prevents normal functioning of the nerve cells.

A final theory of aging involves *free radical damage* which has been linked to a number of diseases like atherosclerosis, cancer, Alzheimer's, cataracts, arthritis and immune deficiency. The continuous bombardment of free radicals in the DNA (nuclear genetic material) of the cells can only be offset by daily repair of the DNA. When the rate of DNA repair slows down, aging occurs.

ANTIOXIDANTS

Antioxidants may prevent free radical damage. *Carotenes* contained in green, orange or yellow vegetables are beneficial. *Flavonoids* found in citrus fruits, berries, onions, parsley, green tea and red wine are also powerful antioxidants. *Vitamins C* and *E* protect elderly people from having heart disease. Vitamin E has been shown specifically to lower "bad" LDL cholesterol in elderly patients with coronary heart disease.

Vitamin E has prolonged the life of cell cultures and improved the longevity of rodents, worms and flies. A recent study has shown that 88 elderly persons fed 200 mg per day of vitamin E had improvement in their immune system and a significant increase in the amount of antibodies produced.

As aging is associated with a decline in the immune system,

which leads to higher morbidity and mortality, vitamin E supplementation should be considered for the elderly. Some gerontologists (anti-aging specialists) even throw in some B6, folic acid and selenium with the vitamins C and E for a powerful longevity cocktail.

B vitamins like *B12* and *folic acid* are essential to prevent homocysteine damage. B vitamins are needed for healthy muscles, nervous system, hair and nails.

CoQ10 may also be involved in anti aging by treating heart failure. It may increase the number of antibodies and thus resist viral and bacterial infections. In her book *Age Proof Your Body*, Elizabeth Somer recommends 30 to 90 mg of CoQ10 to protect cardiovascular function and strengthen the immune system. 120 mg of CoQ10 may slow the progression of Parkinson's disease. However, the best treatment of Parkinson's is the daily intravenous administration of *glutathione* which significantly slows progression of this disease. Only controversial data exist in labeling CoQ10 as an anti-aging agent.

Ginkgo Biloba has demonstrated beneficial effects in improving symptoms associated with aging, like reduced blood flow to the brain, dizziness, ringing in the ears, headache, short-term memory loss and depression.

Ginkgo as well as *pycnogenol* may improve vascular fragility so common in the elderly. *Butcher's broom* is another herbal product used in improving vein health in the elderly population.

A recent study showed the benefits of Ginkgo in some Alzheimer's patients. The pigments in the Ginkgo may have strong antioxidant capabilities that might strengthen the vascular system which nourishes and detoxifies the brain.

Sulfur-containing amino acids like *methionine*, *cysteine* and *glutathione* may be the "roto-rooters" of our blood stream and may protect our elderly population from the deposition of noxious products like pigments and cellular garbage.

Ashwagandha, an Indian herb, described above has also been linked with rejuvenation and anti aging. In India, it is used as an aphrodisiac. Ashwagandha influences the endocrine function (regulating estrogen production) and the central nervous system. As a rejuvenator, it promotes mental and physical stamina.

Gerovital or *procaine* was initially used by Dr. Ana Aslan, of Romania, to help those with circulatory problems and arthritis. Gerovital may also lower monoamine oxidase (MAO) which may be linked with aging (arthritis, senility and neuritis). Table 9 shows the benefits of Gerovital which will, according to Dr. Aslan, allow man to live 30 to 40% longer.

Table 9

PATIENTS TAKING GEROVITAL

1. Live 29% longer than the normal life expectancy.

2. Reduce their sick days by 40%.

3. Experience a cure for their joint pain.

4. Experience more hair growth and less gray hair.

5. Find that loose, flaccid and withered skin becomes smooth and tight.

6. Experience a reduction in memory loss and asthma.

7. Increase their circulation and reduce leg swelling.

8. Experience more energy and improvement in the immune system (fewer colds and flus).

Procaine tightens the skin, helps to regulate blood pressure and irregular heart beat, improves memory and strengthens blood vessels.

Two active ingredients were isolated from Gerovital: *diethyl amino ethanol* (DMAE) and *para amino benzoic acid* (PABA) which offer a wide range of anti-aging properties.

DMAE increases total membrane integrity and a person's life span. This product may help people sleep better and experience a feeling of well being (fewer headaches, less vertigo, and less depression). It also stabilizes heart disease and irregular heartbeat. It has a significant memory-enhancing effect. It may even improve skin-texture.

PABA, on the other hand, slows the graying of hair and improves skin problems.

Mildest cognitive impairment may be correlated to either the onset of dementia or mortality. A British study of 921 men and women, 65 years of age during a 20 year span, found an association between cognitive impairment and increased mortality due to stroke. When the subjects scored low on a mental test, the results correlated closely with an increased risk of dying from stroke.

The same study found that those people who had the lowest vitamin C concentration in the blood had also the worst cognitive function. High intake of *vitamin C* may help protect the brain and its functions.

Acetyl L-carnitine, arginine, choline, the preservative *EDTA*, *5-HTP*, *lipoic acid* and *niacin* were all shown to improve damage in the nerve cells of the brain. *Vinpocetine* and a foreign product called *Lucidril* have been shown to reverse mental decline.

Also, at the Albert Einstein College of Medicine, studies assessing 1,855 elderly people linked impaired cognition with death. Another trial of 2,123 participants in the Framingham Heart Study spanning 10 years also found a solid connection between cognitive impairment and dementia or mortality. A natural product, Galantamine, may even improve the Alzheimer's condition.

Phosphatidyl serine (PS), a naturally-occurring lipid from the brain, may slow and even stop age-related behavioral deficits. PS helps the brain to release neurotransmitters responsible for sending nerve impulses and thus allows better communication between neurons. PS dramatically helps elderly people with cognitive decline.

Researchers concluded that PS has helped people to reverse cognitive aging by 12 years; 300 milligrams of the substance per day is recommended. PS may even reverse the early signs of Alzheimer's disease.

In his best selling book, *Brain Longevity*, Dr. Dharma Singh Kalsa reports that PS significantly decreased the production of stress hormones and depression symptoms.

PS may even reduce fat pads, pendulous abdomens, striae (stretch marks), improve thin skin and easy bruising in the elderly. No side effects were noted.

Ginseng, also a brain enhancer, may help in reminding people of long forgotten behavioral reactions.

Phosphatidyl serine, *Ginkgo biloba*, and *Ginseng* may extend one's life. However, as they improve circulation, accelerate thinking, and improve memory and depression, they also elevate the quality of life.

Therefore, to increase longevity, brain health preservation seems to be the key. Good nutrition and supplementation with the above nutrients may keep our brains functioning longer and our biological clocks ticking forever.

There are certain drugs that have been linked with anti-aging. Anti-diabetic drugs *metformin* or *Glucophage*™ significantly increases weight loss when combined with a reduced calorie diet. This drug has also been suggested as one of the most promising anti-aging, life-extending drugs available, according to Dr. Ward Dean (co-author of *The Neuroendocrine Theory of Aging and Degenerative Disease*). Dr. Dean suggests a dose of 500 mg of *metformin* two to three times a day in people over the age of 40 years. In addition, *B12* should be supplemented, as metformin inhibits B12 absorption. The role of metformin as a life extender is due to its blood sugar-lowering effect. According to Dr. Dean, most adults suffer from subclinical diabetes, and thus Glucophage™ will restore insulin sensitivity to the cells and prevent deadly insulin resistance. Other benefits of metformin related to this action are the decrease of cholesterol triglycerides, and, therefore, of atherosclerosis, improved cellular immunity and suppression of the growth of certain tumors.

Aricept™, a medication that alleviates the dementia and memory loss associated with Alzheimer's disease, may also be a rejuvenator. A new study is underway to determine whether Aricept™ or *vitamin E* can prevent or delay Alzheimer's in patients over 55 with a mild cognitive impairment. Half of these patients may develop Alzheimer's. Both Aricept™ and vitamin E (2,000 IU per day) have been shown to slow the progression of Alzheimer's in patients who already have the disease.

Eldepryl™, a drug with very strong antioxidant properties, is used in patients suffering from Parkinson's syndrome. However, some doctors use this medication as a rejuvenator because it may have life-extending properties. Some other European supplements like *piracetam*, *lucidril* and *modafinil* were all devised to improve alertness, a feeling of well being, and rejuvenation.

Finally, *Sildenafil* or *Viagra*™ has been used to improve sexual arousal and to achieve orgasm in older men. Unfortunately, this drug did not benefit post-menopausal women.

In the future, designer genetically engineered drugs will replace the scalpel in surgeries that remove tumors or do cosmetic surgery. New genes will be created to cure almost every serious ailment. All surgeries will be considered pharmacologic failures. A new protein called *vascular endothelial growth factor* may restore new vessel growth in the legs of diabetics and in the heart of patients with severe cardiovascular disease.

NUTRITION AND AGING:

As described above, lean people survive better. Calorie-restricted rats have been shown to live longer by one-third of their life span. Food may increase injury from free-radical formation. Also, deposition of waste increases from food overconsumption.

The book *Antiaging Plan—Strategies and Recipes for Extending Your Healthy Years*, by Roy L. Walford, M.D. and his wife Lisa Walford, showed that low calorie diets (due to food shortages) were responsible for lowering blood pressure and for improving blood fats in those people studied.

A study of rhesus monkeys reported that a 30% reduction in calories may dramatically raise HDL (the "good" cholesterol) with a reduction in the risk of heart disease.

Eating too many calories may lead to obesity which is associated with killer diseases. As we age, our basal metabolic rate drops, and less food is needed. However, even though older bodies burn fewer calories than younger ones, they actually require bigger helpings of nutrients. Older bodies absorb nutrients from foods less efficiently than younger ones. Their intestinal tract has less absorption capacity.

While vitamins may help prevent heart disease and cancers, enormous amounts of foods are needed in order to ingest all the vitamins needed. Therefore, vitamin supplementation is recommended in the elderly population.

As people age, their thirst signal fades, and they have to be aware of their need to drink to prevent dehydration. Older people also need more fiber than younger people because the muscles in the lower intestinal tract are not as responsive as before.

Not only the sense of smell but also taste declines with age. Elderly people do not eat as much because food does not taste as good to them as it used to. They generally live alone; they have no appetite, and many die of malnutrition. Many diseases are also associated with poor appetite and weight loss. Those elderly who are too slim die soon, as they have lost too many of their immunity cells. It is, therefore, not good to be too fat or too thin.

FOOD AND ITS EFFECT ON THE ELDERLY

To prevent aging, fresh, non-processed foods are recommended. Foods that are high in ribonucleic acid (RNA) have been advocated to increase longevity. Thus, Dr. Frank recommended the consumption of peas, beets, sardines and cucumber, all high in this nuclear substance which may repair damaged nuclear DNA.

Cutting down on fat helps the cardiovascular health of the elderly. While *meat* eating may actually stimulate aging, too much refined sugar and carbohydrates may lead to diabetes and its dire consequences.

Yogurt has also been touted as the "longevity food," par excellence. Centenarians in Europe were described as having had diets heavy in raw cucumbers and yogurt. There seems to be a reason for the success of this old wives' tale.

Cucumbers contain a natural anti-inflammatory substance. Also, researchers at the VA Medical Center in Lexington, Kentucky showed that seven ounces of yogurt each day significantly reduces total cholesterol levels. In addition, probiotics from yogurt increase immunity.

Soy has also been used by postmenopausal women and older men as a cancer-prevention substance. IP6, MGN3, and colostrum as mentioned before, are substances given to patients with a family history of cancer. Antioxidant therapy has been useful in cancer and cardiovascular disease prevention.

Calcium and *Vitamin D* are necessary to combat osteoporosis in postmenopausal women. Saw palmetto, pygeum and lycopene may also prevent cancer of the prostate, so common among the elderly male population.

Glucosamine Sulfate improves the symptoms of arthritis (joint inflammation) that occur so often in the mature population. Boswella, curcumin, cetyl myristolate and methyl-sufonyl-methane are natural anti-inflammatory substances to be given to the elderly population instead of stronger anti-arthritic medications that may cause severe side effects.

Omega-3 Fatty Acids, as well as cherry juice, curcumin (from curry) and finally celery may all beat *inflammation*.

Impotence is common in elderly males and yohimbine has shown positive effects in sexual arousal by increasing arterial blood flow to the penis.

As *cancer* runs in families, frequent checkups with health professionals are recommended. There are many cancer screening tests that should be considered. Hemoccult cards may detect occult blood in the stool which may be related to cancer.

We already know that aspirin has a blood-thinning role. However, some new studies have shown that an aspirin a day also cuts the risk of digestive tumors by 30% to 50%.

When it comes to fiber, the latest study on fiber showed that this substance did not offer any protection against colon cancer. More studies on fiber are needed.

Mammograms are recommended yearly for women who are on HRT and are 50 years or older. Finally, a 24-hour analysis of the urine to check the rates of good versus bad estrogens can also determine whether a woman will have a higher incidence of breast cancer. We recommend indole 3 carbinol or diindolyl methane for all women taking estrogen.

Colonoscopies after the age of 50 reveal polyps and cancers of the digestive tract. Papanicolau smears are also recommended in the elderly to diagnose cancer of the cervix or uterus. For men, total and free PSA are suggested also.

Yearly blood work-ups can also complete the prevention picture. High blood sugar and cholesterol levels can be lowered with dietary intervention and, if necessary, with drugs.

Even though HRT was advocated as a defense against heart disease, the newest study showed no advantage in heart disease risk in patients taking estrogen. The statins that lower cholesterol levels are now thought to be more advantageous in promoting cardiovascular health.

ANTI-AGING AND EXERCISE

The best anti-aging medicine may also be fitness. Physically-fit individuals have reduced cardiovascular disease risk and, thus, decreased morbidity. Even later in life, an exercise regime improves longevity. Remember that for each minute spent on the treadmill, there is almost an 8% decrease in risk of mortality.

What is the best exercise and how much exercise is recommended for the elderly? Exercise may improve memory and reduce the risk of many diseases. The best is to exercise for at least 30 minutes, three to four days a week, at a heart rate of 80% to 90% of maximum. However, many benefits are derived with lesser intensity exercises, using a heart rate of 60% to 80% of maximum.

After age forty, most women lose about half a pound of muscle each year; and as their basal metabolic rate decreases, they gain about the same amount of fat. Strength training may prevent or even reverse these age-related changes. This was explained in Dr. M. Nelson's book, *Strong Women Stay Young*.

Other studies have demonstrated that moderate aerobics and weight training exercises can increase growth hormone levels up to two-and-a-half times; high intensity training pushes that level even higher.

While aerobic exercise may result in long-term release of growth hormone in the blood for two hours, resistance exercise causes spurts of growth hormone production.

If the exercise is too vigorous, deleterious side effects may result. Many anecdotal stories exist of people dying from cardiac arrhythmias while pushing exercise to the limit.

However, it has been reported that music conductors who move their arms frequently enjoy the longest lives! Just performing daily activities seems to produce improvements in health parameters.

Incidentally, weight-lifters do not live long lives because this extreme exercise damages and enlarges their hearts. As a large heart does not function well, these athletes die young.

Keeping our brains busy is important to prevent brain disease. Even retirees should take classes, play games, or engage in intellectual challenges to keep neuronal connections working.

Positive thinking and re-thinking stressful events are important tactics in longevity. Stress is associated with increased levels of glucocorticides (stress hormones) that directly damage the brain area responsible for memory and decrease the immune response to disease.

As we get older, we should re-think our priorities. We will be in a position to avoid any unpleasant situations which may ultimately lead to stress. Every day plan at least half an hour of a pleasant activity and delegate the unpleasant tasks to the bottom of your life's totem pole.

According to Dr. Richard Restak, "You will feel more in control when you avoid the negative results of stress." He also claims that social interactions are crucial for healthy brain aging. Older people who can talk with friends or family members about worries and fears are better able to meet the challenges of daily life.

Dr. Restak speculates that women, who exteriorize their feelings more than men, tend to live longer than men do.

A recent survey at the Royal Edinburgh Hospital in Scotland showed that people who looked 10 years younger than their real ages reported having sex at least three times a week. Is sex the fountain of youth?

While only 30% to 35% of individual differences in longevity among humans can be attributed to genes, the remaining 65% to 70 % may be enhanced by positive lifestyle factors that promote health.

By the year 2030, not only will the whole adult American population be overweight, but it is also estimated that the number of Americans age 65 or over will reach 70 million. Those age 85 and older will be the fastest growing segment of the population. Supercentenerians, who live over 110 years, are destined to become more numerous.

Medical technology must go hand in hand and advance with this increase in older population, as not only age but quality of life is obviously essential.

THE SKIN AND AGING

To make our elderly population happy, physical good looks will be most sought-after. The mature population subjects itself to all kinds of cosmetic treatments and surgical procedures to look younger and more beautiful. According to Helena Rubinstein, "There are no ugly women, only lazy ones." Barbara Cortland concludes that "After age forty, a woman has to chose between her figure and her face." Her advice is: "Keep the face and stay seated."

Those who are positive about their looks are more social and live longer.

As we age, the collagen fibers that give elasticity get disordered instead of neatly roped, and the skin gets thinner by 20%. Sun exposure damages the collagen fibers and decreases the elasticity and resiliency of the skin. The easiest procedure is the peel, either chemical, by dermabrasion or by laser, in order to remove the top layer of keratin of the skin. *Glycolic, alpha hydroxy, beta hydroxy* or *salicylic acids* are supposed to work as a chemical burn to also exfoliate the first layer of the skin.

The rejuvenating quality of *lactic acids* was discovered by Queen Cleopatra who liked to bathe in milk. Josephine Beauharnais, wife of the emperor Napoleon, continued the tradition by luxuriating in a goat milk bath to fight aging.

These acids can also give the skin a softer, more moist look and feel. They may even reduce the appearance of fine wrinkles and age spots. Age spots are caused by an accumulation of cellular debris, known as lipofucsin deposits, from molecules destroyed by free radical damage. The number and severity of age spots are a good indication of oxidative damage and sun exposure.

Chemical Peels at doctors' offices contain products with higher concentrations. **Tetrachloroacetic** acid peels are stronger peels also performed in doctors' offices. These peels burn the top layer of the skin so that there is a renewal of younger skin underneath.

Glycolic or **alpha hydroxy acids** may improve collagen content of the skin, tightening it and improving its thickness. Beta hydroxy acids are more exfoliating and deeper pore cleaners, and may work well with patients who are sensitive to alpha hydroxy acids. Beta hydroxy acids, or salicylic acids, may decrease fine lines, smooth the skin, produce more even pigmentation and decrease pore size.

It is said that the key to rejuvenation of the skin is **exfoliation**. The best exfoliation is produced by a combination of both alpha and beta hydroxy acids.

As stronger concentrations of these acids are supposed to be more effective, a 70% glycolic acid peel has been combined with strontium, a chemical found in sea water and green and leafy vegetables. The addition of strontium blocks the irritation that some patients experience and may allow the acid to stay longer on the skin. Dark-skinned people may also benefit from this combination.

Because skin renewal decreases with age, a study was undertaken to determine the role of the pH of alpha hydroxy acids in skin rejuvenation. Different lactic acid concentrations were used. The conclusion of the study was that for optimal skin renewal, the pH of the lactic acid should be acidic (between 3 and 3.5). The highest concentration of lactic acid achieved optimal results.

While over-the-counter hydroxy acids are available at low concentrations (10%), estheticians may use up to 30%, and doctors use even higher concentrations of up to 70%. New to the market is **Kinerase**™, a wrinkle reducer derived from a plant-growth factor. It improves fine wrinkling, skin texture and mottled pigmentation. In contrast to the hydroxy acids, there has been no reported irritation. Products containing collagen and elastin may also smooth wrinkles in the elderly face.

A relatively recent technique, the *"power peel"* sands the face with micronized crystals and vacuums away dead skin to leave a healthy glow. Greatest improvement comes with a series of four to six weekly peels. An even better technique is the diamond peel which uses a diamond coated wand to exfoliate the skin more gently. A series of 10 weekly diamond microdermabrasion treatments are recommended.

Lasers are high-powered beams of light that may erase everything from sun spots to wrinkles, especially around the eyes or forehead. Because lasers shrink collagen fibers, they tighten the skin. Significant risks are associated with lasers, from pigmentation problems to infection and scarring. However, improvement can last from 10 to 15 years if laser surgery is done properly.

Swiss scientists have discovered a naturally-occurring protein in the skin called *epidermal growth factor* (EGF) that aids in wound healing and skin maintenance. EGF is applied directly to the wrinkles and creates an overall youthful appearance. Dullness and dryness of older skin may, therefore, disappear!

To fill deeper wrinkles, injectable *collagen* may plump up a smile or a frown line. Beef collagen is the most frequently-used product and may be worked around the mouth lines like play dough. As elderly people develop a thinning of the lips, collagen injections around the lips create a more youthful appearance. This injections also dramatically improve wrinkles around the eyes. *Hyaluronic acids* filler, already used in Canada and Europe, will be available soon in the U.S. They are safer and last longer.

Fat Transfer is another procedure in which fat is removed from the patients buttocks or abdomen and injected into the face. In a way, we remove fat where there is plenty to areas where there is a shortage due to aging.

Botox, or purified botulinum toxin, may smooth out crow's feet and forehead lines by paralyzing the muscles in the injected area. However, very rarely, a temporary lid droop may occur with this injection. Recently, Botox is being used to erase fine lines around the lips, to smooth neck lines and even to pull up the jaw line.

Topical Hormones (estrogen and progesterone) have also been used for the purpose of skin rejuvenation. Dr. Joel Hargrove recommends postmenopausal women use 650 mg estradiol and 1,500 mg of natural progesterone in a 10-ounce bottle of Jergen's lotion. This combination dramatically improved skin texture in women. Some investigators have even recommended a 2% natural progesterone skin cream which may result in skin improvement and fading of age spots.

Human Growth Hormone in injections, sublingual drops, or lotion may also ward off aging of the skin, according to Dr. Ronald Klatz.

Antioxidant Vitamins, like vitamins C and E, are also included in some cosmetic products. Vitamin C may tone and firm aging and mature skin. Due to its melanin-reducing properties, vitamin C can improve the appearance of freckles and age spots. Our grandmothers were right after all to employ lemon juice to bleach the freckles on their faces. Vitamin E has been added to many creams and lotions to prevent oxidative damage and reduce the detrimental effects of sun exposure.

Clinical data exists on the beneficial effects of vitamin A derivatives (***Retin A***™ and ***Renova***™). These products, called ***retinoids***, may help prevent age-related skin damage and may rebuild collagen on a cumulative basis. Extensive studies have shown that they improve fine wrinkling, uneven pigmentation and rough skin texture. Improvements persist after they are discontinued for up to four years in contrast with the hydroxy acids, with which benefits stop when no longer used.

According to a commentary in the *JAMA* of May 1998, the hydroxy acids "may puff fine wrinkles" and produce water retention (edema) due to their irritating action. Concerns over those products, however, were possible blood vessel dilation and sun sensitivity. Thus, the recommendation was to use sunscreen whenever hydroxy acids are employed. This commentary also stated that neither vitamin C or E's benefits have been well established in the skin. Even *lipoic acid* and *DMAE* in a cream base have been used as an antioxidant to help smooth skin.

Aloe vera, green tea, wild yam extract and retinol may have some beneficial effect on mature skin; however no data exist to confirm this.

Besides trying to erase wrinkles, the elderly population spends much money and energy trying to fade age spots.

Chemicals called *hydroquinones* may have a bleaching effect on these pigmented areas. *Wildberry* and *kojic* acid extracts also contain a natural whitening agent.

Scars are also worrisome to some older people. *Silicone* in a spray or gel or sheeting may soften and smooth the skin. Besides being an excellent moisturizer, silicone may provide an invisible bandage for optimal healing. Scars are slowly lessened. *Cortisone* or *collagen* injections have been used as well, with some success in raising sunken scars. Laser resurfacing and dermabrasion may also work. Vitamin E has not been proven to work on scars. Merderma™, a gel derived from onions, may produce some mild improvement of scars and even stretch marks. A cream containing gerovital has been used for stretch marks while a cream containing tamoxifen is employed for scars. Clogged facial pores are now extracted with a patch that contains a sticky polymer which grabs onto the skin and yanks out pore plugs as the strip comes off.

Hyaluronic Acid is used in some of the top-selling products on the market. It is a major part of the extracellular matrix surrounding rapidly-dividing cells. It may be responsible for the rapid and scarless healing observed in fetuses. Thus, hyaluronic acid could be used to recapture youth in damaged or senescent tissues. While fetal tissues contain large amounts of hyaluronic acid, low hyaluronic acid is correlated with aging and wrinkling. Recently, hyaluronic acid was used to reduce the incidence of post-operative adhesions, as a viscoelastic agent in intraocular surgery and as a synovial replacement fluid in older joints.

Skin care products containing hyaluronic acid may stimulate new cell growth and healing especially after skin peelings. Fillers containing hyaluronic acid are used in Europe and Canada with much success.

Squalane, an extract from olive oil, is similar to vitamin E. While Japanese people believe that squalane may suppress tumor growth, studies have shown that this product may also stimulate the healing process. Beneficial effects on the skin include a decrease in dryness and smoothing of wrinkles and scaly skin.

Sun protection is very important to combat aging. *Paraaminobenzoic Acid* (PABA) has even been used for many years for this purpose. T*itanium dioxide* has been effective for PABA-sensitive patients. However, the role of sunscreen has been recently questioned, as both UVA and UVB protecting sunscreens did not provide extra protection to those using them.

Hair loss or thinning is another complaint voiced by the elderly. As protein malnutrition has detrimental effects on hair, amino acid supplementation may be the key to achieve beautiful locks. Fish oils (EPA/DHA) may help with thinning hair. *Saw palmetto* extract has also been beneficial in preventing hair loss. A solution combining omega 3 oils and saw palmetto is available for this purpose; 500 mg. of lysine was also advocated as an anti-balding remedy. Hyaluronic acid massaged into the scalp has been beneficial in hair regrowth. *Rogaine*™ and *Propecia*™ are medications that may work in some patients to stimulate hair regrowth.

For those individuals troubled by fat deposits that are diet and exercise resistant, *liposuction* may be the answer. Another option is *Endermologie*, a non-surgical technique developed in France, that uses a vacuum system to enhance skin condition and combat fatty deposits which cause cellulite. Theophylline-containing creams may also reduce the appearance of cellulite in stomach and thighs.

If everything else fails, there is always surgery! Face and neck lifts, tummy tucks and breast uplifts are common medical procedures in the elderly. Kidney, liver and heart transplants prolong the lives of those afflicted with terminal organ disease. Even machines are being produced like pacemakers and "heart mates" to keep our hearts ticking longer.

The aim is, therefore, not only to achieve a longer life (maybe to about 130 years) but also to improve our quality of life, so that we can enjoy our earthly voyage optimally!

In conclusion, we do not need to search for any elusive fountain of youth or reside in any exotic place like Shangri La. Rather, medical technology and new research will continue to prolong our life spans and the quality of our lives.

In the near future, the concept of eternal youth may actually become a possibility!

Chapter Summary

- A genetic predisposition for long life exists and "longevity genes" have been identified.

- Hormonal replacement therapy both in men and women helps longevity.

- Lean people live longer.

- While citrus fruit, fish, milk, yogurt and espresso coffee consumers live longer, meat and fat consumers live less.

- Human growth hormone injections or creams may be the rejuvenating substance of the future.

- Insulin resistance and the combination of sugar protein complexes can produce aging (glycosylation theory of aging).

- Free radical damage may be another theory of aging necessitating antioxidant therapy.

- Many nutritional supplements like Gerovital (containing DMAE and PABA), Ashwaghanda, phosphatidyl serine, and ginseng may help prevent aging.

- Drugs like Glucophage™, Aricept™, Eldepril™ may also rejuvenate the elderly.

- Low calorie diets, foods high in RNA may also prolong life.

- Cosmetic treatments and procedures abound to make the elderly good looking also.

— **Chapter Twenty-One** —

RECIPES

If you have been following my advice throughout this book, you should not even be looking at this chapter! The less you are thinking about food or are in the kitchen cooking, the better off you are!

I know, I know...you have to cook for the family and make them their favorite recipes. All right, continue preparing the same meals; however, make some healthier ones for yourself. Keep one piece of chicken or fish separate from what is intended for the family and prepare it for yourself with vegetables.

Always think ahead about what would be healthiest for you. You already know what to order when you go out; however, home cooking can be a difficult challenge for some people.

The simplest cooking, using the fewest ingredients, is recommended. Armed with the food staple list, go to your local supermarket and purchase as many of the items on the list as possible. Always use cooking spray instead of oil or shortening. I like to use low fat soups like tomato, onion, broccoli, chicken or beef to flavor different entrees.

In general, no specific portion amounts are specified as I expect everyone to improvise upon these basic healthy recipes.

BREAKFAST RECIPES

• Egg White Omelet Spanish Style

Ingredients: *2 egg whites or 2 egg substitutes*
1/2 cup shredded, fat-free cheese
1/2 cup frozen onion and pepper combination

Directions: Spray microwavable dish with non-fat spray. Cook onion and pepper combination in microwave for 1 or 2 minutes (depending on taste). Salt and pepper to taste. Add 1 to 2 eggs and 1 to 2 slices of fat-free cheese; you may put a slice of tomato on it, too. Cook in microwave untill eggs are set and cheese is melted.

• Israeli Style Breakfast

Ingredients: *low-fat cottage cheese*
1 tomato
1 cucumber
balsamic vinegar
olive or canola oil
pepper

Directions: Put a scoop of fat-free or low-fat cottage cheese in the center of your plate and add pieces of tomato, cucumber, and pepper around it. If needed, you may put some dressing made of balsamic vinegar, water and olive or canola oil. Sprinkle with salt, pepper and parsley.

• Oatmeal

High-protein, low-calorie oatmeal with a little sweetener and skim milk is another excellent breakfast alternative. Do not micro-wave for more than 1 minute and do not forget to cover the plate with something to prevent splattering of the oatmeal.

• Shake

A high-protein, low-calorie shake may be taken by those in a hurry; it may be reconstituted and eaten on the run.

LUNCH RECIPES

• Pita With Different Fillings

<u>Ingredients:</u> *1 pita pocket*
1 can tuna in water
or
turkey slices
or
chicken slices
fat-free cheese slices
lettuce leaves
tomato slices
spinach leaves
peppers (cut up)
cucumbers (cut up)
sprouts
fat-free mayonnaise

Directions: Fill a pita pocket with tuna that has been drained, or turkey, or chicken slices or fat-free cheese and any raw vegetable that you enjoy, like lettuce, tomato, spinach, peppers, cucumbers and sprouts. Use some fat-free mayonnaise or dressing if needed.

SALADS

Salads using any of the above ingredients are wonderful fillers. You may also add a scoop of cottage cheese and any other lean protein. Chef salads are popular in the summer; you may use shrimp or sardines in the salad instead of tuna, turkey or chicken.

Shrimp, crab meat or lobster may also be employed if desired. Raw zucchini, carrots, squash or onions may also add crunch to your salad. If you have extra time or have company, you can chop your salad into small pieces. Use as many colors as you desire or have available as they make the meal more appealing. Use salt and pepper as desired.

• Vegetable Salad

Ingredients: *eggplant*
                   onions
                   broccoli
                   zucchini
                   squash
                   cauliflower
                   garlic
                   tomatoes
                   green beans
                   any other vegetables you might like

Directions: The night before you plan to have the salad, slice and cook all the vegetables you have at home, either fresh or frozen (you may use eggplant, onions, broccoli, zucchini, squash, cauliflower, onions, garlic, tomatoes or green beans). Use very little water and keep them a little crunchy by microwaving them for 3 to 5 minutes depending on the quantity. Add salt, pepper, oregano or any spice to taste. While the salad is still warm, drizzle some vinegar and olive oil and store in the refrigerator. You may serve on lettuce leaves with a cherry tomato on top. (Grilling the vegetables is another possibility.)

• Salad Nicoise

Ingredients: *1 or 2 cans of green beans (cooked, fresh or frozen)*
                   balsamic vinegar
                   olive oil
                   1 can of tuna in water
                   lettuce leaves
                   hard boiled eggs
                   tomatoes
                   olives

Directions: Drain the tuna and the green beans. Mix with balsamic vinegar, olive oil and any spices desired. Place the tuna/green bean combination on lettuce leaves and decorate with quartered hard boiled eggs, tomatoes and a few olives.

• Cucumber Salad

Ingredients: *3 to 4 cucumbers*
1 teaspoon salt
1/4 cup lemon juice
5 packets of artificial sweetener
1/4 cup vinegar
fresh or dried chopped dill
paprika

Directions: Use 3 to 4 medium cucumbers peeled and sliced thinly. Put in a bowl and mix them well with the salt. Make a lemonade of 1/4 cup of lemon juice, 5 packets of artificial sweetener and 1/4 cup of vinegar. Pour over the cucumbers and refrigerate overnight. For serving, remove cucumbers from marinade and add 1 cup of fresh or dried chopped dill; sprinkle some paprika on top of the cucumbers.

• Greek Salad

Ingredients: *variety of greens*
onions
cucumbers
tomatoes
oil and vinegar, oregano
feta cheese
calamata olives

Directions: Place a variety of greens on a plate, add some sliced onions, cucumbers and tomatoes (with oil and vinegar and oregano). Put some feta cheese in the middle and garnish with calamata olives.

• Artichoke Salad

Ingredients: *fresh artichokes*
fat-free mayonnaise
or fat free dressing

Directions: Cook fresh artichokes in the microwave with water for about 10 minutes. Cool and serve whole with fat-free

mayonnaise. You may also use canned or bottled
artichokes.

• Mozzarella Salad

Ingredients: *fat-free mozzarella cheese slices*
tomatoes
hearts of palm
red wine vinegar
olive oil
dried basil

Directions: Alternate fat-free mozzarella cheese slices with tomatoes and hearts of palm. Marinate for 30 minutes with
red wine vinegar, olive oil and dried basil.

• Roasted Pepper Salad

Ingredients: *canned roasted peppers*
minced garlic, balsamic vinegar
olive oil

Directions: Marinate drained, canned roasted peppers with minced
garlic, balsamic vinegar and olive oil.

• Beet Salad

Ingredients: *beets (fresh or canned)*
garbanzo beans
fat-free mayonnaise

Directions: Slice cooked beets and marinate them with fat-free
vinaigrette. Mix beets with garbanzo beans and a tea
spoon of mayonnaise for a pink salad effect.

• Fresh Cole Slaw

Ingredients: *cabbage*
carrots
green pepper
fat-free dressing

Directions: Cabbage, carrots and green pepper may be sliced in the food processor or bought already shredded. Add your own fat-free dressing (e.g. poppyseed dressing) and spices to taste.

QUICHES (quiches can be made with many different vegetables.)

• **Spinach Quiche**

Ingredients: *fresh spinach (1 bag) or 1 box of frozen spinach*
4 egg whites
garlic
salt
pepper
fat-free parmesan cheese

Directions: Open 1 bag fresh spinach or thaw and cook 1 box of frozen spinach. Mix with 4 egg whites or 4 egg substitutes and put in a microwavable dish. Add garlic salt, salt and pepper to taste. Sprinkle fat-free parmesan cheese on top. Microwave for 2 to 3 minutes until puffy. Cut into squares or triangles.
You can do the same with pre-cooked broccoli or green beans. Also, add some shredded fat-free cheese or chicken or turkey to the mixture. Some sliced, fresh or canned mushrooms add texture to the quiche.
Sliced tomatoes sprinkled with oregano can also make a colorful topping. You can prepare the quiche the night before and bring it to work to eat cold for lunch.

• **Tortilla or Spanish Omelet**

Ingredients: *1 medium potato*
onions
peppers
1 teaspoon olive oil
garlic powder
salt
4 egg whites or 4 egg substitutes (1/2 container)

Directions: Cook 1 medium peeled potato in the microwave for 1 to 2 minutes. Be careful to put a cover on top to prevent splatter. Dice the potato. Add some fresh or frozen onions and peppers, and cook with 1 teaspoon of olive oil for about 2 minutes. Add garlic powder, salt and pepper to taste. Add 4 egg substitutes or 4 egg whites to the potato-onion mixture. Microwave for about 4 minutes until the mixture puffs up.

SOUPS

Soups can also be made beforehand and re-heated. Mix low-fat tomato, chicken or beef soups. You may add to the soup any vegetables you have in the house (e.g. 1 can of zucchini in tomato sauce or a can of low salt green beans or sliced carrots). Also, some pre-cooked cubes of turkey, chicken, soy or textured vegetable protein (TVP) may be supplemented.

• Gazpacho (cold)

Ingredients: *tomato juice (1-2 cans)*
1-2 cloves garlic
tomato
cucumber
celery
green and red peppers

Directions: Dice one-half cup each of tomato, cucumber, celery, green and red pepper. Add to the chilled tomato juice as desired. This dish may be easily made for company. Pass the crudités separately for your guests to serve themselves.

• Cold Vichyssoise

Ingredients: *1 potato*
low-fat chicken soup
white wine
or
sherry

broccoli
cauliflower
fat-free milk
fat-free cheese

Directions: Cook one potato as described above but mash it this time and add to it a can of low-fat chicken soup. Blend in your spices, the fat free milk and cheese. Cook for 2 minutes in the microwave. You may even add a drop of white wine or sherry if available. Refrigerate and serve cold. You may sprinkle parsley or dill (fresh or dry) on top.

Well-cooked broccoli or cauliflower can be blended and mixed with some fat-free milk and cheeses instead of the potato. These soups can be served hot or cold after they have been cooked for a few minutes in the microwave.

APPETIZERS

• Tuna Fish or Salmon Paté

Ingredients: *1 to 2 cans of tuna or salmon*
lemon juice
fat-free mayonnaise
dill
parsley
hard-boiled egg whites
lettuce leaves
shredded carrots
cucumbers
peppers
tomatoes

Directions: Drain 1 to 2 cans of tuna or salmon. Add lemon juice and fat-free mayonnaise. A little dill and parsley (either fresh or dried) may be supplemented. Hard-boiled egg whites may be chopped into this very well-mixed combination. Make into 1 or 2 balls. Serve on lettuce leaves and decorate with shredded carrots, cucumbers, peppers or tomatoes.

• Sardines on Cucumbers

Ingredients: *oil-free sardines*
               lemon juice
               fat-free margarine
               cucumber
               pimento
               paprika

Directions: Drain a can of oil-free sardines; mash sardines with a fork and add lemon juice and fat-free margarine to make it spreadable. Spread on top of cucumber slices. Decorate with a little pimento or sprinkle some paprika on top.

• Tuna or Salmon Mold (good for company)

Ingredients: *2 cans of tuna or salmon in water*
               1/2 cup fat-free mayonnaise
               1 tablespoon of lemon juice
               1/4 cup hot water
               1 packet of unflavored gelatin

Directions: Drain two cans of tuna or salmon packed in water. Mash the fish finely with a fork. Add 1/2 cup of fat-free mayonnaise and 1/8 cup of lemon juice. Mix 1 envelope of unflavored gelatin with 1/4 cup of hot water. Mix all together and pour in a mold, preferably a fish mold. You may spray the fish mold with fat-free shortening before using it. Refrigerate overnight or as long as needed. Put mold in hot water to loosen; you may need a sharp knife to separate edges. Be careful not to get water into the mold. Reverse mold on a plate. Decorate with salad materials (lettuce, watercress, olive, tomatoes, etc). It is a beautiful luncheon dish to be served with a salad.

CHICKEN RECIPES

• Chicken Breasts

Sprinkle chicken breasts with any spices you like and cook in the microwave for two minutes on each side. Olive oil, lemon juice, and a little paprika and garlic salt add a beautiful color. Make a few chicken breasts in advance and take one for lunch and slice it for use on your salad. Reserve the others for dinner.

Chicken breasts, already cooked and skinned, are easy to use. Finally, drained canned white breast of chicken may be another option whenever one is in a hurry.

Tip: You do not need oil to brown your food. To brown meat, chicken, or vegetables, spray a thin film of non-stick cooking spray over the bottom of a skillet. Preheat skillet and brown the food. If the food starts to stick, add a few teaspoons of water, broth or any other soups or compatible juices.

• Chicken Casserole

Ingredients:	*4-6 cooked chicken breasts*
	low-fat, low-sodium soup
	mushrooms
	carrots
	zucchini
Directions:	Use any 2 cans of low-fat, low-sodium soups (chicken, tomato, beef, broccoli, etc.). Spray baking pan with non-stick spray. Layer chicken and put soup on top. Bake at 325 degrees for 30 minutes or cook on high in the microwave for 10 minutes. Mushrooms, little peeled carrots, and sliced zucchini may also be added to the chicken casserole in the last 5 minutes. Marinades that give moisture to meats prevent carcinogenic product formation.

• Chicken Paprika

Ingredients: *4 chicken breasts*
lemon juice
lime juice
1 can of tomato soup
1 cup red & green pepper & onion slices (frozen)
paprika

Directions: Rub some spices and lemon or lime juice on the breasts. Marinate for 30 minutes. On the stove cook some tomato soup and some frozen red and green peppers and onions. Sprinkle some garlic salt. Add chicken breasts to the soup and cook about 15 minutes on one side. Simmer another 10 minutes on the other side. Sprinkle red paprika on the breasts and serve with the sauce.

Turkey slices can be substituted for the chicken breasts, but less cooking is required. You may also add some chopped tomatoes to the soup either fresh or canned. You may also sprinkle on some oregano, which gives it an Italian flavor. For those who like their food spicy, red pepper may be added.

For company, you may even sprinkle some capers and chopped olives for extra flavor. Drained artichoke hearts are another attractive option. Some people even add a touch of wine to the sauce. For extra-tender chicken, cover and cook in the oven at 325 degrees for 30 minutes instead of cooking it on the stove or microwave.

• Honey-Mustard Chicken

Ingredients: *6 chicken breasts*
1 can of tomato soup
1 cup orange juice
1/4 teaspoon garlic salt
1/4 tablespoon dried tarragon
1/4 tablespoon dried rosemary
1/4 cup honey mustard dressing (reserve until the end)

Directions: Marinate chicken in all ingredients listed above minus the honey mustard dressing for 2 hours or overnight in refrigerator. Cook for 30 to 45 minutes on a barbecue or cook at 350 degrees in an oven for 30 minutes. While chicken cooks, brush with marinade and turn. During the last 10 minutes of cooking, brush the chicken with the honey-mustard dressing.

• **Chicken Divan**

Ingredients: chicken breasts
                low-fat cheese soup
                broccoli spears (pre-cooked)
                paprika

Directions: Cook the chicken breasts in low-fat cheese soup and use broccoli spears as decoration. Sprinkle breasts with paprika.

• **Chinese Chicken**

Ingredients: pre-cooked chicken strips
                chicken-flavored broth
                celery
                green beans
                cauliflower
                broccoli
                mushrooms

Directions: Chop vegetables (fresh or frozen) and add seasonings to taste. Pour vegetables in soup and the mixture on chicken. Cook in the microwave for 6 minutes covered, then cook uncovered until liquid thickens.

• **Chicken Kabobs**

Ingredients: 5 ounces of chicken, cubed
                1 can of chicken broth
                1/2 cup mushrooms (whole)
                1/2 cup green peppers, cubed
                Spices to taste

Directions: Marinate chicken in this mixture for 30 minutes. Place chicken and vegetables on skewers. Place in a baking dish, pour marinade on top and cook in the microwave for 5 minutes. Rotate skewered chicken and vegetables, baste, and cook for another 5 minutes.

• Chicken Stir Fry

Ingredients: *frozen stir fry vegetables*
low-salt teriyaki sauce
pre-cooked chicken strips
1/2 can of chicken broth

Directions: Spray a wok with fat-free non-sticking spray. Add frozen stir fry vegetables and low-salt teriyaki sauce. When almost ready, add some pre-cooked sliced chicken strips. Add up to 1/2 can of chicken broth whenever the mixture gets too dry.

• Chicken and Broccoli

Ingredients: *4 chicken breasts, boneless and skinless*
2 cans of fat-free chicken soup or broth
1 cup cut-up broccoli
1/2 cup thinly sliced carrots

Directions: In a skillet, cook breasts in 1 can of chicken broth for 5 minutes on each side, then remove chicken. Cook the vegetables in the second can of soup until tender. Return chicken to the skillet and simmer at a low heat for 5 minutes more. You can add capers, drained artichoke, fresh or canned mushrooms and sliced olives in the last five minutes.

• Chicken Rolls for Company

Ingredients: *4 chicken breasts*
spinach
1 carrot
fat-free chicken soup

Directions: Pound each chicken breast between plastic wrap with a mallet. Then spread some cooked spinach and one whole carrot on top. Roll chicken tightly in plastic wrap; twist and knot ends. Cook the little bundles in boiling water for about 10 minutes until meat is cooked. Remove the plastic wrap and slice the chicken rolls to form colorful slices with the chicken breast as the outer layer and the spinach and carrot in the middle. Sauce can be made with fat-free chicken soup, blended carrots, and spices to your taste. Place sliced chicken in a fan shape on the plate and drizzle the sauce over it.

VEAL

• Veal Fillets with Vegetable Sauce

Ingredients: *4 veal fillets cut 1/2 inch thick*
16-ounce package of frozen broccoli, baby carrots and water chestnuts
1 can of low-fat chicken or beef broth
1 clove minced garlic

Directions: Stir vegetables and garlic into the broth. Bring to a boil, reduce heat and cover. Put veal fillets in the mixture and cook 15 to 20 minutes or until veal is done, turning once.

• Veal Goulash

Ingredients: *1 pound of veal cut into 1 inch cubes*
1 large onion thinly sliced
1/2 teaspoon paprika
1 can of low-fat tomato soup
1 can low-fat chicken soup
1/2 teaspoon garlic powder
1 bay leaf
1 tablespoon parsley, chopped (fresh or dry)

Directions: Coat a non-stick pan with cooking spray. Over high heat, cook veal in batches until brown and drain well. Remove from pan and stir in 2 cans of soup, add garlic powder, paprica, bay leaf, and onion and then cook for 1-1/2 hours until veal is tender. Add chopped parsley before reheating. Remove the bay leaf prior to serving.

• **Veal Marsala**

Ingredients: *1 pound of veal scaloppini (4 cutlets)*
1 tablespoon flour
1/4 cup Marsala wine
1 tablespoon lemon juice
1/2 teaspoon salt and 1/4 teaspoon ground pepper
1/4 teaspoon chopped parsley
1/2 cup mushrooms

Directions: Pound veal between waxed paper until thin. Then dust with flour on both sides. Heat large skillet and spray with fat-free non-stick spray. On medium heat, sauté veal until brown on both sides (5 minutes maximum). Remove meat. In the same pan, add Marsala wine, lemon juice, mushrooms and pepper, then reduce the amount of sauce, return the veal to the pan until it is thoroughly heated, sprinkle parsley and serve.

MISCELLANEOUS ENTRÉES

• **Stuffed Green Peppers**

Ingredients: *16 ounces of ground veal or ground turkey breast or 1/2 of each*
5 small green onions—finely chopped
2 green peppers
1 can of low-fat tomato soup
1/2 teaspoon garlic powder
1 cup water

Directions: Combine meat, half of the green onions and seasonings in a mixing bowl. Cut peppers in half and clean. Place mixture in pepper halves and brown in a skillet with the meat side down. Pour can of tomato soup or sauce over peppers and sprinkle with remaining onions. Cover and simmer for 25 to 35 minutes. If you are a vegetarian, ground tofu can be substituted for the ground veal or turkey.

• Stuffed Cabbage Rolls

Ingredients: *12 cabbage leaves*
1 can of chopped tomatoes
1 pound ground turkey or veal or both
2 cans of tomato soup
spices to taste
1 can of sauerkraut

Directions: Parboil some cabbage leaves in boiling water. Let cool. Rinse sauerkraut very well to remove salt. Cook sauerkraut with 1 can of tomato soup or sauce, add some frozen onions, peppers and garlic salt. You may add 1 envelope of sweetener to the mixture. Place sauerkraut mixture at bottom of a pan. Brown meat and frozen onions in a non-stick skillet. Drain. Add chopped tomatoes and spices. Put meat mixture in center of cabbage leaves and roll, seam side down. Place the rolls in the sauerkraut-lined pan and bake at 350 degrees for 30 minutes (covered). Also, ground tofu may be substituted for the ground veal or turkey.

• Garden Burger

These burgers are already prepared and need only to cook quickly in the microwave. A small microwave grill is useful for this purpose. You may also use lettuce, tomato ketchup and mustard to achieve a better taste.

• Sloppy Joe

Ingredients   *ground turkey, ground veal or tofu*
tomato soup or tomato sauce
frozen onions and peppers

Directions: Cook ground turkey, veal or tofu with frozen onions and peppers, until meat is brown. Drain fat, if any. Add tomato soup or sauce and spices. Use as a topping on vegetables.

• Meat Loaf or Meatballs
(use ground turkey, veal or tofu)

<u>Ingredients:</u>   *1 lb. Ground meat*
1 egg
1/4 cc bread crumbs (fat free)
1 T ketchup
1 T mustard
1/4 cup cold water
1 can tomato sauce or soup
salt and papper to taste

Directions: In a bowl mix all above ingredients. To prepare meatloaf: spray a baking dish and pour 1 can of tomato soup or sauce (you may add a peeled bard boiled egg in the middle of the meat so it shows when you slice the loaf). Substituting salsa for the tomato soup or sauce may add a different flavor. Cover loaf with plastic wrap and microwave for 10-15 minutes.

To prepare meatballs: the small balls of meat, may be cooked in tomato soup or sauce and simmered till done. For those who do not care for tomato sauce, vegetable soup, celery or any other vegetables can be added instead. Enjoy.

• Spanish Eye Round

<u>Ingredients:</u>   *eye round steak*
1/4 cup olive oil
1/4 cup wine
1/2 cup of water

Directions: Spanish eye round may also be prepared in the pressure cooker. Marinate eye round in water, olive oil, wine and spices to taste for at least 2 hours or overnight. Brown the meat on all sides in a non-stick skillet. Cooking in the pressure cooker for 15 to 20 minutes will allow the eye round to be tender. Carefully remove meat and refrigerate. Slice thin and warm in its own sauce.

FISH RECIPES

Fish can be cooked similarly to chicken, but less cooking time is needed. Only 1 to 2 minutes per side in the microwave is recommended. Turn the fish at least once. Also, whenever the fish flakes with a fork, remove from cooking, as longer exposure to heat will produce drying and overcooking. One may use the oven (5-10 minutes per side), the microwave or the stove, depending on preference. You can use olive oil, lemon juice, tomato juice, or soup, parsley, vegetables for accompaniment. Poached or canned asparagus goes well with any fish.

• Fillet of Sole with Tomatoes and Zucchini

Ingredients: *4 (6 ounce) sole fillets*
1 small zucchini sliced
1 medium tomato, sliced
2 tablespoons lemon juice
1 tablespoon olive oil
Seasonings to taste

Directions: Put 2 fish fillets in medium baking dish. Add one-half of the zucchini and tomato slices. Sprinkle with one-half of the lemon-olive oil mixture. Top with the other 2 fillets. Add the remaining vegetable slices and sprinkle with the lemon-olive oil mixture. Cover and cook for about 8 minutes.

• Broiled Halibut with Mustard

Ingredients: *3 (1-inch thick) halibut pieces (cut in 1/2)*
1/4 cup lemon juice
1/8 teaspoon paprika
1 tablespoon olive oil
3 tablespoons Dijon mustard
2 tablespoons minced onion
2 tablespoons minced parsley
2 tablespoons chopped pimento or red pepper

Directions: Place the 6 slices of fish in a large dish. Combine lemon juice and paprika and pour over the fish. Cover and marinate in the refrigerator for 1 hour. Remove fish and brush with 1/4 teaspoon olive oil. Broil fish 5 minutes, then turn and brush the other side with 1/4 teaspoon olive oil. Broil an additional 3 minutes or until fish flakes. Now combine the marinade, 1-1/2 teaspoon olive oil and mustard in a saucepan. Cook until smooth at medium heat. Add onion, parsley and red pepper. Reduce heat and simmer uncovered for 2 minutes. Stir and spoon over the cooked fish.

• Swordfish Italiana

Ingredients: *1/2 onion chopped*
6 peeled tomatoes or 1 can of chopped tomatoes
1 can of low-fat tomato soup
4 (3-1/2) ounce swordfish steaks or mahi mahi
salt to taste
1 tablespoon fresh or dried parsley leaves

Directions: Cook onion and tomatoes in tomato soup for 4 minutes at medium heat. Add swordfish and salt. Simmer 4 minutes. Turn fish and lower heat. Cook 2-3 minutes more. Place fish on a plate and heat sauce left for 1 minute on high heat. Pour over fish and sprinkle with parsley.

• Baked Salmon Steaks

Ingredients: *2 cups chopped celery with leaves*
    5 salmon steaks
    1 tablespoon olive oil
    1 tablespoon lemon juice
    3/4 teaspoon of tarragon, rosemary, and pepper
    6 lemon wedges

Directions: Preheat oven to 350 degrees. Arrange celery on bottom of dish. Place steaks on top. Heat oil and lemon juice, add spices and spread over fish. Bake about 25 minutes. Garnish with lemon wedges before serving.

• Stuffed Sole

Ingredients: *4 sole or flounder fillets (fresh or thawed)*
    about 3/4 of a pound
    For the stuffing use 1 (10 ounce) package of frozen
    chopped spinach or fresh cooked spinach
    2 beaten egg whites
    1 small carrot, sliced and cooked
    8 pea pods, cooked
    2 tablespoons barbecue sauce (diet)

Directions: Spray 4 (10 ounce) microwave safe custard cups with non-stick spray. Line insides of cups with fillets. Spoon stuffing made of spinach, 2 egg whites and barbecue sauce into the center. Cover with wax paper. Cook for 6 minutes. Slide fish and stuffing into plates lined with steamed carrot slices and pea pods. Makes 4 servings.

• Lemon-Herb Fish Bake

Ingredients: *2 teaspoons oil (olive or canola)*
    1/4 cup dry white wine
    1 teaspoon grated lemon zest
    2 tablespoons chopped parsley
    1 teaspoon ground thyme
    1/2 teaspoon salt

4 individual fish steaks
(halibut, snapper, swordfish or trout)

Directions: Combine oil, wine, lemon zest and juice, parsley, thyme and salt in a shallow baking dish. Place fish in marinade; turn to coat. Marinate 30 minutes. Bake, uncovered, for 15 minutes, basting frequently with marinade. Fish is done when it flakes easily and flesh is opaque. Makes 4 servings.

• Tuna Casserole

Ingredients: *4 ounces of tuna (in water)*
1 package of bouillon soup (vegetable)
1/2 cup water
1 teaspoon parsley flakes
1 teaspoon onion powder
Poultry seasoning to taste
Dill, sage or pepper to taste

Directions: Set oven to 350 degrees. Combine all ingredients in a small bowl and pour into a baking dish. Place in oven and bake for 1/2 hour or until brown. You may also microwave on high until moisture evaporates. You can add this mixture on top of cooked vegetables.

• Tangy Tuna

Ingredients: *4 ounces of tuna in water*
1/2 cup white vinegar
1/2 can of tomato soup
black pepper to taste

Directions: Preheat oven to 350 degrees. Combine all ingredients in a bowl and mix. Place in a baking dish and bake until moisture evaporates.

• Fish Fillets and Vegetables

Ingredients: *4-5 (ounces) fish fillets*
1 package of vegetable soup
Pepper and paprika to taste

> *1 cup broccoli*
> *1 cup zucchini*
> *1 cup tomatoes*
> *1 cup cauliflower*

Directions: Heat oven to 350 degrees. Sprinkle fish with 3 table-spoons of soup. Roll up fish and place in baking dish covered with cooking spray. Sprinkle with the rest of the soup. Place vegetables around fish. Cover and bake for 55 minutes or microwave on high for 20 minutes.

VEGETABLES:

Fresh vegetables are not difficult to tackle. You may use the stove or the microwave for cooking your vegetables.

• **Zucchini and Squash** slices with sliced garlic and onion can be cooked for about 5 minutes on the stove in a skillet which has been sprayed with fat-free spray. Watch that the vegetables do not get burnt.

• **Spinach**, either fresh or frozen, is easier to cook in the microwave with very little water. Add garlic salt and a pinch of nutmeg if available. After cooking, drizzle on some olive oil and serve.

• **Carrots**, **Broccoli**, and **Cauliflower** take a little longer. Cook for about 5 minutes depending on the quantity and check again. You may need to cook them for a few additional minutes, depending on their size.

• **Shredded Cabbage** cooked with tomato sauce, pepper and onions until tender makes a delicious vegetable dish.

• **Frozen Pea Pods** also present themselves as a nice accompaniment to a meal. Fresh pea pods can be cooked the same way in the microwave with a small amount of water.

• **Ratatouille** is another vegetable mixture made from eggplants, tomatoes, peppers, onion and garlic. It is low in calories and may incorporate many other vegetables, like zucchini and squash.

• **Quiches** using **Spinach**, **Broccoli** or **Cauliflower**, are also good choices (as described above).

• **Spanish Potato Omelet** is also a choice to use occasionally.

NOTE: Starches in general should not be used much during the weight loss phase. I recommend them during the weight maintenance phase.

STARCHES:

Even though I shy away from too much starch in the active weight loss phase, in the maintenance phase, some starch may be re-introduced. If you personally have a problem with pasta, rice or bread—if it causes you to overeat or if you have a sensitivity to yeast that provokes bloating whenever you eat bread—then these starches should be limited. I recommend using starches more as a flavoring than as the main meal.

• Potato Paprikash

Ingredients:	*2 to 3 potatoes cooked until tender*
	1 can of tomato sauce
	Frozen onions and peppers
	4 to 6 sliced frankfurters (fat free, soy or turkey)
	paprika
Directions:	Peel and cube the potatoes. Add to a can of fat-free tomato soup or sauce with the frozen peppers and onions (be generous with the onion pepper mixture). Cook for a few minutes. Finally, in the last 5 minutes, add 4 to 6 sliced frankfurters. Sprinkle generously with paprika to give it that wonderful Paprika taste.

• Beans

You can use green beans in any of your recipes. Garbanzo, kidney, red or black beans should be sprinkled on your salads or vegetables as a garnish not as the main meal.

• Rice

When I use rice in my meals I usually use the brown wild rice instant variety. I use the whole rice package and only half of the seasoning packet otherwise the rice would be too salty. I substitute the juice of canned vegetables for the water. I often use tomato sauce or juice. I put so many vegetables and chicken in the rice that the rice hardly shows through.

• Spanish Rice

Ingredients: *1 box of instant brown wild rice*
1/2 packet of the seasonings provided
3-4 ounces of tomato sauce
2 (8 ounce) cans of vegetables with liquids
(may use peas or green beans, carrots or corn)
1 can of chicken (white meat) with liquid
Spices to taste

Directions: Mix all ingredients, put in a microwave casserole, and cook for 10 minutes. It re-heats very well.

• Pasta Primavera

Ingredients: *spaghetti noodles*
mixed frozen vegetables
onion and pepper combination
tomato soup

Directions: Cook 1/2 box of thin spaghetti according to package directions. Add either canned or mixed frozen vegetables cooked *al dente*. You may supplement with the pepper and onion combination (also frozen). Tomato soup or sauce works well with the pasta, but it is not necessary.

Dry oregano flakes and fat-free parmesan cheese may be sprinkled to your taste before serving.

The Sloppy Joe (recipe described previously) works very well with the pasta dishes.

• Orzo Pimavera

Ingredients: *orzo*
                   any vegetable you like
                   canned chicken breast

Directions: Cook the orzo with water in the microwave for about 10 minutes, depending on quantity. Add any vegetables you have in the house, fresh, frozen or canned. Do not discard the juices of the vegetables, rather use them instead of water. Chopped tomatoes, (canned) and frozen onions and peppers may also be added. If you like, add to the mixture some canned chicken breast. The orzo should hardly be seen. Pre-cooked chicken or turkey slices can also be used. In addition, the Sloppy Joe mixture or the meatballs are other ways to serve the orzo.

ADDITIONAL VARIATIONS YOU CAN TRY

Spinach Pasta or cooked orzo with frozen spinach combination is also another option. Sprinkle fat-free parmesan cheese on top.

Couscous is another starch alternative that is easy to prepare. Check the directions on the box. You can also add any vegetables available; I especially like carrots, sweet potato, garbanzo beans and peas with this dish. Sprinkle with nutmeg and cinnamon for a Moroccan flavor.

You can create your own recipes using the staples we have given you. **Roasted peppers** look beautiful on the Spanish rice and a few canned **peas** will provide an attractive color when sprinkled on top of the rice before serving. Fresh or canned **mushrooms** can give salads and main meals an extra flavorful touch.

Canned or bottled heart of **artichokes** (drained) can also be effectively used as decoration for any of the entrees. Sliced **olives with pimento** and **capers** can be used in the rice and chicken dishes for extra flavor and color.

Presentation of the meals is very important for the dieter. The quality of your food presentation more than quantity should be emphasized. Color is another important consideration. Add as many colors as you can to your appetizers and entrees!

DESSERT PREPARATION:

Fat-Free Chocolate or **Vanilla Instant Puddings** are a wonderful ending to a meal. Use the sugar-free variety if you can. Skim milk is a necessity though. You can layer the puddings and create interesting patterns with them.

Get four **graham crackers** and place the puddings in between as a sandwich. You will then have two sandwiches available per person.

Sorbets are also delicious. Serve only one scoop per person and fill the rest of the cup with fresh or frozen thawed-out fruit.

Jell-O is a low-calorie dessert that is ubiquitous, as it is the base for many concoctions. I use the raspberry flavor the most. Instead of using cold water, I substitute a whole bag of thawed frozen raspberries or some other mixed frozen fruit. By using a pie plate, this delicious dessert turns into a healthy crust-less pie.

A store-bought or homemade **Angel Food Cake** may be sliced and fat-free pudding may be used as filling.

Vanilla Pudding may be spiced up with some instant coffee and used as a mocha-like filling.

ADDITIONAL RECOMMENDATIONS:

Dust cakes with cocoa and confectioner's sugar.

Fruit should be restricted during the strict weight loss phase. However, fruit is better than fatty desserts in the maintenance phase.

We recommend cutting up the fruit in small wedges and cubes and decorating your plate with them. Never bring the whole fruit bowl to the table. Do not buy too much fruit at one time so that you feel pressured to eat the ripe ones to prevent throwing them out, thereby consuming more then you otherwise would eat.

Restrict dried fruit which is caloric and too sweet. Buy raisins in small packets only. One packet should be either eaten as a portion of dessert or sprinkled on a whole cake. I find that fruit is delicious and does not need the fattening crust to taste well.

If too ripe, fruit can be cooked with a squirt of juice, artificial sweetener and a pinch of cinnamon or nutmeg. It makes a wonderful "compote" to serve warm or cold.

Fruit can also be poached and served in pretty glasses with a drop of white wine and artificial sweetener. Poached pears are ideal for this dish. A *coulis* (a strained sauce) of raspberries and strawberries can be made by blending these fruits and adding artificial sweetener. Putting these blended products through a sieve removes the fiber and makes a perfect *coulis* which can be drizzled on top of fruits or vanilla pudding.

Fresh or frozen thawed raspberries or strawberries can be served in parfait or champagne glasses. Fat-free vanilla pudding is allowed to fall between the berries. *Coulis* or strained fruit sauce may be drizzled for best visual effect.

Sliced apples or plums or peaches or nectarines can be arranged on a Pyrex pie plate, sprinkled with some juice and artificial sweeteners, and baked in the microwave. A small amount of fat-free liquid shortening or flour may be sprinkled on top if desired. Sometimes a small packet of raisins may also be distributed on the pie.

Cut-up green melons and orange cantaloupes are a cool, refreshing dessert. A few grapes and cherries can be added to decorate the fruit. Remember that grapes, cherries, bananas and watermelon are highly sweetened; therefore, only use a few pieces of those fruits. A drop of grenadine syrup can also sweeten most desserts.

Baked apples can be left unpeeled and simply cored. Drizzle grenadine syrup or orange juice with sweetener on top. Microwave for 5 to 10 minutes or until soft. Cooking time varies according to the quantities used.

Obviously, more elaborate desserts can be produced but with most people being weight conscious, they generally prefer a healthy meal with a healthy ending.

Dinner entrees should be treated the same as the lunch entrees; however, you may start with a salad or soup appetizer before serving the entree.

RECIPE MODIFICATIONS:

Many recipes lure us with attractive pictures in magazines. However, most of them require many ingredients, not usually available in one's home. Modify your recipes by skipping fat and replacing it with olive or canola oil; do not fry—rather use hot soups or tomato sauce to sauté your meats or fish. Instead of potatoes, pasta or rice, use more vegetables. Pasta may be substituted with spaghetti squash. Try low-fat ingredients as much as possible. Omit flour as much as possible. Chocolate may be substituted with cocoa mixed with a non-fat shortening. Use two egg whites for each whole egg in a recipe. Buy sherbet instead of ice cream. Low-fat pudding may also be frozen and eaten as ice cream.

You can also use the rule of what is less detrimental? Fruit is not as bad as cake, and sponge cake is not as bad as a layer cake; low-fat pudding is a better choice than a "mousse au chocolat" or Oreo cookies; berries and melon are better than cherries, grapes and watermelon; and fresh fruits are healthier than dried fruits.

Review all of these healthy recipes, and then make your own customized versions. Be creative while you continue to lose and maintain your weight.

BIBLIOGRAPHY

- **Acids After Myocardial Infarction**. Circulatjon 2002; 105 (16): 1897.1903.

- **Aghakhan**, Moheb M., et al. "Effect of Ephedrine, Caffeine, and Aspirin in Combinations of Weight Loss In Obese Women." *International Journal of Obesity* August 22, 1998, (8 Supplement 3): S264 (abstract pg. 636).

- **Albertazzi**, P., et al. "The Effect of Dietary Soy Supplementation on Hot Flashes." *Obstetrics Gynecology* January 1991, 1998, (1): pg. 6-11.

- **Alexander**, C.M., and Bray G.A. *In The Thyroid*. Werner's Ed, Philadelphia. Lippincolt Company, 1986, pg. 1466-1468.

- **Allura**, B., et al. "Magnesium Dietary Intake Modulates Blood Lipid Levels and Atherogenesis." *PRCC National Academy of Science* March 1990, Vol. 87, pg. 1840-1844.

- **Am** Heart J. June, 2002, 143 (6): 1092-1100.

- **Anchors**, Michael Update on the Phen-Pro Combination and My Views on Obesity in America. *The Bariatrician* Fall 2002, pg. 17 -22.

- **Apgar**, Barbara, M.D. "Do Health Products Really Help Athletic Performance?" *American Family Physician* April 1, 1999. Vol. 59, No. 7, pg. 1990-1992.

- **Aronne**, Louis J., Blank Roy, Foreyt John, and Schumacher Donald. *New Advances in the Treatment of Obesity*. American Medical Communications, 1996.

- **American Journal of Psychiatry**, March 1997. "Prospects for Beating Bulimia." *Science News* March 22, 1997, 1J1 (12), pg. 183.

- **American Journal of Clinical Nutrition** 2002, Vol. 75, Iss. 4, pg 749-753.

- **Avins**, Andrew L. and John M. Neuhaus. General Internal Medicine Section 111-A1, Veterans Affairs Medical Center, 4150 Clement St., San Francisco, CA 94121.

- **"A New Use for the Amino Acid Phenylalanine**. Catecholamines Kick Out the Demons of Depression." *Life Enhancement* July 1999, pg. 22-23.

- **Anderson**, R.E., et al. "Relationship of Physical Activity and Television Watching with Body Weight and Level of Fatness Among Children." *Results From The Third National Health and Nutrition Examination Survey*.

- **Ashy**, A.R., et al. "A Prospective Study Comparing Vertical Banded Gastroplasty Versus Laparoscopic Adjustable Gastric Banding in the Treatment of Morbid and Super Obesity." *International Journal of Obesity* April and June 1998, 83 (2), pg. 108-110.

- **Astrup**, A., et al. "Does Dietary Fat Affect Obesity? A Meta Analysis of Ad Libitum Low Fat Diets." *International Journal of Obesity* May 23, 1999, (5), S102 (abstract pg. 304).

- **Astrup**, A., et al. "Is Obesity Contagious?" *International Journal of Obesity and Related Metabolic Disorders* 1998. AM 22 (4): pg. 375-6.

- **Astrup**, A., et al. "The Role of Low Fat Diets and Fat Substitutes in Body Weight Management: What Have We Learned From Clinical Studies." *Journal of American Dietetic Association* July 1997, (7 supplement), pg. 82-87.

- **Balch**, James M.D., et al. *Prescription for Nutritional Healing*, Avery Publishing Group N.Y., 1997.

- **Barbaro**, G., et al. "Hepatic Glutathione Deficiency in ChronicHepatitis C. Quantitative Evaluation in Patients Who are HIV Positive and HIV Negative and Correlations With Plasmatic and Lymphocytic Concentrations and With The Activity of the Liver Disease." *American Journal of Gastroenterology* December 1996, 91(12): pg. 2569-2573.

- **Beeson**, V., et al. "Successful Long Term Management ofObesity in General Medical Practice." *International Journal of Obesity* August 1998, 2L (8 supplement 3): S290 (abstract pg. 742).

- **Bell**, D.G., et al. "Effects of Caffeine, Ephedrine, and Their Combination On Time To Exhaustion During High Intensity Exercise." *European Journal of Appetite Physiology and Occupational Physiology* April 1998, 77 (5): pg. 427-433.

- **Bender**, Ralf, et al. "Effect of Age on Excess Mortality in Obesity." *JAMA* April 28, 1999; Vol. 281, No. 16, pg. 1498-1504.

- **Berthold**, Heiner K., et al. "Effect of a Garlic Oil Preparation On Serum

Lipoproteins and Cholesterol Metabolism." *JAMA* June 17, 1998, Vol. 279, No. 23, pG. 1900-1901. *JAMA* June 24, 1998, Vol. 279, No. 24, pg. 2010b.

- **BioMedicina**. "What Fat Free Mice Will Tell Us About Diabetes?" *BioMedicina* February 1999, Vol. 2, No. 1, pg. 50-51.

- **Bjorntorp**, P. "Body Fat Distribution, Insulin Resistance and Metabolic Diseases." *Nutrition* September 13, 1997, (9) pg. 795-803.

- **Bjorntorp**, P. "Neuroendocrine Abnormalities in Human Obesity. Metabolism." *Clinical and Experimental* February 1995, 44, (2 Supplement), pg. 38-41.

- **Blackburn**, G.L., et al. "The Effect of Aspartame As Part of a Multi Disciplinary Weight Control Program on Short and Long Term Control Of Body Weight." *American Journal of Clinical Nutrition* February 6, 1997, 5 (2): pg. 409-418.

- **Blair**, SW., et al. "Changes In Physical Fitness and All Causes of Mortality." *JAMA* 1995, 273: pg.1093-1098.

- **Boodman**, S.G. "Childhood Experience Linked to Later Illness: Study Finds Higher Rates of Physical Problems in Adults Who Grew up in Dysfunctional Families." *Washington Post* May 26, 1998, pg. 207.

- **Biots**, Michiel L., et al. "Homocysteine and Short Term Risk of Myocardial Infarction and Stroke in the Elderly: the Rotterdam Study Correspondence." *Diederick E. Groobbee Department of Epidemiologie and Gezundheidsturg, Rijksuniversiteit,* Utrecht, P.O. Box 80035, 3508 TA Utrecht, The Netherlands. *JAMA* April 7, 1999, Vol. 281, No. 13, pg. 1155.

- **Braly**, James M.D. *Dr. Braly's Food Allergy and Nutrition Revolution*. CT. Keats Publishing, INC, New Canaan, 1992.

- **Keller**, Bruce, A.J., et al. "Food Restriction Reduces Brain Damage and Improves Behavioral Outcome Following Excitotoxic and Metabolic Insults." *JAMA* April 7, 1999.

- **Bray**, George A. *Contemporary Diagnosis and Management of Obesity*. Handbooks in Health Care Co. Newton, PA. 1998.

- **Bryner** R.W., et al. "The Effects of Exercise Intensity on Body Composition, Weight Loss, and Dietary Composition In Women." *Journal of the American College of Nutrition* February 1997, 16 (1): pg. 68-73.

- **Balcioglu**, A., et al. "Effects of Phentermine on Striatal Dopamine and Serotonin Release In Conscious Rats; In Vivo Microdyalysis Study." *International Journal of Obesity* April 1998, 22 (25): pg. 325-328.

- **Brody**, Jane E. "New Therapy for Menopause Reduces Risks." *New York Times* November 18, 1994.

- **Burke**, L.M., et al. "Glycemic Index: A New Tool in Sports Nutrition." *International Journal Of Sports Nutrition*, 1998, 8: pg. 401-415.

- **Burton**, Wayne N., et al. "Obesity: Why Is It Worth Another Look?" *American Journal of Managed Care* March 1998.

- **Campfield**, L.A., et al. "Strategies and Potential Molecular Targets for Obesity Treatment." *Science* May 29, 1998; 280 (5368): pg. 1383-7.

- **Carroll**, K.K. "Obesity As A Risk Factor For Certain Types of Cancer." *Lipids* November 1998, 33 (11): pg. 1055-1059.

- **Carroll**, P.V., et al. "Growth Hormone Deficiency In Adulthood and the Effects of Growth Hormone Replacement: A Review by the Growth Hormone Research Society, Scientific Committee." *Journal of Clinical Endocrinology and Metabolism* February 1998, 83 (2): pg. 382-395.

- **Cavaliere**, H., et al. "Addition of Natural Fibers to Orlistat May Prevent Most of the Gastrointestinal Side Effects of Lipase Inhibition." *International Journal of Obesity* May 1999, 23(5) S63: (abstract pg. 165).

- **"Chitosan**: The New Fat Blocking Supplement. There Is Only A Little Evidence It May Cause Weight Loss." *Obesity Research Update* January 1997, Vol. 2, No. 1, pg. 2.

- **"Cholesterol-lowering Margarines."** *Med Letter Drugs Therapy* June 18, 1999, 41 (1055): pg. 56-8.

- **Coakley**, E.H., et al. "Incidence of Obesity-Related Morbidities in Selected. U.S. Cohorts: Results From the Nurses' Health study and Health Professionals. Follow-up Study." *International Journal of Obesity* August 1998, 22 (8 Supplement 3) S11: (abstract pg. 40).

- **"New Cognitive Performance Among the Non-Demented Increases Matality Cognition and Pneumonia."** *Life Enhancement* June 1999, pg. 11-14.

- **Combs**, G.F. Jr., et al. "Reduction of Cancer Mortality and Incidence of Selenium Supplementation." *Med Klin* September 15, 1992, 1997, (Supplement 3): pg. 42-45.

- **Carey**, V. S., et al. "Body Fat Distribution and Risk of Non Insulin Dependent Diabetes Mellitus in Women. The Nurses' Health Study." *American Journal of Epidemiology* April 1, 1997, 145 (7): pg. 614-9.

- **Chon**, M.D., et al. "Effects of Zinc Supplementation on the Plasma Glucose Level and Insulin Activity in Genetically Obese Mice." *Biological Trace Element Research* March, 1998, 61: (3) 30: pg. 3-11.

- **"Cimetidine and Obesity = Conflicting Evidence."** *International Journal of Obesity,* 1999, Vol. 2, pg. 550-551

- **Coyne**, T. A., et al. "Comparative Bioavailability Study of Phentermine Resin and Phentermine Hcl in Normal Healthy Male Subjects." *Obesity Research* November 5, 1997, (Supplement 1) (abstract), pg. 24.

- **Crown**, Loren A. M.D., et al. "Obesity Before Pregnancy is a Risk Factor For Cesarean Delivery." *American Family Physician* March 15, 1999, Vol. 59, No. 6, pg. 1616.

- **Crouse**, et al. "Soy Protein Containing Isoflavones Reduces Plasma Concentrations of Lipids and Lipoproteins." *Thirty-Eighth Annual Conference on Cardiovascular Disease Epidemiology and Prevention* March 18-21, 1998.

- **CRP** Gains Notice as Key Market of Cardiovascular Health. *American Medical News* December 16, 2002, pg. 32

- **Cummings**, S. R., et al. "The Effect of Raloxifene on the Risk of Breast Cancer in Postmenopausal Women." *JAMA* June 16, 1999, Vol. 281, No. 23, pg. 2189-2196.

- **Dalwiski**; et al. "Subtle Hand Changes In Patients With Bulimia Nervosa." *Clinical Orthopedic and Related Research* October 1997, (343): pg. 107-109.

- **Davidson**, Mayer B., et al. "Relationship Between Fasting Plasma Glucose and Glycosylated Hemoglobin: Potential For False Positive Diagnoses of Type II Diabetes Using New Diagnostic Criteria." *JAMA* April 7, 1999, Vol. 281, No. 13, pg. 1203-1209.

- **Dawson**, Hughes B., et al. "A Controlled Trial of the Effect of Calcium Supplementation on Bone Density in Postmenopausal Women." *The New England Journal of Medicine,* 1990, 323(13): pg. 878-883.

- **Decsi**, T., et al. "Reduced Plasma Concentration of Alpha Tocopherol and Beta Carotene in Obese Boys." *Journal of Pediatrics* April 1997, 30 (4), pg. 653-655.

- **"DHEA**: A Better Antidepressant." *Life Enhancement* July, 1999, pg. 16-19.

- **Deheeger**, M., et al. "Physical Activity and Body Composition in 10-Year-Old French Children: Linkages With Nutritional Intake?" *International Journal of Obesity* May 1997, 21 (5): pg. 372-379.

- **DiPasquale**, M.G. "The Eicosanoids and Muscle Protein Synthesis." *Anabolic Research Review* 2 (1): pg. 6-10.

- **Depress**, Jean-Pierre. "Waist Circumference as a Clinical Assessment of Visceral Obesity a Risk Factor for Type II Diabetes and Cardiovascular Disease." *The Bariatrician* Spring 1999, pg. 24-28.

- **Depress**, J.P., et al. "Loss of Abdominal Fat and Metabolic Response to Exercise Training in Obese Women." *American Journal of Physiology* August 26, 1991, (2pt1): E, pg. 159-167.

- **Dionne**, J., et al. "Acute Effect of Exercise and Low Fat Diet on Energy Balance In Heavy Men." *International Journal of Obesity* May 1997, 21(5): pg. 413-416.

- **"Disease Prevention and Treatment**. Scientific Protocols that Integrate Mainstream and Alternative Medicine." *Life Extension Media,* 1997.

- **Ditschuneit**, H.H., et al. "The Effectiveness of Meal Replacement With Diet Shakes On Long Term Weight Loss and Weight Maintenance." *International Journal of Obesity* August 1998, 22 (8 Supple-ment 3) S:13 (abstract pg. 45).

- **Ditschuneit**, H.H., et al. "Metabolic and Weight -Loss Effects of a Long Term Dietary Intervention In Obese Patients." *American Journal of Clinical Nutrition* February 1999, 69 (2), pg. 198-204;

- **Downs**, John R., et al. "Primary Prevention of Acute Coronary Events with Lovastatin in Men and Women with Average Cholesterol Levels." *JAMA* May 27, 1998, Vol .279, No.20, pg. 1618-1622.

- **Dullo**, A.G., et al. "A Green Tea Extract (AR25) Rich in Catechin Polyphenols Stimulates 24-Hour Energy Expenditure and Fat Oxidation in Humans." *International Journal of Obesity* May 23, 1999, (5) S174: pg. 579.

- **Dumensnil**, J.G., et al. "Impact From High Carbohydrate to High Protein Intake on Ad Libitum Energy Intake and Satiety in Overnight Individuals." *International Journal of Obesity* August 1998, 22 (8 supplement 3) S135 (abstract pg. 144).

- **Drummond**, et al. "Evidence That Eating Frequency is Inversely Related To Body Weight Status In Male But Not Female Non-Obese Adults. Reporting Valid Dietary Intakes." *International Journal of Obesity* February 1998, 22(2): pg. 105-112.

- **Dunn**, A.L., et al. "Comparison of Lifestyle and Structural Intermissions to Increase Physical Activity and Cardiorespiratory Fitness. A Randomized Trial." *JAMA* January 27, 1999, Vol. 281, No. 4, pg. 327-334.

- **Eckerly**, Jean Ruth. "Blood Sugar Problems." *Journal of Longevity,* 1999, Vol. 5, No. 2, pg. 30-34.

- **Eddy**, Mark Ph.D., et al. "Insomnia." *American Family Physician* April 1, 1999, Vol. 59, No. 7, pg. 1911-1916.

- **Erasmus**, Udo. *Fats That Heal and Fats That Kill.* Alive Books, 1995.

- **Ernst**, E. "Acupuncture/Acupressure for Weight Reduction? A Systematic Review." *Wiener Klinische Wochenschrift* January 31, 1997, 109 (2): pg. 60-62.

- **Experimental Gerontology** 2002, Vol. 37, Iss 5, pg 629-638.

- **Feldman**, D.L., et al. "Cytoplasmic Glucocorticoid Binding Proteins in Bovine Cells." *Endocrinology*, 1996, pg. 29-36.

- **"Fish Cuts Heart Attack Risk."** *Obesity Research Update* April 1997, Vol 2, No. 4.

- **"Fish Eaters Weigh Less."** *Obesity Research Update* March 1997, 2 (3): pg. 17.

- **"Fish Oils Critical For Dieters."** *Obesity Research Update* March 1997, 2 (3): pg. 17.

- **Flatt**, Jean Pierre. "The Truth About Carbohydrates." *Obesity Research Update* January 1999. Vol. 4, No. 1, pg. 1-9.

- **Folkers**, Karl. "Relevance of the Biosynthesis of Coenzyme Q10 and of the Four Bases of DNA as a Rationale for the Molecular Causes of Cancer and a Therapy." *Institute for Biomedical Research* May 1996. *University of Texas at Austin.* Welch 4.304 Austin, TX 78712.

- **Foreyt**, J.P. and W.S. Poston, II. "Obesity: A Never Ending Cycle?" *International Journal of Fertility and Women's Medicine* March/April 1998, 43(2): pg. 111-116.

- **Foster**, G.P., et al. "Changes In Resting Energy Expenditure After Weight Loss In Obese African-American and White Women." *American Journal of Clinical Nutrition* January 1999, 69(1): pg. 13-17.

- **Frankel**, S., et al. "Childhood Energy Intake and Adult Mortality From Cancer: The Boyd Orr Cohort Study." *British Medical Journal*, February 14, 1998, 316(7130): pg. 499-504.

- **Freedman**, D.S., et al. "Secular Increases In Relative Weight and Adiposity Among Children Over 2 Decades: the Bogalusa Heart Study." *Pediatrics* 1997; March 1999, (3): pg. 420-426.

- **Friedrich**, M.J. "Steps Toward Understanding; Alleviating Osteoarthritis Will Help Aging Population." *JAMA* September 15, 1999, Vol. 282, No. 11, pg. 1023-1028.

- **"Future Diet Pill to Stimulate Metabolism."** *Obesity Research Update* April 1997, Vol. 2, No. 4, pg. 27.

- **Gaby**, Alan R. "Dehydroepiandrosterone. Biological Effects and Clinical Significance." *Alternatives Medicine Review* 1996, Vol. 1, No.2.

- **Gaby**, Alan R. *Preventing and Reversing Osteoporosis.* Prima Publishing Rocklin, CA, 1993.

- **Gadek**, J.E., et al. "Pulmonary and Critical Care Division. Effect of Enteral Feeding With Eicosapentaenoic Acid, Gamma-Linolenic Acids and Antioxidants in Patients With Acute Respiratory Distress Syndrome." *Critical Care Medicine* 1999, 27: pg. 1409-1420.

- **Gann**; et al. "Lower Prostate Cancer Risk in Men With Elevated Plasma Lycopene Levels." *JAMA* May 12, 1999, Vol. 281, No. 18, pg. 1682.

- **Gannon**, Mary, Ph.D. "Dietary Carbohydrate Structure, Digestion and Effects on Blood Sugar and Insulin." *Lecture at the ASBP meeting* October 1999; Las Vegas, Nevada.

• **Gapstur**, Susan M. "Hormone Replacement Therapy and Risk of Breast Cancer with a Favorable Histology." *JAMA* June 9, 1999, Vol. 281, No. 22, pg. 2091.

• **Ghen**, Mitchell J. "The Advanced Guide to Longevity. Medicine. 2001. Partners in Wellness. Ginkgo Extract Shown to Ease Dementia." *American Medical News* October 27, 1997, pg. 9.

• **Golay**, A. and Bobbioni, E. "The Role of Dietary Fat in Obesity." *International Journal of Obesity* 1997, 21 (supplement 3), S:2-S:11.

• **Golan**, M., et al. "Role of Behavior Modification In The Treatment of Childhood Obesity With the Parents as the Exclusive Agents of Change." *International Journal of Obesity* December 22, 1998, (12): pg. 1217-1224.

• **Golozoubova**, V., et al. "Benidipine Induces Thermogenesis In Brown Adipose Tissue By Releasing Endogenous Noradrenaline: A Possible Mechanism For the Anti-Obesity Effect of Calcium Antagonists." *International Journal of Obesity* August 1998, 22 (8Supplement 3) s 187 (abstract pg. 347).

• **Gong**, Candela C., et al. "Analysis Of The Results of Treatment of Obesity In the Hospital Outpatient Department." *Natrician Hospitalaria* October 1998, S 13 (5): pg. 215-220.

• **Gong**, D.W., et al. "Uncoupling Protein 3 Is a Mediator of Thermogenesis Regulated By Thyroid Hormones, Beta 3 Adrenegic Agonists and Leptin?" *Journal of Biological Chemistry* September 26, 1997, 272 (39), 241: pg. 129-32.

• **Grant**, K.E., et al. "Chromium and Exercise Training Effect on Obese Women." *Medicine and Science in Sports and Exercise* August 29, 1997, (8): pg. 992-998.

• **Griffin**, M., et al. "Cellular Cholesterol Synthesis. The Relationship to Post Prandial Glucose and Insulin Following Weight Loss." *Atherosclerosis* June 1998, 138 (2): pg. 313-318.

• **Grundy**, Scott M. "Prevention of Coronary Heart Disease Through Cholesterol Reduction." *AAFP* May 1997, Vol. 55, No. 6, pg. 2250-2258.

• **Gullo**, Stephen. *Thin Tastes Better*. Dell Books 1995.

• **Gura**, T. "Uncoupling Proteins Provide New Clue to Obesity's Causes." *Science* May 29, 1998, 280 (5368): pg. 1369-70.

• **Haapenen**, N., et al. "Association Between Leisure Time, Physical Activity and Body Mass Changes." *International Journal of Obesity* 1997; 21, pg. 288-296. *HWJ* January/February 1999; (13:1:2).

• **Halperin**, A., et al. "PPA Causes More Weight Loss Than Ephedrine and Aminophylline, Thyroid or Yohimbine." *Obesity Research* November 5, 1997, (supplement 1), (abstract pg. 63).

• **Halperin**, A., et al. "Orlistat Plus Sibutramine. A Therapeutic Option For Severe Obesity." *International Journal of Obesity* May 1999, 23 (5): S178 (abstract pg. 594).

• **Hanley**, Jesse M.D. "Can Aging Be Prolonged? The Impact of Non-Drug Procaine on Arteriosclerosis, Senility and Arthritis." *Journal of Longevity* 1996, Vol 2, No. 10, pg. 15-22.

• **Han**, T.S. H., et al. "Waist Circumference As a Screening Tool For Cardiovascular Risk Factors. Evaluation of Receiver Operating Characteristics." *Obesity Research* November 1996; 4 (6): pg. 433-447.

• **Hansen**, D.L., et al. "The Effect of Sibutramine on Energy Expenditure and Appetite During Chronic Treatment Without Dietary Restriction." *International Journal of Obesity* 1999, Vol. 23, pg. 1016-1024.

• **Hargrove**, Joel M.D. "An Alternative Method of Hormonal Replacement Therapy Using The Natural Sex Steroids." *Infertility and Reproductive Medicine Clinics of North America* October 1995, Vol. 6, No. 4, pg. 653- 674.

• **Heaney**, R.P. "Excess Dietary Protein May Not Adversely Affect Bone." *Journal of Nutrition* 1998, 128: pg. 1054-1057.

• **Heymsfield**, Steven B. M.D., et al. "Garcinia Cambogia (Hydroxycitric Acid) As A Potential Anti-Obesity Agent. A Randomized Controlled Trial." *JAMA* November 11, 1998, Vol. 28, No. 18, pg. 1596-1600.

• **"Hypericum Depression Trial Study Group**. Effect of Hypericum Perforatus. (St. John's Wort) in Major Depressive Disorder." *JAMA* April 10, 2002, Vol. 287, No. 14, pg. 1807-1814.

• **Heitman**, B.L., et al. "Dietary Fat Intake and Weight Gain In Women Genetically Predisposed For Obesity." *American Journal of Clinical Nutrition* January 1995, 61(6): pg. 1213-1217.

- **Helmrich**, S.P., et al. "Physical Activity And Reduced Occurence of Non-Insulin Dependent Diabetes Mellitus." *New England Journal of Medicine* 1991, 325: pg. 147-152.

- **Hermann**, J., et al. "Effects of Chromium or Copper Supplementation on Plasma Lipids. Plasma Glucose and Serum Insulin in Adults Over Age Fifty." *Journal of Nutrition for the Elderly* 1998, 18 (1): pg. 27-45.

- **Hill**, James O. Ph.D. "Energy Expenditure and Obesity." *ASBP Syllabus* December 1998, pg. 53.

- **Hirsch**, Alan R. M.D., FACP. *Scentsational Weight Loss*. Simon and Schuster 1998.

- **Hobbs**, Larry. *Lose Weight with Meridia*. Pragmatic Press 1999.

- **Hodgson**, Jonathan M., et al. "Effects of Isoflavones on Blood Pressure in Subjects with High Normal Ambulatory Blood Pressure Levels: A Randomized Controlled Trial." *JAMA* April 7, 1999 Vol. 281, No. 13, pg. 1154.

- **Holt**, Slt., et al. "Insulin Index of Foods: The Insulin Demand Generated by 1000 KJ Portions of Common Foods." *American Journal of Clinical Nutrition* November 1997, 66(5), pg. 1264-1276.

- **Holt**, Peter R. M.D. and Lipkin Martin MD. "Calcium Intake and Colon Cancer Biomarkers." *JAMA* April 7, 1999, Vol. 281, No. 13, pg. 1170-1173.

- **Huang**, M.H., et al. "Preliminary Reports of Triple Therapy for Obesity." *International Journal of Obesity* September 1996, 20 (9): pg. 930-936.

- **Huang**, B., et al. "Association of Adiposity With Prevalent Coronary Heart Disease Among Elderly Men: the Honolulu Heart Program." *International Journal of Obesity* May 21, 1997, (5): pg. 340-348.

- **Hu**, Frank, et al. "Dietary Intake of Alpha Linoleic Acid and Risk of Arrhythmia. Fatal Ischemic Heart Disease Among Women." *American Journal of Clinical Nutrition* 1999; 6, 9, pg. 890-897.

- **Hu**, Frank, et al. "A Prospective Study of Egg Consumption and Risk of Cardiovascular Disease in Men and Women." *JAMA* April 21, 1999, Vol. 281, No. 15, pg. 1387-1394.

- **Humphries**, Suzanne, et al. "Low Dietary Magnesium is Associated With Insulin Resistance in a Sample of Young Non-Diabetic Black Americans." *American Journal of Hypertension*, 1999, Vol. 12, pg. 747-756.

- **Hunt**, C.D., et al. "Effects of Dietary Zinc Depletion on Seminal Volume and Zinc Loss, Serum Testosterone Concentrations and Sperm Morphology In Young Men." *American Journal of Clinical Nutrition* July 1992, 56 (1), pg. 148-157.

- **Nutrition and Cancer**. An International Journal, 2001, Vol. 40, Iss. 2, pg. 125-133.

- **Hyckey**, M.S., et al. A New Paradigm For Type II Diabetes Mellitus: Could It Be A Disease Of The Foregut?" *Annuals of Surgery* May 1998, 227 (5)S pg. 637-643; *Discussion*, pg. 643-644.

- **"Hydrocytrate for Afternoon Cravings."** *Obesity Research Update* October, 1997 Vol. 2, No. 10, pg. 76.

- **Hwang**, Mi Young, et al. "How Much Vitamin C Do You Need?" *JAMA* April 21, 1999, Vol 281, No. 15.

- **Iannuzzi**, A. Celentano E., Panico S., et at. "Dietary and Circulating Antioxidant Vitamins in Relationship to Carotid Plaques in Middle-Aged Women." *American Journal of Clinical Nutrition* 2002; 76:582-587.

- **Ingram**, D., et al. "Case-Control Study of Phyto-Estrogens and Breast Cancer." *Lancet* October 4, 1997, 350 (9083): pg. 990-994.

- **Intensive Care Med** July 28, 2002, (7): 963-8.

- **"Interview with Artemis Simopoulus MD."** *Obesity Research Update* June 1997; 2(1):4.

- **Isojarvi**, J.L., et al. "Obesity and Endocrine Disorders In Women Taking Valproate For Epilepsy." *American Neurologist* May 1996, 39(5): pg. 559-560.

- **"Is High Fructose Corn Syrup Making Us Fat?"** *Obesity Research Update* December 1998, Vol. 3, No. 12, pg. 89-95.

- **Jacob**, S., et al. "Enhancement of Glucose Disposal in Patients With Type 2 Diabetes by 2 alpha Lipoic Acid." *Arznei mittel forschung* August 1995, 45 (8): pg. 872-874.

- **Jakiar**, J.M., et al. "Prescribing Exercise In Multiple Short Bouts Versus On Continuous Bout: Effects on Adherence, Cardiorespiratory Fitness and Weight Loss In Overweight Women." *International Journal of Obesity and Related Metabolic Disorders* December 1995, 19 (12): pg. 893-901.

- **Jakieic** J., et al. "Bioelectrical Impedance To Assess Body Composition In Obese Women: The Effect Of Ethnicity." *International Journal of Obesity* November/December 1998, 22: pg. 243-249, 12:6:82.

- **Jamieson**, James & Dorman, L.E. "Growth Hormone. Reversing Human Aging Naturally. The Methuselah Factor." *Safe Goods, Longevity News Network*.

- **Janney**, C.A., et al. "Lactation and Weight Retention." *American Journal of Clinical Nutrition* November 1997, 66(5): pg. 1116-1124.

- **Johansen**, G., et al. "Growth Hormone Treatment of Abdominally Obese Men Reduces Abdominal Fat Mass, Improves Glucose and Lipoprotein Metabolism and Reduces Diastolic Blood Pressure." *Journal of Clinical Endocrinology and Metabolism* March 1997, 82 (3): pg. 727-734.

- **John**, Cusp Melanie Pharm D. "Herbal Remedies. Adverse Effects and Drug Interactions." *American Family Physician* March 1, 1999, Vol. 59, No. 5, pg. 1239-1245.

- **Joshipura**, K.J., et al. "Fruit and Vegetable Intake in Relation to Risk of Ischemic Stroke." *JAMA* October 6, 1999, Vol. 282, No. 13, pg. 1233-1237.

- **Johnson**, L.N., et al. "The Role of Weight Loss and Acetazolamide In The Treatment Of Idiopathic Intracranial Hypertension (Pseudo Tumor Cerebri)." *Ophthalmology* 1998, 105:2313.

- **Johnston**, C.S. "Substrate Utilization and Work Efficacy During Submaximal Exercise in Vitamin C Depleted Repleted Adults." *International Journal of Vitamin Nutrition Res.* 1999; 69(1): pg. 41-44.

- **JPN J Physiol** April 2002. 52(2) 199-205.

- **Juhlin**, Lennart M.D. "Improvement of Vitiligo After Oral Treatment with vitamin B12 and Folic Acid and the Importance of Sun Exposure." *Acta Derm Venerol* (Stockholm) 1997, 77, pg. 460-462.

- **Journal ofInternational Medical Research**, 2002, Vol. 30 Iss pp 195-199.

- **Journal of the American College of Nutrition**, 2002, Vol. 21, 1ss, pg. 1468-151S.

- **Kaczman**, Tim M.D. *Herbal Support For Diabetes Management. Clinical Nutrition Insights.* Advanced Nutrition Publications 1998.

- **Kahn**, H.S., et al. "Stable Behaviors Associated With Adults' 10 Year Change In Body Mass Index and Likelihood of Gain At The Waist." *American Journal of Public Health* May 1997, 87(5): pg. 747-754.

- **Kallen**, K. "Maternal Smoking, Body Mass Index and Neural Tube Defects." *American Journal of Epidemiology* June 15, 1998, 147 (12): pg. 1103-1111.

- **Kalman**, D., et al. "Effect of Pyruvate Supplementation on Body Composition and Mood." *Current Ther. Res.* 1998, 59, pg. 793-802.

- **Kant**, A.K., et al. "Evening Eating and Subsequent Long Term Weight Change in a National Cohort." *International Journal of Obesity and Related Metabolic Disorders* May 21, 1997, (5): pg. 407-412.

- **Kunz**, I., et al. "Thermic Effect of Food. Influence of Body Fat and Beta Adrenergic Blockage." *International Journal of Obesity* May 25, 1999, (5):S91 (abstract pg. 266).

- **Kats**, G., et al. "Positive Effects of Nutritional Supplements on Body Composition Biomarker of Aging During a Weight Loss Program." *JAMA* March 1998, Vol, No.1, pg. 7.

- **Keebler**, Craig, M.D. "5-HTP in Weight Loss." *American Society of Bariatric Physicians* October 1999, Las Vegas, Nevada.

- **Kelly** Smith, J., et al. "Long Term Exercise and Atherogenic Activity of Blood Mononuclear Cells in Persons At Risk of Developing Ischemic Heart Disease." *JAMA* May 12, 1999, Vol. 281, No.18, pg. 1722-1729.

- **Kendler**, K.S., et al. "Caffeine Intake, Tolerance and Withdrawal in Women: A Population-Based Twin Study." *American Journal of Psychiatry* February 1999, pg. 156-223; 8.

- **Kennedy**, A.R., et al. "The Evidence for Soybean Products and Cancer Preventive Agents." *Journal of Nutrition,* 125:7575-770S.

- **Ketta**, R., et al. "Ephedrine/Caffeine Enhances Abdominal Fat Loss In Females." *International Journal of Obesity* August 1998, 22 (8 supplement 3): S264 (Abstract pg. 637).

- **King**, D.S., et al. "Effect of Oral Androstenedione on Serum Testosterone and Adaptations to Resistance Trainings in Young Men. A Randomize Controlled Trial." *JAMA* June 2, 1999. Vol. 281, No.21.

- **Klipstein-Grobush**, K., et al. "Dietary Iron and Risk of Myocardial Infarction in the Rotterdam Study." *American Journal of Epidemiologe* 1999, 149 (5): pg. 421-428.

- **Knekt**, P., et al. "Antioxidant Vitamin Intake and Coronary Mortality in a Longitudinal Population Study." *American Journal of Epidemiol* 1994, 139: pg. 1180-1189.

- **Kroller**, A. Ph.D., et al. "Regular Exercise and Subclinical Myocardial Injury During Prolonged Aerobic Exercise." *JAMA* November 17, 1999, Vol. 282, No. 19, pg. 1816.

- **Krotkiewski**, M., et al. "Small Doses of Triiodothyronine Can Change Some Risk Factors Associated with Abdominal Obesity." *International Journal of Obesity and Related Metabolic Disorders* October 2, 1997, (10): 92-929.

- **Lake**, J.K., et al. "Women's Reproductive Health; The Role of Body Mass Index in Early and Adult Life." *International Journal of Obesity* June 1997, 21 (6): pg. 432-438.

- **Lancet** May 15, 1999, 353 (9165): 1649-52.

- **Le Bars**, Pierre L. M.D., Ph.D.; Martin Katz M., Ph.D.; Nancy Berman, Ph.D.; Turan Itil M.D.; Alfred Freedman M .M.D., and Alan Schatzberg F.M.D. "A Placebo Controlled, Double-Blind, Randomized Trial of an Extract of Ginkgo Biloba for Dementia." *JAMA* October 22-29, 1997, Vol. 278, No. 16.

- **LeBoff**, Meryl S. M.D., et al. "Occult Vitamin D Deficiency in Postmenopausal U.S. Women with Acute Hip Fracture." *JAMA* April 28, 1999, Vol. 281, No. 16, pg. 1505-1510.

- **Leitzmann**, Michael M.D., et al. "A Prospective Study of Coffee Consumption and The Risk of Symptomatic Gallstone Disease in Men." *JAMA* June 9, 1999, Vol. 281, No. 22, pg. 2106-2112.

- **Lee**, I.M. *Physical Activity, Fitness and Cancer* Bouchard C, Shephard, R.J., Stephenst, eds. Physical Activity, Fitness, and Health. Champaign, IL: Human Kinetics 1994, pg. 814-831.

- **Levine**, J.A., et al. "Fat Free Mass Predicts Susceptibility To Fat Accumulation with Overfeeding." *Obesity Research* November 1997, 5 (supplement 1), (abstract pg. 094).

- **Levine**, Mark M.D. "Criteria and Recommendations for Vitamin C Intake." *JAMA* April 21, 1999, Vol. 281, No. 15, pg. 1415-1422.

- **Lindroos**, A.K., et al. "Dietary Intake in Relation to Restrained Eating Disinhibition and Hunger in Obese and Non-Obese Swedish Women." *Obesity Research* May 1997, 5(3): pg. 175-182.

- **Lobo**, et al. "Reduction of Homocysteine Levels." *American Journal of Cardiology* 1999, 85: pg. 821-825.

- **Loh**, M.Y., et al. "Dietary Fat Type and Level Influence Adiposity Development in Obese But Non-Lean Zucker Rats." *Proceedings of the Society For Experimental Biology and Medicine* May 1998, 218(1): pg. 38-44.

- **Losonczy**, K.G., et al. "Vitamin E and Vitamin C Supplement Use and Risk of All-Cause and Coronary Heart Disease Mortality in Older Persons." *American Journal of Clinical Nutrition* 1996, 64: pg. 190-196.

- **"Lower Estrogen Doses Found To Be Effective."** *American Medical Association News* June 14, 1999, pg. 32.

- **Ludwig**, D.S., et al. "High Glycemic Index Foods, Overeating and Obesity." *Pediatrics* March 10, 1999, 103(3), E26.

- **Luft**, F. "Putative Mechanism of Blood Pressure Reduction Induced by Increase in Dietary Calcium Intake." *American Journal of Hypertension* August 1990, Vol. 3, No. 8, part 2.

- **Manson**, J.E., et al. "Physical Activity and Reduced Occurrence of Non-Insulin Dependent Diabetes Mellitus in Women." *Lancet* 1991, 338: pg. 774-778.

- **Manson**, JoAnn, et al. "Body Weight and Mortality Among Women." *New England Journal of Medicine* September 14, 1995, 333, pg. 677-685.

- **Marchioli**, R., et al. Early protection against sudden death by Omega3 Polyunsaturated Fatty Acids After Myocardial Infarction. *Circulation* 2002, 105 (16): 1897-1903

- **Marcus**, B.H., et al. "Efficacy of Exercise As An Aid For Smoking Cessation In Women." *Archives of Internal Medicine* June 14, 1999, 159 (11): pg. 1229-1234.

- **Mantzovor**, C.S., et al. "Circulating Insulin Concentration, Smoking and Alcohol Intake Are Important Independent Predictors of Leptin In Young, Healthy Men." *Obesity Research* May 6, 1998, (3): pg. 179-186.

- **McCarty**, M.F. "Reduction of Free Fatty Acids May Ameliorate Risk Factors Associated with Abdominal Obesity." *Medical Hypothesis* 1995, 44(4): pg. 278-286.
- **"Meals Per Day**: Three Better Than Five For Losing Weight." *Obesity Research Update* July 1999, Vol. 4, No. 7.
- **Mertens**, D.J., et al. "Exercise Without Dietary Restriction as a Means to Long-Term Fat Loss in the Obese Cardiac Patient." *Journal of Sports Medicine and Physical Fitness* December, 1998; 38 (4): pg. 310-316.
- **"Metformin Increases Weight Loss."** *Obesity Research Update* November, 1998, Vol. 3, No. 3, pg. 81.
- **Miller**, James P. "Lilly's Prozac Gets Approval of FDA For Treating Eating Disorder Bulimia." *Wall Street Journal* November 26, 1996, B8.
- **Miller**, W.C., et al. "A Meta-Analysis of the Past 25 Years of Weight Loss Research Using Diet, Exercise or Diet Plus Exercise Intervention." *International Journal of Obesity and Related Metabolic Disorders* October 21, 1997, (10): pg. 941-947.
- **Molokhia**, M. "Obesity Wars A Pilot Study of Very Low Calorie Diets In General Practice." *British Journal of General Practice* May, 1998, 48 (430): pg. 1251-1252.
- **McKinney**, Douglas E. "Saw Palmetto for Benign Prostatic Hyperplasia." *JAMA* May 12, 1999, Vol. 281, No.18, pg. 1699.
- **Molnar**, D., et al. "Effectivness and Safety of Letigen (ephedrine/caffeine): The First Blind Placebo-Controlled Pilot Study In Adolescents." *International Journal of Obesity* May 23, 1999, (5):S62 (abstract pg. 162).
- **Moore**, M.A., et al. "Implications of the Hyperinsulinemia Diabetes Cancer Link for Preventive Efforts." *European Journal of Cancer Prevention* 1998; American 7 (2), pg. 89-107.
- **Morgenthaler**, John, and Leonard Lane, Ph.D. *5-HTP, the Natural Alternative to Prozac. A Smart Drug Series Special Report.*
- **Moroney**, Joan T., et al. "Low Density Lipoprotein Cholesterol and the Risk of Dementia with Stroke." *JAMA* July 21, 1999, Vol. 282, No. 3.
- **Muller**, J.F., et al. "Significance of a LifeStyle Change in Arterial Hypertension." *Fortschrifte der Medizin* December 10, 1998, 116(34): pg. 20-25.
- **Mulnard** RA, Cotman C.W., Kawas C., et al. "Estrogen replacement Therapy for treatment of mild to moderate Alzheimer's disease." *JAMA* 2000, 283: pg. 1007-1015.
- **Murray**, T. Michael. "Healing Powers of Herbs Reprinted." *Health Counsels Magazine* 1997, Impak Communications.
- **Murray**, Michael T., N.D. *5-HTP The Natural Way to Boost Serotonin and Overcome Depression, Obesity and Insomnia* 1998.
- **Murray**, Michael, N.D. "Osteoporosis Prevention and Treatment Beyond Calcium." *Natural Medicine* Summer 1999, Vol. 2.
- **Murray**, Michael T., N.D. "Which Is Better—Aged Versus Fresh Garlic, Glucosamine Sulfate Versus Chondroitin Sulfate?" *American Journal of Natural Medicine* May, 1997, Vol. 4, No. 4.
- **Must**, Aviva Ph.D. "Overweight in Adolescence Increases Mortality and Morbidity in Adulthood." *New England Journal of Medicine* 1992, 327: pg. 135-1355.
- **Nagata**, C., et al. "Decreased Serum Cholesterol Concentration Is Associated With High Intake of Soy Products In Japanese Men and Women." *Journal of Nutrition* February, 1998, 128 (2): pg. 209-213.
- **Namey**, Thomas C., et al. "High Fat Very Low Carbohydrate Diet Induces Weight Loss and An Improved Lipids Associated With A Degree Of Insulin Suppression In Obese Humans." *Obesity Research* November 1997, 5 (supplement 11), (abstract pg. 109).
- **Nappo**, Francesco, et al. "Impairment of Endothelial Functions By Adult Hyperhomocysteinemia and Reversal By Antioxidant Vitamins." *JAMA* 1999, 281: pg. 2113-2118.
- **Narbro**, K., et al. "Economic Consequences of Sick Leave and Early Retirement In Obese Swedish Women." *International Journal of Obesity* October 1996, 20 (10): pg. 895-903.
- **"Nature Genetics."** *Science News* March 1997, 8 151 (10), pg. 142.
- **"Nature Medicine."** February 1997. Ritter M. "Studies Link Low Hormone Level With Weight Gain." *Associated Press* January 30, 1997.

- **Nelson**, Miriam E. *Strong Women Stay Young*. Bantam Books 1997.
- **Nielsen**, F.H., et al. "Effect of Dietary Boron On Mineral, Estrogen, and Testosterone Metabolism In Postmenopausal Women." *FASEB J* November 5, 1987, pg. 394-397.
- **"Nutrition and Cataracts."** *Review of Ophthalmology* May 1999, pg. 89.
- **"Obesity virus?"** *Obesity Research Update* April 27, 1997, Vol. 2, No. 4.
- **"Obesity and Cancerr-The Latest Information."** The Bariatician Fall 2002, pg. 11-15.
- **O'Brien**, P.E., et al. "Prospective Study of A Laparoscopically Placed, Adjustable Gastric Band in the Treatment of Morbid Obesity." *British Journal of Surgery* January 1999, 86 (1): pg. 113-118.
- **Obrosova**, I., et al. "Diabetes Induced Changes in Lens Antioxidant Status, Glucose Utilization and Energy Metabolism: Effect of DL Alpha linoleic Acid." *Diabetologia* December 1998, 41 (12): pg. 1442-1450.
- **"Olestra Does Not Cause Gastrointestinal Upset."** *Obesity Research Update* February 1998, Vol. 3; No. 2, pg. 14-15.
- **"Omega 3 For Mood Swing."** *Life Enhancement* July, 1999, pg. 24-26.
- **Ortega**, R.M., et al. "Difference In The Breakfast Habits of Overweight Obese and Normal Weight School Children." *International Journal for Vitamin and Nutrition Research* 1998, 68 (2): pg. 125-132.
- **Osganian**, Stavroula M.D., et al. "Distribution of and Factors Associated With Serum Homocysteine Levels In Children. Child and Adolescent Trial For Cardiovascular Health." *JAMA* April 7, 1999, Vol. 281, No. 13, pg. 1189-1196.
- **Palambo**, P.J. "Metformin: Effects On Cardiovascular Risk Factors In Patients With Non-Insulin Dependent Diabetes Mellitus." *Journal of Diabetes and Its Complications* March/April 1998, 12(2): pg. 110-119.
- **Pasman**, W.J., et al. "Effect of Exercise Training on Long Term Weight Maintenance In Weight Reduced Men." *Metabolism: Clincal and Experimental* January 1999, 48 (1): pg. 15-21.
- **Phinney**, Stephen M.D., Ph.D. "Membranes and Genetic Obesity in Humans." *Presented at The ASBP Meeting* December 4, 1998. San Antonio, Texas.
- **Peacock**, J.M., et al. "Relationship of Serum and Dietary Magnesium to Incident Hypertension: The Atherosclerosis Risk In Communities (ARIC) Study." *Ann Epidemiol* April 1999, 9 (3): pg. 159-165.
- **Pereyra**, L., et al. "Eating Attitudes, Dietary Intake and Dieting Behaviors In College Females." *Journal of the American Dietetic Association* 1997; 97 (Supplement) A-48, HWJ January/February 1999, 13:1:3.
- **Pi**, Sunyer F.X. "Comparison of Different Weight Loss Treatments Over 40 Weeks." *Obesity Research*, November 1997, 5 (Supplement 11), (abstract pg. 113).
- **Phytotherapy Research**, 2002 Vol. 16, Suppll 1, pg. 140-144.
- **Pietrobelli**, A., et al. "Fat Loss Decreases and Weight Loss Increases All Causes of Mortality: Results From The Epidemiologic Studies." *International Journal of Obesity* August 1998, 22 (8 Supplement 3), S11 (abstract pg. 39).
- **Prasad**, K. "Dietary Flax Seed In Prevention of Hypercholesterolemic Atherosclerosis." *Atherosclerosis* July 11, 1997, 132 (1): pg. 69-76.
- **"Prescriber's Letter."** *Women's Health* April 1999, pg. 22.
- **"Prescriber's Letter."** *Women's Health* April 2002, Vol. 9, No. 4, pg. 22-23.
- **Prior**, J.C. "Progesterone As A Bone-Trophic Hormone." *Endocrine Reviews* 1997, Vol. 1, No. 2, pg. 386-398.
- **Powell**, T., et al. "Ma Huang Strikes Again. Ephedrine and Nephrolithiasis." *American Journal of Kidney Diseases* July 1998, 32 (1): pg. 153-159.
- **"Preventing Smoking Cessation Weight Gain."** *Obesity Research Update*, January 1997, Vol. 2, No. 1, pg. 3.
- **Proserpi**, C., et al. "Ad Libitum Intake Of A High Carbohydrate or High Fat Diet In Young Men. Effects On Nutrient Balances." *American Journal of Clinical Nutrition* September 1997, 66 (3): pg. 539-545.
- **"Pyruvate Unproven**. UCLA's Dr. Maxwell Speaks." *Obesity Research Update* June 1997, Vol. 2, No. 6.

- **"Quantum Sufficit."** *American Family Physician* April 15, 1999, Vol. 59, No. 8, pg. 2088.
- **"Quick Uptakes**. Cancer Risk in Diet Supplement." *JAMA* April 28, 1999, Vol. 281, No. 16, pg. 1480.
- **Raben**, A. "Spontaneous Weight Loss In Young Subjects of Normal Weight after 11 Weeks of Unrestricted Intake of A Low Fat/High Fiber Diet." *Ugeskrift fur Laeger* March 3, 1997, 159 (10): pg. 1448-1453.
- **Raben**, A., et al. "Replacement of Dietary Fat By Sucrose or Starch. Effects on Ad Libitum Energy Intake, Energy Expenditure and Body Weight In Formerly Obese and Never Obese Subjects." *International Journal of Obesity* October 21, 1997, (10): pg. 846-859.
- **Ramirez**, Johannes M.D. "Hormone Replacement Therapy." *Bio-Medicina* May 1999, Vol. 2, No. 4, pg. 196-199.
- **Ramirez**, Johannes M.D. "Strategies for Preventing Type II Diabetes." *Bio-Medicina* March 1999, Vol. 2, No. 2, pg. 101-108.
- **Ramsey**, J.J., et al. "Energy Expenditure, Body Composition and Glucose Metabolism In Lean and Obese Rhesus Monkeys Treated With Ephedrine and Caffeine." *American Journal of Clinical Nutrition* July 1998, 68 (1): pg. 42-51.
- **Ranneries**, et al. "Low Energy Metabolism In Persons Predisposed to Obesity: Significance of the Thyroid Status." *Ugeskrift fur Laeger* January 1998, 26, 160 (5): pg. 4-647.
- **Raz**, Raul. "A Controlled Trial of Intravaginal Estriol In Postmenopausal Women With Recurrent Urinary Tract Infections." *New England Journal of Medicine* 1993, 329: pg. 753-756.
- **Renna**, Chris and Richard Lohen. "Can Precursors Increase the Use Of Nutritional Precursors With Phen/ Fen?" *Obesity Research Update* May 1997, Vol. 2, No. 5.
- **Renna**, Chris D.O. *Personal Communication*, 1997-1998.
- **Richelsen**, B., et al. "Effects Of GH Treatment for 4 Months in Growth Hormone Deficient Adults on Adipose and Muscle Lipoprotein Lipase Activity and Body Composition." *International Journal of Obesity* June 21, 1997, (supplement 2), S 39 (abstract pg. 92).
- **Richardson**, A.J., et al. "A Randomized Double Blind Placebo Controlled Study of the Effects of Supplementation with Highly Unsatuurated Fatty Acids on ADHD-Relatcd Symptoms in Children with Specific Learning Difficulties Frog Neuropsychopharmacal Biol Psychiatry." 2002; 26 (2): 233-9.
- **"Risk of Coronary Heart Disease Among Women."** *JAMA* June 2, 1999, Vol. 281, No. 21, pg. 1198-2004
- **Ritter**, M. "Appetite Suppressor Found in Rats." *Associated Press* May 1998.
- **Rocchini**, A.P., et al. "Clonidine Prevents Insulin Resistance and Hypertension In Obese Dogs." *Hypertension* January 1999, 33, (1 pt 2), pg. 548-553.
- **Rolls**, B.J., et al. "Energy Density But Not Fat Content Of Foods Affected Energy Intake In Lean and Obese Women." *American Journal of Clinical Nutrition* May 1999, 69 (5): pg. 863-871.
- **Rose**, Johanne L.A C.A. *Natural Approach To Depression. Clinical Nutrition Insights*. Advanced Nutrition Publications Inc. 1998.
- **Rosenson**, Robert S., et al. "Antiatherothrombotic Properties of Statins, Implications For Cardiovascular Event Reduction." *JAMA* May 27, 1998, Vol. 279, No. 20, pg. 1643-1645.
- **Rosner**, S., et al. "Smoking Cessation Rates Improved by an Intensive Weight Control Program and Simultaneous Weight Loss." *International Journal of Obesity*, June 1997, 21, (Supple-ment 2), S 25 (abstracts pg. 55).
- **Ross**, Julia M.D. *The Diet Cure* 1999. Viking Penguin Putnam.
- **Ross** G. Webster, M.D., et al. "Association of Coffee and Caffeine Intake With the Risk of Parkinson Disease." *JAMA* May 24/31, 2000, Vol. 283, No.20, pg. 2674-79.
- **Rothacker**, D.Q., et al. "Effectiveness Of a Garcinia Cambogia and Natural Caffeine Combination In Weight Loss. A Double Blinded Placebo-Controlled Pilot Study." *International Journal of Obesity* June 1997, 21 (supplement 2), 545, (abstract pg. 118).
- **Rouzier**, Neal. "Optimal Thyroid Replacement." *4th Annual Obesity Symposium* October 1999, Las Vegas, Nevada.
- **Rouzier**, Neal. *Natural Hormone Replacement for Men and Women. How to Achieve Healthy Aging* 2001. World Link Medical Publishing.

- **Sadovsky**, Richard M.D. *Beer, Wine, or Liquor, and the Risk of Myocardial Infarction* April 1, 1999, Vol. 59, No. 7, pg. 1926.

- **Sahelian**, Ray M.D. *5-HTP Nature's Serotonin Solution.* Avery Publishing Group. Garden City Park NY, 1998.

- **Sala**, Daniel. "Exercise Monitor Helpful for Weight Loss." *Obesity Research Update* May 1998, Vol 3.

- **Saltman**, R.D.; Strause L.G. "The Role of Trace Minerals In Osteoporosis." *Journal of the American College of Nutrition* August 1993, 12 (4): pg. 384-389.

- **Samaras**, K., et al. "Genetic and Environmental Influences on Total Body and Central Abdominal Fat: The Effect of Physical Activity in Female Twins." *Annals of Internal Medicine* June 1, 1999, 130 (11): pg. 873-882.

- **Schaefer**, F., et al. "Body Mass Index and Percentage Fat Mass In Healthy German Schoolchildren and Adolescents." *International Journal of Obesity* May 1998, 22 (5): 461-469.

- **Schaller**, J.L.; Birchrunville, PA, Fabio Firenzuli MD, et al. St. Joseph's Hospital, Empoli, Italy, Both Letters to The Editor. *JAMA* July 21, 1999, Vol 282, No. 3.

- **Schick**, S.M., et al. "Persons Successful at Long Term Weight Loss and Maintenance Continue to Consume a Low Energy, Low Fat Diet." *Journal of the American Dietetic Association* 1998, Am 98 (4): pg. 408-413.

- **Scho**, Henry C. "The Bariatrician as a Preventive Medicine Physician." *The Bariatrician* Spring, 1999, pg 30-31.

- **Schonfeld-Warden**, et al. "Pediatric Obesity. An Overview Of Etiology and Treatment." *Pediatric Clinics of North America* April 1997, 44 (2): pg. 339-361.

- **Schreiber**, G.B., et al. "Weight Modification Efforts Reported by Black and White Preadolescent Girls. National Heart, Lung, and Blood Institute. Growth and Health Study." *Pediatrics* July, 1996, 98 (1): pg. 63-70.

- **Schwartz**, J. "Fat Fighting Drug Shows Results in First Human Trial. Natural Hormone Helped Test Subjects Lose Weight." *Washington Post* June 1998, pg. A14.

- **Sears**, Barry. *The Omega Rx Zone: The Miracle of the New High Dose Fish Oil.* Regan Books (Harper Collins), 2002.

- **"Selenium** Is Key To Liver Health." *Prescription for Health* October, 1999, pg. 5.

- **Sesso**, H.D., et al. "Coffee and Tea Intake and The Risk Of Myocardial Infarction." *American Journal of Epidemiology* January 15, 1999, 149 (2): pg. 162-167.

- **Severus**, W.E., et al. "Omega 3 Fatty Acids-The Missing Link?" *Arch Gen Psychiatry* 1999, 56 (4): 380.1.

- **Shamsuddin**, Abulkalam M. M.D., Ph.D. *Ip6: Nature's Revolutionary Cancer Fighter.* Kensington Books, 1998.

- **Shults**, C.W., et al. *Effects of Coenzyme Q1 0 in early Parkinson disease: Evidence of Slowing of the Functional Decline Arch Neurol* October 2002, 59 (10):1541-50.

- **Shaywitz**, S.E., et al. "Effect of Estrogen on Brain Activation Patterns in Postmenopausal Women During Working Memory Tasks." *JAMA* April 7, 1999, Vol. 281, No. 13, pg. 1197-1202.

- **Shuckit**, Marc A. M.D. "New Findings In The Genetics of Alcoholism." *JAMA* May 26, 1999, Vol. 281, No. 20, pg. 1875-1876.

- **Simms**, Mic. "Insulin Control Life Extension Program. Lose Weight, Feel Great and Live Longer." *Vitamin Research News* May 1999, pg. 1-16.

- **Simopoulos**, Artemis M.D. *The Omega Plan.* Harper Collins, 1998.

- **Skov**, A.R., et al. "Cimetidine Reduces Weight and Improves Metabolic Control in Overweight Patients with Type II Diabetes." *International Journal of Obesity* November 1998, 22 (11): pg. 1041-1045.

- **Snyder**, K.A., et al. "The Effects of Long Term, Moderate Intensity Intermittent Exercise on Aerobic Capacity, Body Composition, Blood Lipids, Insulin, and Glucose in Overweight Females." *International Journal of Obesity* December 21, 1999, (12): pg. 1180-1189.

- **St. Birketvedt**, G., et al. "Effects of Cimetidine Suspension on Appetite and Weight in Overweight Subjects." *BMJ* 1993, 306: pg. 1091-1093.

- **"Study Suggests a Possible Link Between HiSb Starch Diet and Pancreatic Cancer in Overweight, Sedentary Women (from the Dana FarOOr Cancer Institute)."** *The Bariatrician Fall* 2002.

- **Stampler**; et al. "Vitamin E Consumption and the Risk of Coronary Disease in Women." *New England Journal of Medicine* 1993, 328: pg. 1444-144.

- **Steen** S.N., et al. "Are Obese Adolescent Boys Ignoring an Important Health Risk?" *International Journal of Eating Disorders* November 1996, 20 (3): pg. 281-286.

- **Stephenson**, Joan. "X- Ray Analysis of Hair Reveals Breast Cancer." *JAMA* May 5, 1999, Vol. 281, No. 17.

- **Stephenson**, Joan. "Maternal Smoking, Diabetes Links Described." *JAMA* February 13, 2002, Vol. 287, No. 6, pg. 706.

- **Stevens**, J., et al. "The Effect of Age on the Association Between Body Mass Index and Mortality." *New England Journal of Medicine* 1998, 338: pg. 1-7.

- **Stout**, J., et al. "Effects of 8 weeks of Creatine Supplementation on Exercise. Performance and Fat Free Weight in Football Players During Training." *Nutrition Research* 1999, (2): pg. 217-225.

- **Suskind**, R.M., et al. "Advances In The Treatment of Childhood Obesity." *New England Journal of Medicine* 1988, 318: pg. 461-466.

- **Szmedra**, L., et al. "Exercise Tolerance, Body Composition and Blood Lipids In Obese African-American Women Following Short-Term Training." *Journal of Sports Medicine and Physical Fitness* March 1998, 38 (1): pg. 59-65.

- **Tabada**, V., et al. "What to Tell Your Patients About Alpha Lipoic Acid." *Skin and Aging* November 1999, pg. 81-82.

- **Takada**, H., et al. "Eating Habits, Activity, Lipids, and Body Mass Index In Japanese Children: The Shiratori Children Study." *International Journal of Obesity and Related Metabolic Disorders* May, 1998, 22 (5): pg. 470-476.

- **Takayama**, H., et al. "Long Term Feeding of Sodium Saccharin to Non-Human Primates: Implications for Urinary Tract Cancer." *Journal of the National Cancer Institute* January 7, 1998, 90 (1): pg. 19-25.

- **Tanasescu**, M., et al. "Exercise Type and Indensity in Relation to Cooronary Heart Disease in Men." *JAMA* October 23/30, 2002, Vol. 288, No. 16.

- **Tang**, A.B., et al. Preferential Reduction In Adipose (Alpha) Linoleic Acid 18:3 (omega) Lipids, 1993, 28: pg. 987-993.

- **Tanner**, L. " Obesity in Kids May Be Heart Risk." *Associated Press* December 2, 1997.

- **Tanner**, L. "Results Mixed on Fat Cure Hormone." *Associated Press* June 14, 1998.

- **Tarnopolsky**; et al. "Creatine Monohydrate Increases Strength in Patients with Neuromuscula Disease." *Neurology* March 1999, 52 (1 of 2): pg. 854-857.

- **"The Technology of Immortality."** David Jay Brown interviews Dr. Michael West. *Life Enhancement*, July 1999, pg. 26-29.

- **Thom**, E., et al. "Short and Long Term Efficacy and Tolerability of Hydroxycitrate In The Treatment Of Obesity." *International Journal of Obesity* June 21, 1997, (Supplement 2), S61 abstract, Vol. 82.

- **Thompson**; et al. "Effects Of Human Growth Hormone Insulin Like Growth Factor And Diet and Exercise On Body Composition Of Obese Postmenopausal Women." *Journal of Clinical Endocrinology and Metabolism* May 1998, 83 (s): pg. 1477-84.

- **Tholle**, et al. "Effect Of Q10 On Resting Energy Expenditure In Males." *International Journal of Obesity* August, 1998, 22 (8 Supplement 3), S158 (abstract pg. 231).

- **Thompson**, P.D., et al. "Effect Of Prolonged Exercise Training Without Weight Loss on High Density Lipoprotein Metabolism in Overweight Men." *Metabolism: Clinical and Experimental* February 1997, 46 (2): pg. 217-223.

- **Thueson**, David O., et al. "The Roles of pH and Concentration in Lactic Acid Induced Stimulation of Epidermal Turnover." *American Society of Dermatologic Surgery Inc.* 1998, 24:641: pg. 641-645.

- **Toubro**, S., et al. "A Randomized Comparison of Two Weight Reduction Diets, Calorie Counting Versus Low Fat Carbohydrate Rich Ad Libitum Diet." *Ugeskrift fur Laeger* February 2, 1998, 160 (6): pg. 816-820.

- **"Tracking Insulin Resistance in El Barrio**; News and Comments." *BioMedicina* March 1999, Vol. 2, No. 2, pg. 68 75.

- **"Treatment Cosmetics, Hype or Help."** *JAMA* May 27, 1998, Vol. 279, No. 20, pg. 1595-1596.

- **Tucker**, L.A., et al. "Obesity and Absenteeism: An Epidemiologic Study of 10,825 Employed Adults." *American Journal of Health Promotion* January/February 1998, 12(3): pg. 202-207.

- **Trillin**, Calvin. "I Like Big Seats." *Time* May 10, 1999, pg. 22.

- **Turner**, Robert F.R.C.P., et al. "Glycemic Control with Diet, Sulfonylurea, Metformin and Insulin in Patients With Type II Diabetes Mellitus." *JAMA* June 2, 1999, Vol 281, No. 21, pg. 2005-2012.

- **Ulter**, A.C., et al. "Influence of Diet and/or Exercise on Body Composition and Cardiorespiratory Fitness in Obese Women." *International Journal of Sports Nutrition* September 8, 1998, (3): pg. 213-222.

- **US Dept of Agriculture Food Survey**. Research Group. *How do Americans' Diet Measures Up To The 1995 Dietary Guidelines for Americans* August 31, 1998.

- **Van Puijenbroek**, E.P., et al. "Semen Like Urethral Discharge During the Use of Mazindol." *International Journal of Eating Disorders* July 1998, 24 (1): pg. 111-113.

- **Vasankari**, T.J., et al. "Reduced Oxidized LDL Levels After a 10 Month Exercise Program." *Medical Science Sports Exercise* 1998, 30(10): pg. 1496-1501.

- **Veergaard**, L. "Disfiguring Fat Adds to AIDS Misery." *Associated Press* June 14, 1998.

- **Vinicor**, Frank M.D. MPH. "When is Diabetes Diabetes?" *JAMA* April 7, 1999, Vol. 281, No.13

- **Visser**, M., et al. "Elevated C-reactive Protein Levels in OveR Weight and Obese Adults." *JAMA* 1999, pg. 282:2131-2135.

- **Vgintzas**, A.P., et al. "Obesity Without Sleep Apnea is Associated with Daytime Sleepiness." *Archives of Internal Medicine* June 22, 1998, 158 (12), pg. 1333-1337.

- **Vogel**, Shawna. *The Skinny on Fat, Our Obsession with Weight Control.* Freeman and Co., 1999.

- **Wadden**, T.A., et al. "Exercise in The Treatment of Obesity: Effects of Four Interventions On Body Composition Resting Energy Expenditure, Appetite, And Mood." *Journal of Consulting, and Clinical Psychology* April 1997, 65 (12): pg. 269-277.

- **Wallace**, J.M., et al. "Effects of Hormone Replacement Therapy and Social Stress on Body Fat Distribution in Surgically Post Menopausal Monkeys." *International Journal of Obesity* 1999, Vol. 23, pg. 518-527.

- **Wei**, M., et al. "Waist Circumference As The Best Predictor of NIDDM Compared to Body Mass Index Waist/Hip Ratio and Other Anthropometric Measurements in Mexican Americans, a 7 Year Prospective Study." *Obesity Research* January 1997, S(1), pg. 16-23.

- **Wells**, J.C., et al. "Investigation of the Relationship Between Infant Temperment and Later Body Composition." *International Journal of Obesity* May 1997, 21 (5): pg. 400-406.

- **Westorterp**, K.R., et al. "Relationship Between Physical Activity Related Energy Expenditure and Body Composition: a Gender Difference." *International Journal of Obesity* March 1997, 21 (3): pg. 184-188.

- **Westenhoofer**, J., et al. "Meal Frequency, Mental Performance, and Food Intake." *International Journal of Obesity* May 1999, 23 (5), S115 (abstract pg. 352).

- **"What Are the Diet Patches I've Seen Advertised?"** *Obesity Research Update* March 1997, Vol. 2, No. 3, pg. 24.

- **Whitehead**, J.M., et al. "The Effect of Protein Intake on 24 Hour Energy Expenditure During Energy Restriction." *International Journal of Obesity* 1996, 20, pg. 727-732.

- **Wilson**, James L. "Cause of Obesity and Weight Gain Pinpointed." *Journal of Longevity* 1999, Vol. 5, No. 2, pg. 15-16.

- **Won**, R; et al. "Effect of Exercise on Spontaneous Calorie Intake in Obesity." *American Journal of Clinical Nutrition* September 1982, 36 (3): pg. 470-477.

- **Wolever**, T.M., et al. "Small Weight Loss on Long Term Acarbose Therapy with No Change in Dietary Pattern or Nutrient Intake of Individuals With Non-Insulin Dependent Diabetes." *International Journal of Obesity* September 21, 1997, (9): pg. 756-763.

- **Wolfe**, W., et al. "Variety Associated Body Weight." *Obesity Research Update* 1997; 5:131-141. *H WJ* January/February 1999, 13:1:3.

- **Wolthers**, G., et al. "Different Effects of Growth Hormone and Prednisone on Energy Metabolism and Leptin Levels in Humans." *Metabolism: Clinical and Experimental* January 1998, 47 (1): pg. 83-88.

- **Woods**, S.C., et al. "Signals That Regulate Food Intake and Energy Homeostasis." *Science* May 29, 1998, 280 (5368), pg. 1378-1783.

- **Woo**, R., et al. "Voluntary Food Intake During Prolonged Exercise in Obese Women." *American Journal of Clinical Nutrition* September 1982, 36 (3): pg. 478-484.

- **Wurtman**, R. & **Wurtman** J. *Brain Serotonin, Carbohydrate Craving Obesity And Depression. Recent Advances in Tryptophan Research.* New York, NY; Plenum Press, 1996, pg. 35-41.

- **Wolk** A., et al. "A Prospective Study of Obesity and Cancer." *International Journal of Obesity* August, 1998, 22 (8 Supplement 3), S 12 (abstract pg. 042).

- **Wolk**, A. DMSC. "Long-Term Intake of Dietary Fiber and Decreased Risk of Coronary Heart Disease Among Women." *JAMA* June 2, 1999, Vol 281, No. 21, pg. 1198-2004.

- **Yanoski**, Jack. "Childhood Obesity: Etiology and Diagnosis." *49th Annual Bariatric Meeting.* Las Vegas, Nevada, October 1999.

- **Yoshida**, T., et al. "Nicotine Induces Uncoupling Protein in White Adipose Tissue of Obese Mice." *International Journal of Obesity* 1999, Vol. 23, pg. 570-575.

- **Young**, Ronald L. "Androgens in Postmenopausal Therapy?" *Menopause Management* May 1993, pg. 21-24.

- **Zakrewska**, K.E., et al. "Glucocorticoids As Counter Regulatory Hormones of Leptin: Clues to the Understanding of Leptin Resistance." *International Journal of Obesity* June 21, 1997, (Supplement 2):S31, (abstract pg. 71).